Rethinking the Youth Question

Also by Phil Cohen

Not Just the Same Old Story – Essays and Interventions in Racism's
   Other Scenes
Verbotene Spiele
Really Useful Knowledge
Ananse Meets Spiderwoman (with Linda Haddock)
*Multi-Racist Britain (editor with Harwant S. Bains)
Knuckle Sandwich (with Dave Robins)

*Also published by Macmillan

Rethinking the Youth Question

Education, Labour and Cultural Studies

PHIL COHEN

MACMILLAN

First published 1997 by
MACMILLAN PRESS LTD
Houndmills, Basingstoke, Hampshire RG21 6XS
and London
Companies and representatives
throughout the world

ISBN 0–333–63147–1 hardcover
ISBN 0–333–63148–X paperback

A catalogue record for this book is available from the British Library.

10   9   8   7   6   5   4   3   2   1
06   05   04   03   02   01   00   99   98   97

Typeset by EXPO Holdings, Malaysia

Printed in Hong Kong

For **Ned**, who somehow succeeded in growing up through all this and for all those who didn't

Contents

Acknowledgements

Inevitably in a book of this kind in which personal debts have accumulated over a period of twenty-five years, it is impossible to do more than mention a few of the many people who have helped me on the way. First and foremost there is Stuart Hall, who encouraged me to work out the earliest ideas, and has continued to support my various endeavours over the years. In addition to his intellectual influence, which the reader will easily discern, his capacity to both reformulate old questions and connect theory with politics, often against the grain of current thinking, has been a major source of inspiration.

I have to thank David Downes for arousing my early interest in deviancy theory and subculture, and Jock Young for originally commissioning this book. Colleagues at Street Aid, and the Post 16 Centre (University of London, Institute of Education) in their different ways provided a personal stimulus to develop many of these ideas. At the Institute of Education I was fortunate in having continuing moral as well as intellectual encouragement from Bob Ferguson, Phil Salmon and Anne Phoenix. Dave Robins collaborated on two research projects funded by the Leverhulme Trust, material from which can be found in Chapters 3, 4, 5 and 6. James Curran commissioned the material in Chapter 8 and Ian Taylor Chapter 9, and I am grateful to both of them for their editorial advice. Adrian Chappel and staff at the Cockpit Cultural Studies Department collaborated on the No Kidding project described in Chapter 10, and from Adrian in particular I learnt that Cultural Studies could make sense to children and young people in the classroom. I would also like to thank Alan Tomkins for steering the project through the exciting political minefield that was the GLC, and Dennis Warren for organising the Livelihoods conference, almost single-handed, at the age of 19. I owe a special dept of gratitude to Mike Rustin, Catherine Hall and Bill Schwartz who enabled me to move to the University of East London and introduced me to a fully congenial institutional environment in which to work. They also stood by me at a time of personal crisis, and I am also grateful to all my other colleagues at the Department of Cultural Studies, University of East London, who did the same. During this time Ali Rattansi, Caro Webb and Amal Treacher also showed me what true friendship meant.

I first worked with Angie McRobbie in jointly editing the Youth Questions series and have learnt much from her work on feminism and youth culture over the years. I do not know how she managed to find time to read through all the material and arrange it into something like coherence, but I am very glad that she did. Without her the book would have never seen the light of day. I have also to thank Steven Kennedy, my original editor at Macmillan, for his enormous patience, and Frances Arnold for her enthusiasm and diligence in seeing the project through to completion. Last and most, I would like to thank my partner, Jean McNeil, for the past twelve years and her faith in my ability to keep going when the going got rough.

Chapter 2 was first published in *CCCS Working Papers*, 2 (1972). Chapter 3 first appeared in *Knuckle Sandwich* (Penguin, 1978), subsequently published in the present, revised, verson in *Schooling and Culture*, 4 (1979). The first part of Chapter 4 appeared in *Knuckle Sandwich*, the second in *Youth and Society* (August 1980). Chapter 5 first appeared in Ben Fine *et al.* (eds), *Capitalism and the Rule of Law* (Hutchinson, 1981). Chapter 7 is an edited version of a monograph originally published by the Post 16 Centre, University of London Institute of Education (1986). Chapter 8 originally appeared in the *New Socialist*, 3 and 4 (1982/3), and in its present revised form in J. Curran (ed.), *The Future of the Left* (Polity Press, 1984). Chapter 9 appeared first as Chapter 3 in Ian Taylor (ed.), *The Social Effect of Market Policies* (Harvester/Wheatsheaf, 1990). Chapter 10 is a shortened version of a pamphlet, *Really Useful Knowledge* (Trentham Books, 1990). Chapters 1, 6 and 11 are published for the first time in this volume.

The author and publishers wish to thank the following for permission to use copyright material: Blackwell Publishers for Philip Cohen, 'Losing the generation game' from *Future of the Left*, ed. Jim Curran, Polity Press, 1984, pp. 100–21; Centre for Contemporary Cultural Studies for Philip Cohen, *Subcultural*

Conflict and Working Class Community, CCCS Working Papers Birmingham 1972; National Youth Agency for Philip Cohen, 'Sore thumb: knuckle sandwich revisited', *Youth in Society* (now *Young People Now*), August 1990; Penguin Books Ltd for Philip Cohen, 'Knuckle sandwich' from David Robins and Philip Cohen, *Knuckle Sandwich: Growing Up in the Working-Class City*, Penguin Books, 1987, pp. 89–106 (copyright © David Robins and Philip Cohen, 1987); Prentice-Hall and St Martin's Press, Inc. for Philip Cohen, 'Teaching enterprise culture' from *The Social Effects of Free Market Policies*, ed. Ian Taylor, Harvester/Wheatsheaf, 1990, p. 49–86 (copyright © Ian Taylor, editor); Trentham Books Ltd for Philip Cohen, 'The no kidding project' from *Really Useful Knowledge*, Trentham, 1990, pp. 10–45; Every effort has been made to trace all the copyright-holders, but if any have been inadvertently overlooked the publisher will be pleased to make the necessary arrangement at the first opportunity.

Introduction

Retrospectives

Retrospectives

The essays collected here cover a period of twenty years. The first chapter was written in 1969, in the thick of that peculiar culture war known as 'the underground'; the last chapter is based on a lecture given in 1989, reflecting on the impact of the New Right on education during that decade. Depending on how you cut the birthday cake, the chapters in between could be read in various ways; as the symptomatic journey of a member of the so called '60s generation coming to grips with changing reality principles; or as a series of essays dealing with changing conjunctures in debates around education, labour and the youth question. The argument could also be said to span two 'moments' in which debates in the human sciences pivoted first on the problematics of Marxism and then on Post-Structuralism. Finally, and inevitably, the vicissitudes of personal history intervene, with their own punctuations which may more or less coincide with these other timings, or cut across them....

Such principles of periodisation certainly weave more interesting narrative webs than the simple grid of chronological dating, but whether they place the texts in a more useful way for the reader is increasingly open to doubt. To suggest a provenance along any of these lines is perhaps to give a gloss of retrospective coherence and design to what at the time are necessarily opportunistic interventions. It is often said that social research is a form of disguised autobiography, and there is nothing like writing a life for giving it a unity and a sense of single-minded purpose which it could not possibly possess. But with autobiography there is always the apparently immediate identity between the life of the author and the history of the subject in the text to persuade the reader that, whatever transformations are recounted, they dovetail together to render a continuity of theme.

If a similar pact is to be sustained in work which claims to be about something more or other than the author's life, then it would seem to rely on the even more dangerous notion that what is being offered is the unfolding of a singular intellectual enterprise undertaken by some kind of 'mastermind'. Or else that by bringing together a diversity of otherwise scattered texts under the same imprimatur something like the totality of an 'oeuvre' is being unfolded and put on display.

Both models are derived from the rationale of the retrospective show; they carry the promise that even the most arcane or ephemeral of pieces retain a certain strategic 'relevance', and that early work contains the seeds of 'maturity'. Ironically enough, consoling mythologies like these may be especially vital where the work in question has some pretensions to contribute to social theory, and hence should not, in principle, require them.

The special pleading offered by the retrospective show is not a route which is nowadays available for the epistemologically squeamish. Instead, the republication of 'old work' becomes an occasion for strenuous updating and revision, a way of having second thoughts, or even the 'last word' while persuading the reader that the author is still ahead of the game.

Revisionism is a tempting strategy, in so far as it enables writers to publicly respond to criticism, to change their mind, and learn from their own mistakes. But since, in most cases, readers will not possess the original version with which to compare the text to hand, it is a strategy all too easily co-opted to the authorial desire to be wise after the event, to rewrite the past in the light of present understandings – a symptom of the autobiographical project if ever there was one! If I decided to reject this approach for my own book, I did not think it fair to impose it on others. I have therefore updated the bibliographies with references to the latest, revised editions, and in some cases included new and later work by the same authors where this seemed to me to have a particular bearing on the argument.

My decision – to reproduce the original intact – at first sight seems even less attractive in so far as it implies that these texts have somehow 'stood the test of time', or at least weathered the intellectual storms which produced them, and thus attained the status of 'classics'. But are there any alternative rationales for reproduction which do not rest on such arrogant assumptions?

One could perhaps follow the historical example of the cabinet of curiosities and mount a display of more or less period pieces whose value and interest lay precisely in the fact that they had to be unearthed from dusty archives, out-of-print volumes and obscure journals, in order to be given a new lease of life as 'collectors' items'. But whatever the secret charms of associating the exotic with the antique in this way, it does not recommend itself as a strategy in the present case, given the subject-matter of most of this book. A museum of youth culture might be a suitable project for our fin-de-siècle heritage industry, given its obsession with the archaeology of modernity; but as a rationale for reprinting work which at least in passing, tries to problematise the relation between youth and modernity, it would be something of a contradiction in terms. There are, at any rate, other more urgent considerations, which have to do with the way that debate is currently being played out within the Academy.

It is perhaps not altogether surprising that the younger generation of students and scholars tend to regard anything written more than five years ago as past its sell-by date. The intensity of the pressures to 'publish or perish' means that to keep up with the game you have to make it seem new, even (and especially) when it is not. Academic speed-up tends to the ever more rapid turnover of ever more vapid texts; this planned obsolescence in turn produces a kind of social amnesia. Whatever the gains in decomposing knowledge into a such a highly perishable commodity, it also brings about the compression of memory and attention spans.

This effect would seem to be especially accelerated in the case of 'youth studies'; for in so far as they merely describe the surface shifts and twists of adolescent behaviour, these studies have to be about what is happening here and now, or else they are already yesterday's news. One of the more notable features of this genre is the often wilful ignorance regarding theoretical debates on the youth question which have taken place over the last two decades. We are presented with empiricist 'theory-free' investigations into young peoples' life-styles, patterns of employment or consumption, their occupational aspirations and political opinions, as if this information spoke for itself about changes in sexual or generational divisions of labour, family and class structures, or adolescent cultures, let alone deeper more intangible shifts in the shaping of gender, ethnic or class identities. And this lack of engagement with wider debates in turn underwrites a prevalent view amongst academics that 'youth' is, intellectually speaking, 'old hat'.

This empiricist turn has, however, to be understood as a reaction against the endlessly speculative assertions about the 'postmodern condition' which have increasingly preoccupied those who have held on to a theoretical concern with the youth question. With a few notable exceptions, the absence of grounded ethnographic research to substantiate the large claims for the emergence of symptomatically post-modern forms of identity has left the field open to more basic approaches to generational trend-spotting.

Yet there is another way of 'going back to basics', one which involves remembering rather than forgetting, namely to tell the story of the circumstances which are associated with the production of particular texts. In the 'original' the context is normally assumed to be more or less transparent to the reader, in so far as it is present, implicitly or explicitly in its immediate terms of reference. The text appears in this journal or that book as an individual contribution to a particular shared debate with which it tries to be absolutely contemporary. Whatever more personal remains to be said can then be safely confined to the acknowledgements page. As for any deeper structures of generation they are by definition not available for comment.

The conditions under which the same text is read when reprinted years later, alongside earlier or later work by the same author are almost always the exact opposite of this. Everything that was then transparent has become opaque; nothing can be assumed about the readers' prior understanding of sources or context; on the other hand the underlying rationale which was largely unconscious at the time of original conception is now more accessible to a secondary reading and scrutiny.

To tell the story of the provenance of these texts is thus a way of making them more legible from the vantage point of the contemporary reader, as well as acknowledging the depth of influences which configure the argument. In both senses I hope that the book will contribute to a wider understanding of the genealogy of current debates.

There is, at any rate, another reason why such a logic of retrospection imposes itself in the present case. Although the idea of compiling a book along these lines was a long-standing project, it was only brought to fruition in a period of personal crisis when I was convinced that there was not much time left in which to attend to unfinished business. Although these fears proved unjustified, they did concentrate my mind on the task of reviewing what I had done with my life and work so far!

Unfortunately these are also the conditions most calculated to promote the autobiographical delusion; they offer an open invitation to play at Marat in the bath tub, and produce a grand summation before The Final Deadline. Even if this temptation is resisted, it does not leave the author in a strong position from which to make decisions about what should be included or excluded from a collection. It seemed all the more important then to find someone who was both sympathetic to the project and yet held a critical distance from it, to undertake the task of sifting out the wheat from the chaff.

I was fortunate to find someone who combined these and many other virtues, and who was willing to let me reread the material through another's eyes. This meant, inevitably, that connections which I had taken for granted, because they were at the back of my mind whilst writing the original, had now to be foregrounded and spelt out.

Each chapter is therefore prefaced by a short introduction which tells a story about its genesis. To furnish such myths of origin, for that is what they are, may at least serve to anchor each chapter to its other scene – that once familiar time and place whence it came, but which has now become a foreign country, and to the author as much as the reader. There is always, of course, the danger that by exploring this 'new-won' terra incognita, the past escapes into the present only through the nostalgic retrieve of yet another lost empire of the mind. But perhaps that is a risk worth taking if it creates the basis of a more equitable pact with the reader than the autobiographical one, a pact which does not have to rely on the surplus of meaning artificially created by the always unequal exchange between now and once upon a time....

Beginnings

What links these stories is perhaps a larger and more personal myth of origin; this concerns the way certain recurrent themes impose themselves as objects of enquiry by virtue of a topicality which belongs to what they conjure up from the writer's past rather than simply what they address in the present. The main themes in this book certainly have this common anchorage and it may be helpful to locate their provenance, if only to explain certain idiosyncrasies in the way they are handled.

I grew up in a lower middle-class family on the seventh floor of a large block of private flats in Central London. My father was a junior doctor, from the Jewish quarter of the Gorbals in Glasgow, who had escaped via a scholarship to grammar school, and thence to university. Like the heroes of his socialist, Sunday-school childhood, Jimmy Maxton and John Maclean, he believed that material transformations would set the world to rights. He also thought that a public school education in the Classics was the best training for young minds, an antidote to the Judaeo-Christian tradition for which, as a non-practising atheist, he had little time. He read the *Jewish Chronicle* religiously from cover to cover every week with a pained expression on his face and a faraway look in his eye, so that I was never able to tell whether the source of his discomfiture was abhorrence of the Zionist stance of the newspaper or a sense of distance from the culture and community of his childhood which its contents must have evoked. Perhaps it was both, but I never learnt to decipher *this* Jewish question.

My mother was a no less contradictory figure. She had a strict Victorian upbringing amongst the Welsh shopocracy in Bridgend, where children were subject to the double discipline of mastering social etiquettes which would distance them from miners and other riffraff (my mother's family went to the Church of England up the hill from the Chapel), and of being held at emotional arm's length by parents who considered displays of affection to be 'common'. Even though she learnt both lessons well and tried to pass them to me, she also rebelled against the practical implications. When she was 19 she ran away to London to become a nurse and meet my father in what was always told to me as a whirlwind hospital and wartime romance. This mixed marriage did not go down well in Bridgend and no doubt furnished another cautionary tale about what happened to young girls who ran away to the Wicked City. This may have daunted some dutiful daughters, but my mother was made of sterner stuff. In fact, from an early age she had modelled herself upon Florence Nightingale and subsequently became a fervent disciple of Mrs Thatcher. Like both of them she dealt with the constraints placed upon her ambitions by patriarchal professions by becoming at once her own woman, and her own best man.

The flats we lived in were occupied largely by professional and business people, most of whom were single or childless. A good deal of my early childhood was spent looking down out of the window of my room at the yard of a small council estate which abutted on to our flats. In this confined space large numbers of children could be seen running about, laughing, shouting, fighting and generally carrying on. Their behaviour puzzled me since my own play, which consisted in sending first teddy bears, and then tin soldiers, on imaginary expeditions from which few returned, was so different in its solitary preoccupations. As a result I regarded these children with a mixture of fear and fascination – I was seduced by their social vitality but terrified of actually participating in their rough-and-tumble world. When later on, my parents threatened to take me away from my prep school, if I did not do well enough, and send me to the local elementary school instead, I could not imagine a more dire fate. Unless it was to be sent away to boarding school, where the upper-class bullies who were already making my life a misery would be in permanent residence.

To grow up a mitschling, a Jew to gentiles, and a goy to Jews, whilst perched precariously between threat of descent into the ranks of the local working class and entrée into the charmed circles of a national elite, might seem in retrospect to be a good apprenticeship for a subsequent career as a social researcher. It would have sensitised anyone to the arbitrary constraints placed upon behaviour and belief by particular forms of class culture or ethnicity, and raised curiosity about how and why this had come about. My early induction into what is now called 'identity politics' was heightened by the fierce rows over political matters that frequently broke out at mealtimes between my parents.

In the mythical figures of my grandfathers I did, however, find an alternative resource for inventing a genealogy centred on that sense of singularity which is the lot of the only child. According to legend, my mother's father had played rugby for Wales, drank two raw eggs every morning for breakfast, followed by a pint of beer, and still had the energy to run away with a fancy woman from Cardiff. The possible link between these accomplishments came to intrigue me; by my early teens I had learnt the connection between getting drunk and playing rugby from my schoolmates, but no amount of eggnog did the trick as far as women were concerned.

My father's Russian father was equally promising material for furnishing daydreams of an exotic ancestry far removed from my prosaic life, which I was learning to despise as 'petty bourgeois'. A victim of religious and political persecution under the last tsar, the story has it that he slept with a picture of Kropotkin on one side of his bed and Lenin on the other, and never had a bad night's sleep. For a living he sold blankets door to door in the Scottish coalfields, but by all accounts was more interested in winning converts to the Great Cause than gaining paying customers. For this side of my family romance I liked the idea of someone who could maintain a balancing act, on the high wire of politics, between the two great traditions of Anarchism and Communism.

In both cases what I admired was the fact that these men were mavericks who did not quite 'fit in' to the patterns which were expected of their lives. They offered me a rationale for the feeling of not belonging in the worlds of family and school, a feeling which intensified inevitably at adolescence. Like so many others, I found a home from home in books, in particular books which allowed me to explore at a safe distance the terra incognita of how life was lived 'for real' on the other side of the tracks. Forced to read Cicero, or Caesar's Gallic wars and to turn Pope into Greek iambic hexameters, I rebelled by spending my time reading Sartre, or Ben Traven's stories of peasant revolution, or going on the road with Kerouac, Corso and Ginsberg. Playing truant from Plato's *Republic* to see Truffaut's *Quatre-Cent Coups* (six times!) finally confirmed my romantic identification with teenage misfits who ran from home away to find themselves.

It could have been 'just a phase' but it turned out to be a dress rehearsal for the 'real thing' after all. For this adolescent fugue coincided with the advent of an 'alternative society', in which living by your wits, running away to sea, going on the beat trail and tripping out were all par for the course. As a result I was brought for the first time into contact with young people who really had grown up on the other side of the tracks. A spell working in a hostel for ex-borstal boys convinced me that learning how to survive on the street was vastly over-rated as a source of 'really useful knowledge', even if some of the tricks of this particular trade were to stand me in good stead later on.

The experience did, however, set me off on a search (some might say a wild goose chase) for forms of education which addressed both the immediate and the larger concerns of young people in a way that public school, state school and 'alternative' school in their different ways failed to do. In this way, I hoped, naively, to not only heal the wounds of my own adolescence, but create a framework of serendipity in which I might at last be able to engage productively with those children who had so frightened and fascinated me all those years ago.

Yet such a frame did not after all prove to be accessible from my original starting point. That first position of childish omniscience, from which I had looked down upon a culture about which I knew nothing, mirrored all too accurately the standpoint of an uncritical ethnography, which projects onto the tabula rasa of some 'unknown continent' the figures of its own inner phantasms of The Other Scene. From slum novel to community studies, from urban sociology to subculturalism, working-class life has been portrayed as an exotic underworld, holding out the promise or the threat of overturning 'bourgeois domestic order'. This literature both creates and draws upon a vicarious concern about how life is lived on the 'other side of the tracks'. It is a voyeurism which cares about its objects only because they have first been rendered fascinatingly different by some kind of 'inside story' and then been humanised by the application of a superior reason which demonstrates that 'underneath' they are 'just like us'. From such a vantage point there is much that is shocking but few surprises, since what is discovered is always and already what is suspected to be the case. Looking back it seems as if my early work was pitched in and against the twin impositions of the 'view from below' and the 'view from above'; even as it oscillates uneasily between the two, it is struggling, and usually failing, to find a third position from which to address what is bracketed out by both: the lived interiorities of gender, class and 'race'.

Themes

When we came to discuss the actual selection of work and its organisation into book form, it quickly became apparent that the material fell more or less neatly into three groups: 1) ethnographic studies of youth cultures and other imagined communities of affinity/enmity; 2) historico-structural accounts of sexual and generational divisions of labour, and their institutional reproduction; and 3) essays in educational policy or practice. It was no coincidence that this grouping was also largely chronological, since it corresponded to particular places and times where the work originated and to associated shifts in vantage point.

The youth culture studies (Chapters 1 to 6) were all written while I was directly engaged as a campaigner or community worker with groups of young people in the West End and Inner London between 1969 and 1979. Even when the mode of research was primarily theoretical (Chapters 2, 4) or historical (Chapter 5), rather than ethnographic, it was carried out as an adjunct to the youth cultural and political work, and this undoubtedly shaped the whole approach.

In 1979 I left Street Aid, a legal and welfare organisation for young people which I had helped to set up in the West End, and moved to the Institute of Education to run a series of funded research projects through the '80s. The move from the environment of street culture and 'the underground' to that of the academy was something of a shock. It was like looking at the world from the other end of the telescope. What had seemed overwhelming close up – homelessness, police harassment, drug abuse, overlain by the cultivation of bohemian life-styles – all that was considered of much more distant interest; whilst what had seemed a remote, if lethal, system of power in the state was brought into much sharper and more immediate focus. The move also coincided with the defeat of the last Labour government and the inauguration of Thatcherism. Given the key role which education was to play in shaping the Thatcherite agenda, the Institute turned out to be a very good place from which to observe the changes, and intervene in the debates which unfolded over that decade.

This shift in intellectual and political vantage point led me to reject the culturalism/populism which had dominated the early work. Instead I attempted to elaborate a structuralist approach to the youth question, one which saw it as a specific site of contradiction within and between particular family, educational and labour forms and also focused of the codes of cultural identity through which these tensions might be variously articulated and lived out. Although this essay, which gives this collection its title, consisted largely in an engagement with theory, its purpose was much more practical, as the following chapters make clear. The aim was to make better historical sense of the dislocations which were occurring in the cultural geographies of growing up working-class, and to suggest some of the terms of a new agenda of response on the part of the Labour movement and the left, an agenda which aimed to break with their traditional perspective on the youth question, concerned as it was solely with questions of social integration and welfare.

In fact, the terms in which the youth question is posed on the left have changed dramatically over the two decades. Up to the mid-'70s a Working-Class Hero was still Something to Be, especially, as John Lennon sardonically reminded us, if you were middle-class. Left-wing students wore donkey jackets, and diligently tried to master what was imagined to be prolespeak. The objects of this admiration did not unfortunately return the compliment or live up to the revolutionary expectations foisted upon them. By the end of the 1970s the romantic idealisation of 'the lads' (alias white male working-class youth) had begun to give way to its opposite – an all too ready denunciation of their inherent and irredeemable racism and sexism. As the '80s progressed, feminist and anti-racist critiques of 'macho street culture', and its 'lawless masculinity' focusing on skinheads and football gangs, began to find common ground with New Right diatribes against the 'underclass', which singled out unemployed youth as the bearers of a new Yob culture.

As a result of this shift my work became increasingly preoccupied with how particular versions of masculinity and white ethnicity have been set in motion to mark the territories in and across which the links between growing up, working and class are forged. It seemed important to understand more about the causes and consequences of these links weakening or breaking in order to reformulate the kind of social and political education which

might both address the very real issues of male violence and
racism, and allow young people to explore alternative sources of
identity and belonging. But the nature of my work at the Institute
gave this research a particular focus and direction.

The setting up of a Post 16 Centre, to which I was attached,
pitched me into the thick of the debate over the 'new vocationalism' (Chapter 9), whilst the No Kidding project (described in
Chapter 10) enabled me to work with groups of school leavers at
the ILEA Cockpit Cultural Studies Department on a number of
photographic exhibitions, video programmes and publications
exploring issues connected to the restructuring of adolescent
transitions through youth training schemes.

The issues of cultural identity and difference thrown up by the
advent of 'post-Fordist' forms of education, training and labour
needed, and still need, to be connected to more fundamental
speculations about relationships between individual citizens and
the state in a reconstituted democracy. The experiment of the
Greater London Council, for all its excesses and mistakes,
marked a watershed in connecting these instances in a single
forum of debate. For example, when we asked the GLC for a
grant for the No Kidding project, the application was discussed
in full Council session, and rapidly turned into a debate about
whether cartoons and photography constituted valid art forms,
whether popular culture was a suitable subject for study in
schools, and whether young people should or could be 'empowered' by these means.

Such immediate considerations aside, the period of restructuring posed some new and awkward questions for a generation
which had grown up with the fatally easy assumption that political
radicalism was always 'of the left' and closely associated with youth
culture. At the same time, and no doubt because I was by now
entering my forties, I began to think that the youth question was
too important to be left just to the young! And I was determined,
if at all possible, to avoid the fate of the ageing lecturer in the Biff
cartoon who endlessly recycles his '60s subcultural experiences to
classrooms of bored students. It was time to move on in several
senses, but perhaps also, as I argue in Chapter 7, to go back to
some of the wider and more fundamental issues of theory and
method in the human sciences, which had been lost sight of in
the rush to youth culture.

In order to gain some purchase on this dimension, the work became increasingly involved in exploring the possibilities of an applied Cultural Studies in three linked senses: as a method of critical ethnography for investigating issues in young people's lives, as a practical pedagogy for working around issues of identity and difference with them, and as a theoretical arena within which the youth question could be connected to wider debates. It was the possibility of an approach that connected these different levels, usually so split off and opposed, which excited me about Cultural Studies at this time. Although there certainly was an enormous gulf between debates going on amongst radical practitioners in the world of education or in youth and community work, and those which occupied the high ground of Cultural Studies, this often had more to do with the kind of language used – vernacular and populist on one side, academic and theoreticist on the other, than with the actual agenda of issues being addressed.

The book attempts to take a line of thought for a walk between these two poles, but for that very reason does not proceed in a straight line. It is more of a hop skip and jump across a series of discrete but shifting points of engagement with certain recurrent questions. And it is a line often broken, or occluded, by circumstances which made direct links often difficult to make or follow. Perhaps this was not just dictated by necessity, but was a matter of personal choice?

Samuel T. Maverick and the return to postmodern values

Whenever people ask me what I do I have always had the greatest difficulty in giving a straight one-word answer. I have never been an academic in the accepted sense of the term, though a lot of my work has been based in and around universities. I am not a sociologist or anthropologist by training, though some of the ideas and methods I draw on obviously derive from these traditions. Nor, despite studying history as an undergraduate and spending a good deal of time subsequently in psycho-analysis, could I claim these as disciplines rather than influences. Whilst officially unemployed, I spent several years in the British Library reading voraciously about linguistics, phenomenology and allied subjects, which certainly helped me to move on from classical Marxism, even if it did not turn me into a philosopher of language.

Through all these informal studies I was searching for anything which would help shed light on the conflicts which I saw going on in and around me in the course of the work I was doing with young people.

Does this make the approach 'eclectic'? – which seems to imply a random selection of intellectual ingredients, thrown together to make an appetizing stew, but without much internal logic to recommend the result to the gourmet. I had better leave the reader to judge! What I would like to question, though, is the basis upon which such judgements are often made within academic circles.

A professor of sociology, reviewing some work I produced several years ago, called me a maverick. Although he gave the work a good write-up, he made it clear that in his eyes it was vitiated by the fact that it could not be regarded as a contribution to 'sociology' in so far as it drew heavily on other and heterogeneous sources. I looked 'maverick' up in the OED and was intrigued to find that it referred to a mid-Victorian cattle rancher from Texas who refused to brand his cattle with his name. Whether this was done out of a refusal to take responsibility for any damage done to others' property by his own, or from some high-minded concern with animal rights, is not recorded, though we may have our suspicions. At any rate, by analogy the term came to be applied to 'any masterless person, one who is roving or casual'.

This etymology conjures up a semi-feudal world where runaway slaves, apprentices, gypsies, wandering Jews and scholars comprise a multiple threat to closed orders of knowledge and power. Although this world no longer exists it continues to cast its shadow over the university, where new intellectual aristocracies have been established in place of the old. The new masterminds may no longer be guardians of received wisdom or scholarship from whom a patrimony of specialised knowledge is inherited, but even academic careerists still like to don this mantle on occasion, if only to demand brand loyalty to the particular department of knowledge over which they preside. Anyone who is not authorised with this kind of pedigree then becomes automatically suspect as being not quite the genuine article: in the artisanal metaphor – a jack of all trades, master of none.

At the same time most of the institutional niches which gave people the time and facilities to pursue ideas to see where they might lead have been closed down. In their place we have professional researchers who have to function as mental technicians on short-term contracts, with little influence or control over the direction or use of their work.

Under these circumstances, the notion of the 'freelance' tends to become hopelessly romanticised, being turned into a cross between a brother of the free spirit and Thatcherite entrepreneur. In the world of global information highways, where the ownership of knowledge is dependent increasingly on access to means of dissemination which transcend local stakes and claims, freelances are more likely than ever to be seen as mavericks (if not rogue elephants), even though in fact this is less likely than ever to be the case.

We might reflect that every rancher in Texas would have been able to instantly identify one of Samuel T. Maverick's steers, by the very absence of his brand name; but only on condition that no-one else followed his example, for then, of course, no-one would be able to tell whose runaway steer was whose and the very basis of private ownership of cattle or ideas would be placed in jeopardy. Mavericks are supposed to be loners, not hunt in herds.

Paradoxically, the casualisation of mental labour favours the multiplication of freelances whilst destroying the subversive aspect of maverick thought. Researchers are increasingly impelled to put their name to work which by virtue of the very conditions under which it is produced is impelled by other considerations than the purely intellectual. Moreover as theoretical paradigms impose new principles of standardisation across disciplines, whilst schools of thought become externally more diversified, 'interdisciplinarity' becomes a formula for reproducing rather than challenging the prevailing divisions of academic labour. Although freelances are by definition not bound by these divisions, they increasingly have to locate their work within them if they want to stay in business.

But maybe the game is not so much up, as having its rules changed. We are supposed to be living in a world of 'intertextuality' dominated by 'anxieties of influence', where the line between plagiarism and originality seems ever more thinly drawn. When all the world's a text and all the people in it merely quotations, the ability to correctly identify sources becomes paramount. The maverick text is one which by definition resists easy placement in a canon. But what if that 'transgression' itself gives the text its canonical status? Once the techniques of critical citation are confused with the arts or crafts of authorship, it is enough to permutate familiar elements, to give them a slightly new slant, to create a *succès d'estime*. Postmodernism seems to have institutionalised the principles of maverick thought and turned them into harmless bricolage.

But that is not the end of the story. We are also living in an age when the migration of ideas and populations has accelerated across the globe. Under these circumstances a casual attitude to fences and a tendency to roam may still yield subversive as well as survival value. The more signs that go up warning us that intellectual trespassers will be prosecuted, the more we can be sure that other itinerants have passed this way, and that they may be onto something.

Perhaps this is still too sanguine a view. The biggest fence that remains to be jumped is one that is getting higher all the time – the one which divides theory and practice. I remember talking to a meeting of the ill-fated Socialist Society in the mid-1980s. After my presentation a well-known feminist academic got up and congratulated me on sticking it out with these hard cases, saying how useful it was to have people who were willing to take such risks to bring back the raw material which people like her could then use as the basis of their strategic formulations about education and social change. I am sure she meant it as a compliment! But her assumption was that anyone who spent so much time with 'yobbos' must be suffering from brain damage and could not possibly locate the experience in any wider, or more theoretical frame.

She was certainly correct in thinking that the relation between theory and practice is never direct, and unmediated, nor does it simply occur in some middle ground of 'policy'. This was borne in on me when I was working on designing and evaluating a critical simulation game, called *Livelihoods*, for school-leavers. My collaborator (who was in the process of changing over from being head of a sociology department in a polytechnic to becoming a freelance researcher and educational consultant) insisted that the strategic nature of the game must lie in depicting the changing conditions under which players might trade off street creds against CVs (and vice versa) in order to optimise status or bargaining power. Devising the game made us all too aware of the delicate balancing act in which we also were engaged, between what would be recognised by our peers as serious academic work and what would be regarded by our 'clients' as instructive fun.

In principle it is always possible to combine both sorts of activity and move between these two worlds. But it is getting much more difficult to do so. And this for a number of reasons. The first is the pressure on researchers to produce more in less time and to confine the dissemination of their work to professional or policy-relevant audiences. The second is more complicated and has to do with the way rules of legitimacy and authorisation are currently deployed in knowledge/power games around class, gender and race.

According to these protocols, it is impossible for a white, male, middle-class and middle-aged researcher to entertain anything but an exploitative relationship with clients who are black, working-class, women or young people. The act of research and writing, however sympathetically it is done, denies them a voice and meanings of their own and substitutes an alien perspective. This argument has had a powerful effect on those who lack the required street creds and who now concentrate on enhancing CVs by retreating into the realms of 'high theory' and purely textual research. Whatever might be gained by such a move, it certainly does not end an existing monopoly over the production of knowledge. It has also meant that intellectual work is increasingly at risk of being pulled into one of two rival cultures of narcissism – the first belonging to Eurocentric and Masculinist Forms of Reason and Objectivity and the other to alternative exclusionary discourses of Subjectivity and Fellowfeeling.

What is lost in the process? The notion that research and its writing are an encounter between the Other Within – that other sex, generation, class, or race which is imagined as both limit and condition of what can be known about the Self – and the External Others who are the object of investigations which they always in some sense elude. Those two Others may pass like ships in the night, but they can also communicate in a potential space for what Keats called negative capability. That means, in this context, the ability to turn questions inside-out and hence interrupt the seamless flow of 'interpretations' placed upon utterances or behaviour by the subject-who-knows. Any methodology which forecloses that process through an 'irritable reaching after certainty' is not, in this view, appropriate to the task.

From this standpoint it is not the sources of identification between researcher and informant which are likely to provide the best primary data, but precisely the differences – and the misunderstandings – which emerge in the context of an encounter which is inevitably structured by the very inequalities being studied. It is at the point where a line of enquiry takes you across these familiar front lines into a no man's or woman's land, where it is no longer so easy to tell which 'side' anyone is coming from, that things begin to get interesting, and there emerges a story worth telling. And here perhaps we reach at once the aim and the destination of maverick thought.

Part I

Class, Gender and 'Race' in Urban Youth Culture

Chapter 1

The Writing on the Walls

This piece was written in 1971 and never published. It was an attempt to recollect in something not quite approaching tranquility, the delirium of representations which the actions of the London Street Commune had provoked two years previously. Tagged by the media as 'hippy squatters', to distinguish the movement from respectable homeless families, the Commune was a strange and unstable amalgam of beats, student radicals, junkies, teenage runaways and professional dossers, animated by common confusions about how to make the world a more accommodating place. A brief attempt to build an alliance with the 'New Left' was met with incomprehension and hostile cries of 'What do you produce – syringes?' The Alternative Society of Beautiful People was not much more welcoming! The street communes were, however, a gift for the media, and for pop sociology.

As 'Dr John', I did not particularly enjoy being cast, however briefly, in the role of the nation's 'folk devil', which after all involves playing the villain in someone else's bad B movie! I still remember vividly a nightmare I had at the time, of being pursued through the darkened corridors of 144 Piccadilly by a large mechanical monster with searchlight eyes made up of TV cameras, and spewing out miles of cables in which some of my friends had got hideously tangled up.

The analysis contained here was perhaps an attempt to wake up from that particular paranoid nightmare, to slay the monster or at least get some emotional distance from it, by untangling some of its more seductive coils with the help of conceptual weapons which were then emerging to do what we would now call a 'deconstruction' of images of deviance and the mass media. The desire was not so much to 'set the record straight' as to find out why these images should have had such pulling power, not least over those who were their main focus. The conversations, reproduced in the last section, are used to consider the possibilities of an alternative, and less mediatised, space of representation in which issues of deviance and normality could be publicly debated.

When I re-read the text for the first time since writing it, parts of it made me squirm with embarrassment at the earnestness of the attempt to turn it all into an academic case study; nevertheless, I hope enough of the atmosphere of the events remains to give the reader some sense of being there as an earwitness. Archaeologists of the post-modern might like to note that the slogan 'We are the writing on your walls', which was spray painted on the front of 144, was not then a quotation, even if it subsequently became one. Historians of urban public order might recall that the first time the Special Patrol Group was unleashed in full riot gear on mainland Britain was for the purpose of storming the Street Commune's base in Endell Street, a building which had originally housed a ragged school, and had been renamed by us 'The School for Scoundrels'.

Yes we are
anti-social, unsure, immature
won't work always shirking
our responsibilities.
We don't give a fuck
for your labels and your lies,
we're not selling you any alibis.
We can't wait
till your old world sickens and dies
WE ARE THE WRITING ON YOUR WALLS

Popular chant at 144 Piccadilly

In September 1969, in the symbolic centre of British society, the heart of its capital city, one building became the eye in the teeth of a political storm. 144 Piccadilly: a large mansion, built to imperial proportions in the mid-Victorian period, had been occupied by some 600 or so young people. They came from almost every region of the country, and almost every social background. Ex-borstal boys and ex-public school boys. Sons of hairdressers and daughters of bank clerks. Children of miners and engineers, as well as of industrialists and businessmen. They came together under a banner which read, the London Street Commune. This movement had emerged eighteen months previously, and was to survive in various forms until the end of 1971. Over the three years of its existence, it succeeded in mobilising several thousand people, in a variety of actions around a series of 'impossibilist' demands. Its ultimate failure came as a surprise to no one. But its significance lies in the fact that it represents the largest and most sustained attempt at political organisation by a highly disparate section of disorganised, unemployed and drop-out youth, whose only bargaining power lay in their numbers, their social marginality and their location, on the streets of central London.

The 'Commune of the Streets', as it was then called, first emerged in October 1968, when a group fifty-strong staged a sit-in at a snack bar on Piccadilly Circus. They were protesting at the policy of Forte's, who owned this and many similar cafés in the West End, in refusing to serve beatniks and anyone who 'looked scruffy', wore long hair and was under 25. It's doubtful whether any of these beats had heard of Norman Mailer and his 'white negro' thesis, but, in adopting a tactic from the anti-segrationist movement, their propaganda was quick to draw the parallel, as they saw it, between their own situation of social apartheid – victimised for the very appearance which made them an unofficial tourist attraction – and that of the cheap black immigrant labour in the catering trade, who were instructed to refuse them service. However, their slogan for the occasion, despite – or because of – its intended irony, somewhat backfired. On being handed a leaflet, which demanded in bold print **every Englishman's right to a cup of tea**, a group of High Tory ladies in full regalia, who happened to be passing by, and seeing these white youths being denied their birthright by Asian waiters, became righteously indignant and promptly joined the sit-in – as much to the embarrassment of the beats as of the police, who arrived shortly afterwards to evict them!

Despite its comic aspect, the action was successful. Forte's management, perhaps afraid of bad publicity, perhaps won over by the beguiling nature of the Commune's plea, or for whatever reason best known to themselves, gave way. The 'beatniks' were let back into the various sidewalk 'clubs' they'd established in the West End, and the leadership paused to consider its next move.

Who were they? The majority were older beats, in their middle twenties, who had been 'on the scene', or 'on the road', for several years. Some even dated from the beginnings of the subculture in the late 1950s. As the beats' numbers in the West End had declined – from several thousand to less than a hundred – so this hard core had followed 'the scene' as it shifted its base, from Soho coffee bars to the Duke of Yorks, via 'Sunny Goodge Street', (as portrayed in a song by ex-beat Donovan) and in the mid-1960s to Trafalgar Square, until finally the rump ended up at Piccadilly Circus. This group found themselves a distinct minority in a milieu dominated by well entrenched junkie and petty criminal cultures (drug pushing, prostitutes, street hustling), and a transient population of migrant, unemployed youth, many of them homeless, who had come down to 'The Smoke' from the depressed regions of Scotland, Ireland and the North East, in search of work, and 'life'.

Nevertheless, these older beats formed something of an elite, a respected source of information and advice for the younger, less experienced elements. Their presence was strengthened at this period by the influx of middle class 'drop outs', refugees from the student and underground movement, who drifted into the milieu, often more by accident than design, and who brought with them many of the political ideas and organisational styles they had learnt elsewhere. It was out of the uneasy alliance between these two groups that the core of the street commune movement was to be formed.

After the sit-in's success, its initiators then turned their attention to the omnipresent fact of life for West End youth – police harassment. One of them, road name of Rabbit, described the situation in a typical example of his doggerel talking blues, which he used to improvise and sing to the delight of his friends, and discomfort of his enemies:

> I'm sitting on the Dilly
> I'm getting nicely stoned
> The fuzz are actin' silly

why don't they all go home

Chorus: Oh they ain't let me have a sit down
since I came walkin on
They just give us the run around
you know I'm movin on

They drag you to West End Central
and lock you in a cell
They beat you up, *then* search you
They treat us all like hell

etc.

Policing consisted of routine stop and search, moving on of stationary groups, under threat of arrest (for obstruction) and, at weekends, 'juvenile sweeps' through the all-night cafés and clubs, accompanied by several large 'meat wagons', which slowly emptied of police and filled with young 'suspected persons'. New faces and old-comers were in the front line; the former being checked out as potential runaways or absconders, the latter as potentially 'wanted elsewhere'. As Rabbit indicates, the typical response to this was flight – whether walking the streets from hang-out to hang-out, or moving on from scene to scene in London or even the country as a whole. Given the very high rate of police productivity in this area and the vulnerability/visibility of the population at risk, it therefore took some courage and commitment, as well as cunning, to stay around the 'scene' for any period of time.

The effect of this containment strategy was to establish a kind of demographic equilibrium – eliminating, whether by voluntary or compulsory means, roughly the same number of 'resident' West End youth as there were newcomers at any one time. According to this crude homeostatic principle, as numbers built up, for example in the Spring, harassment increased, until the status quo ante was reached, at which point police activity would slacken off, until the cycle started up once again. This also meant that in moments where demographic and police pressure were both at their height, arrests became systematically arbitrary; drug planting, beatings, frame-ups became routinised and 'democratic', rather than selective devices aimed at specific target groups or individuals. In other words, whenever the subcultural presence in the West End became too visible, to the point where it might be interpreted by the press, politicians, etc. as a threat to public order, then the formal norms of legal rationality, which are officially supposed to govern police behaviour – playing it by the Queen's Rules – would be temporarily suspended; but not to the point of making mass arrests. Such indiscriminate rounds-ups would both alert the liberal watchdogs to the violation of civil liberties *and* threaten the organisational maintenance of the magistrates' courts, remand centres and the police force itself, in their function of processing offenders from arrest to conviction.

It was with this skilfully managed dialectic of legal repression that the street communards now unwittingly came to grips, as they set out on a campaign to arrest the criminal processing of their friends by the judicial machine, and expose the violations to civil liberties. Their activities served to upset the 'demographic equilibrium', for they aimed to turn flight into fusion, moving on into stand and fight.

Street petitions were organised against police harassment, marches to West End Central against police brutality, and letters written to the papers about police corruption. A public rally was organised in Trafalgar Square to make common cause with other oppressed groups, legal advice leaflets distributed, street observers set up to provide an early warning system of police activity, test cases fought on the law of obstruction and, finally (in 1971), a legal advice and welfare centre Street Aid, was established to provide bail, legal aid solicitors and crash pads.

All of this, of course, is standard campaigning tactics. And none of it would have been in the least remarkable, had it not been for the fact that it was organised by young people who lacked *all* the resources which are normally considered essential for this kind of activity.

That is, they lacked a fixed address, sleeping mostly in 'derries'. Their only means of subsistence were what they could 'con', beg, borrow or steal on the street. Their 'office' was a public telephone box in the Piccadilly underground, and a forged GPO credit card. Their propaganda was produced on a stolen typewriter, using stolen paper, and written by people who had spent most of their lives in children's homes. Despite this, the campaign was carried out with neither more nor less efficiency than is usually the case.

At various points along the way, the street communard leadership tried to win the support of groupings who were more organised, if equally youthful, more 'middle-class', if equally 'revolutionist'. The student movement, as represented by the Radical Socialist Student Federation conference of 1968, did not however see Piccadilly Circus as a potential red base, and welcomed the street communards with cries of 'What do you produce? Syringes!' followed by swift ejection. A subsequent intervention at the first LSE sit-in was no less unproductive, eliciting on one side censorious motions concerning the 'flotsam and jetsum of London', and on the other caustic remarks about the sexual potency of the student body, or lack of it.

The 'underground', as represented by its press and welfare agencies, was more consistently approached, and more sympathetic. Its representatives were able to patronise the 'street people' as the bearers of a romantic, even normative, ideal, but only as long as the relationship remained at a safe distance. When confronted with the all too ugly realities of street culture at close quarters, the exponents of the alternative life-style hastily backed off and dissociated themselves from those who were giving the movement a bad name. The street communards' association with the anarchist movement followed a similar pattern: brief honeymoon, sudden divorce.

Commune propaganda frequently put a brave face on this isolation, casting it in a heroic stance of defiance. As one leaflet put it:

> We are fucked about, and kicked around because the Authorities think we are defenceless – unlike the students and workers, we have no bureaucratic organisations to fight for our interests, we don't have the ear of responsible pressure groups, but we are not alone, and we are not without weapons.

Nevertheless, the leadership saw that without external support, they were likely to be defeated from within by the permanent instability of their social base.

Much of their energy was anyway spent on trying to transform its constituency into a more socially cohesive force, and reduce the level of paranoia which was both cause and consequence of its lack. West End youth might be amongst those who had nothing and had nothing to lose, *pace* Bob Dylan, but in practice this meant that they had nothing much to give to each other either, and every reason to grab what they could get away with – 'doss bags', cash, drugs, etc. The dominant mode of exchange was less mutual aid than mutual theft, 'ripping off'.

The leadership's intervention took a severely practical form. They initiated a 'food co-op', whereby earnings from street selling, busking or begging were pooled to bulk-buy enough food to ensure one proper meal a day for everyone who took part. Squads were also delegated to 'liberate' essential supplies from supermarkets, wholesalers and to scavenge street markets.

The food co-op may have been designed to inculcate the beat ideal, but its popularity lay in the material fact that living on the street is the most expensive mode of subsistence: cash conned was immediately, and literally, swallowed up in a succession of snacks through the day. The food stuff thus consumed was both high priced and made an extremely poor diet. It did little to lift the perpetual state of siege against hunger. The food co-op at least did that.

Secondly, the leadership attempted, with somewhat less success, to institute an internal system of social control. The chief aim was to warn off 'bum dealers' – i.e. drug pushers who sold lethal or fraudulent supplies at exorbitant prices. The target was well chosen, they were hardly the most popular element, and the commune's approach to popular justice was nothing if not dramatic.

One of the chief offenders was publicly 'arrested', taken to a derry and tried by a court composed of street communards and his victim. On admitting his guilt, the pusher was forcibly injected with a dosage of his own lethal mixture (Chinese heroin, adulterated with soap powder) and finally dumped, unconscious, on the steps of a West End drug clinic, with a placard round his neck, proclaiming the reasons for his condition.

Such occasional instances of 'propaganda by deed' had very limited impact on the overall level of consciousness of West End youth! Increasingly the leadership had to rely on the leaflets, newspapers, posters and other material it produced in the course of its campaign to formally communicate its aims and ideals to the 'rank and file'. In looking at this literature, it is clear that its aim was less to convert potential outside allies than to serve as an internal information bulletin.

News from Nowhere

144 Piccadilly was seized on by the mass media because it was here that, in the one time and space, *all* the disparate images which had been built up into the Spectacle of Dissident Youth through the two post-war decades suddenly *materialised*, coalesced in a real social interface.

Hippies, Hell's Angels, junkies, teenage runaways, 'revolutionary' students inside, skinheads outside, every category was more or less visibly represented, yet only to become locked in what seemed an essentially private battle amongst themselves. It was a battle which was nevertheless played out in front of a national and international audience, and its evidence was real enough. There were the burnt-out Angels' bikes. There were the young skins of the Millwall end with concussion and gashed faces. There were the junkies rushed to hospital with overdoses. There were the angry parents and probation officers come to rescue 'their' children.

In this dramaturgy it was not just that the phantoms of the Youth Spectacle suddenly took on flesh and blood, but that these diverse social instances, which had previously been insulated from each other, confined to localised or episodic 'irruptions', now, for the first time, imposed their specific presence as subcultural conjuncture.

Imposed their presence, but certainly not their meanings. When, inevitably, the occupation fell – before an efficiently conducted police commando, a large crowd of enthusiastic spectators, the world's press, plus a 'liberated' priest, who came to offer spiritual solidarity to the young squatters but only arrived in time to offer refreshment in Christ to the special patrol group, – when it was all over, the aims and motives of the occupants remained as mysterious to most beholders as their origins.

What the street communards themselves contributed as an interpretation only reinforced the public status of their ambiguity – preserved for posterity in the materiality of a sign, their essential slogan painted on the outside of 144 Piccadilly: 'We are the Writing on Your Walls'.

It was as if the meaning of the event wholly escaped those who took part in it and the only message which could be communicated to the outside world was one which played on a logical paradox of communication itself. But perhaps it would be more accurate to say that this was the only possible meta-statement which could be made about the way their presence had been framed in the means of its broadcast.

The issue of media mystification does not concern the surface details of the event and how they were composed into moral panic. The scenarios of 'Heartbreak Hotel' (the *Guardian*), or 'Sex and Drug Orgy in Filth and Stench of Hippy Haven' (the *People*), 'The Bomb Factories' (*The Times*) or 'Anarchist Conspiracies' (the *Evening Standard*) were seen by the street communards for what they were: pure fabrications. A coherent organisation of appearances for distant and atomised publics. What stood opposed to these imaginary schemes was the sense of an immediacy generated by the fact of confrontation; a collective experience, whose density made it incoherent in the face of the mundane tasks imposed by the logistics of feeding 600 people in a building. Rather than actually recognising themselves in their publicly reflected image, it was more the case of the street communards being forced to misrecognise their meanings in the explanations this imagery contained. With the fall of 144, it was the turn of the commentators (the politicians, the youth experts and all those with an ideological axe to grind) to take over from the immediate image makers (in this case the police spokesman, the high court judge, the property owner, the reporters) and integrate ad hoc judgements into explicit political verdicts.

The scene had already been set with feature articles containing Helpful Hints for Householders on what to do if 'HIPPIES INVADE YOUR HOME TONITE', and quasi-news items beginning: 'Security guards with dogs were on duty at many buildings tonight as hippies threatened to spread their communes throughout London …' The pervasive image, then, was one of the Mob, and inevitably it was the right-wing politicians who exploited it best. One spoke in the Commons of 'these barbarians encamped amidst the ruins of a dying civilisation' (general applause), while it was Enoch Powell who gave the most classical statement of moral panic:

Violence and mob law are organised and spreading today for their own sake. Those who organise and spread them are not seeking to persuade authority to act differently, be more merciful or generous. Their object is to repudiate authority and destroy it. Whatever grievance they have is not to be met by scores of young ruffians and thugs, wandering the streets of our great cities, intimidating the law-abiding members of society. The translation of a want or a need into a right is one of the most dangerous and widespread heresies today, and destroys the very mechanisms by which those wants could be met in an orderly way.

But the left was not to be outdone, one of its spokesmen wrote:

The events of the last week have shown that late capitalism has thrown up social forces in the image of its own degeneracy. This mob of dope addicts, misfits, beatniks and petty criminals are what Marx called the lumpen proletariat, the offal and scum of bourgeois society ... it was gratifying to see that elements of young workers who turned up at the scene put the boot in well and truly on these parasites ...

Along with the figure of the Mob was often added the more general thematic of its locus – the Street: a perennial source of fear and secret fascination. Its permanent inhabitants, and those who make their livelihoods there, have traditionally been associated as carriers of political disorder. The street communards, who celebrated this connection in their name, as well as their propaganda, were inevitably inserted into a familiar moral topography. The return of the repressed from the 'subterranean depths, their sudden volcanic irruption ... the forces of anarchy ... the need for eternal vigilance'. Certainly, there was the paranoid rendition of a 'phantasm of origins', but its social articulation was an effect of the ideological state apparatus itself. As we noted earlier, the dialectics of legal repression consist in the routine elimination from public visibility of all those social forces whose conditions of existence are seen as a threat to official norms of public order. However, in its very nature this is a strategy of containment, not outright suppression. Some of these groups succeed in becoming sufficiently organised to assert the legitimacy of a countervailing public realm. At this point their existence can no longer be contained or officially denied. A strategy of public confrontation and suppression is then required; the due process of law has to be temporarily suspended and the state's claim to legitimacy as a neutral arbiter, above sectional interest is potentially put in jeopardy.

Now it is at this point, where the localised and routine apparatus of social control has broken down, that the mass media, applying its own independent globalising logic to the situation, intervenes. The latent function of their involvement is to legitimate the emergency measures which have to be taken to evict the 'emergent forces' from the bourgeois public realm. This defines both the limits and conditions of media representations, as well as giving the form and tempo of their intervention.

The fact that a countervailing reality, or rather its human bearers, have broken through their encirclement, defines them as 'news'. Suddenly, and apparently out of nowhere, they appear on the front pages, but only for as long as is required for their suppression, i.e. their safe consignment to the routine administrations of the body politic. So that, just as suddenly and inexplicably (to the media public), they disappear back into nowhere ... until the 'next time', leaving behind only the halo of their evanescent threat.

A subcultural conjuncture is always news from nowhere, a volcanic irruption, a non-sense, as well as a non sequitur, from the vantage point of the bourgeois public realm.

Making sense

The phantasm of the 'subterranean depths' held another connection between the Street and the Mob which 144 made palpable: the loss of boundary maintenance. The Street, especially around the city centre, is of course the one space in the capitalist urban structure where all social classes can circulate freely and in their free time; whereas elsewhere they tend to be spatially and structurally segregated in terms of income, residential area or occupation. The anonymity and social promiscuity of the West End crowds, pubs, cafés and cinemas offered the promise of chance encounters, and potential release from constraining identities compiled of family responsibilities, work, etc. But this dissolution of social boundaries is only potential, because an intricate system of informal norms of public order comes into play, designed to reinforce relations of social distance and difference. These norms are backed by the due process of law, and premised on maintaining the free circulation of commodities and keeping the human traffic moving. It was these norms and this Law which the street commune explicitly violated in laying claim to the street and the city centre as its territory – the privileged space of a collective existence – in celebrating, at least in theory, the freedom of the streets. In doing so the commune drew down on itself the second aspect of the Mob – a socially disparate and amorphous mass, whose own lack of boundaries threatens those of the bourgeois public realm at its weakest point.

These themes can be traced in the following quotations from leader comment:

Some of them are well educated, and idealistic in intentions, but their association with long-haired layabouts, some of them not even housetrained, can't do their cause anything but harm....The worst feature of the situation is that there are many perfectly honest decent young people, who have been seduced by the publicity given to the views of this exhibitionist minority.

The majority are engaged in a campaign to create social chaos...their minds filled with the mumbo jumbo of irrational infantile anarchism...these anarchists run the risk of tarring other young people with the same unpleasant brush as they bring to their own activities, from pot smoking to free love. The cost of anarchy is that it can only lead to a tightening of the law.

The West End became filled to overflowing with an ill assorted mob of drifters and homeless youth, the flotsam and jetsam of society, who set up camp on Piccadilly Circus, and proceeded to way-lay passers-by, many of them foreign visitors, with demands for money and food, not only at times completely blocking the pavements, but preventing ordinary citizens from going about their lawful business.

Sometimes the propositions were combined in various permutations. For instance, the leadership was seen as harmless because young idealists, and the rank and file construed as the real threat because out of control. Alternatively, the leadership was especially dangerous because forming an anarchist conspiracy, misleading the 'innocent' rank and file. Here is *The Times'* end-of-term report:

> A distinction must be drawn between the young idealists of Piccadilly, and the drop-outs, the drug addicts and the violent, who made the whole episode so degrading. The idealists were a minority, and their action was misguided. But they were at least trying to provide a direct solution to a grave social problem (homelessness) and in the process they showed a degree of organising ability and spirit. The drop-outs should be put in a completely different category, it was they who determined the course of events, and they should be regarded with no more than the sympathy which should always have been reserved for society's casualties....we need to ensure that money is not given to the work-shy, simply because they cannot be bothered to earn a living themselves...many of the real unfortunates are in want of help in kind rather than cash. A high proportion of drop outs are the product of bad social conditions and poor home surroundings...

By conjugating these propositions, often as here in confusing ways, a whole taxonomy – or, perhaps we should say taxidermy – of deviance was elaborated around the street commune. A system of moral categories was manufactured which, in combination, served as – *or rather instead of* – a principle of historical/ sociological explanation. These categories exist in a purely imaginary space of public discourse, in an empty homogeneous time of modernity outside history, in which the poor are always with us, youth are always rebelling, progress is always being made, and the final collapse of Western civilisation is always and already just around the corner.

The effect was to integrate the question of deviance within the answers provided by the dominant political discourse and its internal disputes. In the case of 144 Piccadilly, this served to link the event with perennial arguments for or against the welfare state, for or against the authority of the family; to allow the lesson to be drawn and the professional moralists, from Bernard Levin to Malcolm Muggeridge to Richard 'Play Power' Neville, to prove once again they were right. It was not surprising, for instance, that the then Labour Minister for Health should act against 'these anti-social rebels without a cause, who have no claim on the compassion of the community', by instructing social security officers to refuse claims to anyone giving 144 Piccadilly as their address. And that this purely symbolic gesture should receive disproportionate emphasis in the media. It would not, of course, be the first or last time that a youth culture was made the silent support of a false debate conducted by others in its name, as official left and right engaged in yet another round of sniping from their respective prepared positions.

What linked these positions was a common stance of voyeurism, the only vantage point offered by the bourgeois public realm on social forces external to it.

In some cases, this was a voyeurism socially committed to its object, which wished to rescue the deviant from an official pariah status and demonstrate that he or she is human like the rest of 'us'; or even more human, because expressing a sense of alienation which is elsewhere denied.

For example, Bernard Levin, in an article headlined 'Why did they reject us?' concluded:

> We do not have to like the radical young, we do not have to bow before their accusations, but for their sake as well as ours, we have got to find out what ails them; why young people, with their lives before them, regress into the womb of hopeless community living, and where and how our society, with all its rewards and satisfactions, has come to seem utterly contemptible to a group which include many who could greatly contribute to it. In finding out what ails them, we may begin to understand what ails us. We have got to start asking these questions seriously.

Meanwhile in sociology departments, Levin's call was already being answered; radical criminologists were making a purely theoretical descent into the lower depths to bring back the good news that schizophrenics, vandals, soccer hooligans, hippies, junkies, were all human too, if it weren't for the dehumanising labels being pinned on them. This project of 're-humanising' the deviant, in and by theory, ended up in practice as special pleading, for greater tolerance in a pluralist society. This worthy plea fell on deaf ears because it was so easily assimilated as a simple liberal variant of the prevailing ideology of deviance.

Opposed to this abstract humanism, was a more concrete and popular form of voyeurism, which saw the issue less in terms of subculture, than as a sub-human, if not super-natural, phenomenon.

The best place to look at this latter kind of voyeurism in action, is in the large crowds which gathered outside 144 during the week of the occupation. Ironically, in the behaviour of *these* crowds (but nowhere else) could be discerned the features attributed to classical bourgeois mythology to the vengeful Mob.

A team of sociology students from the London School of Economics administered a short questionnaire to a random sample of 220 members of this crowd, taken on two successive evenings at the height of the siege. In the nature of the thing it was a somewhat rough and ready exercise. Many of the findings are predictable enough. The median age of the sample was 48. There was a significant proportion of members of ex-service men's organisations, many of whom had spent, or lost, their youth in the Second World War. The most interesting finding concerns the social class composition. What emerged was the overwhelmingly lower middle-class character of the crowd. In the table on p. 37 occupations are re-grouped as far as possible using the framework of definitions adopted elsewhere in this text.

So well over half the crowd sample could be defined as petit bourgeois – from shopkeepers, tradesmen and small independent business folk (traditional) to office workers, technicians and other white collar grades (new). The bourgeoisie and the working class are conspicuous by their absence. In other words, it was those class fractions who are poorly represented as an organised political force within the bourgeois public realm who were most represented in this sample, and from other observations, most in evidence in the crowd. In the questionnaire response, there was a consensus of hostility to the street communards, across both the political and class spectrum. The extreme right were, as might be expected, somewhat over-represented, but there were no significant differences in measured

(%)

1	Professional upper middle class	3
2	Industrial and commercial middle class	2
3	Traditional petit bourgeoisie	28
4	White collar workers, new middle class, inc. students	31
5	Skilled manual	7
6	Unskilled and semi-skilled manual	10
7	Foreign nationals (tourists)	16
8	Unemployed – no job stated	3*

*For OAPs, last occupation before retirement is used. If unemployed, last job or job sought. There were a high proportion of women in the sample: 56 percent. More than half of these were 'housewives'. Housewives were included by their last occupation before marriage, rather than by their husband's occupation. Despite the problems this gives rise to, it was felt preferable to the usual sampling practice at this time. However, it may have served to artificially inflate the representation of Category 4, since many working-class girls take temporary office work before marriage.

range of hostility between Labour and Tory voters. However, voting behaviour is too crude an index of socio-cultural attitude. Within the lower middle-class sample there were significant differences in modes of reaction. The traditional fraction expressed the most extreme degree of hostility of all sampled strata, while the new fractions *expressed the greatest degree of variation of response.* What both fractions had in common, however, was a greater reliance on a single exclusive and all-embracing moral proposition. Within this, the traditional fraction, along with working-class housewives, exhibited the greatest preference for condemning the street communards for personal recklessness, while the new fraction oscillated between structural explanations (alienation, unemployment) and personal attribution. The significance of the different terms through which the moral panic is realised, will be discussed later. It's enough to note here that the immediate scenario of a predominantly middle-aged mob howling for the blood of a predominantly youthful mob responding in kind, the spectre conjured up by the media of an eternally recurrent conflict of generations, is a pure optical illusion. Rather, what was in play was a public confrontation between different fractions or 'moments' of middle and working class formation.

The dialogic imagination

Communication between the crowd and the street communards was not all animal categories and verbal abuse. There were moments when something like a dialogue began to emerge, exchanges whose glimpsed dialectic pointed beyond the closures of moralistic debate. What follows is a transcript of one such encounter between an 18-year-old ex-bank clerk turned street communard and, in turn, an old age pensioner, a skilled worker in his late thirties and – briefly – a student, all of them male. What perhaps should be listened for is the place from which each is speaking, the hidden mediations through which each uses the other as means of communicating his own place to himself.

First Exchange

Charly: If you sit back in your home and read the papers and watch television, then you say you form an opinion about us, but it's not really your own opinion, it's someone else's. Then if you come down and talk to us...

OAP: That's right, then we can see you as we should do.

Charly: You get in touch with reality and your opinion can't stay the same. This is what is happening.

Worker: You're doing yourselves a very bad turn...just turning the public against you. No, you've got no change, boy.

Charly: Well, people are listening now and if you want to carry on, I'll tell you some more things.

OAP: No, we're not listening, we're trying to tell you what to do.

Charly: We don't want to be told.

Worker: No, we're trying to advise you, not tell you.

OAP: We've already told you what to do. Go and find some work and earn some money.

Charly: Go and find some work. You mean some meaningless task.

OAP: No, bigger work. Go and do some.

Charly: You mean hire ourselves out on a time basis.

OAP: No, No, No, you're finished, ain't yer.

Charly: Like a prostitute, sell ourselves for money, regardless of what it is we're supporting by doing this.

Worker: You're...you should be going to work. How can you be enjoying yourself...

Charly: A system which is built to exploit you.

Worker: In a cold hole with mice and rats running about, in a cold old building, and you sit down with whatever you have over your shoulders, and say, 'I'm enjoying myself.' Now, tell me how you're enjoying yourself?

Charly: Well, you see, you get some cannabis resin, and some cigarette papers...

OAP: Yeah (laughter), and then you're away, ain't yer.

Charly: Turned on, sir, is the word, turned on to reality.

OAP: So you don't feel the cold no more, I suppose.

Worker: Some people go and take drugs. They get satisfaction from it. It's up to them. But in the end, it is not a right thing to do, 'cos you've got to face life, and the problems of life.

Charly: You've got to face the problems of life, but first, you've got to identify them. The problems of life are not how to get a car, a new record player, how to gain these and other things.

Worker: Listen, when you take over all these houses, how are you going to maintain them without going to work? Who will do that for you?

Charly: Let's take 144 Piccadilly. It was a building which has been empty for a long time. Obviously it was a very dirty building. The building is now clean – that was our work. We get things given to us by people who realise what we're about and want to help this thing forward. We get paint, furniture, and we liberate things, steal what nobody wants or is going to waste.

Worker: So, you make your living from crime?

Charly: I'm not a criminal. Maybe I've just come out of Ashford [Remand Centre] and maybe I'm going back in again for another couple of months for a period of strict disciplinary training, which, in other words, means 'kick them back into line'. Inside, if you look up, stop to talk to anyone, oh this is bad, you're really rebelling in an incredibly awful way, and you have to be put down hard. And all this because I like to get turned on to reality and all this you, as tax payers, are paying for.

OAP: But, the police, the prisons, they're all we've got. They have to keep you down.

Worker: Say you win, right, you get what you want, are you going to start work then?

Charly: Work? What we're working for is a workless society.

Worker: That means you're not going to work ever. So, if every-one is of the same opinion as you, who is going to give who what? It doesn't make sense.

Student: Well, it does make sense...in fact to most people who study machines for the future and so on, because in about fifty years...

Worker: If you don't work, you don't get food...

Student: The idea of the worker is going to be outdated.

OAP: Work is for the workers and these people are not workers.

Student: Food can be produced quite automatically. In about fifty years time only about ten per cent of the people...

Worker: I'm talking about now. We've heard all this fifty year time rubbish before.

Student: How old are you?

Worker: I'm 37, but I don't...

Student: Did you enjoy your youth?

Charly: What makes you think this man's youth is over? What makes you think that youth is something which ends at twenty-one?

Worker: My youth ended at about twenty-two years, when I got married. From seventeen I left school to twenty-two, yeah.

Student: It's very doubtful if you had a real youth at all.

Second Exchange

Worker: What do you call a meaningless task?

Charly: What do you do?

Worker: I'm an electrical engineer, but that's beside the point.

Charly: You see these things around here, these ads, they're put up by workers, some of them electrical engineers like yourself. They get paid for putting them up, and that is their whole reason for doing it. Now, let's see: there's Carlsberg Lager, Nolita Cameras, Wrigley's Spearmint Chewing Gum, Gordon's Dry Gin, 'A Nice Girl Like You'. All that these things do is create a demand for things people don't need.

Worker: Why is a person not entitled to a Carlsberg, when you think you're entitled to take drugs. You don't *need* drugs.

Charly: People think they want these things, and they have to get the means to get them. They have to get money, they have to work, to get the things they don't really need in the first place, and so they work at putting up these things – all these ads – to condition everyone else to believe they want them as well.

Worker: You're getting yourself tied up in knots. You're going round in a circle.

Charly: What I'm talking about is the circle people's lives go round in.

OAP: What do you want to live?

Charly: I need to eat, I need shelter, that's it.

OAP: And you expect the community, us, to provide you with what you need, a young blood, eighteen or nineteen. You want the world to keep you because you're too lazy to work. How much money have you got now until the end of next week?

Charly: Nothing, but I'm going to go out and sell some *International Times* on the street.

OAP: Yeah, but you don't get enough to make a decent living out of that. Why don't you get a room and pay your rent, then?

Charly: It's enough to live. I wouldn't be happy paying rent when there are so many buildings going to waste.

Worker: Why don't you do what I do? Work hard, save your money, and get a proper place to live? That's what I've done. I've built myself up from nothing. I've got my own house now, and a proper garden and my kids have got a decent start in life.

OAP: Living in that commune...how can I imagine it? I'd feel the lowest form of dog if I'd done that. No, I wouldn't dream of going along with you. I have three meals a day. I have a bath once a week. ...No, I wouldn't dream of walking around like this...half of them look like dogs, don't they? They don't look like human beings do they?

Charly: Bow-wow. Are you convinced I'm a dog?

OAP: (laughs) This one, he's a good one. But have a look at the others?

Charly: Look, sir, if you see me sitting amongst the others, then I'd just be one of the others. If the others were standing as close to you as I'm standing now, you'd recognise their humanity, just as surely as you're recognising mine.

OAP: I got near some of them a little while ago and they made me nearly vomit. They smelt. I had to walk away.

Charly: Very possibly. Some people are filthy. I've seen people of your age group who STUNK. Drug addicts on alcohol. Drug addicts of your generation are called alcoholics, drug addicts of my generation are called junkies...only difference they SMELL and they look far worse than any junkie I've ever seen, and I've been around this scene for a while.

Third Exchange

OAP: This conditioning, or whatever it is...

Charly: Let's take the pattern through. The child is taught to accept established family structure: that is, two people, tied together with legally binding documents to hold them together for the rest of their lives and a couple of kids, their own little box, and together they stand united to face the world. That is what the child is taught as the natural and only way to be. This is the way it's going to be when it grows up. That's conditioning.

OAP: I had no children.

Charly: At 5 years old the child is put into the state schooling system. This teaches it to accept the state or part of it. It is given certain skills, which it can then sell to keep the work-oriented society in existence. At the age of 15, the child leaves school and it's slotted in. Between the ages of 18 and 20 it should start courting and when it reaches the age of 25, it should be married, with

	legally binding documents, to one person for the rest of its life.
OAP:	Which I did.
Charly:	In its own cage, with its own debts, commitments, responsibilities... From 25 onwards all is repetition. Work, work, work, work, work, all the year round, three weeks' holiday a year, at the weekends the man has a pint at the pub. This is freedom. This is life. This is the concept of living which people are brought up and taught to accept, that this is the way they have to live. And, indeed, this is the way they do live. If people were given the full picture, they must say 'It's bad, we don't want it.'
OAP:	I had forty-four years of married life. I never lived in London. I lived ten miles outside. When I was a young man I used to come to London every night of the week with my girl. Pictures and theatres every night of the week. No matter what night it was, I'd go to work, come home and then out we'd go and have some fun. I was earning good money, I'll grant you, as a young-ster, I was earning near £5 a week and I was...it was just after the war...I was working as a mechanic in this garage and I was doing very well. We could afford half a pound of chocolates whenever we went out, and, of course, pictures and theatres, they cost next to nothing in them days. And then we got married and we used still to go out once or twice a week up to London, right up to the time my wife died. And I had forty-four years of married life and I've never regretted that time. Never. I never had no dealings with the police. But you people are chased all over the place. You people haven't got freedom, not like we had. We had all the freedom we wanted then...
Charly:	My mother and her husband, my father, live in a council house in Aidrie in Scotland. They enjoy a good standard of living. They have fitted carpets in the house. They have a television, they have a radio, tape recorder, oh, they enjoy a good standard of living. My mother has been scrubbing floors...she's now forty-six...she's been doing cleaning since she was about

twenty. All these things are the things she has been
working for. These are the things I say she doesn't
need. Yet she's been working for them all her life. Now
she has them and now her children have left home.
She has no happiness. She has got all these things, but
she has got no happiness. I've got none of these things
and I'm happy.

Perhaps the most striking feature of this dialogue is its sharp contrast with the form and content of the official debate. A whole
series of questions are posed here which are excluded from the
interrogations of a moral discourse on deviance and exist beyond
its terms of censure. These questions all turn on *material* conditions of existence: the exigencies of subsistence, the problematic
nature of freedom within capitalist relations of production, the
meaning of work. In other words, they are questions framed from
the vantage point of an alternative public realm. Nevertheless, in
the first two exchanges, these questions are foreclosed, and at precisely the point in the argument where they begin to be posed
explicitly, in political and economic terms, and *where they point to
answers which the sub-culture cannot give*. The virtuosity of Charly's
expositions, which we might add are first hand, the filtering of his
own experience through the concepts he fashioned to make sense
of it, cannot disguise this basic fact. It's worth noting, too, that
the places of foreclosure are all marked by the reintroduction of
moral categories, not here dressed up in elaborate verbiage, but
cut down to the crude stereotypes on which they rest. Even more
significant, is what these 'interruptions' precipitate in the speakers – the falling back on a discourse of generation after generation, the ritual insults of age and youth.

   In the third and final exchange, argument has given way to
affirmation, each speaker placing his point of view in the context
of his own life and in doing so, signifying that what separates
them is *not* youth and age, but history. What is revealed at the end
is what has silently structured this whole encounter between
strangers: the complex of transformations which working-class life
and labour has undergone over half a century, the slow accumulation of cultural discontinuities and dissonant expectations. Three
successive working-class generations are here present to each
other across the three people, who cannot help but be their

spokesmen because they can only relate to each other through their formative experiences of different conjunctures: the inter-war recession (OAP); the welfare state settlement between capital and labour (Charly's parents and the worker); an affluent consumer society (Charly and the student).

In this unlikeliest of settings – a public argument, in the middle of Piccadilly Circus, and its milling Saturday night crowd – these moments in the history of growing up working-class briefly flare up and assert a precise articulation against the eternal dreamtime of youth and modernity which is being advertised and frantically pursued in its midst.

For all that, the meaning of the conjuncture was neither immediately evident, as it would be, for instance, in a strike or a race riot, nor could it be constructed from within, by a pure act of reflection. As the world's press threw themselves on the building of 144 Piccadilly, in an ever more desperate search for the 'real' inside story, perhaps even they began to suspect that the truth, if there was one, was to be found everywhere else but there. Equally, the logic of their situation forced out explanations from the street communards which made a nonsense of their struggle, but which they could only fall back on to make some sense of where it had led them. As, for example, in this statement by 'Doctor John', one of its leading ideologues, a preface to an appeal to form a united youth front, allying skinheads, greasers, students and hippies in a programme of generalised subcultural resistance:

Class warfare has become bogged down as a war of entrenched positions; both ruling class and workers have settled for a stalemate; they prefer to cut their losses and settle for the secondary gains which the status quo provides. For those who become domesticated to it, life in the trenches has its own rewards. But their children are not so happy. They long to escape. There must be something more to life, the real world is somewhere else, perhaps out there. And so a few crawl out into the no man's land between the class trenches. Young people from both sides, at first a few, then in increasing numbers. But as soon as they get there they are hit by a tremendous fusillade from both sides; they have become the common enemies of both classes, traitors to their families and their status quo. Their only hope of survival is to stick together...

Outside 144

What is in fact a metaphor relevant to the formation of lower middle-class student youth is thus projected as an analysis universally applicable to all social classes. It is this universality which precludes the metaphor pointing beyond itself to a concrete understanding of what is specific to the contradictory location of this stratum.

This false consciousness of themselves as the youth vanguard of a new revolutionary class was not of course unique to the ideologues of the 'Street Commune'. In one form or another it was a constant theme in the rhetorics of 1960s' counter-cultural politics. From CND to the YCL, from the New Left groupuscule to the 'life style guerilla'. Each of these movements in their different ways claimed to be building a new world in the midst of a senescent capitalism, even as they were reconstituting a link between youth, culture and modernity which was to prove the life blood of consumerism.

If that irony escaped all those who participated in the spectacle of 144 Piccadilly, it was nevertheless present in the graffiti which became the street communes' iconic monument to its own transient threat. 'We are The Writing on Your Walls' was already a knowing sign made for consumption and reproduction by sociologists, youth experts, and media commentators; in their hands at least it would survive official erasure. For although the events themselves were quickly forgotten, except by those most directly touched by them, and all trace of 'hippy squatterdom' soon vanished along with public interest in the lives of the young homeless and unemployed, the sign itself lived on in popular memory to fight another day. And add its own peculiar burden of representation to the youth question.

Chapter 2

Subcultural Conflict and Working-class Community

At the height of the 'battle for 144', I used to escape from time to time to Westminster Library, or the reading room of the British Museum, to try to get my bearings as far away as possible from the maddening crowds. On one of these intellectual expeditions I came across Louis Althusser's Pour Marx, *still then (in 1969) untranslated. Even though my French was not brilliant and I had to struggle to grasp some of its more intricate arguments, I still remember the sense of liberation I got from its cool dispassionate thinking; for someone who had taken Marcuse and the Great Refusal all too literally, and had followed the exhortations of Debord, and the French situationists, 'to at last create a situation in which there is no turning back', Althusser's counter-injunction to make an 'epistemological break' from such heady Hegelian dialectics came as a breath of fresh air.*

Whatever happened subsequently, we are indebted to Althusser for providing us with a new beginning in trying to understand the seductive power of ideology. With a little help from Lacan, he drew our attention to some of the key ways in which ideology works unconsciously, behind our backs, to captivate us with a certain upside-down image of the world and our place in it. What was new was the emphasis on the everyday

This chapter was first published in *CCCS Working Papers*, 2 (1972), pp. 5–53.

*rituals and modes of address through which people are made to misrecog-
nise themselves as autonomous individuals or subjects, through a discursive process which subordinates them to structures of power over
which they had no control. The appeal of this notion to someone who
was caught up in the events described in Chapter I can perhaps be
readily appreciated!*

*Althusser was mainly concerned with political and moral discourses
which were institutionalised in what he called the 'ideological state
apparatus'. Most of his examples seemed a million miles away from the
world of youth cultures and 144 Piccadilly! There was however another,
related, and equally relevant model of the world turned upside-down provided, by Claude Lévi-Strauss in his theory of mythology. In* Pensée
Sauvage, *and elsewhere, Levi-Strauss demonstrated that myths were not
unitary narratives, but constructed through bricolage – a process which
selected and combined different symbolic elements into a new syncretic
cultural form, and en route magically transformed the underlying structural contradictions in a society into a harmless play of binary
oppositions.*

*Putting these two ideas together enabled me to rethink the class problem-
atics of 1960s youth cultures. Instead of trying to define them in terms of
the real if contradictory social locations of the young people concerned, as I
had done previously (c.f. Chapter 1), it was now possible to analyse them
in terms of their* imaginary *class belonging, and the processes of bricolage
through which particular social contradictions were magically resolved in
different cultural codes or styles.*

*The focus of this analysis was not however the transformation of
bohemianism with the beats and hippies, but the changes which were
occurring in working-class cultures and communities in the 1960s and
'70s, as epitomised by the East End of London. There were two reasons
for this choice. I had moved to Bethnal Green and was living in a street
which housed some of the few surviving Jewish tailoring businesses in the
area. At the same time I had made friends with members of a local skinhead gang – the Collinwood, whom I had first met as 'enemies' at 144.
If nothing else this experience sensitised me to the interplay of continuity
and discontinuity in East End life and labour and the way in which
these might be articulated through youth cultures.*

*A further reason lay in the symbolic place which the East End occupied
in the tradition of English settlement sociology and its post-war revival by
the Institute of Community Studies. I wanted to challenge the view that the*

area exemplified some normative model or ideal type of working-class kinship and community, and that Mods and Rockers were something 'foreign' imported into it from outside.

The text was first given as a talk to a seminar group at the Centre for Contemporary Cultural Studies. The original, longer version was subsequently published in an early number of the CCCS Working Papers. Over the next few years, and unknown to me, since I remained in youth and community work and quite out of touch with developments in academic circles, the paper was taken up by a group at the Centre as the basis of an extended theoretical study of youth cultures and 'rituals of resistance'. This study was primarily concerned with the implications of this approach for developing Gramsci's theory of hegemony and using it to analyse peculiarities of the English class structure. The notion of subcultural bricolage was somewhat ignored, which was perhaps a pity, given that it prefigured so much of the recent debate on post-modern identities. And then, of course, class analysis was pushed aside and the focus of attention shifted to gendered and racialised forms of youth culture. Partly as a result, the initial project of anchoring subcultural analysis to an ethnographic study of structural change impacting on local labour histories or urban geographies was not properly followed through. Nor was such an approach likely to find favour with funding bodies. Today fortunately there is renewed interest in making these connections, in a much more sophisticated way than was possible in this crude first attempt.

The 1950s saw the development of new towns and large estates on the outskirts of east London (Dagenham, Greenleigh and so on), and a large number of families from the worst slums of the East End were rehoused in this way. The East End, one of the highest-density areas in London, underwent a gradual depopulation. But as it did so, certain areas underwent a repopulation as they were rapidly colonized by a large influx of West Indians and Pakistanis. One of the reasons why these communities were attracted (in the weak sense of the word) to such areas is often called 'planning blight'. This concept has been used to describe what happens in the take-off phase of comprehensive redevelopment in the inner residential zones of large urban centres. The typical pattern is that as redevelopment begins, land values inevitably rise and rental values fall; the most dynamic elements in local industry, which are usually the largest employers of labour, tend to move out, alongside the migrating families, and are often offered economic incentives to do so; much of the existing dilapidated property in the area is bought up cheaply by property speculators and Rachman-type landlords, who are only interested in the maximum exploitation of their assets – the largest profits in the shortest time. As a result the property is often not maintained and becomes even further dilapidated. Immigrant families with low incomes, excluded from council housing, naturally gravitate to these areas to penetrate the local economy. This in turn accelerates the migration of the indigenous community to the new towns and estates. The only apparent exception to planning blight in fact proves the rule. For those few areas which are linked to invisible assets – such as houses of 'character' (late Georgian or early Victorian) or amenities such as parks – are actually bought up and improved, renovated for the new middle class, students, young professionals who require easy access to the commercial and cultural centre of the city. The end result for the local community is the same: whether the neighbourhood is gentrified or downgraded, long-resident white working-class families move out.

As the worst effects of this first phase, both on those who moved and on those who stayed behind, became apparent, the planning authorities decided to reverse their policy. Everything was now concentrated on building new estates on slum sites within the old East End. But far from counteracting the social disorganization of the area, this merely accelerated the process. In analysing the impact of redevelopment on the community, these two phases can be treated as one. No one is denying that redevelopment brought an improvement in material conditions for those fortunate enough to be rehoused. But while this removed the tangible evidence of poverty, it did nothing to improve the real economic situation of many families, and those with low incomes may, despite rent-rebate schemes, be worse off.

The first effect of the high-density, high-rise schemes was to attack the customary function of the street, the local pub, the corner shop as articulations of communal space. Instead there was only the privatized space of family units, stacked one on top of each other, in total isolation, juxtaposed with the totally public space which surrounded them and which lacked any of the informal social controls generated by the neighbourhood. The streets which serviced the new estates became thorough-fares, their users 'pedestrians' and, by analogy, so many bits of human traffic – and this irrespective of whether or not they were separated from motorized traffic. It is indicative of how far the planners failed to understand the human ecology of the working-class neighbourhood that they could actually talk about building 'vertical streets'! The people who had to live in them weren't fooled. As one man put it: they might have running hot water and central heating but to him they were still 'prisons in the sky'. Inevitably, the physical isolation, the lack of human scale and the sheer impersonality of the new environment was felt most keenly by people living in the new tower blocks which have gradually come to dominate the East End landscape.

The second effect of redevelopment was to problematize the principle of 'matrilocal residence. Not only was the new housing designed on the model of the nuclear family, with little provision for large low-income families (usually designated 'problem families'!) and none at all for groups of young single people, but the actual pattern of distribution of the new housing tended to disperse the kinship network; families of marriage were separated from their families of origin, especially during the first phase of the redevelopment. The isolated family unit could no longer call on the resources of wider kinship networks or of the neighbourhood, and the family itself became the sole focus of solidarity. This meant that any problems were bottled up within the immediate interpersonal context which produced them; and at the same time family relationships were invested with a new intensity to compensate for the diversity of relationships previously generated through neighbours and wider kin. The trouble was that although the traditional kinship system which corresponded to it had broken down, the traditional patterns of socialization (of communication and control) continued to reproduce themselves in the interior of the family. The working-class family was thus not only isolated from the outside but also undermined from within.

There is no better example of what we are talking about than the plight of the so-called 'housebound mother'. The street or turning was no longer available as a safe playspace, under neighbourly supervision. Mum or Auntie were no longer just around the corner to look after the kids for the odd morning. Instead, the task of keeping an eye on the kids fell exclusively to the young wife, and the only safe playspace was the 'safety of the home'. Feeling herself cooped up with the kids and cut off from the outside world, it wasn't surprising if she occasionally took out her frustration on those nearest and dearest! Only market research and advertising executives imagine that the housebound mother sublimates everything in her G-plan furniture, her washing machine or her non-stick frying pans. Underlying all this, however, there was a more basic process of change going on in the community, a change in the whole economic infrastructure of the East End.

In the late 1950s the British economy began to recover from the effect of the war and to apply the advanced technology developed during this period to the more backward sectors of the economy. Craft industries and small-scale production in general were the first to suffer; automated techniques replaced the traditional handskills and their simple division of labour. Similarly, the economies of scale provided for by the concentration of capital resources meant that the small-scale family business was no longer a viable unit. Despite a long rearguard action, many of the traditional industries – tailoring, furniture making, many of the service and distributive trades linked to the docks – rapidly declined or were bought out. Symbolic of this was the disappearance of the corner shop; where these were not demolished by redevelopment they were replaced by larger supermarkets, often owned by large combines. Even where corner shops were offered places in the redevelopment area, often they could not afford the high rents.

There was a gradual polarization in the structure of the labour force: on the one side, the highly specialized, skilled and well paid jobs associated with the new technology and the high-growth sectors that employed them; on the other, the routine, dead-end, low-paid and unskilled jobs associated with the labour-intensive sectors, especially the service industries. As might be expected, it was the young men, just out of school, who got the worst of the deal. Lacking openings in their fathers' trades, and lacking the qualifications for the new industries, they were relegated to jobs as van boys, office boys, packers, warehousemen and so on, and to long spells out of work. More and more people, young and old, had to travel out of the community to their jobs, and some eventually moved out to live elsewhere,

where suitable work was to be found. The local economy as a whole contracted, became less diverse. Girls, on the whole, negotiated the transition to the new serviced-based economy more easily. They travelled 'up west' to work in shops and offices much more easily than their brothers, who were afraid to leave the protection of their local 'manors'.

If someone should ask why the plan to 'modernize' the pattern of East End life should have been such a disaster, perhaps the only honest answer is that given the macro-social forces acting on it, given the political, ideological and economic framework within which it operated, the result was inevitable. For example, many local people wonder why the new environment should be the way it is. The reasons are complex. They are political in so far as the system does not allow for any effective participation by a local working-class community in the decision-making process at any stage or level of planning. The clients of the planners are simply the local authority or the commercial developer who employs them. They are ideological in so far as the plans are unconsciously modelled on the structure of the middle-class environment, which is based on the concept of *property* and private *ownership*, on individual differences of status, wealth and so on, whereas the structure of the working-class environment is based on the concept of community or collective identity, common lack of ownership, wealth, etc. Similarly, needs were assessed on the norms of the middle-class nuclear family rather than on those of the extended working-class family. But underpinning both these sets of reasons lie the basic economic factors involved in comprehensive redevelopment. Quite simply, faced with the task of financing a large housing programme, local authorities are forced to borrow large amounts of capital and also to design schemes which would attract capital investment to the area. This means that they have to borrow at the going interest rates, which at this period were very high, and that to subsidize housing certain of the best sites have to be earmarked for commercial developers.

All this means that planners have to reduce the cost of production to a minimum through the use of capital-intensive techniques – prefabricated and standardized components which allow for semi-automated processes in construction. The attraction of high-rise developments ('tower blocks', outside the trade) is that they not only meet these requirements but they also allow for certain economies of scale, such as the input costs of essential services, which can be grouped around a central core. As for 'non-essential' services, that is, ones that don't pay, such as playspace, community centres, youth clubs and recreational facilities, these often have to be sacrificed to the needs of commercial developers – who, of course, have quite different priorities.

The situation facing East Enders at present is not new. When the first tenements went up in the nineteenth century they provoked the same objections from local people, and for the same very good reasons, as their modern counterparts, the tower blocks. What *is* new is that in the nineteenth century the voice of the community was vigorous and articulate on these issues, whereas today, just when it needs it most, the community is faced with a crisis of indigenous leadership.

The reasons for this are already implicit in the analysis above. The labour aristocracy, the traditional source of leadership, has virtually disappeared, along with the artisan mode of production. At the same time there has been a split in consciousness between the spheres of production and consumption. More and more East Enders are forced to work outside the area; young people especially are less likely to follow family traditions in this respect. As a result, the issues of the workplace are no longer experienced as directly linked to community issues. Of course, there has always been a 'brain drain' of the most articulate, due to social mobility. But not only has this been intensified as a result of the introduction of comprehensive schools, but the recruitment of fresh talent from the stratum below – from the ranks of the respectable working class, that is – has also dried up. For this stratum, traditionally the social cement of the community, is also in a state of crisis.

The economic changes which we have already described also affected its position and, as it were, *destabilized* it. The 'respectables' found themselves caught and pulled apart by two opposed pressures of social mobility – downwards into the ranks of the casual poor, and upwards into the ranks of the new suburban working-class elite. And, more than any other section of the working class, they were caught in the middle of the two dominant but contradictory ideologies of the day: the ideology of spectacular consumption, promoted by the mass media, and the traditional ideology of production, the so-called male work ethic, which centred on the idea that a man's dignity, his manhood even, was measured by the quantity or quality of his effort in production. If this stratum began to split apart, it was because its existing position had become untenable. Its bargaining power in the labour market was threatened by the introduction of new automated techniques, which eliminated many middle-range, semi-skilled jobs. Its economic position excluded its members from entering the artificial paradise of the new consumer society; at the same time changes in the production process itself have made the traditional work ethic, pride in the job, impossible to uphold. They had the worst of all possible worlds.

Once again, this predicament was registered most deeply in and on the young. But here an additional complicating factor intervenes. We have already described the peculiar strains imposed on the 'nucleated' working-class family. And their most critical impact was in the area of parent/child relationships. What had previously been a source of support and security for both now became something of a battleground, a major focus of all the anxieties created by the disintegration of community structures around them. One result of this was to produce an increase in early marriage. For one way of escaping from the claustrophobic tensions of family life was to start a family of your own! And given the total lack of accommodation for young, single people in the new developments, as well as the conversion of cheap rented accommodation into middle-class, owner-occupied housing, the only practicable way to leave home was to get married. The second outcome of generational conflict (which may appear to go against the trend of early marriage, but in fact reinforced it) was the emergence of specific youth subcultures in opposition to the parent culture. And one effect of this was to weaken the links of historical and cultural continuity, mediated through the family, which had been such a strong force for solidarity in the working-class community. It is, perhaps, not surprising that the parent culture of the respectable working class, already in crisis, was the most 'productive' *vis-à-vis* subcultures; the internal conflicts of the parent culture came to be worked out in terms of generational conflict. One of the functions of generational conflict is to decant the kinds of oedipal tensions which appear face-to-face in the family and to replace them by a generational-specific symbolic system, so that the tension is taken out of the interpersonal context, placed in a collective context and mediated through various stereotypes which have the function of defusing anxiety.

It seems to me that the latent function of subculture is this: to express and resolve, albeit 'magically', the contradictions which remain hidden or unresolved in the parent culture. The succession of subcultures which this parent culture generated can thus all be considered so many variations on a central theme – the contradiction, at an ideological level, between traditional working-class puritanism and the new hedonism of consumption; at an economic level, between a future as part of the socially mobile elite or as part of the new lumpen proletariat. Mods, parkas, skinheads, crombies, all represent, in their different ways, an attempt to retrieve some of the socially cohesive elements destroyed in their parent culture, and to combine these with elements selected from other class fractions, symbolizing one or other of the options confronting it.

It is easy enough to see this working in practice if we remember, first, that subcultures are symbolic structures and must not be confused with the actual young people who are their bearers and supports. Secondly, a given life-style is actually made up of a number of symbolic subsystems, and it is the way in which these are articulated in the total life-style that constitutes its distinctiveness. There are four subsystems, which can be divided into two basic types. There are the relatively 'plastic' forms – dress and music – which are not directly produced by the subculture but which are selected and invested with subcultural value in so far as they express its underlying thematic. Then there are the more 'infrastructural' forms – argot and ritual – which are more resistant to innovation but, of course, reflect changes in the more plastic forms. I'm suggesting here that mods, parkas, skinheads, and so on, are a succession of subcultures which all correspond to the same parent culture and which attempt to work out, through a system of transformations, the basic problematic or contradiction which is inserted in the subculture by the parent culture.

So one can distinguish three levels in the analysis of subcultures; one is historical, which isolates the specific problematic of a particular class fraction – in this case, the respectable working class; the second is a structural and semiotic analysis of the subsystems, the way in which they are articulated and the actual transformations which those subsystems undergo from one moment to another; and the third is the phenomenological analysis of the way the subculture is actually 'lived out' by those who are the bearers and supports of the subculture. No real analysis of subculture is complete without all those levels being in place.

To go back to the diachronic string we are discussing, the original mod life-style could be interpreted as an attempt to realize, *but in an imaginary relation*, the conditions of existence of the socially mobile white-collar worker. While the argot and ritual forms of mods stressed many of the traditional values of their parent culture, their dress and music reflected the hedonistic image of the affluent consumer. The life-style crystallized in opposition to that of the rockers (the famous riots in the early 1960s testified to this), and it seems to be a law of subcultural evolution that its dynamic comes not only from the relations to its own parent culture, but also from the relation to subcultures belonging to *other class fractions*, in this case the manual working class.

The next members of our string – the parkas or scooter boys – were in some senses a transitional form between the mods and the skinheads. The alien elements introduced into music and dress by the mods were progressively de-stressed and the indigenous components of argot and ritual reasserted as the matrix of subcultural identity. The skinheads themselves carried the process to completion. Their life-style, in fact, represents a systematic inversion of the mods – whereas the mods explored the upwardly mobile option, the skinheads explored the lumpen. Music and dress again became the central focus of the life-style; the introduction of reggae (the protest music of the West Indian poor) and the 'uniform' (of which more in a moment) signified a reaction against the contamination of the parent culture by middle-class values and a reassertion of the integral values of working-class culture through its most recessive traits – its puritanism and chauvinism. This double movement gave rise to a phenomenon of 'machismo' – the deployment of masculinities associated with manual labour against groups perceived to threaten the status of both. A dramatic example of this was the epidemic of 'queer-bashing' around the country in 1969–70. The skinhead uniform itself could be interpreted as a kind of caricature of the model worker – the self-image of the working class as distorted through middle-class perceptions, a metastatement about the whole process of cultural emasculation. Finally, the skinhead life-style crystallized in opposition both to the greasers (successors to the rockers) and the hippies – both subcultures representing a species of hedonism which the skinheads rejected.

Following the skinheads there emerged another transitional form, variously known as crombies, casuals, suedes and so on (the proliferation of names being a mark of transitional phases). They represent a movement back towards the original mod position, although this time it is a question of incorporating certain elements drawn from a middle-class subculture – the hippies – which the skinheads had previously ignored. But even though the crombies have adopted some of the external mannerisms of the hippy life-style (dress, soft drug use), they still conserve many of the distinctive features of earlier versions of the subculture.

If the whole process, as we have described it, seems to be circular, forming a closed system, then this is because subculture, by definition, cannot break out of the contradiction derived from the parent culture; it merely transcribes its terms at a microsocial level and inscribes them in an imaginary set of relations.

But there is another reason. Apart from its particular, thematic contradiction, all subcultures share a general contradiction which is inherent in their very conditions of existence. Subculture invests the weak points in the chain of socialization between the family/school nexus and integration into the work process which marks the resumption of the patterns of the parent culture for the next generation. But subculture is also a compromise solution to two contradictory needs: the need to create and express *autonomy and difference* from parents and, by extension, their culture, and the need to maintain the security of existing ego defences and the *parental identifications* which support them. For the initiates the subculture provides a means of 'rebirth' without having to undergo the pain of symbolic death. The autonomy it offers is thus both real (but partial) and illusory as a total 'way of liberation'. Far from constituting an improvised *rite de passage* into adult society, as some anthropologists have claimed, it is a collective and highly ritualized defence against just such a transition. Because defensive functions predominate, ego boundaries become cemented into subcultural boundaries. In a real sense, subcultural conflict (greasers *versus* skinheads, mods *versus* rockers) serves as a displacement of generational conflict, both at a cultural level and at an interpersonal level within the family. One consequence of this is to artificially foreclose the natural trajectory of adolescent revolt. For the kids who are caught up in the internal contradictions of a subculture, what begins as a break in the continuum of social control can easily become a permanent hiatus in their lives. Although there is a certain amount of subcultural mobility (kids evolving from mods to parkas or even switching subcultural affiliations, greasers 'becoming' skinheads), there are no career prospects! There are two possible solutions: one leads out of subculture into early marriage, and, as we've said, for working-class kids this is the normal solution; alternatively, subcultural affiliation can provide a way into membership of one of the delinquent groups which exist in the margins of subculture and often adopt its protective coloration, but which nevertheless are not structurally dependent on it (such groups as pushers, petty criminals or junkies.

This leads us into another contradiction inherent in subculture. Although as a symbolic structure it *does* provide a diffuse sense of identity in terms of a common life-style, it does not in itself prescribe any crystallized group structure. It is through the function of *territoriality* that subculture becomes anchored in the collective reality of the kids who are its bearers, and who in this way become not just its passive support but its conscious agents. Territoriality is simply the process through which environmental boundaries (and foci) are used to signify group boundaries (and foci) and become invested with a subcultural value. This is the function of football teams for the skinheads, for example. Territoriality is thus not only a way in which kids 'live' subculture as a collective behaviour, but also the way in which the subcultural group becomes rooted in the situation of its community. In the context of the East End, it is a way of retrieving the solidarities of the traditional neighbourhood destroyed by redevelopment. The existence of communal space is reasserted as the common pledge of group unity – you belong to the Mile End mob in so far as Mile End belongs to you. Territoriality appears as a magical way of expressing ownership; for Mile End is not owned by the people but by the property developers. Territorial division therefore appears within the subculture and, in the East End, mirrors many of the traditional divisions of sub-communities: Bethnal Green, Hoxton, Mile End, Whitechapel, Balls Pond Road and so on. Thus, in addition to conflict between subcultures, there also exists conflict within them, on a territorial basis. Both these forms of conflict can be seen as displacing or weakening the dynamics of generational conflict, which is in turn a displaced form of the traditional parameters of class conflict.

A distinction must be made here between subcultures and delinquency. Many criminologists talk of delinquent subcultures. In fact, they talk about anything that is not middle-class culture as subculture. From my point of view, I do not think the middle class produces subcultures, for subcultures are produced by a dominated culture, not by a dominant culture. But have subcultures altered the pattern of working-class delinquency?

For during this whole period there was a spectacular rise in the delinquency rates in the area, even compared with similar areas in other parts of the country. The highest increase was in offences involving attacks on property – vandalism, hooliganism of various kinds, the taking and driving away of cars. At the simplest level this can be interpreted as some kind of protest against the general dehumanization of the environment, an effect of the loss of the informal social controls generated by the old neighbourhoods. The delinquency rate also, of course, reflected the level of police activity in the area and the progressively worsening relations between young people and the forces of law and order.

There are many ways of looking at delinquency. One way is to see it as the expression of a system of transactions between young people and various agencies of social control, in the subcultural context of territoriality. One advantage of this definition is that it allows us to make a conceptual distinction between delinquency and deviancy, and to reserve this last term for groups (for example, homosexuals, professional criminals, revolutionaries) which crystallize around a specific counter-ideology, and even career structure, which cuts across age grades and often community or class boundaries. While there is an obvious relation between the two, delinquency often serving as a means of recruitment into deviant groups, the distinction is still worth making.

Delinquency can be seen as a form of communication about a situation of contradiction in which the 'delinquent' is trapped but whose complexity is excommunicated from his perceptions by virtue of the restricted linguistic code which working-class culture makes available. This is especially critical when the situations are institutional ones, in which the rules of relationship are often contradictory, denied or disguised but nevertheless binding on the speaker. For the working-class kid this applies to the family, where the positional rules of extended kinship reverberate against the personalized rules of its new nuclear structure; in the school, where middle-class teachers operate a whole series of linguistic and cultural controls which are 'dissonant' with those of family and peers, but whose mastery is implicitly defined as the index of intelligence and achievement; at work, where the mechanism of exploitation (extraction of surplus value, capital accumulation) are screened off from perception by the apparently free exchange of so much labour time for so much money wage. In the absence of a working-class ideology which is both accessible and capable of providing a concrete interpretation of such contradictions, what can a poor boy do? Delinquency is one way he can communicate, can represent by analogy and through non-verbal channels the dynamics of some of the social configurations he is locked into. And if the content of this communication remains largely 'unconscious', then that is because, as Freud would say, it is 'over-determined'. For what is being communicated is not one but two *different* systems of rules: one belonging to the sphere of object relations and the laws of symbolic production (more specifically, the parameters of Oedipal conflict), the second belonging to property relations, the laws of material production (more specifically, the parameters of class conflict).

Without going into this too deeply, I would suggest that where there is an extended family system the Oedipal conflict is displaced from the triadic situation to wider kin, which then develops into gang formation outside the family. When this begins to break down a reverse process of implosion sets in. In the study of the structural relations for the emergence of subcultures the implications of this are twofold: first, changes in the parameters of class conflict are brought about by advanced technology where there is some class consensus between certain parent cultures, and that level of conflict appears to be invisible or is acted out in various dissociated ways; second, the parameters of Oedipal conflict are becoming recentred in the family context but are refracted through the peer-group situation. It is a kind of double inversion that needs to be looked at not only in terms of a Marxist theory, which would analyse it simply by reference to class conflict and the development of antagonistic class fractions syphoning down vertically into another generational situation, but also in psychoanalytic terms, through the dynamics of Oedipal conflict in adolescence. We need to look at the historical ways in which class conflict and the dynamics of Oedipal conflict have undergone transformation and have interlocked, reverberating against each other.

Chapter 3

Rules of Territoriality and Discourse

Territoriality is now all the rage amongst a younger generation of sociologists concerned with issues of urban crime, public order, race and imagined community. This new work is mainly concerned with exploring the various local/global articulations of place and identity, but tends to treat territorialism itself as a simple, self-evident phenomenon. It is as if the nationalism of the neighbourhood was just the nationalism of the state writ small!

*This early piece implicitly challenges that notion; it insists that rules and rituals of territoriality as they developed within working-class cultures were neither a simple exercise in powers of social combination applied to local amenity and resource, as in the neo-Marxist account of R. D. Sack (*Human Territoriality*, Cambridge, 1986) nor are they the expression of some innate human drive to assert proprietorial rights over the environment, as in the sociobiological model advanced by Robert Ardrey (*The Territorial Imperative*, London, 1977); rather they entail forms of symbolic ownership and control which invest relatively marginalised and powerless groups with a sense of their own self-importance, which is at once strategic and grandiose. Territorialism enables kids on the block to imagine*

The text is a revised version of the short essay which appeared in David Robins and Philip Cohen, *Knuckle Sandwich: Growing Up in the Working-Class City* (Penguin, 1978). The main addition consists of an annotated commentary, which draws out some of the theoretical issues that may be of interest to social scientists. It was subsequently published in *Schooling and Culture*, 4, 1979.

themselves as a kind of local ruling class. It makes 'kings of the castle' or 'lords of the manor' out of those who were regarded as 'dirty wee rascals' in the eyes of the dominant culture. At the same time it promotes rivalries between different street-, school- and estate-based gangs.

I did not look at the historical and psychodynamic dimensions of territoriality, its patterns of gendering and racialisation. These themes are taken up in more recent work around the phenomenon of 'home boys'. The present text concentrates on the formal or elementary structures of discourse which made this construction possible.

What we refer to as 'territoriality' is a symbolic process of magically appropriating, owning and controlling the material environment in which you live, but which in real, economic and political terms is owned and controlled by 'outsiders' – in our society, usually by private landlords or the state. It applies, therefore, almost exclusively to working-class areas. And it has to be understood in class terms.[1]

In Britain, the defeat of the radical political culture which culminated in Chartism, produced as its legacy community structures which evolved inwardly, and served to create an almost separate society. The sense of place, of neighbourhood, became intimately bound up with a sense of class, a sense of one's place in society. And, since the mid-Victorian period, this fact has been exploited by town planners and municipal reformers, who, often for the most divergent of reasons, saw the political advantages of having a parochialised working class, split up into small units, each divided against the other by fierce local loyalties.[2]

Territoriality is, therefore, deeply ingrained in most working-class cultures, even if its functions are diffused through a number of institutions – the local pub, shops, and local political, religious and cultural associations of every kind. But young people have only one institution to support this function, and a fragile one at that – the gang! The same historical processes which pushed the parent culture inwards on itself, pushed working-class youth to its periphery, as the residual legatees of street culture.

So the street becomes the arena where the Growing Up game is played out, a social space and time of apparent freedom from the more insidious forms of parental censorship and control. Here the peer group assembles itself to enact its rivalries, and so the game of identities and differences between the sexes and between the generations can begin.[3] In early childhood this takes the form of fantasy games; later, without losing this component, it takes on a more organised ritual form, and finally becomes elaborated by teenagers into collective narratives or myth, at a time when the game is getting rather more serious. The basic rule of this game is not that 'any number can play', but rather that certain people can't. Because they are too little or too big. Because they are boys or girls. So, at the heart of the game lies a symbolic interdict, but one which in this particular environment has no material support.[4] Any number *could* play; the waste ground and street is there for all. This opens up a whole possible area of ambiguity, of distance and relation. The function of territoriality is quite simply to eliminate this problem at its source, by providing a material basis for a system of *positional* rules which preserve the boundaries of the loose-knit peer group network in the street, and assigns the entire youthful population, big and little, boy and girl, to a place which cuts across these distinctions, a place which is marked by an unequivocal question: Friend or Foe? As we will see, the question is posed in a way which already contains its own answer in an inverted form, irrespective of whether the conflict of affinity/enmity involves traditions of feud between groups, or isolated incidents between individuals who may not even know each other. Territoriality is always a *social* process. You may feel that you belong on the Pakington Estate, just like your mum and dad do. But you'll never belong in The Pakington – one of the North Bank's top fighting crews – until you demonstrate that symbolically the area belongs to you. And that demands a ritual display of aggravation against a rival crew. The logic of this whole process, therefore, comes out best in accounts of fights. Here is one such account:

> Whenever you have parties, there's one thing you should never do, is invite kids from two different areas like, say, round here and the Angel ... never invite kids like that, cos they're so close, yet they're so far apart, if you see what I mean. I went to this party, that was a liberty. There was this fight, see, it was over this bird, Sharon, and my mate Rusty starts having a go at her. He says to her: 'Bird, or no bird, you need a slap.' Whack! She

starts screaming at him: 'You wait, I'll get my bloke.' So he says: 'Go and get him.' So her bloke comes back and says to Rusty: 'Did you hit my bird?' 'Yeah.' So he says: 'All right then, outside'. And he starts giving him a kicking and so I was fighting his younger brother. But Sharon's sister's gone and got her brother's mates and they jump in on me and so Rusty's bird's brother jumps in ... there was a bit of a ruck, and there were three other kids with the bloke who was having a go at Rusty, and one of them threw a bottle at the ceiling and it smashed everywhere. But that fight was broke up and I went outside, and there was this bloke from the party and he started saying, 'A kid in a white shirt threw it,' and I had a white shirt on, and he said it again, and he was looking at me, 'A kid in a white shirt'. So, I said to him, 'Look,' I said, 'it wasn't me,' but he kept saying it and the way he was looking at me. I said to him, 'Go away will yer.' And I turned me back and walked back into the party and he sort of whacked me. I fell on the floor, I was kickin' me feet up in his face, he couldn't get near me. Then someone pulled him off ... it was silly really. You could say there were three lots: there was us, there was the kids from the Angel, and these kids who'd come with this bird Sharon. The kids from the Angel, they know some of us, and we know some of them, and one of our lot, Johnny, was fighting one of the other lot Sharon was with, but when the Angel seen it, they thought Johnny wasn't with us like, he was with the other lot, 'cos they didn't know him, of course, and they thought he was starting all the trouble, so they're all running to hit him, and we were running into them to help him. And like, it's almost like us fighting the Angel, 'cos of these other four kids with Sharon who weren't with anyone, if you know what I mean. They were brought there to stop trouble and they started it. That was the only thing that was wrong ... they invited kids from different areas which is all wrong ...

The complexities of this account have *nothing* to do with any failure of the speaker to conceptualise what is going on. The restrictions of its syntax are those of narrative structure as such. The speaker is explaining a complex system of rules, concretely, through the description of an event in which they were violated, and I challenge the reader to produce a better, more logically

connected account. In fact, the whole thing could be read as a
kind of Talmudic commentary, whose intricacies could only be
rendered more economically by translating them into a meta-
language, such as the abstract propositions of symbolic logic. The
territorial rule which is being broken is clearly stated:

That was the only thing that was wrong ... they invited kids
from different areas which is all wrong ...

But underneath this lies a system of relations defining affinity and
enmity, who's on whose side, in what situation, here very much
stated in the context of kinship and its obligations. These rules
could be put formally as a set of propositions:[5]

1. The friend of a friend is a friend
     (+)   (+)   =   (+)
2. The enemy of an enemy is a friend
     (−)   (−)   =   (+)
3. The friend of an enemy is an enemy
     (+)   (−)   =   (−)
4. The enemy of a friend is an enemy
     (−)   (+)   =   (−)

These propositions can be built up on each other to the nth
degree without destroying the symmetry of the rule, e.g. the
friend of an enemy's enemy's friend is still a friend. The system
serves to support and structure the interlocking social networks
which expand out from the family, through the peer group to the
solidarities of school and workplace. But this also contains a
problem. Friend/enemy are categories which define each other
by exclusion. But, as the rule expands through a network, it may
generate feedback loops in which 'John' finds himself simultaneously assigned to opposite categories by others in the group who,
nevertheless, are applying the rule consistently throughout. But
where rules are positional − here, quite literally, a function of
place − no-one can be friend AND enemy without dissolving the
whole system into an infinitely negotiable seesaw of person-
to-person perceptions. When this happens, 'John' is caught in an
untenable position in the network, the inevitable focus and scape-
goat of its tensions. This would be a chronic occurrence if the

only categories in play were friend and enemy. But each logically implies a negative 'qualifier': 'not a friend', 'not an enemy', which are less strongly marked oppositions, and give the system the necessary flexibility to integrate those like 'John', by assigning them to a relative position between the two extremes of affinity or enmity. The way these four sets interact could be mapped as follows:

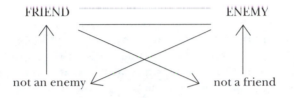

These are the means which enable people to locate each other, confidently and with precision, on a scale between best mates and worst enemies. Fortunately, in the real world, they don't require the assistance of logicians to do this. These operations don't derive from abstract ideas about friendship etc., but are a system of ideological practices which are all too painfully 'concrete': *the rituals of recognition* which regulate everyday encounters, all the way from the simplest of routine greetings to the most elaborate ceremonial challenge. In working-class cultures, recognition is always of a *difference*, either one that is shared and therefore releases a display of friendliness, or one that isn't and releases a show of hostility. If such rituals also involve a *mis*recognition, it is because these differences are interpreted as contingent 'qualities' emanating from – and hidden – 'inside' individuals, rather than what they are: the structural properties of a system of relationships governed by positional rules. It is a misrecognition of the grounds of IDENTITY.[6]

Frequently, individuals enter the social field of the peer group whose positions are not contextually, i.e. territorially, defined. They are simultaneously 'not a friend' and 'not an enemy'. The group's strategy, therefore, consists in attempting to provoke the 'stranger' into the public declaration of a difference which will enable him to be located as One of Us (friend), or One of Them (enemy). The paradigm of recognition usually takes the form of ritual insult. At its simplest, not a word is spoken. Just a silent exchange of glances: taking a screw at someone, someone taking a screw at you.[7] This may be only the first stage of an escalating sequence which culminates in a punch-up. In between, a whole repertoire of insult may be displayed, which includes repartee, taking the piss, practical jokes, and so on. This is the baseline of a whole working-class tradition of wit and humour, which provides the material for the stand-up comic of music hall and working-men's club, just as it sensitises the kids to the linguistic and other skills involved.

Now imagine the following scenario of a male middle-class teacher or youth-worker with a progressive outlook, confronting a group of working-class lads. Culturally, it is an encounter between strangers, and each side brings its own rules into play to deal with the situation. The teacher will be motivated to establish non-authoritarian relationships with 'the lads' – to be defined as their friend. And he goes about befriending them, using the techniques he has learned for establishing relationships with strangers in his own social milieu. He will try to *negotiate* an area of common *subjectivity*, based on eliciting signs of *similarity*, in this instance perhaps by trying to create contexts which will demonstrate elective affinities in terms of a generational life-style e.g. rock 'n roll, movies, clothes, etc. 'The lads,' however, will be trying to elicit expressions of difference as a function of the teacher's objective position – and may be making jokes about his appearance, mannerisms, accent, etc. The teacher has two options. He can turn the other cheek to their cheeking him. In which case, they will probably consign him to a residual category – not a friend, not an enemy, but a mug – and the insults will simply escalate. Or else the teacher can stand on his dignity, lose his temper and assert his authority by threats or actual punishment. In which case, 'the lads' have won anyway because they have located him unambiguously as an enemy.

The problem for the teacher, then, is to decide at what level to respond. Is 'the lads' behaviour good-humoured 'play', and so just play along with it? Or is it real aggression, calling for counter-measures? There is no way for him to step outside the communication frame so as to tell. And, whichever way he responds, he is unlikely to be vindicated by 'the lads' responses. If he plays along, then he has lost control – the pupils may not stop short of trying to wreck the classroom or youth club. But if he cracks down, they may turn round and accuse him of misreading the situation – he can't take a joke, etc. – and he's lost the one thing he was trying to achieve, a friendly, easy-going relationship with them.

The distinction between this use of ritual insult and the techniques of the wind-up merchant, is one of degree rather than kind. The latter is simply more professional in their approach to the victim, more conscious of the mechanism of manipulation.[8]

Both play on a special effect created by articulating two different kinds of statements:

1. Those that are simply *informative* about a state of affairs, in which the speaker is not necessarily represented as the grammatical subject, and where the utterance itself does not affect the social context in which it is made; as opposed to

2. *Performative* statements, in which the speaker is always present as the grammatical subject, and through the process of utterance enacts the reality the statement denotes, and/or defines the social context in which it takes place.

For example: a young person is up at a magistrates court on a charge. S/he is asked to plead guilty or not guilty. If s/he pleads guilty, then that is defined as a performative statement, the offender is judged to have judged him or her self. If the plea is not guilty, however, this is treated as purely informative. The accused is then called to the witness stand to take the oath to tell the truth. This is formally a performative statement but, substantively it carries little weight. The defendant is then cross-examined, all statements being treated as purely informative. When it is the police turn to take the same oath, its performative resonance is read as carrying right through the evidence. The magistrates then give their verdict and pass sentence (performative statements). In our society, the ability to make performative statements is the virtual monopoly of the class whose job it is to lay down the law, open garden fetes, close factories, launch ships or party-political manifestoes. It is power which legitimates these kind of statements, just as they in turn legitimate these people's authority.

But there is a special case where those with no power make use of performative statements, as a means of exerting control over each other, or against those in authority over them. And that case is ritual insult, as in the following example.

One evening on the Wall by Monmouth Estate, Tommy arrives looking like David Bowie, complete with make-up and streaked hair. Chorus of hoots, wolf-whistles, and jeers from the Wall. Then Nick, who used to be a close friend of Tommy, but is now more involved with his motorbike, starts to have a go at him. 'Where's your handbag, dearie? Going out with your fella, then? You little fairy.' Ruffles Tommy's hair. Tommy is trapped. On the face of it, he's confronted with a simple informative statement: 'You're a fairy,' which he could deny on the same level: 'No, I'm not.' But Nick's insult contains a meta-statement which pre-empts this response; an injunction which says: 'Go on then, if you're not a fairy, then show us you're not.' The obvious way for Tommy to show the Wall that he's not in fact weak, effeminate, passive, or any other attribute of being a fairy as far as they are concerned, is to smash Nick in the face. But Nick is the bigger and the better fighter. He would lose and be humiliated in the process – showing himself to be weak. Now Nick knows all this as well as Tommy and so do the other members of the Wall. The only other option open to Tommy is to cap Nick's insult with a counter-jibe which is equally effective. But he's not much good at repartee – certainly not up to Nick's standard. So he just stands there for a moment, red-faced, and then drifts off, promising revenge under his breath. His departure is followed by more jeers and whistles. What has happened is that Nick's original statement has assumed a real performative function. Tommy has *become* in his own eyes, and those of his mates, even if temporarily, a 'fairy'.

Here is another example where the mechanism is even clearer than the above. A boy and girl are playing together. The boy is four, the girl five.

BOY: (chanting) You're a baby, you're a baby.
GIRL: (crossly) No I'm not. I'm five. I'm older than you. And bigger than you, so there.
BOY: No, you're not. You're a baby. Yes you are, you're a baby.
GIRL: (now very upset) I'm *not* a baby. I'm not. I'm NOT.
BOY: Yes you are, etc.
At which point the girl bursts into tears and runs away, calling for her mum.

BOY: (triumphantly calling after her) See, I told you, you *are* a baby.

It is no coincidence, of course, that both these examples bear on the determination of age and gender roles in the peer group. For within this culture, in which images of maturity and masculinity are both linked to a paradigm of physical hardness and where consequently the display of emotion becomes the despised attribute of 'the weaker sex', to be a baby or a 'fairy' are about the worst insults that can be levelled. Ironically, it is in the 'free' play of the peer group, through the media of its apparent revolt, that the deep structure of sexism in the parent culture is most actively reinforced for the next generation.

Ritual insults are most likely to lead to physical injury when there is no way of walking, as opposed to talking, your way out. Then what counts is not a reputation for wit, but for being able to handle yourself in a fight.

As the term 'hardness' suggests, what is involved is a technique of bodily control which puts the practice of motor skills (climbing, running, etc.) at the disposal of mastering the immediate environment of the working-class city. Being able to settle disputes with your fists also ensures that your words need no further emphasis!

Techniques of cognitive and bodily control not only serve the same social function, in establishing distance and closure, the boundaries between Us and Them, they also derive from a common symbolic order to which the working-class child has traditionally been apprenticed. This order can perhaps be most easily observed where both techniques are most strenuously practised and locked together – street games.

These games have usually been classified according to differences in their surface features: different types of activities (seeking, chasing, duelling, etc.), or different local or regional characteristics (dialect, historical colorations). But perhaps these could be most usefully regarded as so many empirical variations of an underlying structure, both formal and elementary. I suggest that the work this unconscious structure does, through the practices it sustains, is to link the dialectics of identity and difference to those of separation and possession.

One of the most popular chasing games played around the Monmouth, by both sexes and assorted age-groups from 7 to 14, was called Cops and Robbers. Two teams are first chosen, this in itself being an important element of foreplay, as preferences and animosities are sorted out. Then a base is decided on and marked out. The scenario is that the robbers have pulled a bank job, and the cops have to arrest them before they can get back to the safety of 'home'. The game ends when all the robbers have either been caught or made base, the teams then swapping roles, and the winning team being whichever has the most homes after an agreed series of games.

At first sight it seems a simple enough chasing game; but it is not enough for the robbers to simply evade the clutches of the law – they have to get to base to do so. Equally, the cops not only have to get their man, but usually have to do so *beyond* a certain agreed distance from base. It is not enough for one team to simply defend the base or for the other to get as far away from them as possible: the rules of the game prohibit such a stalemate. Much of the tactical skill and enjoyment consists in the way both sides try to outmanoeuvre each other, the robbers perhaps using a decoy to draw the cops away, the cops in turn attempting to lure them into a trap through taunts and gibes.

These rules derive from a system of formal oppositions. They bear initially on an instance of separation or lack (of the robbers from home, of cops from robbers) which assigns a task, whose successful accomplishment demands the overcoming of certain obstacles by means of a variety of ruses; success in turn produces an instance of possession ('safety' or 'arrest) which supresses the original lack. Finally, the rules pivot on an interdict, the violation of which means failure. The system could be represented as follows:

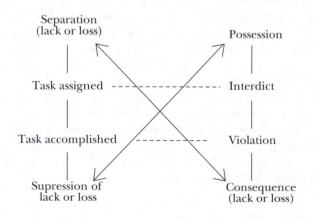

In the case of Cops and Robbers:

	SEPARATION	INTERDICT	VIOLATION	POSSESSION
<u>ROBBER</u>	to get back home	without being cought by cops	is caught	gets to safety
<u>COP</u>	to catch robber	before the robber gets home	fails to make arrest	catches robber

task assigned   failure   success

It is no coincidence that what is found embedded in these games is the same system of symbolic functions which, as object relations (of identity and difference), rule the subject's means of being his or her age and sex. What is being occupied in the game is nothing but a series of places of desire, of exchanges between them, marked by the presence or absence of their object. Yet, instead of being locked inside the family and its fantasy-systems of theft and gift, debt and sacrifice, instead of being frozen in an untenable or overtenanted place in the parental discourse, these games, and the whole material culture of working-class childhood, enable people to 'play' with all these places in a supportive social setting outside adult censorship. The same historical forces which confined the political aspirations of the class to the limits of occupation or community, also produced a system of extra-familial apprenticeship. This does *not* mean that this kind of formation annuls or abolishes oedipal structuration, rather it displaces some of its effects which are elsewhere condensed. As an example, consider how kids become 'best mates' within the framework of the peer group, without undermining its social cohesion. Many of the in-jokes, confidences and other forms of exclusive communication defining best friends, which we observed going on amongst the younger boys on the estate, become intelligible as a single meta-statement not, as might be expected, about their relationship to each other, but about their respective parents. The proposition could be written as: 'I hate my mum but I like my dad.' It would be wrong to take this simply at its face value, as an expression of 'real' feelings – of ambivalence and identification which are censored in the family discourse. This may indeed be the case in some circumstances, but it does not explain the general prevalence of the construction: this, in fact, comes from its underlying function as the statement of an oedipal interdict, and the consequences of its violation, bearing on the dialectics of desire. The proposition has to be rewritten to include the discursive function of its 'hidden' interlocutor. This function articulates what is unsaid to the surface syntax, primarily by embedding qualifying clauses in a recursive system of signifiers which represent the speaking subject to another subject. We can restore the chain of repressed statements as follows:

I (love)   hate   mum
                          like   dad
I (boys must not desire but must) love mum/dad
I (must be a man)   like   dad
(not a woman   like   mum)
I like you (because you are (a boy) like me) (but boys must not desire their own sex)

The law which binds two boys together is also what defines the limits and conditions of their friendship: it is a law about the possible relations between those of the same sex but different generations, and between those of the same generation but different sex. Its symbolic function comes from the way this law is *contextualised* or articulated to a *peer group* ideal, an ideal which reproduces a paradigm of solidarity. This does not imply that young people do not use these settings and structures perversely, i.e. individually, as means of 'getting their own back' for losses or lacks inflicted by 'other scenes'; nor that Street Games Named Desire do not get them into trouble with the law. But the law in question is less likely to be that guaranteed by language, than that of the institutions of private property and public propriety.

Growing up under capitalism is to grow into a series of quite *material* separations: of the family from its means of subsistence, of education from social production, and, resuming them both, of labour from the means of production. It is these separations which those institutions legalise and guarantee.

Yet no-one grows up by living directly and consciously these separations; rather they are lived through the disavowal of their effects in practices of imagined kinship and community. In the case of working-class culture, these practices can also challenge the ideological premises of property and propriety.[9] But to become grown-up also means to have grown out of these 'kids' games', to discover new and more material ways of being your own age and sex. Increasingly, it also means to be confined to a special space of social isolation, for in the capitalist city there remain few legitimate places, outside the control of property or propriety, for working-class youth to be – even the depopulated streets are often unofficially 'out of bounds'.

Having nothing to do, nowhere to go, equals boredom. Working-class young people are already apprenticed to the condition at school, in preparation for their working lives. Yet they escape from the tedium of classroom or workshop into 'free time' only to encounter there another variant of the same. In dealing with it, they bring to bear not just the techniques they have learned to interrupt oppressive routines elsewhere, but those they have mastered earlier in dealing with the immediate environment of childhood. *Mucking about* takes on an added dimension when it gets to grips with the specific boredom of free time – a lack of *being*, as much as having or doing. Above all, a lack of consequence.

Killing boredom means making something happen out of nothing. An action that produces a consequence becomes an event. An event is whatever is remarkable, recountable to your mates. Mucking about thus becomes subsumed under rules and rituals which invest it with narrative functions; and these in turn correspond to the same symbolic order which regulates street games. The tasks the peer group assigns itself, to suppress its lack of being, always and already bear on specific interdicts – the do's and don'ts which rule their lives. In this game of consequences, it is never just a question of having or doing this or that. It is the privileged way the group possesses itself, a means of coming alive. To infringe an interdict successfully yields up stories spiced with obstacles overcome, ruses worked. Failure equals the ignominious return to boredom and inconsequence. The following account is of one episode in a continuous and collective narrative given to us by a 16-year-old lad:

Well, one night, we was just walking about, not doing nothing, you know, and then Billy says 'let's go up the market', and then Jacko sees this ladder and he starts mucking about on it, and we get up on it, onto the roof of this shop, and it's a flat roof and there's all this gear lying about, old chairs, telly, the lot, and Jacko says we could get a few bob for scrap. And then Billy, he's looking out for us, and he starts screaming 'here comes the Old Bill', so we scarper quick don't we ... but they wasn't really, he was having us on, so we weren't too pleased I can tell you, but it was all a load of rubbish there really, so we went home.

This particular story relies for its dramatic effect on the ambiguities of what is playful and what is serious; what begins as killing boredom by larking about on a ladder, shifts into a proposition to make money by contravening certain sections of the Theft Act. Billy, however, gets bored and so creates an event on his own account. By crying wolf for the law, he not only interrupts the serious business, but exposes the element of pretend in the whole *mise-en-scène*. His mates are angry, but perhaps also secretly relieved. Billy's wind-up at least forestalled any serious consequence, while still conforming to the rules of this game: he knew his mates had no means of knowing whether the alarm was real or not. Here the ruse constitutes a performative statement. They let him off, because he has done the same for them; in symbolic terms the task they set themselves has been successfully accomplished, any dissonances of pride in daring taken care of by the sour-grapes effect – it was not worth the trouble nicking anyway – and so they go home, everyone's honour satisfied.[10]

In looking around for materials with which to fabricate remarkable events, young people tend to seize on whatever is nearest to hand. And that often means violating a territorial interdict which has done more than anything to sustain ideologies of private property and public propriety in working-class cultures: don't shit on your own doorstep (if you want to draw the line under your own feet). This interdict not only demarcates between 'rough' and 'respectable', but tends to reproduce these terms on either side of the great moral divide in a series of infinite gradations of social status.

Killing boredom, though, is not done by attacking "ideologies", but the physical plant in which they have become enshrined. Here theft and vandalism are equivalent and equally accessible modes of action. Smashing windows, setting fire to derelict houses, damaging cars, are often simply junior versions of older childrens' exploits in breaking and entering, taking and driving away.

Since the first construction of mass estates, vandalism has been the Number One problem for tenants' organisations and housing authorities alike. Repairs on some estates can more than double annual maintenance costs and become a major item of deficit in public-housing finance. A whole gamut of solutions has been proposed: more police surveillance, vigilante patrols, mobile trouble-shooters, the reintroduction of resident caretakers, adventure playgrounds, youth clubs. Whether these proposals aim at prevention or cure, repression or safety-valves, they fail to see that the common denominator of these behaviours is not 'violence' or 'wanton aggression' but their material premise as *discursive* practices.

And, far from being 'anomic', the behaviour which goes under the name of vandalism should be seen as an attempt to reassert rules – rules of territoriality, foci and boundaries of peer group rivalries – in a social space which has become virtually illegible for this purpose, and not least through the intervention of town planners. In some inner-city neighbourhoods, the only way for young people to assert the dialectics of belonging is to efface or deface the official landscape in favour of their own landmarks of community which they create by these means. However indefensible such behaviour may appear, it is the only means at their disposal to build a defensible space.[11]

Ironically, the more enlightened attempts to deal with the problem, by providing local youth with places to be, things to do, often end only by opening up new arenas for vandalism. Such leisure activities may be authorised, but, by the same token, young people themselves are not the authors. Far from killing boredom, they call for the creation of remarkable events.

The reason for this is not hard to find. The byzantine processes whereby local authorities provide such facilities are almost completely invisible, or incomprehensible, to their eventual users. It is something They do for Us. But if these facilities are mysteriously 'given', kids over about eleven are well aware that they have not been made a present of them. These places do not in fact belong to them, either in the sense of economic ownership or of political control. Yet the organisers want *members*, active adherents to some normative ideal, rather than merely passive consumers. So they tend to construct imaginary contexts of belonging. Painting the youth club. The Members' Committee.

Secondly, these facilities operate with formal rules of territorial inclusion (the catchment area), and informal rules of ideological exclusion (public propriety as a behavioural ideal). The result is twofold. The provision tends to detonate existing patterns of territorial affinity and emnity, as rival groups struggle to assert magical forms of ownership or control. And they trigger behaviour designed to test empirically whether these facilities really do belong to their members, are their's to do what they like with. In either case, waves of petty theft and vandalism ensue and ensure that these places serve to kill boredom, if not in quite the way intended.

The positions taken up within the youth constituency toward such provisions, whether as active members, users, or actors at a distance, serve to reiterate many of the rough/ respectable distinctions within the parent cultures. But no longer in any simple or predictable way.

The divisions of labour at the point of production, between skilled and unskilled, are not only themselves being eroded: they are no longer reproduced in the moral economy of the working-class neighbourhood. The old labour aristocracy may once have succeeded in living apart in micro-districts of their own, just as they spun a cocoon of institutions – mechanics institutes, friendly societies and the like – around themselves, in order to make substantive the connection between superior occupational and moral status. Equally, unskilled and casual labour may have elaborated a material culture based on more rudimentary forms of social closure, notably in their oral and fighting traditions. But these systems of cultural apprenticeship have largely broken down, as has the great divide between them. In the mass estates of the inner-city, black and white, skilled and unskilled, established and outsiders, self-employed and unemployed, hard cases and soft touches, live side by side in no pre-established terms of harmony or conflict. The sense of place and class are no longer so intimately tied together. Other means have to be found to re-establish the broken links in the chains of cultural transmission.

And through these means, too, the divisions of labour, rather than the 'unity of the class', come to be enlarged.

Notes

1. Interest in territoriality has mainly come from cultural geographers and urban planners concerned to develop a theory of environmental perception. This research has, therefore, been largely preoccupied with the question of how personal space is constructed (R. Stea, *Maps in Minds,* London, 1977), how mental maps of the city or region vary between social strata (P. Gould and R. White, *Mental Maps,* London 1986), and how environmental perception affects the social usages which different groups make of urban facilities. A good review of the literature, is to be found in B. Goodey, *Perception of the Environment,* (University of Birmingham Centre for Urban and Regional Studies, 1986). The seminal contributions to this field, for our purpose, are those of Kevin Lynch, *The Image of the City* (Cambridge, 1960) and Deiter Prokop, 'Image and function of the city', in *Urban Core and Inner City* (London, 1966). Erving Goffman also has some suggestive insights in *Behaviour in Public Places* (London, 1985). The research of Schegloff on the conversational devices associated with the use of place names, touches on some of the discursive aspects of territorial rules of affinity and enmity. The weakness of all this research, is that it fails to locate territoriality within wider structures of power. The classic phenomenology of the working-class city is provided by Jack Common, in *The Freedom of the Streets* (1938), a profound and often brilliant essay by a highly original working-class writer of the period. Marxist research has largely concentrated on the political economy of urban growth and crisis for example in work of M. Castells *The City and the Grass Roots* (London, 1983) and David Harvey, *Social Justice and the City*; (Oxford, 1988). This work tends to ignore the micro symbolic forms of identification which are, however, decisive for understanding many contemporary urban phenomenon including the growth of racism in the inner city. This issue has recently been taken up by cultural geographers writing within a post-structualist framework. See, for example, P. Jackson, *Maps of Meaning* (London, 1989).
2. This is a highly simplified statement of what has come to be known as the Anderson/Nairn thesis on the origins of working-class corporatism or labourism in Britain. The key texts by Perry Anderson and Tom Nairn were published in *New Left Review* between 1968 and 1978. In explaining why the British working class should have evolved a separate but subordinate culture of its own, with such a peculiar combination of defensive strength and offensive weakness, Anderson and Nairn adopt a consciously macro-historical perspective, which

leaves unexamined many of the concrete mediations which are required for a full understanding of the phenomenon. For example, what are the social structural processes which reproduce corporatist political cultures at a micro-level? What are the effects of specific discontinuities in these processes due to changing articulations within the class structure (i.e. the question of subcultures)? How far does the political function of labourism change in different conjunctures? Recent work in the field of social history has begun to tackle some of these problems, particularly in the context of a continuing debate on the nature of the labour aristocracy. Some of the major contributions are: R. Q. Gray, *The Aristocracy of Labour* (London, 1981); J. Foster, *Class Struggle and the Industrial Revolution: Early Industrial Capitalism in Three English Towns* (London, 1977); S. Meacham, *A Life Apart* (London, 1977); G. Stedman Jones, *Outcast London* (London, 1984); W. Tholfsen, *Working-Class Radicalism in Victorian England* (London, 1976).

3. This notion of the symbolic function of peer-group rivalry is derived from the psychoanalytic theory of Lacan.

Lacan's theory of narcissism, from the celebration of the specular capture through the formation of an Ideal Self, to its transubstantiation into an Ego Ideal, has the virtue of re-establishing the dialectic between the social function of mastery and the imaginary rivalries through which it is exercised in, for example, the peer group. M. Safouan, in *Etudes sur L'Oedipe* (Paris, 1975), gives the most rigorous statement of the Lacanian position; less satisfactory, but more accessible, is the account by F. Dolto in *Dominique* (London, 1974). In the present text, I have tried to begin to outline some of the material and historical mediations through which this particular aspect of the symbolic order is inserted into the social realities of growing up working class. This is a dimension wholly missing from Lacan's own work, and indeed quite inimical to his metaphysics of desire. However, some of his associates have more recently begun to open up such a perspective, notably in a discussion of the role of unconscious phantasy in social systems and popular discourse, c.f. Pierre Legendre, *L'Amour du Censeur* (Paris, 1974), and the contribution of J.-P. Valabrega to the symposium on *Le Desir et la Perversion* (Paris, 1978). It is also necessary to reintroduce a diachronic framework so as to adequately specify the play of *generational* difference in the assumption of sexual identity. How else to explain how people actually grow up?

4. We are not talking about the highly-structured gang, organised into age grades, each with its own hierarchy, etc. These seem to occur only if there are strong ethnic territorial rivalries between interfacing parent cultures, as in Catholic/Protestant interzones in Liverpool, Glasgow or Belfast. The interdict here becomes explicitly parental: 'Because they're Proddies', etc.

5. The problem of how to formalise these socio-logics, and isolate the rules of transformation through which they become embedded in

different contexts of communication, depends for its solution largely on establishing a methodology appropriate to the relevant unit of analysis – not words or sentences or bits of behaviour, but statements generated by discursive practice. The most promising approach at present stems from work being done in the field of narrative grammar. I have particularly drawn on the work of Alan Dundes, *Analytic Essays in Folk Lore* (The Hague, 1977), A. J. Greimas, *Narrative Semiotics* (London, 1990) and William Labov, *Language in the Inner City* (Oxford, 1977) – none of these being of course responsible for the uses to which I have put their models and formulations in applying them to an essentially different purpose.

6. It is just this function of misrecognition which is obscured in the accounts of ethnomethodology and symbolic interactionism. The rationalism of the former and the subjectivism of the latter fail to grasp that discursive practices are reproduced, not by some immanent logic, however 'dialectical', but from *material* premises within various modalities of class ideology (behavioural, moral and political). It was the immense achievement of Basil Bernstein's work on socio-linguistic codes (*Class Codes and Control,* London, 1977) to have isolated some of the ways in which the class subject is 'legalised' as a speaking subject, and thus to have introduced a key mediation between systems of unconscious representation and the material history of class cultures. If his work did not develop that connection, it was perhaps because at that time it did not break out of its dualistic premise both within linguistics (competence/performance) and a social psychology of perception (personal/positional). Bernstein's concept of social structure could, thus, only be Durkheimian rather than Marxist. This problem is also found in the work of Mary Douglas on classification and ritual (c.f. *Natural Symbols,* Harmondsworth 1980 and *Purity and Danger,* Harmondsworth 1978), but she has also developed a model of the correspondence between styles of cognitive organisation and strategies of social closure, which is highly suggestive for understanding principles of class cultural stratification.

This research has added an essential, hitherto missing, dimension to the theory of ideology. It is perhaps unfortunate that the contributions of both Louis Althusser (c.f. *Lenin and Philosophy,* London 1977) and Michel Foucault (c.f. *The Archaeology of Knowledge,* London, 1979) focused almost exclusively on the apparatus of scientific discourse and dominant ideology. This has raised the suspicion that such constructs as 'interpellation' and 'episteme', whatever their general theoretical validity, have little *heuristic* application in the study of popular ideology and cultural practice in their own 'write' – i.e. as something other than the effect of power on them. For example, the concrete mechanisms of rumour and gossip, trade talk and trouble talk and the other peer-group usages of language and literacy in which the archeology of working-class knowledge is enshrined articulate powers of social and discursive combination, whose meaning are not reducible to their functions of resistance or transgression *vis-a-vis* the 'dominant ideology'.

7. At the level of fantasy, *and only there*, this kind of 'screwing' has the same connotation as the other kinds (i.e. sexual and criminal), breaking in to a forbidden 'inside' belonging to somebody else.

8. For an analysis of the techniques of the wind-up merchant see Dick Hebdige's highly original study included in *Resistance Through Rituals* (London, 1978).

   It should be noted that the approach to ritual insult suggested here differs in several respects from the classic statement by Labov – particularly in stressing the extra-linguistic dimension of power and authority. In doing so, I have drawn on Emile Benveniste's revision of J. L. Austin's original distinction between types of statement (see E. Benveniste, *Polyphonic Linguistics*, The Hague, 1981).

9. For a discussion of the concepts of separation and possession within the Marxist problematic c.f. L. Althusser, *Reading Capital* (London 1971). For an historical account of the development of institutions of public propriety, and the role of the police in their enforcement, see the discussion in Chapter 5 of this volume.

10. The structures which allow such ambiguities to be played with also ensure that these lads have no difficulty in distinguishing between the terms of what is imaginary and what is real. Yet it would literally be a very different story if that dialectic was foreclosed by fetishising either or both of its supports in phantasy or material practice.

11. In the past decade, in both Britain and the USA, there has been no shortage of 'radical' town planners, who have proposed environmentalist solutions to the problems of vandalism and delinquency along the lines of constructing physical spaces which simulate, and support, the social control functions of territoriality, c.f. for example, Oscar Newman, *Defensible Space* (New York, 1961), Jane Jacobs, *The Life and Death of Great American Cities* (Harmondsworth, 1972), Colin Ward (ed.), *On Vandalism* (London, 1973). These urbanists urge that residential environments should avoid the extremes of privatisation found in the modern suburb mass estate and the public anonymity of the city centre, but should instead return to the scale of 'the urban village', a self-policing communal system. These solutions are situated in that current of radicalism whose symptomatic slogan is 'small is beautiful' i.e. small-scale capitalism and petty commodity production is more 'human' hence morally superior to Monopoly Capitalism and machinofacture. The notion of the urban village as a bulwark of the People's Liberties against the encroachment of centralised bureaucracies, etc., is a theme which unites populists of all persuasions in the advocacy of a parochialised working-class.

    In more practical terms, the attempt by these planners to recreate the conditions of the 'self-policing community' may have some temporary effect in reducing local levels of juvenile vandalism and crime by facilitating adult surveillance, but by definition this only pushes the problem elsewhere – into neighbouring areas which experience a concomitant increase. It is, thus, a purely cosmetic solution, favoured by central and local government only because it is cost-effective and requires no real redistribution of power or resource. The contexts of 'community' thus created remain, in our definition, purely imaginary, and in no way increase the level of real political control exercised by the population over its environment.

Chapter 4

Knuckle Sandwich and Sore Thumbs

In 1975 I became involved with a group of community activists who tried to set up an 'alternative' youth and community centre on a large rundown GLC (Greater London Council) estate near King's Cross. The project was largely inspired by the romantic populism of the 'Libertarian Left' of this period. But if we had hoped to build the New Jerusulem in this most unpromised land, we were quickly disillusioned by the local realpolitik. The derelict pub which we had occupied and converted with the help of a Council grant became a battleground for a whole range of competing interests all claiming to represent 'the community'. Our uncomplicated vision of cultural negotiation was no match for a tactical alliance between local villains who saw the chance of some easy pickings, and conservative elements amongst the council tenantry alarmed at the prospect of their young people being corrupted by long-haired lefties from Liverpool Road. One night, shortly after it had opened, the pub burnt down under mysterious circumstances, and the tenants' association acquired enough insurance money to build the bingo palace they really wanted.

Knuckle Sandwich *tells this cautionary tale and tries to draw some political conclusions from it. The publishers, however, were more interested in the book's potential as an inside story about how life was lived*

The first part of the main text of this chapter (pp. 86–102) originally appeared in David Robins and Philip Cohen, *Knuckle Sandwich* (Penprin Books, 1978); the second part (pp. 102–8) was published in *Youth and Society* (August 1980).

on the other side of the class tracks. They put a photograph of a fist on the front cover and a suitably lurid description of the contents on the back, and no doubt hoped it would hit the bestseller charts. It never did, but the presentation did help to tarnish the book's reputation in certain quarters...

The blame is not all the publisher's. The book is subtitled Growing Up in the Working-Class City, *but it was largely preoccupied with mapping the cultural geography of adolescent masculinity and girls' place within it, rather than privileging their own separate point of view. Not surprisingly the book was lambasted by feminists for its masculinist standpoint. Even though we had definitely not celebrated the laddish culture of violence which we described, we had certainly failed to frame it with an equally strongly weighted account of working-class cultures of femininity. The extract from the book given here (pp. 87–102) illustrates how we accounted for the lads') culture, and is followed by a response to the feminist critique (pp. 102–8). Taken together I hope they will give some flavour of the debate.*

Knuckle Sandwich

Forms of 'hardness' can still be anchored in street-fighting traditions where these survive; the Monmouth and Denby estates, with their complement of second- and third-generation Irish families, still contained the traces. Accounts of Famous Fights were passed from father to son in local families. Phil would rhapsodize at length to his mates about the time old man MacIlroy, half-pissed, had taken on all the menfolk of his very extended family at a sister's wedding, and still had time to call for more beer. Young Neil told how old man Allen had one day for a bet drawn a line across the bar-room floor at the Black Horse, and challenged all comers to cross it; he won his bet. These legends are not just part of a rich oral tradition; they are also supposed to instruct the next generation, how, where and when to put their boots and fists, and the occasional broken bottle, where their mouths are.

In faithfully recounting these stories, Phil and Neil were carrying on a discourse which speaks to a shrinking audience. In earlier years much family talk would have been sustained by a whole network of popular institutions which linked into a wider community context, and even into the professional fight game. It is no coincidence that professional fighters have traditionally been recruited from the ranks of first-generation immigrant families struggling to survive in a hostile environment. Irish, Jews, Blacks – all have successively thrown up champions. Rinty Monahan, Kid Berg, Harry Mizler, Bunny Sterling: these are the names remembered in the annals of the British fight game. But at street level, there were thousands of lads from similar backgrounds who sought to emulate them.

Before the war a young man would first show promise with his fists in neighbourhood gangs. These fights were not just to defend territory but to assert the physical integrity of the parent culture, which was under attack in so many other ways. The next step might have been for friends, or workmates, to put up money to arrange a fight 'on the stones', perhaps to decide who was neighbourhood champion. Sometimes fights were arranged between champions of rival ethnic groups or different areas.

Fights on the stones had their own rules – though not exactly the Marquess of Queensberry's. In the factory yard or the back alley, a crowd of interested parties would gather, most of whom had bets on the outcome. Friends would officiate in the corners, and you were judged to have lost when you could no longer carry on. Many contests would be catchweight – a small wiry man fighting a larger would provide an added David and Goliath fascination. Throughout the proceedings, a trusted member of the fraternity would 'hold the purse' (the bets laid) for all to see, while another would keep a lookout for the police.

These fights were not only an important apprenticeship into the fight game itself. A good street fighter would attract the attention of the network of local patrons of boxing. These were usually self-made men – the timber merchant, the publican, the haulage contractor, and other variety of the species – the local fixers, bookies, fences, 'scrap dealers', the villains, many of them ex-fighters themselves. Patronage could take various forms. In the field of heavy casual labour, where work could be an extension of training (most notably in the markets and docks), 'a word in your ear' would get the young novice preferential treatment. If a lad showed he was coming good in his early fights, patrons would readily be found to put up money for promotions, where money could be made. Not by the lad, of course. Most of his earnings would be taken by the manager, trainer and so on. All these were needed before the boxer could obtain a licence and be allowed to fight. Most professional fighters remained part-time. The young novice's earnings from the ring was simply a supplementary income, from a few shillings for taking on all comers at the fairground booth to a few pounds for a night's work at Shoreditch Town Hall. But even this was useful when times were hard, as they so often were during this period, especially for immigrant families.

Graduation into the ranks of the professionals inevitably excluded the novice from the street-fighting scene or the barroom brawl. To get involved outside the ring would mean losing his licence, and a severer than usual sentence from the magistrates. Nevertheless, the status as well as the stigma of his early background followed him into the ring. A two-fisted style of fighting evoked echoes of street culture and its underlife, and this was recognized by an audience composed equally of his local following and 'the experts'. A fighter like Pat Rafferty or 'Two Ton Tony' Galento, good at settling arguments with their bare fists but found out in the ring, constitute a central legend of professional boxing. The fighter against the boxer, brawn against brains, instinct against science – such archetypal oppositions are contested in flesh and blood and give the boxing spectacle much of its conscious drama.

Into this exclusively working-class domain, the boys' club movement at the turn of the century attempted to introduce a different ethos. The amateur code of the gentleman stressed the virtues of fitness, consistent training, abstention from vices such as drinking and smoking, and above all the art of being a good loser, rather than a born one. The club gymnasium rather than the back alley was the place to learn to box properly, yet it was still a manly place for boys to settle arguments. By the 1920s, in London clubs like the Gainsford Covent Garden and Repton in the East End, boxing was disinfected of its unsavoury connections with gambling and petty crime, not without some tension of course between the small hall boys and the grafters, and the advocates of self-improvement through self-defence, as each competed to recruit youngsters to their respective codes.

Today, with the obvious exception of the black immigrant community, recruitment into boxing, both professional and amateur, is confined to a diminishing number of old-established 'fighting families' (for example the Walkers of the East End, the Mancinis of Notting Hill, the Straceys of Bethnal Green, the Tibbs of South London gang fame). The fight game itself has become a backwater of remembrance of an ageing fraternity, while the amateur tradition of the boys' club has been left behind in the slipstream of post-war youth culture. The distance between the rituals of the ring and those of contemporary teenage violence has assumed the proportions of a great divide; while the first have ossified into an almost perversely formal ceremonial, the latter have become increasingly unstructured.

Sixteen-year-old Bobby Munro was generally recognized as the best fighter for his age on the Monmouth; so good in fact that he complained that no one would take him on. He enjoyed a scrap 'as long as its fair and friendly' but he wouldn't pick a fight 'to get the practice' because it only got you into more trouble, i.e. it would be breaking the code. Why didn't he solve the problem by learning boxing at a nearby youth club, which specialized in the noble art? This advice was anathema to him. Youth club boxing and his own fighting culture were for him totally incompatible. It wasn't just that the techniques were different; they represented two different moral universes.

And he wasn't going to change sides. At school his expertise at sabotaging classroom order and his reputation with his fists had been equally recognized by a succession of teachers, who tried in vain to persuade him to develop the latter skill through boxing for the school, as a way of getting him to abandon the former! But as far as Bobby was concerned, boxing was unnatural. 'We was given fists to fight with. If we'd've been meant to fight with them things [boxing gloves] we'd 've been born with them … All them geezers running around with skipping ropes, they're like a load of nances.'

Bobby came from a fighting family. Thirty years previously his father had successfully made the transition from street fighter to boxer, precisely through the youth club. Lads of that earlier generation and background could never have made a statement like Bobby's – that boxing was soft. But in the intervening period, the occupational or other close-knit community structures which had supported the father's solution have disintegrated – whether through urban redevelopment or changes in the division of labour.

Yet a more positive force finally prevented Bobby following his father's steps into the ring. The post-war period saw not just the decline of local boxing traditions, but subcultures whose styles and idioms constituted a non place realm of identity for massive sections of working-class youth (i.e. teds, mods, rockers, skinheads, greasers). This meant that for the first time fighting techniques were no longer regulated, and transmitted through the parent culture, but directly through the peer groupings of youth. Certain aspects of the old 'hardness' were conserved, but only as a purely symbolic element of ritual display, integrated along with the other systems, dress, music, argot, which in varying forms and combinations gave these subcultures their distinctive 'code'. Most recently, however, the coherence of these codes has been subsumed by traditional symbolism or else their component parts have evolved into separate, specialized and highly dissociated 'styles' or 'interests' of their own.

One product of this has been the emergence of the fighting *crew*, a legacy of the skinhead era. As the skins declined in numbers and influence, as their argot was assimilated back into the mainstream of working-class culture, as their dress was taken over by commercial interest as a generalized youth commodity, as reggae was reappropriated by black youth, or 'taken up' as a specialized 'thing', as the drugs and life-styles of middle-class youth made ideological inroads, so the elements of ritual display became increasingly impoverished, denuded of symbolic content. The one element which remained, precisely the one which had been so fetishized by the mass media as the sign of the skinhead, was 'aggro', and it was this which the rump of hard-core skinheads seized on and elaborated, in a purely material sense, as the matrix of a new style. The fighting crew was born. Inevitably such crews developed in those areas where the subculture had been strongest and parent culture weakest. They remain locality- based, but violence is only marginally related to the protocols of territory – which now provide the pretext, rather than the structuring context of 'aggro'.

Micky Spyer was a member of one such crew in an area of South Islington which had been a skinhead stronghold.

Well, some of us go to work, and then we go to clubs, or pubs sometimes, to have fights, but the weekends are best, that's when we have the big fights, with about ten of us outside the fish and chip shop. You've got to fight to protect yourself and you can get a bit of a name and you've got to protect it, you can't just bottle it and walk away, and then you get really slagged off ... There's about ten of us like, we're all together, all mates from round the flats ... and when we get into fights then the birds we're with fight with the other birds [i.e. of the other crew]. They're worse than us, they use bottles as well, they're fucking mad sometimes ... They're all good fighters in our crew, well, that's the idea, isn't it, there's a few no good, well they just hang about with us like, they're not really in it. If a kids not a good fighter than he don't go about with us and that's that. If we think a geezer's all mouth and not really a good fighter, then we just have a fight with him to show him up ... they're the real idiots, the right mouthy geezers.

Elements of the old fighting code can still be seen in this account, but they no longer have any work to do. The code no longer has any purchase on social reality outside itself. And not surprisingly this results in a kind of regression of age roles in the fighting crew.

The kind of routine fighting which characterizes young children's groups in the playground or street is both random and highly competitive, but still playful, essentially 'friendly'. Its function is both to learn and display fighting prowess, as well as to establish hierarchies of prestige within the peer group. The fighting crew of older youth remains fixated at this stage; the same mechanisms are carried over, but with one big difference – now they operate for 'real', and are projected on to randomly selected 'enemies' outside the group. In terms of sex roles though, this development must be seen as also containing a progressive aspect. For, as Micky's account makes clear and as our own observations corroborated, what had been a male preserve, and an index of male sexual dominance, opened up to the opposite sex. But the credit for this belongs not so much to the crew itself, as to the advent of Bruce Lee on to the silver screen. For Bruce could not only be idolized by girls in traditional terms as Supermale, his films demonstrated that the so-called weaker sex could master a technique which meant that they could fight on equal terms with boys – and win. Even if his girl fans didn't in practice follow the way of the dragon, Bruce Lee ratified their entry into the precincts of the fighting crew.

The traditions of the martial arts imported from the Far East thus provided a new source of orientation, but not just for these crews. They appealed to larger sections of youth precisely because they spoke to a widespread sense of cultural displacement experienced during this period, 1972–4. In kung fu, kendo and karate, fighting technique is cultivated as an end in itself, a pure metaphysic of bodily control, split off from external reality, rather than what it had always been in the working class, a means of social control. In addition, the mass media intervened to blend all three elements, the native brawling tradition, youthful styles of aggro, and the martial arts, into a single *mise-en-scène* of contemporary violence.

There were no fighting crews on the Monmouth or Denby estates at this time (summer 1973). If there had been, then they would certainly have provided a 'solution' for lads like Bobby Munro. But the older fighting code still exerted an influence on most local youth, albeit at an increasing distance. The way Neil or Phil talked about fights or fighting was still a long way away from Micky Spyer's account. And those lads whose personal styles of aggro went over the limits were quickly isolated as 'nutters' and steered clear of as far as possible.

This did not mean that interest in karate and kung fu wasn't high. Many of the members of the Wall gang boasted of their prowess in such matters. But none showed any signs of expertise, or the inclination to submit themselves to the rigorous physical and mental discipline needed to acquire it. One night over the summer months, a group from the Wall went up the West End to see Bruce Lee in *Fist of Fury*. Afterwards, one of them attempted to emulate his newfound hero by chopping down a window. Result: a cracked arm and seven stitches! The irony of the story is that the imagery of kung fu appeals most strongly to those kids who are often least equipped, in real terms, to master its techniques. The majority of the Wall, for example, had long since rejected the whole ethos of physical self-discipline and sustained effort which goes with success in organized sport.

The girls too had their stake in the martial arts. Since there was no fighting crew, they formed one of their own. This they modelled after the sixties bike gangs – a number of the lads were roaring around the estate on Suzukis at the time, and so provided the initial 'image' to emulate. The Denby Lady Hells Angels Club was formed. The girls didn't have bikes, of course, but they did have Bruce Lee, and they set off to practise their skills on the boys. There was nothing pretend about this. One lad was set on by a group of girls and so badly beaten up that he had to be sent to hospital. Needless to say, this aggro did nothing to alter the girls' fundamental one-down position in the local youth culture – as in other areas of their lives.

Enter the dragon

In other words, the fascination of kung fu movies for these kids was not simply due to the fact that they presented a new and exotic fighting style. Their interest was much more sociological.

Bruce Lee in his movies finds himself, just as much as his fans in real life, caught up in a social system which he neither understands nor controls, because it is 'remote controlled' by superior, often institutional, forces, whose power is as hidden as it is all-pervasive. But unlike the heroes of the Western, gangster or fantasy stories (which in movie or comic form constitute these kids' staple cultural diet), Bruce Lee shuns the advanced weaponry of 'the Man' to fight back, just as he scorns ideological ruses. He takes on the technology of 'the system' armed with nothing but his fists, and his superior techniques of body control. And unlike these kids, he manages to salvage victory out of defeat.

The *mise-en-scène* of martial arts movies is, however, already familiar to the audience – from their comics and film-going, as much as from the narrative context of their everyday lives: rival mobs fighting over territory, plenty of ritual insults, even more physical injuries. For example, if we compare the narrative structure of *Fist of Fury* with the kids' own story-telling about the exploits and encounters they live through, we can see an almost point by point correspondence between the two. The story of *Fist of Fury* goes like this: The leader of the kung fu school has died. He has left behind a scroll of instructions on how his disciples are to carry on the tradition. It contains a key *interdict*[1] — kung fu is to be used only in self-defence, and in the last resort when attacked. While the members of the school are pondering this, and their *lack of a leader* and how to replace him, in other words the *tasks* the founding father has *assigned* to them, they are interrupted by a visit of a 'mob' from a rival, Japanese school of martial arts. They have come not to praise the name of the dead master, but to *insult* him – and issue a challenge to his disciples to take them on in unarmed combat to see which of the two schools is superior. The elders hold to their master's instructions, and refuse to be provoked, so the Japanese leave, jeering at their cowardice, and taking with them the 'sacred text'. The kung fu school are in a dilemma. A *new task* has been *assigned* –to retrieve the scroll, but its *accomplishment* will inevitably mean *violating* the founder's *interdict*. They are caught in a *trap*. Young Bruce Lee rises to the challenge, even though he knows that it means banishment from the school. Alone and outcast, or rather since this is a movie with Hollywood pretensions, aided by an attractive young female accomplice who runs away from the school to join him, he succeeds in *avenging the insult* and retrieving the scroll. But this only brings further trouble from the Japanese mob, and the familar pattern of *attack* and *counter-attack* follows. In the process, Bruce Lee of course takes the place of the dead master, the school has found a *new leader*. But the authorities present them with an ultimatum: either Bruce Lee surrenders or the school is closed down. Bruce knows that he has successfully *accomplished* the *task* set by his dead teacher – the reputation and tradition of the kung fu school have been secured by his victories in battle – and will survive his own death. But if the school closes down everything he has fought for will be lost. So he gives himself up. And the school is left back where it was at the beginning of the story, *lacking a leader*.

The fascination of the content of such movies for working-class kids thus goes side by side with their unconscious recognition of its narrative style or 'grammar', as one which is identical with their own. They can read it effortlessly. Sometimes, at the level of motif, the links are more explicitly recognized, as in this poem written by a 13-year-old girl from Denby estate:

> *Tribute to Bruce Lee*
> When you were young, you used to roam
> the streets and alleys of Hong Kong
> You learn't your martial arts and then
> you tried it out on everywun.
> You led a gang or so they say

and terrorized the town
a rebel you will always be
nowun can keep you down
Your dead i know I've seen the proof
your image still lives on
you're worshipped now throughout the world
even tho youre gone
The waterfronts you used to go
to fight and show your skill
you always wun cos youre the guy
nowun could ever kill
You never thought of death i know
cos death woud mean defeat
and thats the thing you never knew
how to win or beat.

In recent years there has been a lot of talk to the effect that violence in the mass media has produced the teenage rampage – working-class kids acting out the images and situations they see portrayed on the screen in real life. It should be clear from the analysis so far that what is in play is the linkage of two forms of 'collective representation' which have radically different historical origins and institutional supports. If the linkage is possible at all, it is because there is an objective correspondence between some oral traditions in working-class culture and *some* genres produced by the mass media. It is a correspondence of form, rather than content, and where it doesn't exist, the impact of the mass media on working-class consciousness is entirely negligible. Finally, both in the history of the class, and in the life history of those growing up into it, the narrative forms of oral culture predate those of the mass media and constitute a kind of permanent infra-structure, which condition and limit the effectivity of the latter.

The following discussion between two 14-year-old best mates living on the Monmouth may help to illustrate this. They are trying to reconstruct a subcultural past which they've experienced only at second hand, through the stories told by elder brothers or from what they've read in newspapers or books, or seen on TV or film. Images drawn from the mass media are inextricably interwoven with those drawn from real lives around the estate. But

although they may be 'overdramatizing' this past, it is done with a
self-critical awareness and no sentimentalism:

FRANK: Well, when I was young I used to really like the mods,
but I couldn't stand the rockers. I thought they were a load of
hooligans, you know. But as you grow older you kind of find
out they was as bad as each other. I used to think of the rockers
going round with chains and hatchets and things like that, but
the mods used to go round just as much with bare fists. They'll
just mob a couple of rockers, splatter them against the wall,
rearrange their faces a little, and then the kid will go and get a
couple of rockers to get the kids that got him and do exactly
the same back ...

TERRY: And when you was little, remember people used to come
up and say 'who do you want, mods or rockers?' and there was
two lots of gangs of us round here, one supported the rockers,
and the other mods, and it just went on like that and there was
fights over that.

FRANK: You know people used to reckon the teddy boys were the
biggest, but the skins were thousands, tens of thousands all over
Britain, and they were in the papers every day like the teds ...
Skins, bovver, all over the papers. Skins hit Brixton, Skins hit
this, Skins hit that ... there was a book out not long ago, you
know it was really good, but it was a load of bollocks as well, if
you know what I mean. It was called *Skinhead*. It was all about
this geezer called Joe Hawkins and his mob and all the fights
they used to have down Southend and all that. And after that
he was sent to jail. And after he came out and became a suede-
head and by the time you finished the book he was back in
prison again for stabbing some Paki in the throat, with an
umbrella, blood running all over him and that was that.

TERRY: It's like that film we see the other night, didn't we. *Heavy
Traffic*. There was three greasers and they was trying to get this
other kid to have it off with this bird, 'cos to become one you
got to do it, you know, overnight, and anyway this kid doesn't
know what to do, so they start mucking him about, hitting him
over the head, and you see all the blood coming out, and
they're pulling out chains and all sorts, and in the end they was

all flaked out on the floor with half a leg missing here and
there, and that. It was really tasty, but I don't think it's like that,
'cos me brother had a mate who was a greaser and he had a
bike, you know, a big BMW, and he went on runs, the lot, but
he never said anything about anything like that …

The Mary Whitehouse brigade would by now be getting quite
excited picturing two young psychopathic thugs who set out each
night to brutally translate these media fantasies into reality on
whoever they can get their hands on. Concerned liberals may be
worrying that these two lads are internalizing a 'stereotyped image
of deviance', and acting up to *that*. The truth, however, is quite
otherwise, and far more mundane.

Both Terry and Frank were popular members of the Wall fraternity, and well liked on the estate generally. Both their families
were decidedly 'respectable' Irish, though not well off. They
both had a reputation locally as 'comedians' and in fact had
quite a nice little double act going. They both knew how to
'handle themselves' and, for that reason, rarely got into fights.
Equally, they'd both been in the odd bit of bother with the law,
but only for trivial 'offences' to do with hanging about the Wall,
and not involving violence of any kind. They didn't see themselves, and weren't seen by anyone else, as deviant, or as in any
way different from the majority of the young people on the
estate.

It becomes evident from this that such lads readily draw on the
resources of the mass media where it supports their imaginative
capacities as story-tellers of their own lives.

Sometimes there is an objective correspondence between situations portrayed in a given movie and the more subterranean
realities of living in a 'hard' working-class area. In the following
account, Terry draws on a media analogy to make the distinction – correctly from our own observations – between different
roles in a well-known Islington fighting crew. But towards the
end, media imagery spills out of its context and 'takes over the
account'.

TERRY: … you usually find it's a dim bitch that's got all the
bottle. If you look at *Clockwork Orange*, the one in there, he was
dim, he had all the bottle there. You usually get that in crews …

like we've got this kid, he's called Willy, he's as dim as they come, and every time there's a fight he don't care what the odds are, he just steams in, but then this other kid, they more or less take him for leader, Steve Taylor, when the fight starts off, he's usually at the back, he may be the best fighter there, but he's clever like. So it's the poor mugs blind at the front that gets the first chunk of lead and all their face just going splut all over the place and all you hear is chop chop and little groans and grunts, and little kids crawling out with half their jaws missing ...

But this doesn't mean that Terry, Frank or any of the other lads have any difficulty in 'telling' fantasy from reality *when it matters*. The major subterranean tradition of violence in this part of London was carried on by the fraternity of professional villains whose base was in the Cross Keys pub opposite the Black Horse. The local lads' attitude to these men was nothing if not ambivalent. They admired their trappings of affluence, the expensive suits, cars and the rest, and the fact that they had got this without having to work. But the other trappings of their trade, the scars, the broken noses, their justified reputation for calculated violence, the spells in prison, this inspired only fear. They might watch at a safe distance, but they didn't aspire to be any part of it.

FRANK: But then you get these really hard nuts, about twenty and up. You know, there's really big fights. Like we were up the hospital the other day, and this geezer come in, he works up the Riverside,[2] and he's been slashed across the face and he's been stabbed twice in the back by some other geezer from another mob, reckoned he should have the job or something, so he puts him out of commission like. I think that's pretty stupid, you know, but if any of that lot are around, the kids stand around like little goody boys ...

In fact these lads have a very solid, and material sense of their own reality – and it is from that base-line that they criticize its distortion and misrepresentations by press and TV. For example, another lad, in his early twenties, a keen Arsenal supporter but now grown out of the North Bank, comments on a TV discussion

programme in which a panel of experts have given their views on
the nature and causes of contemporary teenage violence:

> Well there was this geezer sitting there who thought he knew all
> about it, but he didn't know nothing if you ask me ... He was
> going on about soccer hooligans and how they carry on down
> the ends, and he says, well, it's all because they don't like the
> middle classes taking over the game, getting in the act like.
> Well, anyone who ever been down the North Bank'll tell you
> they don't give a sod for the students and all the other wankers
> and pooftas that turn up. They never go down the end anyway,
> they're too scared. All the North Bank care about is their team
> and the other end and that's all there is to it.

The Great Chinese Take-Away Massacre

One incident which was recounted in numerous versions by Monmouth and Denby kids during the time of the Black Horse disco
came to be known as the Great Chinese Take-Away Massacre. The
following is a synopsis of these accounts.

One evening, after they came out of the pub, a group of Black
Horse regulars went down to the Chinese take-away on the main
road. After getting their food, they were standing outside, talking
and laughing, when a squad car pulled up. A young police constable jumped out and pushed his way through the lads to Brian,
who was in the centre of the group. The PC told Brian to Break it
Up and Move On as they were causing an obstruction. Brian
replied to the effect that he didn't know eating chop suey in the
street was against the law. At which, with the ceremonial utterance
'don't get clever with me, you Irish bastard, I'm having you,
you're nicked', the constable proceeded to bundle Brian into the
car. The rest of the group crowded round, jeering. Two other
young policemen got out, smacked a couple of the boys in the
mouth, and grabbed a third and bundled him too into the car,
which then sped off, leaving the survivors to elaborate the more
or less heroic nature of the encounter to themselves and their
mates.

They didn't do what middle-class youths might have done in
similar circumstances and what advocates of children's rights
advocate – namely, become morally outraged at the injustice they

had suffered. It didn't occur to them to go round to the police station to make a complaint, for example, or to write a letter to their MP or to the local paper or to the NCCL. This has nothing to do with their lack of the communication skills which such strategies imply. Rather these boys have an implicit awareness of their specific class position *vis-à-vis* authority. The rule here is that you try and steer clear of the law if you can, but at the same time you don't let the law dictate what you should or should not do. If you or your mates get nicked, then that's it. It's a fairly routine fact of life, and there's nothing you can do about it.

The first thing to notice about such street encounters between kids and the police is that at one level both sides start from the *same* rules in the *same* context and recognize the fact that they share a common code as members of the same culture. Consider the following account by a 14-year-old boy from the Denby estate:

We was walking down the road, me and my mate, we were just talking to each other and because this copper had nothing to do, he wanted to try and get us up the old bill, and he said we was taking the mick out of him, and he was, you know, like a flash copper. And my mate, he's looking at the copper and giving him bad looks, and then the copper takes his helmet off and says 'Go on then, hit me' and my mate's dying to hit him but he knows if he did, the copper could get him nicked, and then the copper goes, 'I'll take the lot of you on in the garage.' But what could we do? We couldn't, could we? Then we've had it, haven't we?

There are no ambiguities of recognition in this account; it's a meeting between, not strangers, but positionally known enemies. The issue is 'Who rules round here?' Such encounters are always prestructured in terms of rules of territoriality, and unfold in the form of a street challenge between two rival mobs. In this account we can see the classic sequence of ritual insult taking place; the initial informative-performative bind (taking the mick), the exchange of looks, the invitation to physical injury. The immediate pretext of the incident is, however, explained here in terms of the copper's boredom on the beat. This is not just a projection on the lad's part; it corresponds to sociological fact. Young police officers not only get bored on the beat but respond, just like any other working-class lad, by an intervention designed to generate a consequential narrative event. Often it is not only a question of getting into the action and having something to report but, where an arrest ensues, getting off the beat and getting back to the warmth and comfort of the station (not to mention an additional perk of the following morning off to appear in court). Late at night and in bad weather the temptation must be irresistible. Drunks, unlicensed street traders, and footloose kids provide the stock in trade for the policeman on walkabout or panda patrol.

So what began as a ritual exchange between 'equals' quickly escalates into a highly unequal confrontation between one mob, which has the full weight of the State apparatus behind it, and the other which has only each other. Magistrates' courts, borstal, detention centre – these institutions are all too visible in the mind's eye of the kids, from either their own past experiences or those represented by mates or relatives. The copper, however, acts *as if* this was not true, as if these institutions did not exist, and all that was happening was a fight between equals. He symbolizes this by taking off his helmet – his badge of office. Needless to say the kids aren't conned – they'd like to have a go, but they know that if they do they've 'had it'. In fact the 'fair deal' the copper is proposing is nothing of the sort, as both sides are fully aware. If these lads do square up and succeed in beating the copper in a 'fair fight' – a somewhat unlikely outcome since they are two pint-sized 14-year-olds against a six-foot fourteen-stone full-grown man – then next day they are very likely to find themselves up in court charged with assault, or worse. The alternative is to take a beating, and even then there is no guarantee that they won't be arrested into the bargain, although it is much less likely. The only other solution – the one these boys opted for – was to back down, apologize, or in some other way extricate themselves. Every way, they lose. But for some lads, like Brian, and in some encounters, like the Great Chinese Take-Away Massacre, it is actually *less* humiliating to be arrested than to suffer the indignity of being beaten up or of backing down.[3]

Sore thumbs

Since its publication in 1978 *Knuckle Sandwich* has had quite a lively reception in youth and community work circles, not all of it favourable! One of the central concerns of the book was to show that the attempt to develop alternative styles of youth work and education reached an impasse in the mid-'70s, because it was based on a drastic misconception about what was at stake in growing up working-class. Certain forms of middle-class radicalism were counterproductive, and likely to provoke a backlash from working-class young people. In this respect, unfortunately, I think events have largely proved us correct.

Nevertheless, some of the criticisms made of the book were quite justified. It has rightly been attacked for its overwhelming emphasis on boys' culture; indeed it should more accurately have been subtitled *Growing up Masculine in the Working-Class City*. One of the reasons for this deficiency is that, as men, we found it impossible to develop the kind of relationship with girls on the estate which would generate a detailed account of their special predicament. But I do not think that this entirely lets us off the hook. That we were able to generate so much material from the boys was partly because we allowed ourselves to become implicated in macho norms which, to some extent, we manipulated to cut across the differences in class and culture, which would otherwise have impeded our efforts.

The real criticism, therefore, is not that we failed to deal adequately with the issue of girls' sexuality and social subordination, but that we did not devote enough attention to the assumption of gender roles, or the function of masculine ideals in the local culture. I think this was partly because we did not adequately follow though our own indications about the tension between wage-earning autonomy and domestic dependence as central to working-class adolescence. Had we done so, the patriarchal linkages between the sexual and generational divisions of labour under capitalism would have emerged as the main focus of the argument.

This does not mean that we identify totally with all aspects of the feminist position especially its separatist tendency. In the early 1970s feminism had yet to make an organised impact on youth work. In part, this was due to the fact that feminists in this period ignored the generational dimension of patriarchy almost entirely.[4] However, subsequent attempts to identify a common ground in which middle-class feminists can relate to working-class girls, as bearers of a common oppression, are fraught with difficulties and contradictions. In fact, many of these problems are comparable to those faced when attempting to develop libertarian methods of education and youth work – especially in cases where the same strategies, e.g. consciousness raising, are deployed.

Women are not, by definition a social class, any more than youth. Yet as non-class agents, women and youth are always placed in positions of social subordination within specific and antagonistic class cultures. So in some contexts, for example in struggles against the law of the state which condemns them to second-class citizenship, women and youth from different classes can find a common cause. But in other contexts, such as struggles concerning housing, education and employment, they often have different and conflicting interests.

This is not to deny the importance of the women's movement or youth movements, or their relative autonomy from class politics, but to suggest that there is no simple unmediated principle of alliance between working-class girls and middle-class women, any more than there is between young workers and students. The separatist, (though not the socialist) feminist position obscures this point; which has direct practical implications.

To take a specific example, the relation between socialist and feminist styles of youth work has scarcely begun to be posed. Yet this is an increasingly urgent task, especially in the fields of sex education and adolescent counselling. How do we tackle the chauvinism of working-class boys, for example, in a way that does not simultaneously undermine the cultural sources of their class combativity and intensify their sexual anxieties? Clearly this is a problem which calls for delicate but precise handling, and one which it is incumbent on male radicals to tackle, as well as the women's movement.

Somewhat similar difficulties have arisen in the anti-racist movement, as a result of its intervention into youth politics. In *Knuckle Sandwich*, we tried to show that the growth of working-class racism could not be accounted for in terms of 'false consciousness', or as the effect of some diabolical scheme by the bourgeoisie to divide and rule the masses. The phenomenon has to be understood and fought in its own working-class ground, as constituted by the rules and rituals of territoriality through which the most powerless and disorganised sections of the working class fabricate imaginary contexts of origin and belonging. These practices, centred on ritual insult and physical challenge, literally embody a peer group ideal of 'hardness' and are the major ways in which white working-class boys traditionally establish their ethnic credentials over 'outsiders'.

We tried to show how easily this sense of ethnic identity might undergo a racist transformation, in conditions where the Black and Asian working class was seen to possess rival credentials. Working-class racism thus either takes the form of a defence of public proprieties, associated with aspirations to social betterment within the white parent culture, or a defence of the imaginary kingdoms of the street, associated with juvenile gangs.

Normally these two instances are in conflict; racist ideology unites them. Nevertheless, it is an unstable 'synthesis' and one which the National Front has found very hard to organise into a political force. Unfortunately, working-class racism is also resistant to such strategies as multi-cultural education, for this approach sets out to dissolve antagonisms based on ethnic differences, by also dissolving antagonisms based on class. What the advocates of a 'pluralistic' society do not seem to realise is that while ethnicity is indeed a matter of identity and difference, class is to do with domination and subordination. It is the way these two kinds of relations become interlocked and confused with each other as 'race relations' that is the problem! If the anti-racist message is preached by groups such as priests, teachers, youth workers, politicians, etc, who are seen as the voice of middle-class authority, it is likely to provoke just that residual working-class chauvinism which supports racist practices.

Anti-racist alliance

The achievement of the Anti-Nazi League and Rock Against Racism was to cut the anti-racist message free from these associations, to give it a youthful, anti-authoritarian and populist idiom. But the medium (music) made its transmission dependent on the all too volatile affinities and enmities of purely subcultural 'politics'. The attempt to forge an anti-racist alliance between teds, punks, skinheads, mods, etc. had no real organisational base and was bound to fail. The symbols – a badge, a tee shirt, a hair style, slang, etc. – float free of any fixed ideological context, allowing endless permutations and ultimately enabling young people to follow two-tone bands like The Specials *and* racist groups like the British Movement, without experiencing any sense of contradiction. Our conclusion was that anti-racist work had to reach beneath these surface idioms and gain some purchase on the underlying class problems.

In the final section of *Knuckle Sandwich* we tried to outline one possible method of undertaking non-sectarian, non-evangelical political education work, based on socialist principles. We outlined four main principles for this kind of detached work with groups of young people in working class environments:

1. It should aim to make explicit the class analytics embedded in the structures of peer group narratives.
2. The educational group should focus its work on issues of power and powerlessness and seek to make these issues a special object of discussion and collective action.
3. The function of the teacher should be to transmit his or her skills to the group, so that some of its members become confident enough to set up their own groups.
4. The group must be anchored in a wider working-class community, so that it serves as a forum for political expression and representation by young people.

We subtitled the programme, ironically, '*a modest proposal*'. It is not a formula for turning out disciplined converts to the Labour Party, or Socialist Workers' Party, nor has it much to do with the kind of 'political literacy' that Professor Crick and the Hansard Society are concerned with. The educational group aims to explore working-class consciousness so that its members can decide for themselves which are the useful and progressive elements, and which the reactionary and self destructive elements.

Improvisation

The fact that the group generates its own educational materials as it goes along, means that the keynote is one of constant improvisation. Youth workers are perhaps more used to doing this than professional teachers. It also raises the question of how far this approach depends for its success on discovering gifted teachers outside the normal channels – people who have an intuitive grasp of the underlying principles – and how far it can be incorporated within existing programmes for professional teachers and youth workers.

I am not sure what the implications of this type of work are for the Youth Service as a whole. It certainly tries to give more power to the elbow of those who want to move away from a glorified child-minding role, but does it perhaps also point to a changed relation between 'youth providers' and their youth constituencies? Like most socialists, we believe that it is important to try and strengthen the democratic trends with the Service, against its more traditional and paternalistic tendencies.

The professionalisation of the Service has been all to the good in this respect, in so far as it has meant that young middle-class radicals have increasingly supplanted policemen, priests and the lesser urban gentry as youth workers. Our criticism of this development has been directed at stressing that it represents only a transitional stage, and that there is a permanent danger of reverting to a modern version of the liberal imperialist 'solution' to the youth question, unless this is consciously resisted.

In order to advance, it seems to me that the Youth Service has to recognise the necessity of evolving a form of internal democracy, corresponding to, but not identical with, the forms of self-organisation common to its overwhelmingly working-class clientele. This means translating the existing norms of youth participation into substantive control by users over the planning, administration and use of facilities. It means the labour movement having a far greater structural, as well as personal, involvement in youth provision, both inside and outside the workplace. Clearly, such a shift in power raises wider issues concerning the class struggle within the state, which cannot be dealt with here. But it should be evident that these changes will not be engineered from above. The kind of youth work we are arguing for would help build up the pressure for change from the grass roots.

Such initiatives must form part of a wider process for, to leave the last word where it belongs, with Jack Common.

Actually the kind of intimations I have been dealing with are common property amongst many, many people, who have far greater authority than I to speak of them. When they are codified it must be by collective counsel, a general squaring up of common experiences. To do it any other way, would be to commit an act of isolation. One has to be careful of that, even in small matters.[5]

Notes

1. The italics illustrate the narrative functions.
2. The newly opened Riverside Sports Centre recruited a number of local professional 'hard men' to police the place after repeated fights and vandalism. As this story reveals, there was some 'competition' for the job among the fraternity.
3. Encounters such as those described here were common experiences for young people in this part of North London, and we listened to many accounts similar to those just quoted. To try to check their frequency we asked four members of the popular Wall hangout opposite the Black Horse to keep a record over four weeks of the occasions on which they were stopped by the police. Two of them had court convictions for minor offences, the other two didn't. One was a fringe member of the Wall, two were regulars, and one we judged to be 'hard core'. We should stress that none of these young people had a hard delinquent status in the area; they all had relatively well-paid jobs, and one in fact was going to evening class twice a week to qualify for an apprenticeship.
    There were fifteen separate incidents recorded over the period. Ten of them took place in situations where they were with mates, including each other. Eight took place after 10 p.m. In only two cases were boys lawbreaking in any recognizable form. Once they were caught joy-riding in a relative's car. The other instance concerned a pub fight when the police were called. The remaining incidents all took place in the context of street challenge: either on the Wall itself (5), or outside cinemas, cafés and other youth hangouts (7), or when just walking about (3).
    All this might be expected. But in comparing the experiences of the four lads there is a surprise: there was no appreciable difference in either the frequency or the seriousness of encounters between the two lads known to the police and those who were not. Nor did their degree of involvement in the Wall fraternity seem to make a difference. There seemed to be a fairly equal and random distribution of incidents. Obviously this has a lot to do with the short time-span of this piece of research, and may be something of an 'optical illusion'. If this kind of getting into trouble is situationally determined, we should expect that the stronger and hence longer a young person's

commitment to the Wall, the more likely that routine, random police harassment would be registered in terms of court appearances and convictions. So over a longer period of research, differences between the lads might begin to show, if not necessarily in any predictable way But what it also points to is that it is essential to distinguish the kind of processes which determine degree of commitment to the Wall from the mechanisms which produce a young 'apprentice gangster' of the Billy Sheahan variety. There are cases in which these two may mesh in, but they are likely to be the exception rather than the rule.

4. A notable exception is the research undertaken by Angela McRobbie into working-class girls' cultures. For a witty critique of the youth research from a socialist feminist perspective see her contribution in the August 1980 issue of *Screen Education,* and her book *Feminism and Youth Culture* (London, 1992).

5. Jack Common, *Freedom of the Streets* (1938).

Chapter 5

Policing the Working-class City

The research reported here arose out of a comparison between different types of police harassment directed against groups of young people in the city centre and on council estates in the inner city. I had, of course, experienced the sharp end of city centre policing at 144 Piccadilly. Subsequent experience of working with young people in North Islington (described in the previous chapter) made it clear that a very different set of protocols and procedures were being applied in this case.

The work of Isaac Balbus, an American Civil rights lawyer, and in particular his book The Dialectics of Legal Repression, *seemed to provide one possible theoretical framework for understanding differential policing in terms of the internal constraints and contradictions of this particular state apparatus. At the same time Gramsci had taught us that the state governed not only through forms of physical deterrence and coercion but through processes of moral compulsion tied to cultural norms of what was appropriate and possible public behaviour. Might it not then be the case that the kinds of systemic contradiction which Balbus talked about derived in fact from the way the police force combined both a coercive and moral role?*

The second line of thought concerns the impact of policing on divisions within working-class communities. Gramsci's notion of corporatism, which had been extensively used by the Centre for Contemporary Cultural Studies

Ben Fine *et al.* (eds), *Capitalism and the Rule of Law* (London: Hutchinson, 1981).

(CCCS) to explain the evolution of English working-class cultures as a separate and subordinate formation, still rested on a too unitary or mono-lithic model of the process. This essay represents an early, and hence still rather crude (and no doubt some would say 'preFoucauldian'), attempt to understand technologies of social control in a less reductionist manner.

It appeared in a collection of papers from a conference organised by the National Deviancy Symposium in which general theories of Law and the State were, perhaps for the first time, placed at the top of the agenda of debate. It was perhaps out of this encounter, whose awkwardnesses are reg-istered in this text, that a space was subsequently opened up for the wider dissemination of Foucault's work on disciplinary regimes, not only within criminology, but across the human sciences generally.

The changing role of the police force has increasingly become a central theme in the current debate on the left over the road to socialism in advanced capitalist societies. Those who argue for the parliamentary road are almost invariably committed to a civil lib-ertarian position – that the powers and practices of policing can and must be made accountable to democratic institutions of control, as part of a broader struggle to transform the state. Consequently the attempt is made to radicalize and extend the functions of the traditional 'Liberal Watchdog', and to give a structural edge to the 'rotten apples' thesis concerning police behaviour.

On the other side are those who maintain they are holding to the revolutionary road, and who argue that state power must be seized or smashed, through the autonomous organization of pro-letarian struggle. For the ultra left, the police force is the brutal repressive arm of the ruling class, which must be confronted and shown up for what it is at every opportunity. This could be called the 'all coppers are fascist pigs' thesis, and generally goes with the view that Britain is on the way to becoming a police state.

Campaigns against legal repression (against the 'sus' laws, against the extension of powers of detention and arrest) cannot help but highlight the crisis of bourgeois democracy, and the rela-tion of state to civil society, even if the gulf between street activist and academic Marxist seems to grow even wider. But are the terms of the theoretical debate adequate to the task of formulat-ing principles of political practice?

At present the argument seems to be bogged down in a series of antinomies:

> *Either* the freedoms and structures of accountability which characterize bourgeois democracy contain within them the conditions of their socialist transformation, *or* they are pure sham, designed to mystify the masses, and must be exploded

> *Either* the state can be transformed so it reflects, or is subordinated to, the institutions of civil society *or* civil society is the basis on and from which the apparatus of the state is to be eroded, and ultimately destroyed.

Like all debates that go round in circles, the arguments continually pass each other going in opposite directions. But that would at least indicate that there is some 'common ground'. And there is.

Civil libertarians and ultra-leftists agree that there is a fundamental contradiction in the mechanisms of bourgeois democracy, between the formal and substantive aspects of law enforcement; between, for example, the neutral and impartial administration of justice, enshrined in juridical ideology, and the material practices which ensure there is 'one law for the poor, another for the rich'.

Where they diverge, of course, is on what to do about it. For the ultra-left it is a question of stripping away the appearance of neutrality, to reveal the hidden essence of class justice; for the civil libertarian, of suppressing the residual elements of class practice, so that the formal principles become substantive guarantees.

Marxists like to pride themselves on having gone beyond such either/or positions, and the Manichaean division of the struggle into goodies and baddies. Yet they are not able to account for the fact that this superior dialectical view is nowhere reflected in their political practice, other than by appealing to the usual get out clauses about the 'relative autonomy of theory'. Yet what if the problem turned out to be theoretical after all? What if it lay in the terms which Marxists themselves have contributed to the debate?

Several recent studies have suggested that the problems lie less in the terms themselves than the way they are used to generate false dichotomies. Balbus (1973) argues that the police force must be considered in its structural specificity as a site of contradictory practices, between those which are required to guarantee public order, those which safeguard the legitimacy of the state as a neutral arbiter of justice, and those which are required for the organizational maintenance of the force itself, as a bureaucratic apparatus. These contradictions are reproduced in a whole series of split perceptions about the functions of the police, which is reflected also at the level of public debate.

Edelman (1979) has argued that juridical ideology is not something confined to the law courts; it is a representation of a material transformation which class relations undergo in the sphere of commodity circulation and exchange, and as such penetrates the basic conditions of subjectivity in capitalist society. The law gives class subjects legal being; it determines the most intimate relations between parents and children, as well as the most public aspects of everyday life.

What both studies point to is the need for additional concepts to denote the range of institutions and practices, which are not wholly 'in' the state or civil society but are interpenetrated by them, and which serve to both condense and displace their contradiction on the terrain of class conflict.[1]

The terms 'bourgeois' and 'proletarian public realm', popularized by the Frankfurt school, seem to me to be useful here, once they are divested of their idealist problematic (see in particular Negt and Kluge 1973 and 1975). For they can be used to make sense of a space of articulation between *specific habitats of class practice*, and *specific conditions of legal subjectivity*, a space which is far from metaphysical and, as I hope to show, has a very material history. For it is here and nowhere else that the policing of the working-class city takes place.

Cuffs and capes

The modern police force emerged out of the crisis of urban administration in the Victorian city. It was the first branch of the British state to develop an ideological as well as a purely repressive function. As such, the official task of policing was both to protect the institutions of private property, and to enforce statutory norms of public order primarily designed to ensure the free circulation of commodities, including the commodity of labour power.

In London especially, the metropolitan force was both the strong arm and the advance guard of municipal reform.[2] As a population formed by pre-industrial and rural conditions crowded in and colonized the archaic urban infrastructure, it became less a question of enforcing their segregation from the upper classes than of policing their usage of social space and time so that it did not obstruct the traffic of industry and commerce. The potential sources of obstruction included not only strikes, political mobilizations and organized crime, but also the develop-ment of street cultures and their irregular economies, upon which whole working-class communities came to depend as a means of local livelihood and identity against the anarchy of impersonal market forces. In such areas as these, the question 'Who rules around here?' was no mere metaphor of a class strug-gle waged essentially elsewhere: it was itself that struggle. For here the new instruments of bourgeois law and the traditional instru-ments of popular order became quickly locked in a brutal, if everyday, confrontation. Inevitably the slum neighbourhoods adjoining the inner industrial perimeter, with their volatile, visible and organized social systems, mounted the most violent and sus-tained opposition to these new urban reformers in blue. Islington was no exception.[3]

Henry Mayhew noted in the 1850s that the costermonger com-munity was in the vanguard of resistance. To 'have' a policeman was the bravest act a coster could perform, and those who were sent down were regarded as local martyrs and heroes. When they came out of prison, subscriptions were organized. Coster boys adopted 'guerrilla' tactics based on superior knowledge of the local terrain, waiting hidden down an alleyway until the policeman came past, lobbing their stone or brick, and then just as quickly disappearing. Mayhew suggests that the costers' hatred of the police was due to a residual Chartist influence amongst them, but his own evidence suggests that the main motive was economic rather than political. As one coster told him (Mayhew, 1851, p. 22):

> They drive us about, we must move on, we can't stand here and we can't pitch there; they are trying to drive us out of business.

Resistance was not confined to the coster colony around Chapel Street market and the Pentonville Road. From the 1880s onwards, as Islington became increasingly proletarianized in the south and the middle class retreated northwards behind the barriers of property and income, it was those traditional occupational groups concentrated geographically and socially between the two, still tied to the irregular street economy, its seasonal patterns of casual labour and drift migration, who became the special targets of policing. For nearly half a century Popham Street and Packington Street off Essex Road, and Gifford and Bemerton Streets off the Caledonian Road, saw numerous affrays between constabulary and local populace. The local press records 146 such incidents in these areas between 1880 and 1920 – inevitably only those leading to arrest, and hence presumably only a fraction of the real number of cases.

A report in the *Islington Gazette* of January 1881 gives some sense of these occasions. A certain Mr Savoury, a horse-keeper in his mid-twenties who lived in Gifford Street, was charged with assault and wounding a policeman. On the Sunday night, after the pubs had closed, there had been a fight in Gifford Street and a crowd of a hundred or so had gathered round to watch and cheer on their man. The police arrived to break it up and proceeded to arrest one of the contestants. This infuriated the crowd who set on the policemen, gave them a thorough beating, and rescued the prisoner. Mr Savoury had apparently played a leading role in the counter-attack, and when a policeman drew his staff to arrest him, he grabbed it and 'knocked him about so severely that he's been under the surgeon's hand ever since'. In court the next day, a large crowd from Gifford Street turned up to support their hero, only to see him sent down for six months' hard labour, the stiffest penalty the magistrate could inflict for such an offence at this period.

It is interesting to note that in evidence the police claimed that they had intervened to 'quell a riot', whereas in fact, by breaking up the popular recreation of a Sunday night spar, their actions had actually provoked one.

The ancient tradition of collective self-defence still existed in this area two generations later, as shown by a report (*Islington Gazette*, June 1924) from the 1920s. A policeman arrested a local woman in the Caledonian Road, when a large hostile crowd – but this time *mainly of youths* – gathered round to rescue her. Stones, cans, bottles began to fly, and one nimble 16-year-old errand boy wriggled his way through the crowd and tripped up the police-man. However, the police had become increasingly efficient at dealing with these situations: reinforcements were summoned, and several more arrests were made.

Even arrest might not be the end of the story. One Islington resident (Mr Malone: oral testimony) recalled how in his youth, before the First World War, the police would strap a particularly obstreperous offender on to an open stretcher and wheel him back, still followed by the crowd, to the station. Once there, the crowd would wait outside and, if they heard a noise, claim the police were beating up the man, even on occasion retaliating by stoning the windows. He also remembered how during this period, in the tenements where he lived, the arrival of the police on what was regarded as the residents' own territory would be greeted by a hail of flower pots, and this was not an infrequent occurrence of his childhood!

What outraged these communities was not just the law's attack on what they regarded as legitimate means of livelihood or sec-ondary income – these were in any case being increasingly eroded by wider and purely economic forces – but the criminalization of traditional street pastimes which were solely recreational. From the 1870s onwards, it was young people who were particularly singled out on this front. Mayhew (1851) noted that street gam-bling, in the form of pitch and toss, held a special fascination for the costers, Kings Cross being a popular venue:

> It is difficult to find in the whole of this numerous class a youngster who is not a desperate gambler ... every attempt by the police to check this ruinous system has been unavailing and rather given a gloss of daring and courage to the sport.

In the 1850s, men as well as boys had been addicts of pitch and toss, but by the 1920s adults had taken to other forms of betting, notably of course horse-racing, while pitch and toss had retained its popularity as an integral part of general street youth culture, now reinforced by the imposed leisure of unemployment. Secondly, while pugilism was being taken off the streets and refined in the boxing club, the rise of the professional football club had given a powerful impetus to its amateur emulation in the back alley.

During the 1920s, Islington police seem to have made a special drive against these two sports, and it is therefore not surprising to find that they account for over half the reported arrests of juveniles during this period. Given the scale of these activities and the local police's limited manpower, there was no attempt at mass roundups. Instead the police attempted a more selective strategy of arrest. They concentrated harassment in those streets associated by reputation or tradition with *adult* crime. The geographical distribution of arrests for street football (which has no possible criminal connotations) closely follows that of youngsters for playing pitch and toss, which *may* conceivably have been used as a cover for working as bookies' runners. Policing tactics thus consisted of general physical intimidation coupled with systematically arbitrary arrests.

Another Islington resident, Mr Spendriff, remembers:

> If we'd been playing football or something in the street, there used to be a policeman – we used to call him Flash Harry – and he used to throw his cape at you as you'd run away. He'd throw it right between your legs. Yes. He'd just cuff you round the ears and let you go. (oral testimony)

Cuffs and capes seem to have been the favourite methods of discipline, as they could be applied apparently randomly against isolated kids. Officers who specialized in such attacks were of course especially feared and hated. Here is a vivid account of one such incident in Chapel Street in the late 1930s:

> There was this copper, he was a real bully; all the kids were scared of him. In those days the Law was mostly brawn, big fellas, and they'd clout you as soon as take a look. Well there was this one, he was called King Kong – you know, after that monster in the film. Well, one day, it was around Christmas time and I'd been helping my uncle out on the barrow and he'd given me a few bob for myself; so I was quite chuffed, thinking what I was going to spend it on, and just walking along thinking my own thoughts, and then WHAM! it was like I'd walked into a lamppost or something. And it was this copper, King Kong. He must have been standing in a doorway 'cos I didn't see him. And then

he just came out and got hold of me and smacked me in the teeth. You know I was so shocked I couldn't do nothing, say anything. I just sort of looked at him and he smiled and said 'Well son, if you want to know what that was for, I'll tell you: disturbing the peace. And you'd better scarper off home before you get another one for whistling about like you own the place'. And you know what it was – I'd been whistling in the street, and it was agin the law he reckoned. Anything like that, the littlest thing, you'd get the Law down on you. But they rarely took you to the station – just belted you! Of course in them days you sort of expected it, same as the teachers gave you, or the old man if you didn't behave. So it was all the same sort of thing. (Mr Spencer, oral testimony)

The sense of shock registered is not then at the actual violence metered out. That is accepted as a normal feature of relations between adult authority and youth. What does hurt is the sudden and arbitrary nature of its occurrence.

Nevertheless, in the decade after the First World War, the whole pattern of relations between the police and the working class in North London had begun slowly, but subtly, to change from outright physical confrontation to an unwritten system of tacit negotiation. The antagonism was not resolved, but it was pursued by means other than street beatings and set-tos. The reasons for the change are complex: they are partly to do with changes in the conditions and composition of the local working class, partly with the position of youth within the generational division of labour, and partly the result of the changing function of the police force in the developing structure of the capitalist state. Let us look at each in turn.

The years after 1919 saw the disintegration of many of the material supports of traditional street culture. The casual labour market generated by the irregular economy declined; while the associated criminal subculture split off and became the preserve of an increasingly professional fraternity, whose scale of operations and organization embraced not just Islington but also Kentish and Camden Town. Secondly, access to job opportunities was no longer so dependent on highly localized social networks of information and patronage. Apart from odd jobs, the street corner labour exchange was actually less efficient than the official version under conditions of widespread, and not just local, unemployment. Thirdly, the local Irish presence had tended to become both geographically more dispersed and culturally more entrenched, largely through its involvement in trade unionism and local labour politics. The traditional techniques of hardness and brawling expertise, while still called on, tended to play a supporting rather than a leading role. Concentrations of the old 'dangerous class' had been broken up through sustained harassment or rebuilding. Campbell Road was demolished to make way for a factory. Slum tenements began to give way to municipal housing. Clissold and Finsbury Parks, Highbury Fields, various youth clubs, uniformed organizations, all claimed a share of youthful energies from the overpoliced streets. Finally, the expanding lower middle class consolidated *their* presence in residential neighbourhoods previously monopolized by the carriage trade, and added to the weight of civic consciousness in numerous local institutions patronized by manual workers and their families. Furthermore, the sheer physical fact that large numbers of the men and boys, who had previously dominated the traditional street culture, were away from it during the war years, meant that women and children were left in charge and, in a sense, domesticated some of its functions.

All these changes, small in themselves, uneven in their development, nevertheless combined to alter the contexts of policing and the practices of social control at street level. In the process, the local working class had become more sedimented, less autonomous, their public behaviour to an extent domesticated by an urban environment which was beginning to bear the first marks of properly capitalist planning. But this does not mean that it had become sedentary, dependent, or privatized.

In part, the patterns of street and neighbourhood usage remained remarkably consistent, given the changes in economic infrastructure. It was the moral ideologies associated with that use which were modified, harnessed to specific working-class notions of *public propriety.*

The notion was one of the great distinguishing characteristics of the labour aristocracy; and by the 1870s it was firmly established as an active principle amongst the large colonies of skilled print and railway workers in Islington. Nor was it just a notion, for these groups spun a whole cocoon of institutions around themselves to make substantive, and to preserve, the connection between superior occupational and moral status. What this in practice meant was a more or less ritual avoidance of contact with street cultures, a preference for more rational recreation over its popular diversions. It meant drawing a socially, and often geographically, visible line between the two habitats of working-class subjectivity – here the workshop, there the street – serving as a principle of territorial affinities and enmities. But if the skilled worker drew a line under his own feet, it was not always so neat or so visible for his children. Nevertheless, up until the First World War there were two quite clear-cut apprenticeships into working-class masculinity and manual labour. Those for whom apprenticeship was a material institution were kept firmly under the patriarchal thumb of the master craftsman in the workshop and, because of their prolonged financial dependence, kept under the parental thumb as well. From this basis, the parent culture had little difficulty in extending its strategy of social closure to embrace the free time of its youth. Those new institutions of public propriety the woodcraft organizations and the boys' clubs, were dominated by the children of skilled workers – and of course in many cases it was only they who could afford the cost of membership.

There is no greater contrast than with the way coster boys and girls were informally apprenticed to their street trade. The aristocracy of the irregular economy ensured that their children started learning the trade almost as soon as they could walk. By the time they were 12 or 13, girls as well as boys had familiarized themselves with all the essential tricks of the trade, as well as having learned how to negotiate the local underlife and still stay out of trouble with the law. Just as importantly, they were often able to save enough from what they earned on the family barrow and through odd jobs to hire a pitch of their own, and set up in competition with their parents. Even more scandalous in the eyes of juvenile reformers, almost as soon as they reached puberty coster boys and girls could afford to leave home, rent lodgings and live as husband and wife. With money in their pockets, their own bosses, free from irksome family constraints (which did not, however, mean that they were not part of a close network of kin and could not rely on it for support when times were hard), no wonder coster youth were often the envy of their peers, the local youth style leaders, and their style was dead set against public propriety and all it stood for!

In between these two extremes stood the mass of unskilled and semi-skilled manual workers and their families. It was this stratum which now began to move away from the moral economies of street culture, and find in the institutions of public propriety a means, not just of respectability, but of material advancement.[4] For them, involvement in trade unionism and local labour politics has been the great pathway to these twin goals. Labourism is the working-class politics of public propriety and conscience, and it is no coincidence that its spokesmen have always been in the vanguard of those advocating the strictest legal repression of 'hooliganism', 'juvenile crimes', and working-class youth cultures in general. In Islington, the rise of the New Unionism and, after the war, of the Unemployed Workers Movement not only organized the hitherto unorganized, but helped give them a stake in the new urban order that was taking shape. Unemployed men still gathered at the unofficial labour exchange on the High Pavement of Essex Road, but to talk politics or racing results rather than to jeer at passing toffs or spit at the police, as was their regular habit in the 1890s. Their courting children no longer scandalized the older citizenry by obscene catcalls or by jostling them off the pavement, as they were recorded as doing up until 1914. By the 1920s, the monkey parade had retired to the greater privacy – if not decency – of Highbury Fields.

A railway porter summed up the span of change neatly enough, comparing his own childhood before the First World War with that of his son before the second:

> When Johnny was growing up in the flats, people had started using flower pots to grow flowers in. When I was a lad there, they kept them empty to throw at the Law. (Mr Elder, oral testimony)

But perhaps the most sensitive indicator of change comes from comparing the accounts given by mainstream-strata young workers about their encounters with the law before and after the war. In the descriptions of the pre-1914 period, the policeman remains a shadowy almost anonymous figure. A van driver recalls one such childhood encounter:

They were generally all stereotyped. Big black moustaches – you couldn't tell one from the other. All we knew was they was all down on us the same. We never got a chance to recognize them; we were too busy running away. (Mr Freeman, oral testimony)

But in the accounts of the 1920s and 1930s the portraits are filled in. Personal idiosyncrasies are mercilessly characterized, not least in nicknames. Wee Willy Winkie. Droopy Dan. Flash Harry. King Kong. Terms, certainly not of endearment, but of some familiarity. These are no longer shadows, but larger than life figures in the scenarios of youthful experience. This growing personification is one index of the gradual ideological penetration of 'The Law' into the basic conditions of working-class life during the period.

Another is the way certain aspects of routine policing became perceived as part of public ceremonial, a legitimate drama punctuating working-class life, as in this account *circa* 1920 by a warehouseman, then in his late teens:

Well, the police, you could tell the time by them. The posse we used to call them. At ten o'clock at night you'd see them marching down the road, relieving the various beats … Course, Saturday nights, if you wanted to enjoy yourself, you'd go down with your mates to see the drunks being brought in to the station. (Mr Jackson, oral testimony)

So instead of an angry crowd representing a whole neighbourhood, solid with one of their own in the nick – a not infrequent occurrence in the earlier period – here, a quarter of a century on, we have a group of footloose youngsters enjoying the spectacle of arrest as a free Saturday night entertainment.

It is impossible to be absolutely certain how typical these different responses were, or how accurate the accounts. But since they are all drawn from the mainstream elements, rather than from the extremes of rough or respectable, it seems likely that they do register substantive qualitative changes in popular attitudes to policing over this period. Given that police and court records were not available, it is difficult to construct any precise quantitative index of change. However, by comparing local press reports of 'disturbances' from 1880 to 1935, a distinct pattern begins to emerge:

1. After the First World War the number of reported incidents of public disorder per year drops considerably. On the other hand, there were episodic disturbances associated with local political activity – meetings and marches against unemployment and fights with local fascists.
2. After 1919 the reported size of the crowds involved in 'non-political' disturbances falls, sixty to eighty being a pre-war figure and twenty to thirty postwar. The ratio of reported arrests rises as the size of the crowds falls.
3. The age and sex composition reported also changes, men, women and children figuring in the pre-war reports, while in the 1920s and 1930s the accounts increasingly mention the predominance of male youths. This is also reflected in the details of those arrested, the age distribution progressively narrowing over time to the 14- to 18-year-old band, with a complement of slightly older, often unemployed, lads!
4. The most frequent places of disturbances remain remarkably consistent across the whole period; but in the post-war reports a number of new landmarks of confrontation make their appearance – for example, the Carlton Club, and the Coffee Stall in Essex Road, both of which are described as hang-about centres for youth and the unemployed.
5. In the 1920s and 1930s disturbances were almost exclusively concentrated at weekends and public holidays, whereas in the earlier period they show a slightly broader distribution through the week and throughout the year, though here again weekends and holidays show a peak concentration.
6. More significant was the fact that the reported occupations of juveniles arrested shows a higher concentration of those in 'street trades' in the later period than in the earlier.

This evidence points both to the changing configuration of the parent cultures and the changing pattern of juvenile employment. Increasingly it was wage-earning and unemployed boys who were left behind on the front lines of street confrontation with the law, as their parents increasingly identified the etiquette of public propriety with the exercise of parental responsibility. But the visibility factor is not enough in itself to explain the concentration of police activity on street-corner youth. The introduction of legislation against street-trading by juveniles, the stricter enforcement of elementary school attendance after the war, separated them conspicuously from their younger brothers and sisters at the same time as their elders and betters retreated from the scene. Second, the creation of new categories of juvenile offence also created greater pressure on the police to enforce them. Third, the polarizations within the local youth constituency between the apprenticeships of the workshop and those of the street was diminishing. Not only was the irregular economy in decline, but the interwar years saw the decline of many of the Finsbury workshop trades, and the migration of skilled labour to the new light industries being set up in West London. Juvenile labour became increasingly concentrated in shop and distributive trades, a small army of messenger boys was taken on by the post office, while the railway continued to employ a considerable number of van boys. Office work in the City claimed many girls from domestic service and laundry work. These jobs were still often dead-end and low-paid, but at least they were *decasualized*, even if the attitude of young workers to them was not.

All of this served to articulate the conditions of juvenile labour more closely to the institution of juvenile delinquency, to make substantive in policing practice the imaginary connection between a dangerous place (the streets of the working-class city) and a dangerous time (youth).

Of course it also gave impetus to those who were busy constructing safe places (youth clubs and organizations) where working-class youth could have safe times (rational recreation). But here it must be noted that Islington was not penetrated nearly so early or so thoroughly by the agencies of religious evangelism and philanthropy, as many other working-class areas (MacLeod, 1974). Here, for a long time, the police were the sole agency of urban reform. This factor, coupled with the survival of the irregular street economy, and the presence of a well-organized criminal community, explains why it took the police much longer to establish public propriety in Islington than many other inner cities. The great watershed, which occurred in the 1914–18 period for Islington, undoubtedly occurred in many industrial areas by the 1870s and 80s (Storch, 1976).

That this could happen at all is due to the decentralized nature of the apparatus of enforcement; its key particularisms – the logistics of police operations, and the cultures of local resistance – interact to determine the actual tempo of change in different urban contexts. However, if we want to underline the 'law' of this uneven and combined development, we will have to look in more detail at the structural processes which underlie the constraining variables of policing the working-class city.

Relations of force

The picture given so far has been no simple one of urban pacification. We have seen that the limits imposed on policing by working-class resistance were as significant as those imposed on street cultures in the name of public propriety. The proletarian public realm retained its historical individuality as a nexus of institutions and practices, through the very means of its accommodation to the capitalist city.

But what effect did these relations of force have on the internal development of police structures and functions? It seems to me that the British police have become, almost uniquely, a dependent part of a wider apparatus; we might call this the 'educational state system' – the system which educates the subjects of capital about the state, and about their legal conditions of existence as 'individuals' in 'civil society'. It is no coincidence that working-class kids call police 'The Law' because it is from them that they receive their physical and moral education about the place they occupy as legal subjects in class society. Especially where 'father's word is law', it is the policeman whose name is taken in vain as its support. As for those who refuse to learn their lesson, they are notoriously confused about which or whose law they have transgressed – the law of patriarchy or of propriety. For in the institution of public propriety, the two are indeed chronically conflated.

But this in turn has imposed a peculiarly contradictory role on the police themselves. The British bobby is called upon to perform two basic and distinct tasks:

As the moral entrepreneur of public propriety, and by implication arbiter of deviance, he performs a purely expressive function of community welfare and is expected to do so impartially, as a public servant, in contexts occupied solely by what appear to be individual citizens in need or distress. This aspect of the job is necessarily very labour intensive.

As the administrator of a juridical ideology of crime, in which the bourgeoisie has enshrined its version of the rights of capital and the obligations of labour, he performs a repressive function in a policing context where there are two categories of client – the legitimate and the illegitimate possessors of property. This aspect of the job has become increasingly capital intensive.

How these two sides of the job operate in practice is best described by a rank-and-file policeman in a novel he wrote about the force in the 1960s:

It was as though there were two police forces. One was real, the one which caught criminals, and the other one was the one that existed in some high-up's office in the Yard. The real police force was there to catch criminals the best way it knew how; and if you couldn't get them down according to Judges Rules, you got them down in your own way. The real police force worked in and around police stations; the real police force *worked*.

The other one was the one the Press wrote about, the one the taxpayers believed in. It was full of unsung heroes with blue eyes and honest English faces … *that* police force helped old ladies across the road, in between spells of taking finger prints and running four-minute miles. That police force gave you a pain in the arse. Not only didn't it exist, it *couldn't*. If it did, the prisons would be empty. And the senior officers knew all about the real police force … But for some reason, once you got up that end of the ladder you started forgetting what it was like. Police duty as it was done became a dirty word. And let some poor sod get caught out in something – whether it was a bit of exaggeration in a magistrate's court, or laying someone else's old woman – and they all raised their clean little hands in horror. 'But this is terrible', they would say, their own dirty skeletons locked out of sight, 'to think a policeman could do a thing like this'. When what they really meant was, 'Some bloody reporter's going to get hold of this and splash it on the front page'. (Brock, 1968)

So the combining of expressive and repressive functions seems to lead to a whole series of conflicts within the police force itself, and in its relations to other institutions which police the boundaries of the bourgeois public realm.

Normally a capitalist state develops forms of representative democracy and public accountability, which reproduce the conditions of bourgeois hegemony through a process of active consent. Normally, therefore, its powers of physical coercion are called on as a last resort, and against those who have first been publicly outlawed as legal subjects by a variety of ideological mechanisms. But the police force is in a peculiar position here, as an agency of the state which has to penetrate into the heart of civil society if it is to be effective, which has to win active consent to its presence if it is to do so, but which both directly and immediately represents the state's powers of physical coercion. The situation is critical when it comes to policing the working-class city. For, as we have seen, in those areas which were characterized by a backward, small-scale economy, the police force was charged with introducing elements of urban discipline into a population which had not yet fully experienced industrial discipline. And these districts sustained popular cultures which incorporated quite highly-developed countervailing norms of law and order, which could only be totally eliminated by outright repression. It was thus decisive that police intervention in the life of these areas should be seen as the neutral administration of a rational system of justice, rather than the brutal extension of bourgeois class power; if the police were to be seen as legal subjects, not as class subjects, it was necessary to evolve for these 'difficult' neighbourhoods a policing strategy which would maintain the legitimacy of the force's role, as much to the world outside as within itself, by representing the illusory unity of its functions against the manifest reality of their contradictions.

The routine practices of policing were, therefore, designed to conform to the same principles of formal legal rationality[5] as the judicial system they serviced with 'offenders'. Only this kind of bureaucratic accountability could give the appearance of the police and the judiciary being independent of each other, and both being independent of political pressure and vested interest. So the policeman on the beat was trained to apply standard protocols of surveillance, investigation and arrest to all citizen subjects, irrespective of class, colour or creed; just as the magistrate was supposed to apply universalistic rules of evidence, definitions of crime and punishment, with similar impartiality in the court.

As we have seen in Islington, however, the universality of the legal subject could only be substantiated by systematically violating the due process of law in the manner of its enforcement: which, in turn, undermined the whole enterprise of legitimation. The alternative strategy, observing the full letter of the law, would only generate mass arrests, which would overstretch limited manpower resources and threaten the bureaucratic system of processing offenders. The case of street football and gambling illustrated how concretely the problem arose, and also how the police evolved a method of dealing with it: by a partial suspension of formal legal rationality, turning half a blind eye to the rule book; and by the partial suspension of statutory norms of public order, turning the other half of the blind eye to a good deal of minor infringement. Such a strategy enlarged the autonomy of the rank-and-file police over and against the higher white-collar echelons whose job is to maintain the bureaucratic accountability of the organization as a whole. But equally, the calculated use, or abuse, of discretionary powers produces a highly arbitrary system of policing, which undermines the official posture of the force as neutral arbiters of justice. The force is still confronted with the impossible choice of enforcing law *or* order.

In the event, an answer was found by modifying the operational definition of public order, thus producing mediation from within the police apparatus itself.

The statutory definitions, as we have seen, consisted of universalistic rules of public behaviour applied to isolated economic agents going about their lawful business, which in practice meant going from A to B in the shortest possible time. These norms enter into a whole series of legal regulations which criminalize any other kind of public behaviour – the laws against being a suspected person, loitering with intent, causing an obstruction, behaviour likely to cause a breach of the peace, insulting behaviour, definitions of riot and affray. These rules and regulations are, therefore, especially strategic in the city centre, where the symbolic institutions of power are concentrated and where different social classes – elsewhere residentially segregated – congregate in large numbers. Their function here, then, is to outlaw the social promiscuity of the urban crowd, as well as its potential political thread, by reinforcing its characteristics as an atomized mass.

Now initially, and at the time when large numbers of the so-called 'dangerous and perishing' classes still lived crowded together in close proximity to the citadels of power, the police attempted to apply the same norms of public order to these residential areas as to the central place itself. As the problems of enforcing these norms became apparent, and as the urban poor were evicted from the city centre, the policing strategy changed. The innovations consisted precisely in differentiating between the two urban contexts. While statutory norms were still routinely enforced in the centre, in the new heartlands of the working-class city they were increasingly used only as an emergency measure, to justify the last resort of physical repression. In their place, a system of informal, tacitly negotiated and particularistic definitions of public order were evolved which *accommodated* certain working-class usages of social space and time, and *outlawed* others. What were ratified were those practices which articulated the institutions of patriarchy and public propriety within the class habitat; what were outlawed were those practices of women and children which challenged the monopoly of those institutions over the working-class city and its legitimate usage. The new norms in effect imposed a system of unofficial curfew, informal out-of-bounds, to define what were the wrong people, wrong age, wrong sex, in the wrong place and the wrong time. And 'wrong' was defined in the simultaneous terms of a moral ideology of deviance and the juridical ideology of crime. A kind of guilt-by-association was insinuated into these norms: if you were a legal subject caught following a less than pedestrian line of desire,[6] or a class subject caught out of your legal place, you were not only out of (statutory public) order, but had broken a moral code of respectable public behaviour. The first condition supplied the criminal offence, the second justified arrest. Here are some generic examples which may help illustrate how these norms operate:

1. Two smartly dressed young women are standing outside a Wimpy Bar in mid-afternoon talking to each other. All things

being equal, they will be assumed by the law, as well as by the general populace, to be two housewives having a gossip while out shopping. However, the same two young women doing exactly the same thing in exactly the same place at midnight will, all things being equal, be assumed to be prostitutes waiting for a pick up.

2. A group of working-class lads walking home down a main thoroughfare late at night, joking and singing, will be more likely to be subject to routine intervention by the law than a similar-sized group of girls, behaving in the same way. If two of the lads leave the main group to stroll through the back streets to get home, they will be twice as likely to get stopped and questioned if they pass through a cluster of middle-class residential streets on their way, than if their route passes exclusively through a working-class district.

3. A group of school-age boys or girls who decide to venture downtown for a look around the city centre one evening are likely to be picked up by the police and taken to the police station for interrogation, whereas if they were behaving in the same way (window shopping, eating bags of crisps) in their own locality, they would be unmolested. In one context they will be regarded as potential delinquents and morally 'at risk', while in the other they are simply normal boys and girls doing an everyday thing. However, if Arsenal win an important home game, and they go up west with a crowd of their mates from the North Bank to celebrate, but in fact spend their time wandering about as above, they will be regarded as extremely well-behaved. They may, on the other hand, also discover that on such an occasion they can get away with public behaviour which, if repeated in their own home areas or in a middle-class suburb, would be regarded by residents as constituting a riot, and by the law as behaviour likely to cause a breach of the peace.

4. Today, a group of young people can play football in most working-class streets without scarcely provoking interference by the police. Fifty years ago, their grandparents, doing the same thing in the same place, were highly likely to incur summary arrest and fines.

Once you have learned the ground rules, there is nothing haphazard or arbitrary about the application of these discretionary norms.

The principles of variation are rigorously determined by the strategic priorities of policing under different sets of circumstances, and those priorities are in turn determined by the need to maintain a balance between the conflicting demands of observing the letter of the law and the organizational maintenance of public order. The new methods set out to impose a principle of negotiation between the external policing of the neighbourhood and its internal systems of social control. More concretely, it was an attempt to forge an alliance between the spokesmen of proletarian patriarchy and propriety and the enforcers of bourgeois law and order. Here, uniquely, the police force and the labour movement perform complementary functions of political socialization – though, from a socialist standpoint, entirely negative ones. For the combined effect is to limit the access of working-class polity, while outlawing as potentially deviant the very 'public realms' they have had to construct to reaffirm some kind of social existence in the face of their disenfranchisement as speaking subjects within the class habitat. But more recently, in a period which has seen a general weakening of the links between sexual and generational relations in the reproduction of labour-power, their massive reinforcement at this superstructural level of 'community relations' has, if anything, served to sharpen working-class perceptions of the situation.

If the alliance at the top has been remarkably successful, the negotiation of informal norms at the grass-roots has been far less smooth. Firstly, because the constant drive towards increased accumulation of capital demands the continual recomposition and relocation of its labour force. Not only is this process resisted, thus unleashing community struggles which go far beyond the confines of public propriety, but it throws up new social forces (for example, immigrant workers) whose material cultures also challenge these constraints. If outsiders are to become established, informal norms must be negotiated anew. The fact that their very presence threatens the delicate equilibrium of existing tolerances means that the police normally respond by falling back on the more or less brutal reimposition of statutory public order when policing these groups.

A degree of immunity from this kind of direct legal repression has been won by the more sedimented sections of the class; but only by surrendering some of the means by which they once policed themselves. And these welfare functions, once confiscated, become the cutting-edge of the police campaign for active consent and public support. In many of the rougher inner-city neighbourhoods, however, and despite everything that municipal reformers can do, a strong countervailing sense of moral and social cohesion has survived. In these conditions, if the local police show one very public face in defence of order and another, more private one, in the enforcement of the law, they are likely to be condemned as two-faced.

Far from disappearing, the contradictions between the two sides of police work have intensified. They continue to undermine each other, while taking on new, more mediated forms. For example, the welfare function only remains credible if its implication for law enforcement (that is, the scrupulously impartial adherence to due process of law) is also observed. But in criminal work the emphasis is inevitably on productivity, increasing the ratio of arrests, and this in turn means bending the rules. This is also a problem for organizational maintenance. The more resources allocated to increasing the efficiency of repressive policing, the more manpower has to be poured into 'community relations' to restabilize the public image of the force. The more technologically sophisticated, and hence impersonal, the systems of surveillance, the more home-beat coppers are needed on the ground. The more manpower is drained here, the more rationalization is needed in policing methods in the other departments. The more this push-me-pull-you process accelerates, the more essential and the more impossible becomes the task of representing the repressive edge as a natural extension of the welfare wedge – the Sweeney as the legitimate offspring of Dixon of Dock Green.

In the post-war period, and especially during the last decade and in the inner city, the situation has come to a head. Increasingly in these areas the police have had to reply on apparatuses outside their control – notably, the mass media – to construct local emergencies which would sanction the reimposition of statutory norms through the systematic violation of the due process of law. If it was so easy to fabricate imaginary scenarios of lawlessness, hooliganism, mob violence and general rampage, we should remember that the survival of distinctive habitats of class subjectivity is necessarily a scandal, as well as a source of secret fascination and fear, in a Welfare State dedicated to equality of opportunity. Whatever social or political force manages to emerge from its invisibility, to break through the cover of routine surveillance and control, is by definition an emergency. And if it is 'bad' news, it is because it is always news from nowhere, a non-sense as well as a *non sequitur* from this vantage point. The restoration of order simply demands that this bad news return back into nowhere as quickly as possible. The separate tempos of police and media intervention thus work in counterpoint to each other, never in simple harmony.[7] If the police were relatively successful in isolating and attacking the new dangerous classes, they had also to pay the price of increased dependency on sources of legitimation in civil society. It was to prove a costly trade-off; for, as their own behaviour came increasingly into the public limelight, so many of the carefully negotiated norms and other special arrangements which constituted time-honoured station practice came suddenly to be redefined as 'corruption' because they did indeed violate principles of neutral administration and due process.

Yet the suppression of these practices could only endanger the organizational maintenance of local forces, already heavily under strength. The only alternative short-cut to getting results consisted in reverting to the more overt techniques of physical intimidation. Either way the image of public service and accountability was damaged, and exposed the force to even greater political pressure from watchdog groups. Inevitably, the push-me-pull-you process took its toll of the internal command structure of the force. The division of police labour became ever more specialized, and generated tensions between rival departments, each jealously guarding its professional autonomy. But the conflicts that have begun to shake the foundations are not merely institutional: they have distinct class connotations.

We have already noted the latent antagonism between the local beat coppers and their superior officers. The former are naturally concerned to safeguard their discretionary powers which alone allow them to gain intimate working knowledge of neighbourhood underlife, and to successfully perform the delicate balancing act between productivity and acceptability. But however they

negotiate their presence in the community, they are still accountable to their superiors. These latter are usually college-trained
administrators (Trenchard's Boys) who are preoccupied with a
different set of priorities, above all the need to balance the
demands of organizational maintenance with the observance of
procedural norms. This is only one instance of a wider conflict
between those whose conditions of police work require that they
take account of the existence of 'the working-class city', and those
whose position of public accountability requires that they do not.
So, for example, a basic antagonism quickly developed between
station staff, in charge of maintaining negotiated order in their
local manor, and the new elite cadres like the Special Patrol
Group and Regional Crime Squads, organized on paramilitary
lines, whose explicit and peripatetic function was precisely to
restore statutory order without regard for any of the factors constraining the operations of the local force.

Increasingly then, a split has tended to develop in the occupational socialization of the police force between its professional
ideology and its material cultures. This too has a history (see
Pilling, 1971).

Even as late as the Edwardian period, especially in industrial
areas, policing was still regarded as a normal working-class job.
Artisans and skilled men would get a job on the local force when
times were hard, and return to their 'real' trade when seasonal or
cyclical demand picked up. Police culture was that of a working
class temporarily in uniform. But with the growing professional-
ism of police work, the growing diversification of skills based on
mental as well as manual labour, a quite distinctive occupational
culture emerged. The force now tended to attract working men
whose aspirations, for whatever reason, fell short of their long-
term prospects in the labour market. Recruits were mainly
married men, often with considerable work experience in civilian
life – but their entry into the force signified a far more permanent
shift. This was reflected in the fact that police work had come to
be seen as a highly deviant occupational choice within the range
of working-class job opportunities. Police PROs tried to turn this
to good account by promoting a middle-class image of the force
as a 'vocation' and a 'career'. But, for the raw recruit, the reality
was of course quite otherwise, and so very different working-class
paradigms were brought to bear. The trade magazine of the force

is still obstinately called *The Job*, and, as its pages stress, it is one of society's dirty jobs and pretty underpaid at that. The ideology of public service, as in other sectors, backfired and produced growing trade-union militancy amongst the rank and file. Paradoxically, this militancy is an effect of the social isolation of the policeman from the mainstream of working-class life. The extent of social closure within this occupational community is indicated by the tendency of police work to become a family tradition – son succeeding father from generation to generation. There are other, no less idiosyncratic, factors at work in recruitment. Chief among them in the post-1945 period is the increasing *juvenilization* of the force. National service in the 1950s was an important feeder here, and so of course was the mounting level of youth unemployment in the 1970s. But cultural factors are equally important. The effect of such mass phenomena as the Teds, the Mods and Rockers, and the Skinheads on those young people who remained within the confines of parent cultures wedded to public propriety, should not be underestimated. In working-class districts where subcultures were strong, ultra-conformists could easily be isolated from the mainstream of local peer-group life. It may be significant then that those young constables I spoke to in Islington,[8] who had all joined the force after 1965, though they gave very disparate and personal reasons for doing so, were almost unanimous in saying that what they liked best about the job, what they had missed previously, was the sense of comradeship – the fact that you had mates you could depend on, who would back you up no matter what. This peer group ideal seemed, by all accounts, most strongly exemplified in the section house where the single lived; here horseplay, petty pilfering and strenuous parties seemed the order of the day. While they displayed deference to the symbolisms of Authority, these working-class youth were quite active in a whole culture of insubordination, with its own quite elaborate rituals of misrule. All this seemed to be officially tolerated, though not encouraged, as a necessary safety valve for young men subject to rigorous discipline at the bottom of the command structure – good for bonding them into an efficient crime-fighting unit. Just as it served as a defence against what was perceived as social ostracism by the local community.

The result had been to narrow the scenario of law and order down to a battle between two rival gangs, both composed of

young, single, working-class males, each seeking territorial control
over the class habitat – but with this difference, that one mob
have the full weight of the state behind them, the other only
themselves and their mates to fall back on. The scores they have
to settle still revolve around the question 'Who rules?' But they no
longer revolve around the material stakes of a class struggle, as it
was with the costers in the 1880s. Now the struggle is purely symbolic. Nevertheless, it is one which has all too real a consequence
for those who are on the losing side.

It is in fact a battle which the police force cannot afford not to
be seen to be winning. And increasingly they have fallen back on
the repressive weight of the state as represented by the juvenile
penal system in order to hold their own. It is the closed world of
'The Institution', acting at a distance through him, which confers
on the beat-copper his secret power in his dealings with the rival
mob. Higher police productivity has come to mean not so much
higher rates of arrest, or even conviction, but more deterrent
levels of judicial sentencing – higher rates of imprisonment. One
lad sent down for a short sharp shock in a detention centre,
instead of being let off with a fine, came to be seen as a more
efficient expenditure of scarce police resources than cautioning a
dozen of his mates and visiting his parents. But this solution is not
without its problems. It often means artificially escalating the
charge and/or fabricating evidence in order to ensure conviction
and higher sentence; yet this might mean endangering the
posture of formal legal rationality which the force might be
anxious to preserve in public settings such as the court. Equally, it
might mean a higher proportion of contested cases and jury trials;
further, the routine processing of offenders by courts, and with it
the bureaucratic equilibrium of justice, would be put under
strain. Nor does the problem stop there. As a log jam of cases
builds up, so the remand centres would clog up with those awaiting trial. However useful from the policing viewpoint, the deterrent effect of this preliminary taste of institutional life,
overcrowding and deteriorating conditions could only lead to
unrest amongst both staff and prisoners. As a consequence, local
judicial practices have had to be unofficially adjusted to take
account of variants in policing strategy. A secondary system of
informal norms of sentencing and treatment has evolved; but this
does not always reflect police priorities – indeed it may run

directly counter to them. Inevitably, the result is to produce wide-spread discrepancies between different areas of the city and different parts of the country, and vicious anomalies between crime and punishment in individual cases. Hardly the best advertisement for legal universalism.

To sum up, I have tried to suggest that the structural contradictions in policing practice derive from the force's peculiar historical position within the British state. In Gramsci's terms, it was the first branch of the state to exemplify a shift in ruling-class strategy from a war of manoeuvre to a war of fixed position (see Anderson, 1977). This pioneering role was forced upon it by the underdeveloped nature of the local state administration in a period of rapid urbanization, and at a time when long-established structures of popular recreation and justice retained powerful material supports. The response of the police to its predicament partially succeeded in imposing the elements of a properly capitalist urban discipline in the name of public propriety, but signally failed to resolve its own contradictions. These have sharpened into chronic conflicts within the force itself, and in its relations to a whole series of environing institutions. The current crisis in the policing of the working-class city has become a crisis of legitimacy for the bourgeois public realm as a whole.

Notes

1. Anderson (1977) argues this; his article is also a good introduction to the whole post-Gramscian debate on state and civil society.
2. See Storch (1976) for an empiricist reading of Victorian policing.
3. All historical material refers to the London borough of Islington. This research consisted of an analysis of local newspaper reports from 1875 to 1935 and of oral testimony collected from residents who grew up in Islington between the world wars. I am grateful to Lucy Bland for collecting much of this material, and also to the staff of the Islington library service for their help. The Islington Bus Company is collecting oral testimony on the political history of Islington during the inter-war period, and I am grateful to Neil Martinson for enabling me to consult that material.
4. See Walters (1975), an autobiographical account of working-class life in Islington between the wars. It gives a very good picture from the point of view of a spokesman of public propriety who lived in 'notorious' Popham Street.
5. For a full discussion of this concept see Balbus (1973).

6. A comment on the ironic fact that urban planners use the term 'line of desire' to indicate the direction of maximum pedestrian flow between fixed points, for example from tube station to office, or from home to shops.

7. The objective effect of so-called 'moral panics' is therefore one of *reassurance* that the bourgeois public realm is alive and well and has triumphed once again over adversity. This aspect is ignored by Cohen (1973).

8. I gathered this information through participant observation while a youth worker in Islington between 1971 and 1974.

References

Anderson, P. (1977) 'The Antinomies of Gramsci', *New Left Review*, 100.

Balbus, I. (1973) The *Dialectics of Legal Repression* (New York).

Brock, E. (1965) *The Little White God* (London).

Cohen, S. (1973) *Folk Devils and Moral Panics* (London).

Edelman, B. (1979) *Ownership of the Image* (London).

Negt, O. and Kluge, A. (1973) *Offentlichkeit und Erfahring* (Frankfurt).

Steedman, C. (1984) *Policing the Victorian Community* (London).

Storch, R. (1976) 'The Police as Domestic Missionaries', *Social History*, 4.

— (1979) *Popular Culture and Custom in 19th Century England* (London).

Walters, H. (1975) *The Street* (London).

Chapter 6

On the Wrong Side of the Tracks: The Cultural Geography of Adolescent Racism in a White Working-Class Community

The late 1970s saw a marked rise in youth unemployment and also in the level of popular support for the National Front, especially amongst white working-class boys growing up in multiracial neighbourhoods. The left was quick to seize on the connection as confirmation of its prevailing economistic theory of racism.

A critique of this model is the starting point for the ethnographic research reported in this chapter. Its aim was to understand the construction of white ethnicity, and its processes of racialisation in terms of specific subject positions which might be adopted within working-class cultures, positions which could not be reduced to socio-economic status.

For this purpose the study drew together many of the ideas about youth culture, territoriality and public propriety which had been developed in previous work. At the same I tried to draw out some of the implications of this approach for anti-racist youth work. The initial success of the Anti-Nazi League with its two-tone concerts, and its slogan 'NF equals No Fun', had concealed some of the more intractable problems posed by the discourse of commonsense racism. In so far as this discourse encouraged ambivalence, and indeed oscillated perpetually between accommodation and aversion to the black presence, it was not amenable to challenge from the types of moral, symbolic or doctrinaire antiracism then currently in vogue. Indeed, these antiracist rhetorics with their idealisation of black cultures were so much grist to the mill of racist envy and its strategies of disavowal. How then to engage with the deeper reaches of the racist imagination, and shift white ethnicities onto another terrain? This is an issue which was destined to run and run …

Starting points

The persistant increase in racial violence through the 1980s underlined the importance of understanding and tackling the forms of popular racism which circulate within white working-class communities. The report on Burnage School in Manchester indicated the problems which can arise from a failure to engage the active sympathies of white parents and pupils for anti-racist policies. The New Right was able to make political capital out of the event by posing as a champion of parental rights against a 'dictatorial' Labour-controlled Education Authority and/or as a defender of 'non-political' education against supposed anti-racist 'indoctrination'. In this context the idioms of class racism were not merely articulated to Popular Toryism via the pages of *The Sun*, but gained a wider and more respectable currency as part of a great debate about education and the new National Curriculum.

It is, of course, to be expected that the right will exploit situations such as Burnage, to condemn the whole enterprise of anti-racism. But this will only 'work' in so far as the anti-racist movement itself fails to critically appraise its own policies and practices, and instead retreats into the kind of moralistic and doctrinaire positions which the Macdonald Report indicated to be part of the problem. However, some of the difficulties which have occurred in schools which have seriously attempted to implement anti-racist policies arise from a different source; there has been a profound failure to appreciate the secret power and pleasure which the racist imagination confers through various media of popular culture;[1] as a result many teachers have tended to overestimate the effect of multi-cultural or anti-racist curricula in changing attitudes or behaviour, and to underestimate the subtler kinds of pupil resistance which they encounter. Inevitably, where educational methods are not achieving the desired outcome, there is a tendency to fall back on purely disciplinary measures. And this in turn fuels the myth that anti-racism is authoritarian.[2]

If a way is to be found out of this kind of impasse then perhaps we need to look again at some of the theories of ideology and white working class racism which have informed current educational practice.[3] Broadly, there are two schools of thought. The first argues that racist beliefs originated historically with colonialism, and were then insinuated into working-class cultures through various media of propaganda, and/or through the agency of the labour aristocracy itself. In some versions the argument still relies on crude conspiracy theories of the 'divide and rule' type;[4] increasingly a more sophisticated model allows for a more intricate process of institutional mediation whereby racist beliefs are not only internalised but modified and given a special working-class articulation.[5] This theory has the advantage of allowing the Left to hold on to a view of the English proletariat as a potentially revolutionary class, albeit one corrupted by bourgeois society, imperialism or its own leadership. But it has some difficulty in accounting for the specific appeal of popular racism, since this is viewed as merely a pale reflection of the bourgeois code. This does not put the theory in a strong position to explain those contexts and conjunctures where the subordinated forms of popular racism come into conflict with the institutionalised racism of the State. Yet it is the terms of just this contradiction we need to grasp if we are to win the white working class over to anti-racist positions.

The second main group of theories starts from the opposite direction: racist ideology is not something which penetrates working-class culture from outside, but is immanent in its particular conditions of existence. It is these conditions which are held to determine the distinctive form and function of popular racist beliefs. There is, however, considerable divergence of opinion as to the nature of this 'immanence' and which conditions are the salient ones. At one end of the spectrum we have arguments centred on some notion of deprivation. If working-class people blame unemployment, bad housing etc. on ethnic minority immigrants, it is because their culture has not equipped them with the cognitive or experiential resources to 'know any better'. Unable to abstract from or reflect critically on their immediate situation, they mistake symptom for cause and easily fall prey to the irrational explanations offered by racism.[6]

At the other end of the spectrum lie various theories of 'false consciousness'; here working-class racism is a spontaneous ideology produced by the phenomenal forms of capitalist society, forms which conceal, mystify or invert real relations of exploitation. According to this model, the real movement of capital, governed as it is by unequal exchange, and the international division of labour is concealed behind its visible effect – the invasion of immigrant labour into sectors of the metropolitan economy hitherto reserved for indigenous workers. Popular racism represents – and legitimates – this 'displacement effect' by constructing a set of purely imaginary relations of circulation based on notions of kinship and blood as a means of defending an exclusive reproduction of racialised labour power.[7]

The false consciousness model does in principle admit structural factors, which deprivation theories, dependant as they are on social psychology, tend to leave out of the picture.[8] The two positions have more in common, however, than is usually recognised. Both operate with deficit models of working-class culture (albeit defining and locating that deficiency very differently in macro or micro terms); both see education as playing a key, compensatory, role, in relaying Marxist analysis or liberal values, respectively, to counteract the mystifications of racism; and both suffer from rather similar theoretical limitations, in being unable to adequately explain why some working-class people are more or less racist than others, or how different modalities of racism can come into being within the working class, or why they should vary in normative strength in different times and places.

Recently there has been a series of attempts to go beyond the external/internal, structural/cultural dichotomies, or at least to incorporate elements of both within a single analytic framework. A lot of this work has focussed on the environmental or market conditions which prevail in particular communities of labour.[9] Thus, it has been argued, in contexts of interdependence between black and white, such as the hidden economies of the inner city, racist practices will be attenuated; where there is little need for networks of mutual aid and/or strong competition for jobs and housing racist atttitudes and beliefs will intensify. The equation more jobs and houses equals less racism is undoubtedly an attractive one for the Labour movement, in giving its economistic demands the status of a moral crusade against racism;[10] as for the Left, the idea that marginalisation creates unity between black and white youth on the front lines of confrontation with the State strikes an all too responsive chord with a certain kind of romantic populism.[11]

The main difficulty with these arguments is that they do not match the available evidence. We all know that it is in so called 'white highlands' areas, where there is little or no contact or competition with ethnic minorities, that resistance to multi-cultural or anti-racist education has proved most intransigent .[12] Equally, as this study will show, shared material conditions of unemployment or police harrassment may actually serve to polarise relations between black and white youth.

Underlying many accounts is the notion that under certain circumstances, racism may amount to a 'rational choice' for sections of the white working class. In other words it may be in their short-term self-interest to exclude immigrant workers from local labour markets, or more generally, to freeze ethnic minorities out of access to scarce resources.[13] Now it may be one of the functions of popular racist discourses to legitimate such practices. Indeed, Marxist functionalists base their analysis of working-class racism on just that.[14] But the trouble with both rational choice and functionalist models, is that they accord such discourses the status of realist accounts without in any way problematising their construction, as such. In this way the claims of racism on 'common sense' are recognised, but the ideological mechanisms which establish those claims are ignored, or seen as a simple expression of political or economic forces.

Actual patterns of race relations within specific working-class communities can clearly not be reduced to local economic conditions, any more than they can be read off from global determinants. Popular racism is no more a product of ignorance or superstition, than it is a rational pursuit of working-class interests. It is from this starting point that the work of Gramsci takes on its full intellectual salience.[15] The Gramscian perspective enables us to identify the distinctive features of different racist discourses in terms of the role they play in maintaining various strategies of class and ethnic hegemony; but this is not something which can be established *a priori*; it requires detailed research into particular contexts and conjunctures.[16] At the same time, common sense racism is no longer seen as the mechanical effect of the dominant ideology or 'false consciousness'; it is produced though an active process of negotiation, of accommodation and resistance between conflicting class racisms. As such it is a site of multiple contradictions, continually shifting its ground, renewing its idioms, and by the same token, always open to political and educational intervention.

Gramscian interpretations of the construction of 'race' in post-war Britain have tended to focus on the role of the ideological state apparatus and the race relations industry.[17] Yet is it just as important to understand how popular racism works 'on the ground' intervening and interpreting local community histories. It is on this basis, perhaps, that we might begin to compose a comparative cultural geography which could inform an anti-racist strategy more sensitively attuned to the particularisms of place and time. In what follows I have made an initial essay in that direction.

The *mise-en-scène*

In this study of a white working-class community in London in the late 1970s, I am concerned to understand the positions adopted by a group of adolescent boys, both towards their black peers and towards the organised racialism of the National Front. A series of discussions was organised with a group aged 15 to 17. This was part of an action research project whose aim was to investigate the effect of delayed or broken transitions from school to work on patterns and processes of political socialisation, and devise strategies of educational intervention.[18] The dramatic increase in youth unemployment during the 1970s coincided with the rise of support for the National Front, and in the level of racist attacks by white youth on sections of the black community. Was this just a coincidence? Was there a direct causal link between unemployment and racism in the inner city? Or is there some more complicated and hidden process of change going on within white working-class cultures? We set out to examine these questions through a project in which we tried to develop a community-based strategy for anti-racist youth work. We concentrated this intervention on groups of young people who held pronounced racist views: some of them were known to be responsible for racial attacks and/or were active members of racialist organisations; others did not take an active part, but supported from the sidelines. We were particularly interested in whether it was possible, by purely educational means, to detach the followers from the dedicated 'hard core' as a preliminary to shifting the former towards an anti-racist position, and weakening the influence of the latter.

The area we chose for the study had a long history of settlement by different ethnic groups. The industrial development of West London during the inter-war period had drawn in large numbers of Irish and Jewish working-class people, and their presence had been consolidated after the war. Both groups had become actively involved in local politics, through trades councils, trade unions and the Labour Party.

The Kipling Estate (see diagram) had been built during the 1960s as part of an urban renewal programme to rehouse families from rundown areas of Hammersmith and Shepherds Bush. The estate formed part of a migration corridor leading out from the slums to the better-off western suburbs. So when families first moved into the estate, hopes were high. The move represented a step in the right direction, a step out and up from poverty and squalor. These hopes were shortlived. The huge blocks soon began to reveal hidden flaws in design and finishing. The lifts broke down continually, the heating systems were erratic and the landscaping of the estate was compared (unfavourably) to the effects of the Blitz; there was a virtual absence of shopping facilities or community amenities. Graffiti soon provided an alternative landscaping effect, while less creative forms of vandalism attacked the windswept stairwells.

An all-too-familiar story, but one which, in this case, began to take on racist overtones. The white families on the estate increasingly came to associate their deteriorating living conditions with the presence of black people. A number of Asian families had moved in to some of the terraced housing in streets bordering on the estate. For many of these council tenants, owning your own house was a dream as far removed from life on Kipling, as life on Mars. To see these prosperous Asian families moving in to these 'dream homes' was experienced, as one Kipling resident

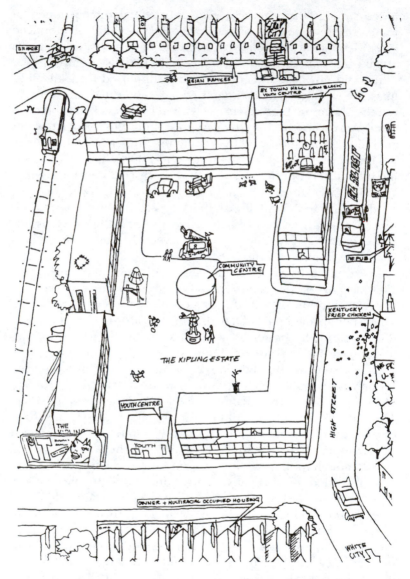

put it, as 'adding insult to injury'. Another sore point was the fact that the Council had converted part of the town hall into a youth centre used predominantly by Afro-Caribbean youth. The High Street became the front line of racial tension, where black and white gang territories collided; fights and other violent assaults were a frequent occurrence.

This then was how the situation was built up through the early 1970s. The local newspapers carried a number of stories, doing little more than glossing local rumours, to the effect that Asians were keeping goats and slaughtering them in their backyards, or were overcrowding their houses with members of their families who were illegal immigrants. Afro-Caribbean youth were supposed to be spending their time mugging little old ladies, and peddling drugs. The National Front, if it did not initiate these rumours, certainly capitalised upon them. It maintained a strong presence in the area throughout this period, and one of the pubs on the High Street became a well known meeting place, where leading members of the NF used to drink. The Kipling Tenants Association had increasingly come under NF influence, and two of its leading lights were card-carrying members. What had begun as a campaign to get better services from the Council, had turned into a movement to 'clean up the area by getting rid of the blacks'. Local youth and community workers viewed these developments with alarm and despondency. There had been a number of nasty racial incidents in local youth clubs, and an increasing number of 'ordinary decent kids' (as one worker put it) were being attracted to racist positions.

It was against this background that we were invited to undertake an experiment in anti-racist youth work on the estate. Its aim was clear enough: to persuade young people that problems such as bad housing, unemployment and lack of amenities, had nothing to do with the presence of black people. Indeed, they suffered from these problems to an even greater degree. Rather the cause lay in local state or central government policies, and the failure of the Labour Party to change them. However, this was not to be a conventional exercise in political education – to set socialist truth against racist lies. There was no need to go into the finer points of epistemology, to realise that such an approach would fall on deaf ears. Instead we were committed to an approach which would work with and through the lived culture of these young people, to help them recontextualise their experience so that it no longer had to be made sense of in racist terms. Instead of preaching the anti-racist message at them, something many of them had already learnt to resist at school, we would start by listening to what they had to say, letting them talk their racism out to the point where its limited repertoire of meanings was exhausted, and they might be more receptive to other views.

These 'race talk' sessions (of which the transcript on pp. 150–4 is an example) were tape-recorded and sometimes played back at a later date. This was a device to shift them into a more reflexive and self-critical space in which they might not only begin to listen to themselves and each other, but question what they heard. However, our role was fraught with dangers. Listening posts are all too easily used as sounding boards; silence may be taken for sympathy, especially by those who are used to shouting others down. This is an ethical as well as a tactical issue. Youth workers are by definition in the business of establishing relations of trust. This often makes us privy to information about criminal or anti-social behaviour. We may make it clear that we do not approve but we do not as a rule shop our clients to the police. Our professional code of conduct includes the rule of confidentiality. Yet in a context where we were deliberately eliciting 'race talk', we were forced to listen to accounts of the most sickening violence, as well as the usual repertoire of racist jokes and jibes. There was clear evidence that two of these boys were committing systematic racial assaults, and getting away with it. Their identity was a matter of fairly common knowledge. They were known to the police who claimed to be powerless to act because there were no 'reliable' (by which they meant white) witnesses. Should we present our tapes to the police and demand action? The status of such evidence would anyway be challenged and was probably inadmissible in a court of law. Instead we decided to use our work to help put general pressure on the police to defend the local black community. In the group itself we made our own anti-racist position clear. We did not condone their activities; in fact we condemned them. But while they were talking they were not putting the boot in. It was the connection between what they said or felt, and what they did that we would explore with them. Within the framework of the group discussion we would neither censure nor collude, but seek to refer them to alternative means of understanding and acting on their situation.

We considered whether to try and involve girls in the group. We decided against it for several reasons. Firstly, as is evident from the tape, the girls on the estate had been cast in the role of passive supporters rather than activists. We neither wanted to reproduce that position in the group, nor as men did we feel adequately equipped to explore the connection between these girls' subordination and their racist views. Secondly, it was the boys who were responsible for the racial harrassment and we were under considerable pressure to do what we could about that. So although we were not entirely happy about it, we decided to opt for all boys groups, with a mental footnote to the effect that we would keep an eye and ear open for the sexual dynamics of working-class racism. All this only underlines the crucial importance of feminist initiatives in anti-racist youth work, and the lack of such work in the area at the time.

Our group met once a week, for approximately two hours. Its membership was drawn from a larger pool of lads who were either unemployed or bunked off school, and spent most of their time just hanging about the estate. Having somewhere warm to go was thus one of the attractions. The most regular attenders constituted a friendship group. Two of them were hard core young NF supporters, two were 'camp followers', and one lad had already distanced himself from these activities, although no less racist in his view of black people. One of the immediate problems was thus the group dynamics. The NF spokeslads were quite dominant personalities, with a reputation as local style leaders, and initially did most of the talking. Yet a context centred on talk, also privileges other roles, in particular those of storyteller and wit. This opened up a space in which others could begin to have their say, and voice some of their misgivings. As the sessions progressed, an increasing flow of semi-jokey asides made it clear that the camp followers wanted to dissociate themselves from certain central aspects of NF propaganda. The crunch came when, sensing that the tide was turning against them, the 'hard core' suggested that we invite the local NF youth worker to address the group. He would put the arguments better than they could, and convince even us of the justice of their cause. For whatever reason the 'youth worker' failed to turn up at the appointed time, which was of course interpreted by the others as 'bottling out', with the result that the hard core decisively lost face. They had put themselves out on a limb, and could not now climb down. However, it was precisely at this point that they were at their most dangerous, something we did not sufficiently appreciate at the time. The next week they 'forgot' to show up, but they had not forgiven us.

A few days later there was a mysterious fire at the youth centre where the sessions had been held. This was their answer (although nothing, as usual, could be proved). It had the desired effect of halting the proceedings. Indeed, owing to the hostility of the tenants' association it was not possible to find another base, and so the project was all too abruptly terminated. Yet it was something of a pyrrhic victory for the NF. Their bluff had been called, and they had 'shown themselves up'. The hard core were effectively isolated and the peer group broke up. The others drifted away from racist involvements, even though far from converted to the anti-racist cause. One of the hard core was shortly afterwards sentenced to borstal, for an attack on a 13-year-old Asian boy, and the other was also sent down, for a non-racial offence.

There were some immediate conclusions to be drawn. It was possible to intervene in the peer group dynamics of racist discourse, to split the hard core from the followers. The experience confirmed our belief that with the hard core, the only effective method was to take them out of circulation and teach them a lesson that if they persisted in racial violence then they would either end up behind bars, or be subjected to physical counterattack. In so far as the police are not prepared to take the necessary measures, then the black community simply has to look to its own self-defence. With the 'followers of fashion' it is a different story, and here an open-ended educational process could be effective. Yet isolated initiatives like this without a wider base of community involvement and support, can do no more than win small-scale victories, and remain vulnerable to attack. If anything like a concerted strategy of anti-racist youth work is to evolve, it will clearly have to be based on a finer understanding of the different modalities of racism, and where they are coming from. It was with this in mind that we turned to the race talk sessions to see if a closer analysis would give us some clues as to how to make further progress.

From the other side of the tracks[20]

You got into a fight the other night. What happened?

Well, there was a *fair fight* between one of my brothers and this coloured kid, right? They started one on to one. And my brother won, right? And half of the blacks said 'Right, let's leave it at that.' But the other lot come down the next night, and the night after that, and the night after that, all week they come down, about 40, 50 of them, from all over, Shepherd's Bush, Notting Hill, White City...

Black City (laughter)

... and there was just our lot, from the estate.

What started the first fight?

I dunno, you never know, do you, it just happens...

Are most of the people on this estate white?

It used to be, didn't it? (general assent) But not no more, since they started bringing coloured families in. Now it's about half and half.

In this fight did all the black people come from outside the area?

All from outside, weren't they (general assent) ... Well, *one* lived here, the rest came from outside.

Would you go outside the area to fight blacks?

No, not really. You see, if we went outside our area we'd get nicked. Remember that time the police come down, and they said 'If you're on your own territory we'll nick the others. But if you're outside, we'll nick *you*.' So we let the blacks come down to us, we didn't go looking for them. And on the Friday night we was fetching bottles and sticks and everything, and we hid them ready. And the Old Bill came down and found them and nicked *us*, even after what they'd said. And we got done for conspiracy to cause GBH. Nine of us got done. But the blacks, they just let them go. They just put them in the meat wagon and dropped them up town.

Why do you think the police let them go?

Race relations ... Race Relations Act. If the coons get nicked they start complaining, saying the police are nicking them unfairly. That was in the paper, about suss or something...

Do you think the police in this area are biased against young white people?

No, they're not biased against white people, they're biased against *us*! They know quite a few of us, don't they, and if they see you they nick you. But if they see a bunch of black kids hanging around they won't nick them.

... Blacks reckon the opposite; they reckon the police are picking on them.

... Nearly every day round our area you used to get searched. They come over if you were in a group. If you hang about after 10 o'clock they come over and say 'If you lot ain't out of here in five minutes you're nicked, the lot of you!'

... Yes, there used to be a bigger lot, you know, like 18, 19. Now they're off and married, so *we* hang about and we get the trouble.

What did your parents have to say about all this?

Well, they saw there was more of them (the blacks) than us. And they saw the Old Bill nicking us, and letting the coons go. And they was right behind us.

Yes, cos they seen all the trouble from the balconies, you know.

Everyone was looking over the balcony. There was a big audience. *Everyone* was out. Some of the older blokes, they come out, and they started fighting as well! [Laughter] One bloke come down from the flats with just a pair of trousers and a vest on, and *he* started having a go!

Yes, when they see all the white kids getting nicked, all the parents was going mad about it.

And we got a petition!

Yes, we just went round the houses and we said to the people you know, why we was getting nicked, and they just signed their names. We got 100 names in three days!

Is it a very violent neigbourhood?

It can be. It can be very bad. It ain't that violent really unless some trouble breaks out, and then everyone comes out. Like if a big gang of blokes come down against us, within about two minutes everyone would be there, 'cos the word just gets passed along. Like if there were five kids sitting on the wall, within two minutes loads would come out the pubs and that, to help them.

What are the girls doing while all this is going on?

Well … er … it depends. Sometimes they egg you on, you know. Most times they just hang about and watch if there's a fight. If there's real trouble with the blacks, most of them don't want to know. But a few of them, they're worse than us, ain't they?

How long have you lived here?

All my life, so 16 years.

7 years

3 months

11 years

So at least three of you have lived here most of your lives. How would you describe growing up in this area?

It was good when we were smaller; it was much better … wasn't it?

Yes.

Where our flats are, all it is now are green and trees and everything. There used to be rubbish dumps and mud and all that, and we used to have a laugh there, you know what I mean.

There used to be a lot of older houses, and we used to all go in them. But they've been knocking everything down.

I mean, we can't even have a bonfire round our way now, can we? Without them phoning the police.

Now we've got *one* club down there and that ain't much of a club either, it's falling down. [Laughter] It's got a post in the middle holding the ceiling up! And that's the only club. Well there is a new one, but they won't open it. A brand new club, and they use it for old people (contemptuously); bingo and that.

A year ago, right, we was in there, we went in there for a meeting, right, and this bloke's going: 'Yes, we'll have boxing, weightlifting, everything. Next thing we know, old pensioners are using it in the daytime, and that's it! It's closed now.

What other changes have there been?

Well, they just keep building flats, don't they? They're opening a new lot now at the top of the road there. It just keeps on getting bigger and bigger. It's nearly one of the biggest in London now.

And how many houses have gone to blacks in just the last few years? That's where my first house was, where they are now. I don't reckon they should build more flats; there's too many flats now. I reckon they should build some houses.

No more big estates?

No (*very emphatic agreement from all of them*). They should build little houses, you know ... small blocks of flats.

You know, even when we went on holiday to the Isle of Wight, some people had heard the reputation of our estate – on holiday! Unbelievable!

Yes, we all went to the Isle of Wight – about twenty of us, wasn't it? We was down at the seaside and that, and people come from, you know, outside London, and we talked to them, and they, you know, asked where we come from and we said South Acton, and they said 'Oh, that's a rough place, ain't it?'

London is a drag. [Laughter] It is! I ain't joking. I mean, you live out in the country and you can have the time of your life. But when you're stuck in a hole like this ...! We're like baked beans in a tin can. [Laughter] There's nothing to do down our way; you can't even play football! You get a game going and it's 'Go away! We'll call the police!'

And I don't know the last time when they cleaned the place!

I used to live down by the factories. It used to be brilliant down there. We had such a massive back garden it was unbelievable!

A first reading

If you are told that the transcript is from a discussion by young racists, you are likely to assume without looking further, that everything in it is an expression of racist ideology. Yet there are chunks of it, when the boys are talking about their childhoods, or what it is like to live in high rise flats, when you could be forgiven for thinking that these are 'ordinary decent kids' talking about quite typical working-class experiences. So do we have a simple juxtaposition of race and class discourses, or are they interleaved in a more complicated way, so that the racism is given a specific class voice, and the class perceptions taken on racist undertones? The issue is of quite crucial practical importance, for in the first case it may be relatively easy to separate out and oppose race and class consciousness, whereas in the second, it is a much more tricky business.

Perhaps this issue will become clearer if we look in more detail at what is said, and what is left unsaid, in the transcript. It begins with a collective account of a fight between a white and black boy. It is not a question here of who started it, or what was the immediate cause. It may have been triggered by an exchange of insults, or it may have been an argument between two 'friends' over a girl. It is perhaps significant that we are not told. What concerns us though, is how the incident is represented, how it is racialised through its narrative construction.

It is through such stories, and through the medium of rumour and gossip, that racism is reproduced and made into common sense. These narratives do not simply exaggerate or distort reality 'after the event'; they actively enter into the way race relations are constructed at the level of everyday social encounters.

Perhaps the first point to note here is that the fight is represented as having nothing to do with race or racial conflict. It is a *fair fight*, one to one, if not according to Queensbury Rules then at least working-class ones. But the black boy loses – at least in this version. Then what happens? According to the story, half the blacks accept the verdict. These are the 'good niggers'. But the other half do not. They try and change the result. These are the 'bad niggers', the ones who cry foul against the British notion of 'fair play', and who in fighting back also implicitly challenge the verdict of a history which assigns them a congenitally inferior place. There is of course no sense from the storyteller that the victory of his brother in the fight might have any wider racial significance for him. Yet in the way he characterises the responses of the black youth it clearly does. The hidden message is that if things had gone the other way, and the white lad lost, then the result would have been accepted. It is the blacks who are 'badly out of order' in demanding revenge and escalating the conflict. Yet it is precisely in and through this construction, that the white

lads put themselves in a superior position – as guardians of both
popular justice and public order, and by implication of a civilised
way of life against the 'law of the jungle'.

It is at this point however that the official guardians of law and
order enter the story. Perhaps the most surprising thing about the
way the police role is characterised is that they begin by stating a
version of these boys' own code of conduct; for the first 'law' of
territoriality in the working-class city is that you are safe in your
area because it belongs to you in so far as you belong in it.[21] But if
you are out of your territory then you are vulnerable to attack.
The police restate this rule in terms of differential risks of arrest:
'If you're in your area we'll nick the others, but if you're outside
we'll nick you.' This is presented as a fair rule, in so far as it is
applied evenhandedly to keep the two sides apart. All part of
British fair play. Yet no sooner do 'the Law' state the rule, than
they themselves are made to break it. They arrest the white youth
who are on their home ground, and let the black youth go. Thus
the police who start out being associated with the position of
white youth end up by 'changing sides'. For in the account the
Law are made out to be just as much 'out of order' as 'the blacks';
the former break the code of territoriality, and the latter the
unwritten rules for fair fights.

These white boys expressed the same sense of moral indignation in describing the behaviour of both. They feel themselves to
be the innocent victims of a conspiracy organised through race
relations legislation, to promote the interests of the black community at their own expense. They, meanwhile, are left as the
heroic defenders of British justice and 'fair play'.

However, when they were asked whether they thought the
police were biased against white people, they emphatically
answered 'No – they're prejudiced against *us*.' Did this mean that
the police were picking on them because they were racialists? Far
from it unfortunately. As the group itself made clear in discussing
how they were following in the footsteps of their older peers, it
was the fact that they were a street gang in a 'hard' working-class
area, and that many of them already had a delinquent reputation,
if not a criminal record, which singled them out for special attention from the Law. There follows a brief discussion about whether
black or white youth suffer worse harassment, in which one of the
lads does actually state the black point of view. But if the parallels

between the two situations cannot be explored further it is not only because it would threaten their racial conspiracy theory. It is because of real contradictions in policing strategy, contradictions which these lads are here struggling to make sense of.

In the policing of white working-class communities, the strict letter of the law is rarely applied.[22] Instead a set of informal, nego-tiated norms of public order have evolved, in which a blind eye is turned to certain practices in order to keep a sharper eye open for certain others. The result is to push adolescent boys, especially those who belong to highly visible youth sub-cultures, into the front line of street confrontation with the police, and to isolate them from other sections of their community. However, in the policing of black communities no such accommodation to their codes of conduct has been made until very recently. The official statutory norms of public order have been applied according to the strictest letter of the law, and all sections are equally at risk of arrest. Black youth are thus not as isolated as their white counter-parts; if the police pick on them, it is experienced as an attack on their whole community. Thus the way in which black and white youth are constructed as suspect categories follows quite different principles, even though the effect is the same. This policing double standard is what makes it so easy for these white boys to feel that they are being singled out in a way that their black peers are not. Ironically, with the shift to community policing strategies in black areas following the 1981 riots, the position of black youth subcultures is brought much *closer* to that of their white counterparts.

However, what is significant about the present incident is the way these young racists are able to use the circumstances of their arrest to move closer to the black situation, in the sense of repre-senting it as an attack on the whole community, and how a racist interpretation of the event succeeds in mobilising adult support.

Normally working-class parents are quite disapproving when their children get into trouble with the law, and do little to give them support. But in this case the opposite occurs. The adults not only give these lads their moral support, some of them actually come down and join in the fighting. To understand what is at stake here, you have to know something about the different codes of practice through which the moral economy of working-class com-munities is reproduced. There are two main ones. First, rules and rituals of *territoriality*, which have just been mentioned, and which have historically been associated with, and linked the positions of youth, masculinity and the 'rough' working class. These construct symbolic sites of belonging in communities which by definition neither own or control their own environment. These sites are almost exclusively 'maintained' at street level by young men, who stake out neighbourhood boundaries through the medium of peer group or subcultural rivalries. The political geography of the working-class city is also governed by protocols and principles of *public propriety*. These are associated with the place of adults, women and the 'respectable' elements. They define what is private and what is public space, and lay down appropriate rules of behaviour in both. They maintain norms of social distance and reciprocity which allow people to keep themselves to themselves, whilst relying on neighbours in times of need, and also set limits to the degree of solidarity expressible in public. These protocols operate through institutions like tenants associations, trades unions and various kinds of voluntary association or community organisation.

Public propriety dictates, for example, that girls should be largely confined to the great indoors, and any that do hang around on the streets are 'slags'. Whereas rules of territoriality insist that a boy who keeps off the streets cannot be 'one of the lads'. The two codes are thus complimentary in reinforcing gender roles, but they can come into conflict at the level of generational relations. In the account of the fight and the adults' role, this tension forms the basis of a comic incident: 'One bloke comes down from the flats with just a pair of trousers and a vest and started fighting.' In other words he is breaking out of the moral strait jacket of public propriety in a double sense – it may be OK to wear just your vest indoors, but it is definitely not decent in public, and of course he is an adult, joining in a 'kids fight' based on rules of territoriality. However, the tension is here represented as dissolving into an almost ceremonial display of communal solidarity against the external black threat. The fight is portrayed as a piece of street theatre, the crowds lining the balconies, the women cheering the lads, the moment of comic relief with the man in the vest wading in, and so on. And if the fight itself is an exercise in territorial self-defence, then its aftermath, the organising of a petition to protest against the 'unjust' police intervention, is pure public propriety in action.

In its propaganda the National Front has tried to racialise both codes. Its appeal to youth has largely been in terms of the blacks invading white territory and the need to fight back. At the same time, the NF addresses adult voters in the tones of a 'responsible political party' and focusses on 'outrages to public propriety' as represented by the conversion of a town hall into a black youth centre. Still the tension between the two codes, and their respective constituencies has persisted, even inside the National Front, leading to splits and a large defection of youth to the more street activist British Movement. The tension is also expressed in the form of split perceptions of the two 'coloured' communities. Our group saw all Afro-Caribbeans in terms of an agressive street presence, whilst Asians, in contrast, were portrayed as performing bizarre rituals behind closed doors, offending the 'proprieties' of English family life.

The difficulties which the NF have had in recruiting and holding their potential support amongst the young white working class are well known, and parallel the failure of socialist youth movements.[23] The reasons have less to do with political ideology, than with the constraints placed on youth sections by party elders and by the bureaucratic maintenance of the political machine. The National Front was No Fun, for the same reason that the Labour Party isn't much fun – it involves attending lots of boring meetings, and doing lots of administrative chores. Still, it is some testimony to the success of the Anti-Nazi League's campaign that the NF members in the discussion group were curiously defensive about certain aspects of party ideology. They denied that the NF was a fascist organisation, and asserted they 'had other policies'. They portrayed themselves as having been forced to join by circumstances beyond their control. One of the lads, in a typical reversal, blamed his racism on black people: 'If they hadn't come over here there would be no need for a party like the National Front.' Some were more ambivalent than others. 'I'm not proud I joined,' said one, but another thought that 'membership strengthened you and gave you back a sense of pride'. One thing the whole group were united about was their contempt for both the main political parties. Mrs Thatcher was condemned for electoral opportunism in making her famous speech about the swamping of the British way of life; Labour were blamed for having let the blacks in, and let down 'their own kind'. Here was an example of how racism was being given a distinctive working-class voice. For although some of the group were reading NF literature, and making use of some of the arguments therein, their racism was not primarily a matter of theoretical doctrine, or even of political programme. This political education just gave a secondary gloss to a deeper, more unconscious process of political socialisation, which operated through the medium of a 'body politics'. This became clear in the way they talked about their relations with black youth.

What comes across, first of all, is these boys' sense of being threatened by what they see as the superior strength and social cohesion of their black peers. They feel outnumbered, even if, in statistical terms, they are not. The sense of immigration as a remorseless invasion is echoed in their characterisation of the black build-up to the return fight: '40, 50, from all over, they come down the next night, the night after, all week ... The tone of mounting panic is arrested by a joke 'White City ... Black City', which like all jokes represents in condensed form what is most feared: in this case the take-over of their area. Significantly, two of the group had actually lived on the White City estate at a time when it was occupied predominantly by white families. Only later, after their move to Kipling, had the estate become used by the Council as a 'dumping ground for blacks'. They are now afraid that history will repeat itself, and their estate will 'go the same way'. The role of the local state in regulating the movement of populations is rendered invisible, and black people themselves are held responsible for their 'occupation' of substandard public housing. In place of the state there is simply a 'hidden hand' of history which they feel powerless to confront. In this way institutionalised racism (here a racialist housing policy) and popular racism are made to feed off each other.

There is something else involved in these lads' version of the 'numbers game'. The presence of black youth has come to signify for them a power of social combination which they feel their own community no longer possesses. Although they are quick to stress how many people they can mobilise, the overall impression they create is of a beleaguered white minority, doing a heroic Custer's last stand. But the other side of this is a secret envy for qualities which they feel black youth have, and which their own culture has come to lack. This comes out in a little vignette of the street encounter outside the Kentucky Fried Chicken. The white boy is indignant at having his chips 'nicked' but he also admires the cheek. He might think of doing the same but he wouldn't have the bottle. Yet this secret admiration is no sooner hinted at than it is denied. As we were to see, this was a highly systematic pattern of disavowal.

Meanings and modalities

It was by looking at the way they constructed their autobiographies that we hoped to get to grips with some of the deeper structures of these boys' racial feelings. As soon as they started talking about their childhoods a change came over the mood of the whole group. Anger and frustration gave way to a pervasive sense of sadness and loss. The picture which some of them painted was of an idyllic time and space of unbounded freedom and fun. Yet this was no conventional childhood utopia where the sun always shines and the grass is always green. Quite the reverse. It was anchored to an all too real, or rather surreal image and place: a rubbish dump, a row of derelict houses. Here they could literally muck about without a care in the world. This first territory where they could construct their own sense of order out of the materials to hand, was contrasted with the official externally imposed order of the municipal landscape with its 'No Ball Games' and 'Keep Off the Grass'. But what on earth has this to do with a racist interpretation of history? It was only by a circuitous route, following various chains of association that we finally arrived at the connection. In several of the boys' cases, their own infancy had coincided with that of the estate. As they grew in size so did the blocks of flats. This was experienced on a number of levels. As the municipal bulldozer erased the site of their childhood play, so at the same time its forms were increasingly curtailed, and ruled out of order by other state agencies, for example, by the school and the police. Yet this was not lived as simple transition from a state of freedom to one of imprisonment. It was experienced as a process of deterioration and decay in their day-to-day environment. Their experience of growing up was, as one of them put it, of everything getting worse and worse. They had come to associate this process with the growing influx of black people. It was these people who were being dumped on them, who were turning the area into a rubbish tip, and who were no better than human rubbish themselves. In other words 'the blacks' are made to take on the symbolic properties associated with their childhood, but in a purely negative sense. The blacks have now not only robbed them of the future (by taking their jobs, their houses, and even their exams) but they have stolen their childhood past. This was signalled directly in the case of the boy who claimed that a black family have occupied his childhood home, but it is a theme in many of the other life stories as well.

It is possible to glimpse here how autobiographies are re-written according to a racist grammar in contexts where the links between growing-up-working-class are getting harder and harder to make in any real terms. For example, none of the lads in our group were following in their fathers' footsteps into work, let alone the same trade. There was also a breakdown in the pattern of cultural apprenticeship which has traditionally occurred within the manual working class. This was illustrated in a number of ways. The boys talk with some pride of following in the footsteps of their elder brothers, getting into trouble with the law. But this is a tradition confined within the youth culture, and its rituals of male territoriality. As for the role of adults, this is portrayed, in the very moment of celebrating a link between the generations, as taking the form of a regression. It is the men who come down from the balconies to join the boys, to be 'one of the lads' again. This is the opposite of the traditional apprenticeship in which the old hand teaches the youngster the ropes. These boys feel they have nothing to inherit from the older generation; that is partly why they envy the roots radicalism of black youth. The sense of betrayal this produces comes out strongly in their hostility to old people on the estate. There were no happy evocations of 'gran' in these boys' childhood memories, only anger at the way the OAP club had prevented them from using the community centre.

In a period when the landmarks and signposts which hitherto connected growing up, working and class, are being bulldozed by complex economic and political processes, racist ideology seemed to offer a seductively simple map which gave these young people back a sense of pride in where they had come from and where they were going. Their real birth places, the streets and playgrounds of their childhood may have melted into air, but once inserted in a racist topography, they take on the 'substance' of all these lost solidarities in serving as the imaginary origin of a larger destiny. These youngsters' involvement with the NF thus gave them access to a mode of political apprenticeship which magically retrieved an inheritance which at some deep level they felt had been destroyed, and told them it was OK to blame it all on black people.

Yet this was a storyline which some of them still found hard to believe. No one in our group actually felt comfortable about proclaiming themselves the territorial standard-bearers of a master race. Any more than they thought writing 'Kipling Rules OK' on walls made them in reality into a ruling class. Nationalism of the neighbourhood was, however, something they could practise and indeed connect to a racialised sense of territory. 'White Youth Rules OK' was quite an easy transition to make. The next step, to entail their own personal sense of being working-class born and bred, within a national/popular mythology of the rights of the 'freeborn Englishman' was considerably more difficult to sustain; certainly there is more to it than parading the Union Jack and singing Rule Britannia at football matches; yet it could be done by some. The final leap of the racist imagination – to associate an imperial legacy of 'white rule' with a proletarian birthright to break the stranglehold of Jewish Finance Capital over the body politic – defeated all but the hard core. Whenever we pushed the NFers to enunciate this position they did so defensively while the rest of the group dissolved into giggles.

So what is it about this version of racism which resists translation into the more florid realms of fascist and imperialist imagery associated with full-blown white supremacism? Turning back to our group we asked them to explain to us just why they had become active racialists to see if this would shed any light on the question. Throughout our discussions they insisted that their negative evaluation of 'coloureds' – little distinction was made between Afro-Caribbean and Asian in *this* context – was founded on the 'fact' that they were directly responsible for the deteriorating conditions of the local white working-class community. If we challenged this belief, the group shifted tack and argued that 'blacks were getting a better deal' in terms of housing, jobs, and especially policing. If that view was challenged, they reverted to the former position, and so on and on. This was a *local* conspiracy theory of race relations in which two quite discontinuous structural processes – black immigration and inner city decline – were conjuncturally, and causally, linked. However, this link was *not* constructed in purely material terms; the presence of black youth in 'their' area was represented primarily as a *cultural* challenge. Housing and youth provision constituted strategic sites linking the two levels; this was the interface within which racism could be made into 'common sense' and endorsed by continual reference to 'experience'.

We might call this a *racism of relative deprivation* in which the ethnic minority is at least recognised as a competitor or rival, and in that sense a peer; even if here the comparisons are never not invidious, they resist incorporation within the totalising discourses of fascism or white supremacism. This was the majority position in our group, and one elaborated by the style leader-cum-spokeslad:

> When they started coming over a lot, people started thinking that the white people was going homeless and poor, and the coloured geezers was making a bomb. A bloke who's poor has only gotta see a black in a big flash car and he thinks 'the bastard'.

There was also, however, a minority report delivered by the hard man of the group who volunteered the following bit of auto-biography:

> I was only little, I must have been about seven or eight, and I got into a fight with this coloured kid at school. I couldn't stand them even then. I gave him a good kicking. There was blood everywhere, most of it was his, all over my shirt it was. I needed seven stitches. So they took me to the hospital. I got in there and I couldn't believe my eyes, there was this Paki doctor. I wouldn't let him touch me. I just run out, you know. I couldn't stand being handled by one. They don't wash or keep themselves clean. They smell – they really do. I don't understand how they let them become doctors. I'd rather bleed to death.

Here is a body politics of racism founded on a logic of *absolute negation*. Black people are regarded as totally alien, wholly 'other', they are everything that white people are not, and vice versa. No similarity, no basis of comparison is therefore possible; this racism is focussed on the fear of physical contamination and moral pollution, symbolised here in images of dirt, smell and blood. To be near to, or touched by 'one of them' apparently induced in this boy intense feelings of panic and rage. Clearly this absolutist position can all too easily be converted to a global conspiracy theory. If this does not happen as often as might be expected, it is because this position is no sooner articulated than it tends to be relativised by the class discourse within which it normally remains embedded. Indeed, it is a characteristic of popular racism, whether or not it is politically organised, that it regards immigrant workers as both a source of unfair competition which should be regulated, *and* as an alien or subhuman species who should be removed from the face of the earth. The dialectics of race and class consciousness are here completely enmeshed. Firstly, to regard someone as a fellow competitor on the labour market is also to potentially recognise a kinship of circumstance based on class. To suppress that possibility, it is necessary to construct an imaginary, 'species-specific' community of labour.

However, as we have seen, such a construct is only constituted through practices of territoriality and public propriety, grounded in specific localities where 'immigrants' are already settled, and local workplaces where 'aliens' are *de facto* workmates. So the perception of their otherness is always and already detotalised, and tied to specific contexts of usage.

We had an example of how this operates in our group. They spent a good deal of time fantasising about ways of physically exterminating black people, but invariably they ended by rationalising this project through a recital of local (and usually trivial) grievances. Yet as soon as we tried to recontextualise *this* material within an alternative frame of reference (i.e. to break the links they had forged between black immigration and inner-city decline) they reverted to expressions of total racial disgust at the black presence. This oscillation, though it made our task doubly difficult, did at least serve to inhibit the appeal of more global conspiracy theories.

We are talking here about the interaction of two complementary positions within the same field of racist discourse, *not* the conjuncture of two radically different kinds of race thinking. The difference is that one focusses on socio-cultural qualities and the other on physical characteristics; yet both underpin the same 'congenital' image of the body politic, the same imaginary kinship of labour powers. In some cases, as with our 'hard man', this construction is anchored to an immediate body image; he felt the black presence to be a total threat to his personal physical integrity, his basic sense of self. However, it is perhaps important to stress that this was not simply an individual aberration. The conditions under which racism becomes an existential ideology are not at all reduceable to the vicissitudes of the psyche. Moreover, the same fear of physical invasion can take a more 'socialised' form in the rituals of street racism; here collective boundaries are articulated through the medium of a peer group, rather than an ego ideal. Similar mechanisms can be found at work behind the moral niceties of public propriety, even if the main weapons are rumour and gossip, rather than boots and bricks. Finally, the closed shop practices of certain trade unions have served to institutionalise a similar process of exclusion from the body politic of labour. These are different registers or modalities but they all belong to the same code and relay the same message as far as the black community is concerned.

What though of those who are not actively involved in any form of harrassment or discrimination? Do they have a qualitatively distinct standpoint, one in which 'class consciousness' has prevailed over racial prejudice? Or do they simply keep their racism to themselves? Our group continually claimed that they were simply voicing and acting out the beliefs and sentiments of the silent white majority in the estate. But how true was this? We were able to interview a small control group of boys aged 16 to 17 who also used the youth club, but who were not known to be actively involved in racial harrassment, or to be associated with the NF. However this group knew our NFers quite well, and remained on speaking terms with them even after the fire. This confirmed our view (and their claim) that the latter were popular on the estate. However the 'control' boys were also noticeably careful to keep their distance. This was not, we discovered, out of distaste for racialism as such, but because to be associated with the NF spelt 'trouble'. Yet there was more to it than that. For example, the control group did not have the same ontological stake in racialist explanations of their predicament. They did not see the development of the estate as a process of degeneration associated with an influx of black people. In fact, they did not feel themselves threatened by the black presence to nearly the same extent. Their attitude was one of calculated indifference or patronising tolerance. Their general view was that 'most blacks are OK; they don't bother us and we don't bother them'; although still 'some of them are bastards'. They did not condemn or condone the activities of the NF, but privately voiced the opinion that they were 'nutters'. One of the control group claimed an Afro-Caribbean boy as a best mate and to have stood up for him in a fight, but this was the exception rather than the rule. Most of the kids thought it natural that whites and blacks 'preferred their own kind', and they were strongly against mixed marriages. They took it for granted that as members of an ethnic majority they should have more going for them, although some also thought that black people deserved decent jobs and housing, provided this did not affect their own positon. We might call this a racism of *relative privilege*; it adopts a *laissez faire* stance, especially towards institutionalised forms of discrimination. Yet as soon as these privileges are felt to be challenged in some way, for example by programmes of positive action in employment, then there is an immediate shift to a more interventionist model, usually accompanied by expressions of outraged public propriety.

It was clear then that we were dealing with a spectrum of discrete positions, each with its own modalities and supports, but that they were linked and there might be a pattern to the shifts which took place between them, at the level of individuals and groups. One example of this had already come to our attention. We called it the 'Jekyll and Hyde' effect because in one context (e.g. when talking to us) young people would adopt a relatively privileged position, and voice their sympathies with the plight of 'blacks in South Africa' whilst in another (say with their friends when they thought we were out of earshot) they would revert to a racism of relative deprivation and start complaining about the way white people were being treated as second-class citizens in their own country. These were the 'two facers' to which our NFers so contemptuously referred. But this was not the only instance. There were also some who had formed very close 'best mate' relationships with black youngsters, but who confided to us, or other youth workers, the most intense feelings of racial hostility to 'blacks in general'. This was a much more extreme swing – from a position of absolute identification, in which any difference is annulled, to one of absolute negation, in which difference is everything and rules out any possibility of positive identification. This pattern of ambivalence is canonised in the proverbial 'some of my best friends are …'. It is *not* the effect of an oscillation between racist and anti-racist positions, but part of a strategy of disavowal intrinsic to racism itself. There have always been 'good niggers' to set against the 'bad'. The ritual disclaimer enables people to support racist immigration policies whilst dissociating themselves from the policies of the National Front, or to rock against racism, because they are 'into' reggae music, whilst continuing to beat up black people on the streets.

In fact, at the level of youth culture these 'split perceptions' have increasingly solidified into a double standard of ethnic representation. At this period White youth adopted or adapted Afro-Caribbean styles, whilst continuing to despise and reject Asian cultures. White 'soul boys' or 'Rudies' showed off their mastery of creole or rasta slang, before they went off 'Paki-bashing'. It is all the more unfortunate then that the 'two-tone' music sponsored by the Anti-Nazi League, in stressing the subcultural linkages between black and white youth, should have tacitly underwritten the double standard by privileging Afro-Caribbean over Asian styles.[24]

In effect, certain elements are selected from Afro-Caribbean culture and privileged because they are associated with the street code of manual working-class masculinity; in contrast certain elements are selected from the Asian cultural heritage because they can be made to signify petty bourgeois and effeminate traits. The full formula (where + indicates idealisation and – denigration) for the double standard could thus be written:

Afro-Caribbean : Asian :: proletarian : petty bourgeois
as   +   –   +   –
Masculine : Feminine :: Manual : Mental
   +   –   +   –

This is the most elaborated version of a structure of disavowal which is built into the code of working-class racism.[25] The code is centred on the construction of a white proletarian ethnicity in which race has replaced generation as the subject of an idealised patrimony of labour powers. Rival ethnicities are either assimilated to this patrimony, or else set up as the despised object of its exclusionary practice.

What is at issue here, of course, are not real differences, but contrasting stereotypes produced by the racist imagination. Whatever the actual proportion of the British population from the Indian subcontinent who own shops or small businesses, as against factory workers or lawyers, it is the former who are taken as typical, not the latter. Equally, while there is a significant minority of Afro-Caribbean youth who engage in a variety of more or less macho subcultural styles, there are even more who do not, yet it is the former who are regarded as representative of the whole black community. Amongst the white youth we worked with, militant Sikhs continued to be regarded as 'wimps' while the pacifist Rastas were 'heavy'.

The patriarchal basis of this system should now be made clear. The sexual double standard is transposed into split perceptions of ethnicity and these in turn are articulated to signifiers of class division to produce the final imagery of 'race relations.[26] One implication of this model is that patterns of discrimination will vary systematically between boys and girls. For, to shift from the standpoint of relative racism (in which ethnic minorities are

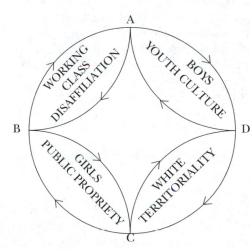

Key

Positions within working-
class racism

A Absolute identification
B Relative privilege
C Relative deprivation
D Absolute negation

envied or let be) to one of absolute identification or negation, it is necessary to assume a position of superiority vis-a-vis *one's own* peer group. And for working-class youth this is mainly done on the basis of gender. Working-class boys are therefore much more likely to flip between the two extremes, whereas girls, in so far as they are still confined within the protocols of public propriety, will tend to oscillate between racisms of relative privilege and deprivation. This was certainly true of the girls who hung around with the NFers; whereas even the 'control' group of boys veered towards absolute positions when it came to comparing respective demerits of Asians and Afro-Caribbean youth.

Gender, however, may not be the only shifter. Young people who want to better themselves may appropriate aspects of other cultures in order to symbolise their *disaffiliation* from working-class origins. In doing so they may move from a racism of relative privilege to a position of positive identification with ethnic minorities. This is especially likely to occur amongst those who have stayed on into further education to avoid the dole. Although this shift represents a welcome step away from the more active forms of racialism, it should not be confused with the assumption of an anti-racist position as long as it remains locked into the equivocation of 'some of my best friends are ...'.

It was therefore possible to construct a model showing the interaction between the four modalities: We were not able to test this model through additional fieldwork, but it was one which we found useful in trying to unravel the tangled and complex web of racist representation which we had met. It was, however, difficult to relate our findings to those of other investigators. Although we broadly agreed as to the *extent* of racist beliefs within white working-class communities, our picture of its meanings and modalities was rather different, or at least more differentiated, so that it was difficult to make any point-by-point comparison.[27]

Postscript

We were well aware of how dangerous it can be to generalise on the basis of a local case study carried out at a particular point in time. However, no longitudinal research based on a properly differential typology of racism has ever been carried out in this country. To generate some rudimentary control on our results we therefore decided to return to the 'scene of the crime' some five years afterwards to see what had changed and what had stayed the same.

By 1986, the estate itself looked decidedly the worse for wear, despite some localised attempts at do-it-yourself improvement. The proportion of black families had increased only slightly; in statistical terms the most significant change was the dramatic increase in youth unemployment. Two out of three school leavers was now either on a training scheme or the dole. The pattern of racial prejudice had also changed considerably. Local support for both the National Front and the British Movement had declined, racial attacks took the form of sporadic harrassment against individual targets, rather than routine or sustained confrontations between groups. The ethnic double standard had become by now fully established as commonsense and had even developed a material base. A small gang of unemployed white youth had organised a protection racket directed against Asian families who had shops in the area. If the money demanded was not forthcoming a mounting scale of reprisals occurred starting with the daubing of slogans through smashed windows and rubbish tipped through doors, to break-ins and setting fire to premises. In one case the children of an Asian shopkeeper who refused to pay up were viciously beaten. The group had no liking for Afro-Caribbeans either but were also too scared of them to do more than hurl a few insults behind their backs. Working-class racism had thus established its own obscene version of moral economy.

Other unemployed youth adopted a different tack. Many had become involved in the local hidden economy and had considerable dealings with Afro-Caribbean peers on that score. This was not confined to the drugs scene, but embraced various kinds of otherwise legitimate self-employment, linked either to youth culture (e.g. running discos) or community needs (e.g. cheap repairs and others goods or services). This group had developed an attitude of grudging respect for their 'partners in crime' either on account of their hardness ('you don't mess with them') or their style ('sharp'). These economic activities had not, however, won them over to an anti-racist position. Far from it. They continued to despise the *Asian* community and fully endorsed the views, if not the actions, of the protection racketeers. A further development also reinforcing earlier trends was the way the racisms of relative privilege and deprivation had become anchored to experiences on youth training schemes.[28] Those who were on schemes where there were good prospects of getting a job, were far more likely to adopt a *laissez faire* position, 'blacks were no problem'. These boys were not predisposed to question why there should be so few black trainees on these high status schemes. In contrast, for boys on schemes where prospects were far less good, 'race' was a highly charged issue, albeit one which was mostly kept under wraps. Many of them deeply resented being on schemes dominated numerically by black youth; in their eyes this only confirmed the popular view that the schemes were rubbish. They were not predisposed to question the institutionalised racism of the Youth Training Scheme (YTS) any more than their counterparts on 'better' schemes. Moreover, they did not make such a great distinction between Asians and Afro-Caribbeans. All coloureds were rubbish. However, they did make some exceptions to this rule. Those coloured trainees who distinguished themselves in various acts of resistance to the regime, were given a degree of approval, 'OK for a black'. So there was some evidence that experiences of YTS were providing a relativising framework of comparison.

One conclusion was inescapable from all this. There was no straightforward correlation between youth unemployment and working-class racism. A change in the level of the former, could not account for shifts in the pattern of the latter.

The problems this raises are both theoretical and practical. Once we abandon the classical base/superstructure model, in favour of the relative autonomy principle, we have to find a new means of analysing the functions of ideology.[29] Amongst other things, this means we need a methodology that can identify the specificity of different types of (racist) ideology, whilst at the sametime locating these particular instances within a general theory of their common structural properties.[30] So, for example, we need to establish the microfoundations of popular racism, as this study has attempted to do, and to locate that evidence, at another level, in terms of a macro-historical analysis of the peculiarities of the British social structure.[31] Only when both dimensions are in place can we proceed with any confidence to the kind of theoretically grounded comparative analysis required to construct a political and cultural geography of contemporary racism. This is turn will help us, at a more practical level, to develop more particularised forms of anti-racist policy, sensitively geared into the specificities of local contexts and conjunctures, whilst still co-ordinating them within a more general framework of strategic intervention.

Notes

1. For an attempt to develop such an analysis, drawing on elements of Marxist and psychoanalytic theory, see P. Cohen, 'The Perversions of Inheritence' in P. Cohen and H. S. Bains (eds) *Multiracist Britain* (London 1988), and also P. Cohen, *Home Rules* (London, 1993).

2. For an account of the moral panic against anti-racism see N. Murray 'Anti Racists and other Demons', *Race and Class*, 27(3) (1977).

3. One of the best introductions to the current debates on ideology, of particular relevance to an analysis of racist discourse, is still the short book by G. Therborn *The Ideology of Power and the Power of Ideology* (London, 1980). See also G. Ben-Tovim and J. Gabriel, 'Marxism and the Concept of Racism', *Economy and Society*, 7(2) (1978), J. C. Guillaumin, *Racism, Sexism, Power and Ideology* (London, 1995).

4. For an example of the divide and rule thesis see D. Edgar 'Racism, Fascism, and the Politics of the National Front,' *Race and Class*, 19 (2)(1977).

5. For an example of what has been called the 'stratified diffusion' theory see the excellent study by D. Lorimer, *Class, Colour and the Victorians* (Leicester, 1978).

6. This common sense explanation is popular amongst teachers. For a discussion of this see P. Cohen, 'Popular Racism, Unpopular Education', *Youth and Policy*, 24 (1988).

7. The notions of 'displacement effect' and 'imaginary relations of circulation' are developed in P. Cohen 'The Perversions of Inheritance', although not within the problematic of false consciousness. The difficulty with the original formulation of Lukacs *History and Class Consciousness* (trans. 1971) is that any form of non (totalising) class position is regarded as objectively 'false'.

8. The work of J. Gabel, *False Consciousness* (Baltimore, 1975) attempts to apply a Lukacsian model to understanding both racism and schizophrenia. In equating the two, he effectively dissolves the structural aspects of reification into social psychological phenomena.

9. For an example of comparative local studies, see E. Cashmore, *The Logic of Racism* (London, 1987). For a study which stresses linguistic and socio-cultural variables, rather than material ones, see R. Hewitt *White Talk, Black Talk* (Cambridge, 1986).

10. For a critical analysis of Labourism, and economistic theories of racism, see R. Miles and A. Phizacklea, *Labour and Racism* (London, 1982).
11. For a critique of the romantic tendencies of utopian populism on the Left, see D. Heyermacher, *Profits of Hope, Prophets of Doom* (New York, 1976).
12. See for example the discussion in C. Gaine, *Still no Problem Here*, rev. edn (Stoke on Trent, 1995).
13. See M. Hechter, 'Rational Choice Theory and the Study of Race and Ethnic Relations', in J. Rex and D. Mason, *Theories of Race and Ethnic Relations* (Cambridge, 1986).
14. For a functionalist account of working-class racism, see R. Miles, *Racism and Migrant Labour* (London, 1982).
15. For a general introduction to Gramsci's work which draws out its relevances to contemporary theoretical and political issues see C. Mouffe, *Gramsci and Marxist Theory* (London, 1979).
16. See P. Cohen 'The Perversions of Inheritance' (op. cit, 1988), for an attempt to develop such a reading in the context of English social history.
17. See, for instance, CCCS, *The Empire Strikes Back* (London, 1982) and M. Sarup, *The Politics of Multi-racial Education* (London, 1986).
18. The Political Socialisation Project was funded by the Leverhulme Trust and was based in the Department of Sociology at the London Institute of Education from 1978 to 1981.
19. See for, example, P. Parmar, 'Gender, Race and Power', in *Multiracist Britain* (1988).
20. This tape was made by my colleague D. Robins as part of the ethnographic research undertaken by the Political Socialisation Project. He is not responsible for the analysis of the material given here. See *We Hate Humans* (Harmondsworth, 1984) for a different treatment of this material.
21. For a discussion of the general role which territoriality plays in maintaining the 'corporatism' of working-class cultures, see Chapter 3 in this volume.
22. For a historical analysis of policing and public propriety, see Chapter 5 in this volume.
23. For further discussion of this point, see Chapter 8 in this volume.
24. For a discussion of the cultural politics of the anti-racist movement during this period see P. Gilroy and E. Lawrence, 'Two-tone Britain' P. Cohen, *Multiracist Britain* (1988).
25. For an analysis of some of these negotiations, which fails, however to highlight the implications of the ethnic double standard, see S. Jones, *Black Culture, White Culture* (London, 1987).
26. For an analysis of some of the gender dynamics in popular racism see P. Cohen, 'Tarzan and the Jungle Bunnies: race, sex and class in popular culture', *New Formations*, 5 (1988c).
27. See, for example, the research reported in A. Phizacklea and R. Miles, 'Working-class Racist Beliefs in the Inner City' in their book

Racism and Political Action (London, 1979). My typology, developed originally in the early 1980s, has some points in common with that of Cashmore's (1986), though the analytic framework is different.

28. For an analysis of institutionalised racism in youth training schemes see the chapter by J. Solomos in *Multiracist Britain* (1988). Also his *Racism, Black Youth and the State* (London, 1989). For a more detailed ethnographic account see R. Holland, *The Long Transition* (London, 1989).

29. See the discussion of Bentovim and Gabriel on this point.

30. For a general discussion of the relation between macro and micro levels of analysis within Marxism see A. Levine *et al.*, 'Marxism and Methodological Individualism', *New Left Review*, 162 (1987).

Part II

Transitional Subjects

Chapter 7

Rethinking the Youth Question

By the early 1980s two things had become clear. The project of finding a replacement revolutionary subject for the 'proletariat' was doomed to failure; and youth cultures were extending their range of bricolage into new domains of race and gender, whilst becoming ever more fully integrated within the dynamics of what was variously described as post-Fordism or post-industrial capitalism. These developments inevitably affected youth research. Marxists, such as Paul Willis,[1] still held on to a basically functionalist model of social and cultural reproduction to explain the restructuring of youth labour and school transitions, whilst subculture theory went post-modern in the work of Dick Hebdige and others[2]. In the case of the youth research programme funded by the ESRC; the brief flirtation with theory and critical ethnography was over[3]. There was a determined return to empiricist studies which tracked school-leavers' transition routes, measured their aspirations against qualifications, quantified their consumption patterns and correlated the lot against crude indices of gender, age, race and 'class'.

It was against this background that 'Rethinking the Youth Question' was written. It came out of a course at the Institute of Education, and hence necessarily took the form of a critical review of the major schools of thought which had informed educational and social policies towards

Originally published as a monograph by the Post 16 Centre, University of London Institute of Education (1986). This chapter is an edited version of the monograph.

young people since the war. In and through this reading, and especially through a consideration of some of the classical theories of human development focusing on generational relations and adolescence, I tried to argue the case for the continuing intellectual and political importance of the youth question. It was not just a matter of going back to the classical themes, but of a critical revision. By identifying four codes – of vocation, inheritance, apprenticeship and career – and briefly tracing the history of their articulations in particular kinds of youth question I tried to lay down the elements of a general theory of cultural identity formation which would be serviceable for this purpose: no doubt a hopelessly over-schematic (not to say ambitious) project. The concept of a cultural, as opposed to a socio-linguistic, code referred to the construction of identities through the transmission of skills and competencies which were realised in the form of what Bourdieu calls 'cultural capital'. The central idea explored here is that there are different types of cultural capital, and that they are not all confined to the governing, or so-called educated, classes but are also associated with particular types of manual labour, and are strongly gendered.

The study sets out a programme of research into the genealogy of these codes, focussing on their function as autobiographical grammars and on their 'habitus' in particular forms of family, education and labour process. This is a project which was not followed through directly and which, indeed, to do properly would require a large-scale piece of comparative historical research: something I have saved up for my 'retirement'! In the meantime I developed some of the ideas in the case studies which follow in Chapters 8, 9 and 10.

Old heads, young shoulders

It is often said that socialists have a bad habit of advancing towards the future looking back over their shoulders at the past. This is not perhaps the best of positions from which to engage with a present in which so many of our traditional assumptions have been upset by deep and subtle shifts in our social structure. Instead of struggling to remain contemporary with the society we are seeking to change, it is all too easy to read social changes through the grid of the particular ideas and experiences which were strategic in forming the historical generation to which we belong.

The fact is that the youth question has to be continually rethought in the light of the changing circumstances of the times. Yet if we look at the political and theoretical assumptions which continue to govern so much of youth policy-making we find that all too often it is a case of old wine in new bottles.

Labour politicians, for example, continue to recognise only two possible modes of youth politics: the narrowly electoral and the violently extra-parliamentary.[4] The shock of the scale of the party's defeat in the 1983 election did for a time concentrate its mind wonderfully on the youth question. For the first time in its history it lost the youth vote, partly as a result of an unprecedented rate of abstention amongst first voters, and partly as a result of a general rightwards shift. The party therefore sought to rejuvenate its image by various forays into 'media kidology', courtesy of Tracy Ullman, Billy Bragg and Co. The polls then showed that the youth vote had swung back to Labour. Therefore it is concluded that Labour does have the right youth policies and it only remains to find better and brighter ways of communicating them. The subsequent riots in Tottenham, Brixton, Handsworth and elsewhere once more shattered this electoralist dream. Yet those young people whose only remaining form of collective bargaining was to riot, did more than confirm the great fear of the Labour Party. They indicated the failure of the existing welfare state solutions to the youth question, to which the Labour Party continues to be committed. Bigger and better youth training schemes, continuing education, more leisure centres, even so-called community policing, are clearly not adequate responses to the needs and demands of the new, and seemingly permanent, reserve army of youth labour which has been thrown up by Britain's industrial decline. If the Labour party does not succeed in developing a strategy which speaks directly to the predicament of this other young England, who will almost certainly *not* vote for them or any other political party, then it does not deserve to win the youth vote at all.[5]

It is increasingly claimed that what appears at first sight to be political apathy in fact represents a profound cultural revolution. Young people are rejecting the alienated forms of organised politics in favour of a new style of personal politics influenced by feminism, environmentalism and the peace movement. This may not lead them to riot, vote Labour or go on Right to Work marches, but they are nevertheless in the vanguard of the changeover into a post-modern society.

In a period in which material power is ever more concentrated at the commanding heights of economy and state, while the symbolic power of the consciousness industries grows apace, it seems to me that the claims being made for these new movements is probably exaggerated. There is a limit to which affinity groups and peer networks can sustain protracted campaigns and/or outflank the powers that be. The importance of black and gay youth politics is not that it might constitute the elements of some mass youth movement – that is an old socialist dream whose attempted realisation has always led to disaster – but that by their very existence they challenge the dominant pattern of youth provision and its bio-political premises. These premises are widely shared by politicians, policy-makers and professionals. They can be summarised as follows:

1. Youth is a unitary category, with certain psychological characteristics and social needs common to the age group.
2. Youth is an especially formative stage of development, where attitudes and values become anchored to ideologies and remain fixed in this mould in later life.
3. The transition from childhood dependence to adult autonomy normally involves a rebellious phase, which is itself part of a cultural tradition transmitted from one generation to the next.
4. Young people in modern societies experience difficulty in making successful transitions and require professional help, advice and support to do so.

I have called these premises 'bio-political' because they constitute youth as a specific type of population and as a site of particular political interventions. This youthism first crystallised in the 1880s during the first great debate on the youth question. In the intervening period youthism has been progressively – or rather regressively – institutionalised in youth policy and practice. Moreover, it has been shored up by a vast amount of social scientific research, to the point where it has become, if not gospel, then at least unquestioned commonsense. It is these theoretical underpinnings which have to be challenged if we are to begin to rethink the youth question in and for the 1990s. Not in order to be bloody-minded or clever at other people's expense, but because the old maps of working-class or middle-class adolescence – whether they were drawn by Marxists or settlement sociologists or psycho-analysts – no longer work, no longer serve as an adequate guide either for youth professionals or for young people with whom they work. But if social scientists do indeed have to go back to the drawing board, then perhaps we should at least first look at the range of theories which are currently on offer.[6]

Back to Methusaleh: biologism, historicism and some other old-fashioned stories

It is not at all easy to define the specificity of the youth question without falling back on the notion that young people constitute some kind of unitary category, governed by certain key features of adolescence. After all, a lot of people say, puberty is puberty, and unmarried youth always pose a problem of integration in any type of society. The youth question is as old as Methusaleh, and as universal as the life cycle itself; only the answers change.

The classical theories (Stanley Hall, Karl Mannheim and Talcott Parsons) all set out to challenge that commonsense view. If they only succeed in relativising it, giving it a pyscho- or sociological rationale, the reason is not hard to find. They all start from the notion of youth as a biological given, with certain inherent and invariant (usually psychological) properties, and only then introduce cultural or historical mediations to analyse its variant forms of social expression. The essential drama of adolescence thus concerns the irresistible forces of Nature (the sexual drive unleashed by puberty) meeting the immovable objects of Culture (the institutions of social integration). There is considerable disagreement as to the outcome, the precise mechanisms of mediation, etc., but this is possibly less significant than the fact that in all these theories *sexuality is naturalised in explaining how a generation is socialised.*

Hall's psychology of adolescence, Mannheim's sociology of knowledge and Parsonian functionalism might not at first appear to have much in common beyond their gender blindness and ethnocentricity. Yet they all ultimately rest on the same equation – Nature : Culture :: Individual : Society. The formula itself has dominated western thought since at least the 17th century. Hobbes, for example, thought that individual human natures were nasty and brutish and had to be subordinated to the social contract if culture was to survive. Rousseau, of course, gave a diametrically opposed reading to these terms, insisting that it was in the nature of individuals to develop forms of human co-operation if they were not corrupted by society and its cultural demands.

The Rousseau/Hobbes debate was central to the developing debate on childhood and its moral status which so interested educationalists and philanthropic reformers in the 18th and early 19th century. But it was not until the advent of Darwin, and more particularly social Darwinism in the latter part of the century, that the debate began to focus on the notion of adolescence itself. This was largely due to the work of Stanley Hall. In his *Psychology of Adolescence* (1905) he argued that the development of the individual recapitulates that of society, and both consist in an evolution from a state of primitive wildness to one of civilised maturity. The reason that adolescence was such a period of emotional storm and stress was because young people were being pulled in two opposite directions – back to the primitive states of the stone age baby and forward towards the rational and enlightened state of 'modern man'.

It is interesting that this characterisation of adolescents as a hybrid species (half animal, half human) corresponds almost exactly to the position assigned to colonial populations and the domestic working classes in the discourse of liberal imperialism. Indeed in Britain the youth question was originally constructed in these terms, as part of a moral panic about the future of the race. But for Stanley Hall himself the more immediate reference was to the way young white middle-class Americans were being whipped up into states of mass hysteria and conversion by a new style of religious evangelism in the 1880s. Why were the children of the most 'civilised' section of American society behaving with the 'primitive abandon' attributed to the native Indians? The answer was 'adolescence'!

No one today would dare to take literally Hall's notion that in growing up we all move from behaving like members of a hunting and gathering tribe to behaving like members of the modern world. Yet his central notion of recapitulation (ontogeny repeats phylogeny) has continued to inform both developmental psychology and, as we will see later, psycho-analysis. His characterisation of adolescence as a period of emotional upheaval has been popularised through countless channels and today is enshrined as the dominant, commonsense definition of youth. It certainly continues to inform the civilising mission of much youth provision.[7]

Karl Mannheim seems to offer a completely different reading of the youth question. For him it is a question not of adolescence but of generation. And generation, he insists, is a social construct, a function of shared cultural symbolisms or locations, not a biological given, or a demographic category determined by date of birth. Generations, in other words, are social groups who believe they belong to a common movement of history, or are formed by the same conjuncture. The generation of May '68, the 'lost generation' of the First World War are examples of this kind. It is not clear in Mannheim's account why youth should be the privileged bearer of this special generational consciousness, or zeitgeist, and what relation it bears to processes of class formation. What is clear is that behind much of what he writes lies the student unrest and counter-culture which emerged in Germany after the First World War, and which rejected the 'Old Germany' in the name of a variety of romantic Utopias. Their country's defeat and the indiscriminate slaughter of trench warfare undoubtedly did give many young Germans a strong sense of belonging to a common generation. Yet Mannheim extrapolates from this rather special situation to argue for something like a historical law of generational conflict – the irresistible force of ideas and symbols through which each new generation defines its identity (and difference) always meeting the immovable objections of the 'old guard'. Thus Mannheim's historicism leads him to a formulation very similar to the biologism he is at such pains to reject. And perhaps this is because he fails to give generation a material location as a division of labour within both the family and the wider society.[8]

In the theories of Talcott Parsons and his followers, the Darwinism of Stanley Hall, and the historicism of Mannheim are subsumed in a functionalist synthesis. Not only is the working of the 'social system' modelled on that of the biological organism, but its evolution also is seen as a process of progressive differentiation of functions, parallel to that which the 'personality system' undergoes in adapting to them. However, what is new and import-

ant about the Parsonian model is the way it seeks to specify the
youth question in terms of particular structural tensions arising
out of the transition from traditional to modern society.[9]

The argument can be simply stated. In traditional (or what we
would call pre-capitalist) societies, the family fulfills all the vital
functions of reproduction – economic, biological and cultural. It
unites education, material production and primary child care in a
single social system. Thus family relations and patterns of socialisation provide an adequate and effective model for later life;
there is a basic continuity between the roles which the child
learns within the family and the roles which the adult is called
upon to perform in the wider society. However, in modern industrial societies this is no longer the case. The family has been
divested of its educational and occupational functions, and these
are now organised on a quite different basis from the roles which
regulate parent/child interaction. Occupational roles, unlike
family roles, are specialised rather than diffuse, instrumental
rather than expressive, allocated on the basis of achievement
rather than ascription, and their performance is judged by 'universalistic' rather than 'particularistic' criteria. In other words
there is a basic discontinuity between the pattern of family socialisation, which continues to be organised along traditional patriarchal lines, and adult roles, which are organised in terms of market
rationality and impersonal bureaucratic structures, knitted
together by an ideology of competitive individualism. The position of youth is then located at the maximum point of tension
between these two 'value systems'. Parsons suggests that this is
partly the effect of extended schooling, in both separating young
people from the world of the family and segregating them from
the adult world of work and politics, whilst simultaneously organising them into age grade hierarchies.

The result, he argues, is the emergence of adolescence as a
period of 'structured irresponsibility', a moratorium between
childhood and adulthood. This new space in the life cycle then
allows the emergence of peer groups and youth culture, whose
latent function is to mediate between traditional and modern
value systems, by incorporating elements from both. Thus adolescent peer groups enable their members to both distance themselves from family roles and to rehearse future occupational roles;
youth cultures reproduce the patterns of emotional dependence

and security, the particularisms of place, and diffuse roles characteristic of primary or childhood socialisation, whilst enabling young people to master the competitive and instrumental techniques required of adults in the workplace. So however 'bizarre' or 'deviant' their behaviour may appear, their function is essentially adaptive.

Now it has to be said straight away that Parsons own accounts of youth culture are essentially about what it was like to be a white male adolescent in middle-class America during and after the Second World War. The attempt to apply his model to understanding the position of working-class or ethnic minority youth has inevitably led to a pathological view of their cultures. Thus, for example, black youth cultures are not regarded as a response to white racism, but as the product of a disjunction between the traditional value orientation of their families, and the 'modern' values of industrialism, individualism, etc., which they encounter in white society! A somewhat similar scenario has been constructed to explain the persistence of delinquent gang cultures in working-class neighbourhoods in the inner city.

The underlying model of Social Darwinism emerges clearly here; its notion of evolution as differentiation led to a disastrous misreading of family forms in the transition to capitalism, and especially the way a patriarchal order came to be reconstructed out of the new relations of production. As we shall see, this is crucial for understanding the specific features and position of youth labour which emerged in the 19th century, on which so much of what we now regard as the youth question is built. But no sustained intellectual attempt has since been made to engage with the problems raised by these classical theories. Subsequent sociologies of youth have either uncritically absorbed the classical premises (especially the psychological ones) or else evaded them in favour of an alternative starting point in the hope that somehow this will lead onto new terrain.

The effect, however, has been to open the way for a new wave of 'youth theory' to carry to an extreme the Darwinian or historicist tendencies of the classical texts. So we currently have the attempt by sociobiologists to apply ethological theories of animal behaviour to understanding human body language in general, and teenage body language in particular.[10] And then we have the psycho-historians trying to discover the secret of cultural evolution by studying the early toilet training practices of the commercial bourgeoisie in 17th-century Flanders.[8] And whereas Parsons or Mannheim did at least seek to identify and localise the youth question in terms of some notion, however inadequately phrased, of a transition from feudalism to capitalism, the new school usually do not. They are looking for transhistorical patterns of human behaviour, which can be explained in terms of a limited set of psychological or instinctual repertoires.

The aim appears laudable enough. It is to demolish the myth, perpetuated in the earlier theories, that there was some golden 'pre-industrial' age where youth was closely integrated into family and community life, where it enjoyed positive roles and rites of passage, and where relations between the generations were essentially harmonious. For the patterns which the psycho-historians and socio-biologists are interested in tracing as far back as classical antiquity, are all patterns of adolescent conflict. However in their search through the dustbins of history for any scrap of evidence which would suggest continuity, they have often committed the most ludicrous kinds of back projection. St Augustine becomes James Dean's kid brother (yes, they were both suffering from an adolescent identity crisis); wandering bands of young bachelor knights in mediaeval Europe are compared to the Wandervogel in the Weimar Republic and American hippies on the trail to Katmandu (they all had a thing about mystical quests, romantic love, and preferred their poetry sung, it seems); West Ham supporters fighting the Stretford End become reincarnations of rival plebeian factions clashing on the terraces of the Colosseum in Imperial Rome (you guessed it, these are young lower-class males ritualising their innate aggression through the medium of territorial rivalries). The coming out of the debutante in 'Society' mirrors the initiation of young girls in tribal society and so on.[12]

There has never been a shortage of parallels for researchers who are prepared to look at youth history through the wrong end of the telescope and abstract symbolic forms from the social relations and material contexts which give them meaning. The result of doing so is quite simply a misreading. Let's take one concrete example from the above list.

Detailed historical research[13] has shown that wandering knights were invariably younger sons whose fathers were not able or willing to provide an adequate patrimony to ensure a successful marriage.

Their chivalric codes and military adventures had a severely practical function – to master the martial and social arts, and thus enhance their attractiveness as suitors, or to acquire land and other possessions for the same purpose. The institution of knighthood thus did for the lesser nobility what the 'putting out' of young people as apprentices and servants to other households did for artisans and peasants – it postponed marriage, absorbed surplus offspring and generally eased the strains which inheritance systems were undergoing in reproducing these class positions in the later Middle Ages. The chivalric codes, *chansons de gestes*, etc., which comprised the 'youth culture' of this warrior caste have therefore to be understood in their historical specificity, within a particular set of feudal social relations, at a certain moment of their development.

Needless to say, the German students and middle-class youth who joined the Wandervogel movements of the 1920s were reacting to a rather different set of circumstances! The version of the Middle Ages to which they tried, symbolically, to return was a highly idealised one, where the *chansons* – the lyrical evocations of Nature and Romantic Love – were celebrated, while the *gestes* – the acts of violence and pillage which were the real substance of military adventures – were conveniently ignored. But such a disassociation is readily understandable in a generation which had been almost wiped out by the advent of mechanised warfare in the trenches, a slaughter they blamed on an unholy alliance of 'old men' – industrialists and Prussian aristocrats – whose attempt to rejuvenate the German state and economy had ended by destroying most of its youth. If the pacifist Wandervogel were so easily converted to the militaristic Hitler Jugend, it was precisely because Nazi ideology was a mixture of modern racism and mediaeval 'Volkgeist' brilliantly calculated to 'cover' the most brutal actions with the most romantic of songs. But if, half a century or so later, a proportion of the student generation which organised the peace movement against the Vietnam War retires hurt into the mediaeval phantasy world of *Lord of the Rings* or 'Dungeons and Dragons', then we are clearly in a different situation again; for here what began as opposition to the brutal irrationality of the US military adventure, a youth movement at least partly informed by a Marxist critique, ended in retreat from public involvement into a private world ruled by magic and violence of the most irrational kind. An emotional as well as historical regression, yet one inscribed in the tablets of Hippiedom (one at least of which reads 'you're never too old to have a happy childhood'), awaiting only the moment of political defeat to become law.

Now I suppose it is just about possible to explain all three cases as so many variants on adolescent or generational conflict.[14] But the closer we look at them, the more superficial the similarities and the deeper the discontinuities between them become. And this happens whenever we try and understand youth phenomena concretely as part of wider context and conjuncture. There are, of course, different tempos in history; some of shorter, some of longer, duration. But not even Kondratieff, let alone Keynes, could have dreamt up a long wave of youth history lasting eight centuries and spanning both feudalism and capitalism!

Whenever continuities of this order are postulated we can be sure of two things: youth has been extrapolated from its different forms of social and cultural reproduction and reduced to a common quasi-biological substrate; and/or youth is constructed as the passive bearer of a cultural tradition – a tradition of misrule. In both cases young people are allowed to enter history only on the most reified terms – through the measurable disposition of their bodies (viz. rates of illegitimacy, age of puberty or other demographic indices) or through customary practices which have the weight of a no less congenital destiny.[15]

It is, of course, the case that for periods before the present century, this is the only kind of reasonably reliable data of collective behaviour which is available. The problem is not so much the nature of the evidence as the uses to which it is put in attempting to construct a history of youth. Many of these difficulties stem from the ambiguity of 'generation' as a heuristic concept. It is in principle possible to distinguish three types of generation:

1. a sibling generation – a cohort of children born to a cohort of parents;
2. a peer group generation – those who belong to the same normatively defined age group, within the same social location;
3. a historical generation – all those who identify themselves either contemporaneously or in retrospect as belonging to the same historical conjuncture or process.

Under different sets of conditions these three types of generational memberships may be combined in a variety of ways, or not combined at all. In so far as youth history is the study of these sets of conditions, it involves a notion of social history which goes beyond both demography and cultural anthropology, and includes the political and economic dimensions of reproduction.

The work of Mannheim and Parsons fails to clarify these problematics. But the more recent attempt to go beyond the classical theories seem to me to fall well short of the mark. They either fall back on a unitary category of 'youth' as the basis of historical comparison, or worse still, construct a transhistorical model of adolescence.

The classical errors are not only conserved, they are compounded. Socio-biology biologises the social; it certainly does not provide us with a material history of the youthful body and its social techniques. Psycho-history either psychologises the historical or historicises the unconscious. It has nothing to tell us about the changing ideological basis of particular modes of production of subjectivity in different periods or types of society. Within these perspectives it becomes impossible to locate the youth question in terms of a specific set of economic, social and cultural transformations. Yet it is precisely because the models bequeathed us by Hall, Mannheim and Parsons are inadequate for the purpose, that we have to try to construct new and better ways of periodising youth history, rather than to abandon the project altogether.

What then is the point of trying to draw these historical parallels at all? If it is not theoretically justified, are there overriding political reasons for the exercise? It is sometimes argued that by demolishing the myth of some golden age of youth, before the advent of sex 'n'drugs 'n'rock 'n'roll, the power of moral panic over public opinion can be broken. For example, if it can be shown conclusively that young people in 19th-century urban communities were *not* more obedient to their parents, or more respectful to their 'elders and betters', indeed were *more* lawless and violent than their counterparts today, then the Thatcherite call for a 'return to Victorian values' may lose some of its appeal. Even granted that the power of such slogans is primarily emotional and is unlikely to be countered by facts, is the argument likely to be won on these terms? It does not follow, for instance, that if one accepts that young males have always been addicted to some form of public violence, one is thereby convinced of the futility of repressive measures. The reaction is just as likely to be the opposite: Thank God respectable tax-paying citizens nowadays have got the police, detention centres and the courts to protect us (and deter them), whereas the poor burghers of mediaeval Paris or 17th-century London only had each other to rely on for self-defence!

Another line consists in trying to use historical evidence to persuade the older generation that the 'good old days' never were, and that young people today are not fundamentally worse behaved than when they themselves were young. This is a subtext in many oral history projects undertaken by schools.[16] I personally doubt whether it is much consolation to an elderly couple who have been kept awake all night by a teenage party in the flat next door, to be told, as one community worker tried, that rock'n'roll was latterday 'rough music' and all part of an ancient tradition of youth misrule! The fact is that historical knowledge in itself no more leads to tolerance than age leads to wisdom. If elderly people tend to idealise their own youth and compare today's youngsters invidiously, this is not just the selective action of memory on autobiography, it has at least as much to do with those specific changes in working-class family and community life that have made young people more visible, and the elderly both more numerous and more vulnerable. No amount of historical bridge-building between the generations is likely to alter that.

The most important case for constructing historical parallels is that focusing on the perennial association between the juvenile and the delinquent helps expose the scapegoating mechanisms whereby youth is made to represent a whole series of conflicts which originate elsewhere in society, e.g. in the class structure. In this view the youth question is by definition diversionary, deflecting public attention and resources away from what can and should be changed (political and economic conditions) and towards something which is essentially unchangeable (adolescent behaviour).

Now this view does have to be considered very seriously. Youth professionals of every kind do have a material stake in the youth question – it is the source of their livelihoods. Indeed, this could be put more strongly. However critical our awareness of the ideological implications, we have a vested interest in moral panics about 'youth problems' (e.g. about drug abuse, or homelessness, or street crime) because they help generate public support for our projects. It has not been unknown, in these days of a thousand cuts, for hard-pressed researchers or agencies to even start a moral panic or two of their own about young people 'at risk' in order to put pressure on funding bodies. There is nothing like a scare story about teenage glue-sniffing in the local paper to drum up trade – more clients *and* more cash! Moral panics after all deal in self-fulfilling prophecies and it's an open trade secret that the supply of a particular kind of provision tends to stimulate the demand for that type of service. *Any* kind of historical analysis which points up the compulsive repetition of this pattern in the development and expansion of both state and philanthropic interventions over the past century is to be welcomed – even, and especially though it challenges our 'civilising mission'.[17] However, it does *not* follow from this that the youth question should be abandoned, only that it needs to be formulated in a more critical and reflexive way. That means rethinking the whole relation between the youth question and young people themselves, or more precisely, stopping confusing the two levels of reality by collapsing one into the other. The recent history of youth research in this country only serves to highlight the issue.

Since the 1950s youth research in Britain has been almost exclusively 'social problem' oriented. Settlement sociology had always focussed attention on those groups who resisted its civilising mission; the advent of the welfare state saw the full flowering of this tradition. The inner-city neighbourhood, as a site of multiple deprivation and the working class family as their pathological support, continued to be held responsible for the persistence of delinquent sub-cultures.[18] To this was added a growing concern with other, less traditional kinds of cultural and political deviance amongst the young, especially the new styles of Bohemian revolt and political protest which seemed to signify a wholesale rejection not only of capitalism, but the 'socialist' welfare state. Was this the effect of affluence, or social mobility or symptomatic of wider social changes? Most of the studies in this genre surveyed cross-sections of young people in the hope of establishing intra- or inter-generational patterns of change in behaviour or moral values.[19] The youth question was effectively reduced to the notion of a 'generation gap' to be measured by some kind of political arithmetic.

One result of all this was that through the 1960s the majority of young people who did not take drugs, drop out, run away from home, become wildly promiscuous and engage in street violence or petty crime were pushed to the sidelines of academic concern. Youth research endorsed the great moral divide between sheep and goats, between the respectable young citizens who join youth clubs, and the 'rougher elements' who do not – a division institutionalised in the pattern of youth provision since the 1880s. Even research which sought to argue that delinquency or truancy were rational responses to working-class predicaments, failed to problematise the links between moral and economic status which continued to govern both state and philanthropic policies towards youth.[20] Moreover, the fragmentary nature of youth research, its positivism and lack of theorisation, are directly attributable to the fact that it limped along in the wake of moral panics about this or that 'problem category'. Yet by the late 1960s the emergence of middle-class counter-cultures (not to mention other phenomena of the so-called 'Youth revolt') had disrupted the moral economy of provision to such an extent that for the first time it became possible to seriously question prevailing definitions of the youth question.

Critical revisions: from sub-culture analysis to reproduction theory

The first major attempt to reformulate the relation between young people and the youth question came in the late 1960s and perhaps not suprisingly centred on the significance of the youth cultures of this period.[21] Earlier analysis had tried to assimilate teds, mods, rockers, skinheads and the rest to existing models of working-class delinquency or adolescence, with some allowance made for the impact of 'American imports' such as teenage fashion and rock 'n' roll. The new approach stressed the centrality of changes in the post-war British class structure for understanding these youth cultural forms, in particular changes in patterns of kinship, labour and urban structure. It was argued that these changes created a series of tensions or discontinuities in the reproduction of class cultures, and these in turn were reworked into a series of stylistic oppositions between youth cultures. Considerable attention was therefore paid to decoding the meanings of different styles of clothes, music, territoriality, and the other languages of peer group interaction; the relation between these symbolic forms and the class location of the young people who adopted them was argued to be *imaginary*, not real.

For example, skinhead style might signify a particularly chauvinistic version of proletarian ethnicity, but that did not necessarily mean that everyone who dressed Skinhead was working-class or a racist. The 'answers' given by a youth culture to the 'questions' posed in a class culture should therefore be distinguished from the social problems which its adherents might (or might not) have. To confuse the two levels was to endorse the popular 'ageist' prejudice, which read off the social and moral characteristics of young people from the physical appearances they affected.

Subsequently the original focus on class gave way to an emphasis on ethnicity and gender as the major youth cultural dynamic. At the same time the terms of the analysis shifted.[22] 'Life' was bracketted off from 'style' and style took on a life of its own. The analysis of real relations of social reproduction and their imaginary transformation (displacement, condensation, etc.) was gradually abandoned in favour of interpreting signifying practices in terms of their own internal devices of meaning. An idealist semiology replaced a positivistic sociology; the observation of 'teenage behaviour' gave way to the reading of texts in which youth functioned as 'signifier' or 'signified'. The youth question was thus radically disconnected from young people; it became simply the the site of a multiplicity of conflicting discourses; youth had no reality outside its representation, no history other than the discontinuities which govern the present. All this is certainly an antidote to the biologism/historicism of the classical theories! But it really will not do.

The trouble with what might be called the 'storm and dress' theory of youth culture is that by making clothes, music and the other body languages do all the talking, not only are young people themselves reduced to silence, but there are not even the most basic controls on interpretation. Perhaps this is as well since many young people when asked about the meaning of their style are apt to reply 'its just about being different'. But if we want to go further than this manifest truth we will need to avoid the metaphysics of post-structuralism and look instead at precisely what it is that the style conceals from its wearers – which is not just a code, but a chain of associations to a set of contradictions which are actually, however unconsciously, being lived.

Take, for example, the male uniform worn by Scuttler gangs in Manchester in the late Victorian period. By all accounts this included fustian trousers and corduroy jacket, set off with a studded belt and silk muffler. It is no coincidence that the first two items were the traditional badges of the artisan, that aristocrat of organised labour, and the second two were originally adopted by costermongers to mark out this elite of the hidden economy from lesser fry amongst street traders. Thus we have represented, magically reconciled at the level of a youth style, a major intra-class division. But it is more specific than that. For we have to consider what links as well as separates these two positions. It is clear for instance that working-class lads did not distinguish between artisan and coster culture in terms of general moral/economic status, but via the rather more immediate issue of the polar types of sexual and occupational apprenticeship they afforded.

Coster boys and girls could often save enough pennies from working their parents' stall to hire a barrow and set up on their own; by the age of 13 or 14 many had moved into lodgings and set up home together. In contrast, the growing up of the aspiring artisan was a much more frustrating and drawn-out affair, involving an often lengthy period of courtship before he had served out his time and could afford to get married. This difference, which dramatises a key tension in male working-class adolescence (e.g. between domestic dependence and wage-earning autonomy) is given condensed expression in a 'tension' within the style itself: between the coster elements, which are primarily for sexual display, and the more 'functional' and hardwearing artisan ma-terials, which indeed often doubled as working clothes.

What both constrains the selection of these 'signifiers' and makes their combination possible, is what artisan and coster cultures have in common despite the gulf in material conditions between them – namely the fact that entry into both kinds of trade was largely restricted to kith and kin, and excluded out-siders, especially immigrants. In both cases skill was constructed as special patrimony, girls were expected to marry 'within the trade', boys to follow in fathers' footsteps, and there were numerous sym-bolisms to assert a 'congenital' link between origins and destiny. The conflict between this code of inheritance with its passive reproduction of positions, and the code of apprenticeship with its more active process of appropriation is correspondingly intense; it is both signified and mediated in the youth-cultural form. But what is perhaps more important is the way this form is thereby invested with an ethnic dimension. It is certainly no coincidence that Scuttler gangs were based in and around the Irish districts of Manchester; their territorial rivalries were, to say the least, overdetermined by that fact. The Scuttler style in one sense symbolised everything from which the Irish working class were excluded. In adopting it, Irish youth could *magically* realise and harmonise the contradictory aspirations of their own community. For the Scuttler, style was about wish-fulfilment, about wanting to have the best of both artisan and coster worlds – to combine the sexual precocity and independence of the young barrow king, with the patrimony and pride of skill afforded to the young journeyman.

What is unconscious in the youth culture, is thus the same as what overdetermines its forms – a certain history of hidden contradictions of gender, ethnicity and class. By definition this history has to be researched from other sources than the iconographies furnished by the youth culture itself. In the case of the Scuttlers we need to know about the political geography of Manchester at this period, the pattern of Irish migration and settlement, the organisation of the juvenile labour market, the family and occupational cultures of artisans and costers, etc. Failing this all we will see in the Scuttlers is a generalised picture of 19th-century street gang culture – precisely all that Victorian commentators at the time saw in them.

A somewhat similar caveat is needed in trying to apply the methods of discourse analysis to historical texts as a way of constructing an archaeology of the youth question. For instance, it is certainly worth looking at parental primers and 'advice to the young' books published in different periods. For it is through these texts that some vital connections between scientific discourse and commonsense understandings are made. But there is a very real danger that certain genres will be presumed strategic, certain texts given more importance than they warrant, simply because their formal structures yield the most succinct grammars of theoretical or behavioural ideology. But whether we are looking in the sermons of 17th-century Puritan divines, the etiquette books of the 18th-century aristocracy, the Victorian literature of self-improvement or contemporary manuals of popular psychology, what we need to know is not just how these texts work in terms of their characteristic devices of meaning, but if they worked in the other, more material, sense of influencing the policies and practices of the groups or institutions to which they were addressed. And to answer that you need to know what the texts themselves cannot tell you – their mode of circulation, how they were read and by whom, and the role their readerships played in forming public opinion and popular attitudes. Only then would a picture emerge of which kind of prescriptive text was strategic in a particular conjuncture. Failing that wider evidence a quite misleading impression can result. For instance, it would be quite wrong to construct a geneology of vocationalism which dated the essential break with precapitalist ideologies of training and discipline in the mid-17th-century English revolution. For although Puritan tracts addressed to the young did combine a vision of life's journey as the unfolding of an inner quest with a new emphasis on the need to master the practical accomplishments of a chosen calling, they had no measurable impact on actual processes of education and apprenticeship at the time; in that sense they were not strategic. The decisive shift seems to have occurred much later, in the mid-Victorian period, through the medium of self-improvement literature.

The problem with this kind of discourse analysis is that it collapses theoretical and behavioural ideology into one another: the tensions and discontinuity between what 'professional experts' say, and what young people (as clients, pupils, etc.) feel and do is allowed to appear only in individual heroic actions of defiance against the 'technology of Power'; In other words this resistance is deprived at once of its collective meaning, and of its constitutive role in determining actual strategies of containment and control.

The cultural politics which have been inspired by these various 'new wave' theories has largely been about trying to deconstruct the links binding young people to the youth question. The aim is to open up spaces of representation in which they can formulate their own desires and demands beyond the constraining images of deviance imposed on them by the promoters of pop music and moral panic alike. But in practice the overwhelming focus on practices of leisure and pleasure (and usually the more spectacular, subcultural ones at that) has tended to collude with the impact of the consciousness industries in ignoring the mundane worlds of family, school and work which most young people still inhabit.

However, the collapse of the so-called 'alternative society' of the 1960s, the manifest incapacity of youth cultures to live up to the impossible political expectations foisted upon them, coupled with the collapse of the youth labour market and customary transitions from school, meant that the more bread-and-butter aspects of the youth question forced their way back to the top of the agenda. The relation between education and production, rather than between parent and youth culture, became the focus of analysis.

Most of this research [23] started from the premise that state schooling, and in particular its more hidden regimes of knowledge and power, play a decisive role in perpetuating and legitimating the various social divisions of labour under capitalism. Further, there is a permanent structural tension between the *ideological* forms of educational dis/qualification (which are highly conservative) and the technical division of labour (which is highly dynamic); it is not just that educational supply and economic demand are usually out of synch, but that a specific contradiction (base/superstructure, state/capital, or forces/relations of production) appears at a specific moment in social reproduction – in the transition from school. From this perspective it is irrelevant whether the school regime is liberal or authoritarian, whether it seeks to educate the whole person or inculcate work discipline, its latent function is to ensure that the majority of children are disqualified from entry to middle-class jobs, whilst simultaneously ruling the informal cultural apprenticeships of working-class life and labour out of academic order.

It has to be said straight away that this attempt to ground the youth question in a materialist analysis of reproduction was a welcome advance over previous accounts of schooling and the transition.[24] We are no longer presented with an abstracted individual who first becomes a child in the family, then a pupil at school, and finally a worker in the labour market – a unilinear development punctuated only by these institutional transitions and their attendant 'role conflicts'. Instead we have, at its best, a dialectical model of how a system of class places is reproduced in and through the processes which form the class subjects to fill them. However, the model has its problems, most of them connected with its functionalism. The synchronic (the system of positions or places) is privileged over the diachronic (the 'shifters' which articulate the life-historical process), the latter merely unfolding as a preordained destiny. The tension between the two orders, which is, after all, what makes 'youth' such a weak link in the chain, where it is recognised at all, is treated reductively as an instance of global contradiction so that its specificity is no sooner grasped than lost. For example, in all the discussion about the mental/manual division and how it is transmitted from generation to generation (the relative roles of family, school and occupational structures, sociolinguistic codes, etc.) the *generational* division of labour itself is scarcely mentioned, let alone conceptualised. It is simply regarded as a quasi-automatic process of replacement of older workers by younger, regulated by purely external factors such as state legislation or the labour market. This in turn can lead to overestimating the impact which these factors have on working-class strategies of transition from school.

For example, it has been suggested that youth unemployment has had an 'infantilising' effect, in prolonging economic and hence emotional dependence on parents. Now certainly it may have prolonged and deepened the tension *between* domestic dependence and wage-earning autonomy, but while that may intensify certain structures of adolescent feeling, and certainly tends to reinforce the double standard of parental treatment of sons and daughters, it does not necessarily lead to psychic regression, or destroy the cultural frameworks of growing up working class. The reason is not hard to find. While the state may legislate the age of entry or exit from the official labour market, and employers may practice wage by age differentials (especially in the hidden economy), the generational division of labour is much more broadly based and finely calibrated than that. It is as much regulated by the domestic life cycle as by the trade cycle, by family roles and their sexual division as by occupational roles and their technical specialisation. Above all, each class culture throws its own grid of representation over the life cycle, and what is a mark of maturity in one may be a sign of backwardness in another. In the case of working-class culture these wider principles of periodisation and predicament have proved as adaptable to economic change as they are resistant to ideological penetration and

reform. New markers of maturity are continually being improvised, often by transgressing the bans on participation in adult
activity, laid down by various kinds of protective 'under age' legislation. Thus the official routes and signposts are often ignored, or
put to very different meaning and purpose. Any attempt to
remove young people from the labour market will meet resistance
as long as full-time waged work continues to draw for them the
key dividing line between becoming an adult and remaining 'a
kid'. But equally no one should underestimate the cultural
resources that are available to young people who continue to
grow up working-class, even when there is no work.

Another related area which reproduction theories have tended
to ignore, due to their lack of sensitivity to 'diachronics', is the
role of the family in school transitions. Kinship networks and
family ideology are at least as important as school or peer group
'counter cultures' in positioning young people differentially
within the field of transitions. Indeed, the sheer variety of
working-class experience that the inclusion of family mediations
introduces into the picture tends to be an embarrassment to
Marxist functionalists. But the result of ignoring the family, as well
as generational divisions, is that the status of youth labour itself
remains unclarified. The fact that youth labour has been historically constituted as servicing or proto-domestic labour, that it is
bracketted with womens' work, over against both skilled work and
the family wage, the consequence this has for the different ways
working-class boys and girls learn to labour or negotiate the transition from school, all this, until very recently went largely unre-
marked and un-researched.[25] Yet we cannot understand the
specific vulnerability of youth labour to both hyper-exploitation
and structural redundancy, unless its generic 'feminine' features
are fully grasped. And this also has implications for a theory of
youth culture which is grounded in the main political and economic realities of adolescence.

On patriarchy and adolescence

It was only with the advent of a fully-fledged feminist perspective
into the field that some of these issues began to be taken up, both
theoretically and practically. Inevitably, the main focus of the fem-

inist critique has been on the overwhelming gender blindness of youth research. Several decades of work by male social scientists had done little or nothing to challenge the popular view that youth was boys being boys, usually in the street, while girls went on practising being little wives and mothers somewhere else, usually indoors, where from this vantage point they were both out of sight and out of mind.

Much of the emphasis has therefore been on establishing the autonomous rationale of girls' cultures (especially that of working-class girls) as a form of resistance both to the brutal sexism of male peer groups, and to the patterns of gender typing and discrimination built into the educational system and the labour market.[26] Girls' transitions and adolescent roles have been shown to be constructed along quite different lines from that of boys, and these differences are sometimes asserted to cut across class divisions as well. Some feminists have argued that the youth question itself is so implicated in patriarchal assumptions that it can only be addressed from a sexist standpoint. In any case, given the continuity between girls' and women's culture, and the close link between mothers and daughters, common bonds of gender override generational difference, so that the youth question is an irrelevance.

Other feminists, whilst endorsing much of this critique draw the opposite conclusion. To understand how patterns of sexual domination/ subordination are both reproduced and resisted, they argue that it is necessary to look at their processes of generational transmission. Moreover it is important for girls to fight against the pressure which might either infantilise them or lock them into a position of chronic maturity from an early age. Laying claim to a youth culture of their own is at least half the battle. All the more so, in so far as they find themselves trapped between contradictory discourses of adolescence and femininity.

Without entering into the details of this debate, it seems clear that the term 'patriarchy' (i.e. the rule of the father) by definition requires us to take account of both gender and generation, and to consider them in their interconnection. The simplest 'law' of patriarchy could be formulated as: male/female: adult/child, where the first term of each pair corresponds to a position of domination, associated with a variety of presumed capacities, and the second to a position of subordination linked to their presumed lack. Even this elementary structure throws more light on the youth question than taking either of the pairs on their own. Take, for example, the notorious double standard whereby boys split girls into two mutually exclusive categories – despised 'slags' and idealised 'virgins'. This seems to occur in cultures where boys, as children, are explicitly placed in a quasi-feminine position of subordination vis-a-vis male elders (e.g. elder brothers, fathers, uncles, elders in the community or workplace). Through various practices, sexual teasing, practical jokes, etc., the adolescent boy is shown up as 'soft like a girl' in order to provoke him into the counter-assertion of 'manhood and maturity'. In order to show that he is grown up, i.e. to move from the status of child to adult, the boy therefore not only has to distance himself from his mother, but to dissociate or suppress his own 'feminine side'. It is precisely that split structure of feeling which is projected back onto girls to fix them in the double standard, as either despised objects (whom anyone can have and no one therefore wants) or unattainable subjects (who are desired because they are nobody's baby, but hold out the promise of a mother's love). The sexual and economic power of male elders is thus not confronted directly; rather their role is assumed by the boy through a series of displacements of its terms, played out in relation to women.[27]

If this analysis is accepted, the issue now becomes whether this kind of patriarchal order is universal, or historically specific to certain types of society, whether it cuts across class-cultural divisions, or always takes on class specific forms. Again, without going into too much detail, it might be worth taking one concrete case in point – the cultural apprenticeships of working-class boys in modern Britain. Perhaps the first thing to stress here is the complementarity between its sexual and occupational forms. We noticed this in passing in discussing coster and artisan codes, but it can be spelt out in more detail.

Historically, youth labour has been massively concentrated in the distribution and service trades, and in labour-intensive sectors of manufacturing industry. If they have been confined to the lowest paid, least skilled positions within these sectors, this has nothing to do with any real qualities, or lack of them, which young workers may possess. It has everything to do with 'customary practice' in confining lads to fetching and carrying of goods, the servicing of clients or customers, or lending a helping hand to the adult worker. Sometimes all three were combined in the same job, sometimes there was a progression from one to the other, but the essential point is that boy labour was proto-domestic labour: it was modelled on women's work in the home. This was under-scored by the social relations of the workplace. The lad was expected to make the tea, run errands, sweep up and generally serve as a skivvy for the older men, whether he was officially 'mated' to one of them or not. He was also subjected to a good deal of teasing, often of a sexual kind, designed to show him up as 'soft' and 'incompetent' in various ways. All this was part of the initiation of the 'virgin' worker, something that had to be endured, in order to eventually 'make the grade' as a full-fledged workmate. Normally this would involve the 'apprentice worker' demonstrating that he was just as 'hard' as the older men (such as when it came to dealing with the bosses) as well as emulating their supposed sexual prowess with women.

Sexual apprenticeships complemented the occupational form. Indeed, in some trades the sexual initiation of the young lad was undertaken by an older woman, at work, egged on by her work-mates. Usually these women were unmarried, and regarded as especially unattractive by the men; certainly the initiation con-tained a sadistic element. In the second stage however the sexual apprentice 'got his own back' in exercising his new found mastery of technique, over younger, preferably virgin girls, who once, 'had', were relegated to the same 'slag bag' as the 'Big Berthas' of the first phase. Finally the 'sexual improver' would find a 'steady' and enter the phase of courtship – essentially a form of apprenticeship to marriage and to the role of the 'family man'.

The system could be summarised as follows:

Sexual apprenticeship	*Occupational apprenticeship*
1. The initiation of the virgin boy by an older woman.	1. The 'feminisation' of the virgin worker who is 'mated' to an older man.
2. The practice of sexual mastery over younger girls.	2. The counter-display of 'hardness'.
3. Going steady, the apprenticeship	3. Making the grade as a

of courtship to marriage and the 'family man'. workmate amongst 'the men'.

It is clear from this that the linkage between certain techniques of masculinity and manual labour was forged from a radical *disavowal* of the feminine status assigned to youth by the generational division of labour. An *imaginary* sexual division is used to maintain real inequalities between youth and adult labour. Perhaps this will seem less bizarre when it is realised that under the traditional apprenticeship system, both official and informal, old workers directly handed on to youth the very skills which would enable the new generation one day to replace them; moreover, employers often used youth labour to dilute skilled work or bid down the adult wage. On both counts the young worker might be perceived as a threat. Add to this the fact that the relationship between 'instructor' and apprentice was very like that of father and son, and the sources of oedipal tension become all too apparent. How was conflict to be minimised? Through rituals of initiation which displace the terms of conflict with elders into non-antagonistic forms. In the process, boy labour is kept in its quasi-feminine place, as a 'generic' instance of incompetence and unskill. In addition, the resulting wage (by age) differentials serve the interests of capital, cutting labour costs and providing a reserve army of youth labour.

However, none of this would be necessary or possible were it not for the peculiar way in which skill is constructed within the class culture – not so much a socially achieved practice as an inherent property, at once a birthright and legacy, 'something you grow up with', which 'runs in the family' or 'in your blood'. Growing up working-class has for many meant an apprenticeship to such an inheritance – a patrimony of skill entailed in the body and its techniques, forging a quasi-congenital link between origins and destinies. This can make occupational succession seem almost mandatory, with each generation of workers holding its job in trust for the next; at the limit it can mean that children are only recognised by parents as so many chips off the old block – the son is told he has a footballer's feet, a carpenter's hands, his uncle's appetite, his grandfather's chin, etc.

There is, however, something of a tension between the two codes. For what is construed under the code of apprenticeship as a sign of active appropriation, under the code of inheritance appears only as a principle of passive reproduction and this has customarily been 'resolved' through the mediation of cultural forms which treat everything outside the body and its apprenticeships as belonging to an alien sphere, outside the boundaries of kith and kinship established by the class inheritance. In particular it was through symbolic forms of territoriality that the sense of being 'working-class born and bred' was invested with a positive ethnic dimension; at the same time this form enabled working-class boys to disavow aspects of their feminine positioning by projecting it onto properties associated with other despised cultures – for example, Asian cultures.

This example answers one question – working-class partiarchy *does* have distinctive features which are not found elsewhere. But it raises another even more difficult question concerning the relation between social and psychic reality, between real relations of reproduction, and their unconscious representation.

You might expect this to be the province of social psychology, but you would be wrong. This discipline traditionally concerns itself only with the surface structures of social interaction and conscious belief. Thus for example, social psychologies of adolescence seek to demonstrate that self-image is directly related to social status; ethnic minority or working-class youth are consequently held to suffer from a 'poor self-image'. Equally the achievement of economic independence is equated with greater emotional independence from parents. We already had cause to question that association in discussing the impact of youth unemployment on growing up. Perhaps we should now add: there is no necessary correspondence between positions within the psychic economy of a particular phantasy system, and positions within the capitalist economy. There is, however, a complex and variable relation between these two 'sets', a series of mappings of one onto the other, involving various kinds of transformation (displacement, condensation) between the two. Some of this was glimpsed in the discussion of sexual and occupational apprenticeships. Certainly no one should assume that because the reality principles of this system of socialisation have broken down, the pleasure principles attached to these subject positions have lost their power to animate social relations. They most certainly haven't!

Social psychology in so far as it gives a sociological gloss to developmental psychology brackets out all this. Even the 'individualism' of adolescence remains taken for granted in most accounts – certainly it is not connected either to the behavioural ideology of the market economy, or the mechanisms of defence mobilised by the psychic economy of the divided self. No theory which remains premised on a static model of individual/society is likely to engage this issue, or to explain how a particular set of social divisions converge to split the subject in a particular way at adolescence.

Psycho-analysis and 'youth'

It is here that the revolutionary character of psycho-analysis should appear. For here we have a theory and practice devoted to understanding the language of the divided self. The ego is not taken at its own (high) evaluation, but treated as the flimsy social construction of an imaginary identity, to paper over the emotional cracks opened up by structures of difference. Psycho-analysis sets out to de-centre the subject, to shatter the ideological premises of individualism. This is one reason why it has held such a fatal fascination for middle-class intelligentsias, who live by a highly individualistic code, and long to transcend it. Nevertheless many of the stock-in-trade ideas – the feminine position of boys, the persistence of infantile structure in adult life, the presence of the parent in the child – retain their power to subvert common-sense views of 'growing up'. In particular they challenge what might be called the Whig interpretation of life history, the notion that growing up is a process of progressive enlightenment in which the subject moves from a state of childhood innocence or ignorance, to the eventual wisdom (or cynicism) of old age. More than a trace of this model can be found in sociologies of youth where transition is seen as a one-way process – the transition from school to work, or childhood to adulthood. Freud's concepts of regression, compulsion to repeat, and transference, show that model up for what it is, an example of retrospective wish fulfilment, a convenient adult myth. Psycho-analytical research properly requires us to abandon the notion of transition, in favour of the notion of *transposition*.

This is a more dialectical construct of the life-historical process – the unconscious mapping of past positions onto future ones as the basis for (mis) recognising the present in the very moment of consciously going beyond it. Certainly we need some such concept if we are to delve beneath the surface structures of the life course, and its 'autobiographic illusions' so as to engage with a more hidden curriculum vitae.

How is it then that psycho-analytical ideas have been so easily and so widely dismissed by sociologists of youth? One reason is that in discussing adolescence, psycho-analysis has revealed all its weaknesses and limitations, and almost none of its strengths. It is almost as if the theoretical advances that have been made in understanding the 'other scenes' of childhood are thrown out of the window as soon as adolescence is reached. No wonder Anna Freud called adolescence the stepchild of psycho-analysis!

To some extent this was inevitable. The discovery of infantile sexuality had as one of its immediate consequences the dethronement of adolescence; for puberty was no longer the start of sexual life, it was now seen as merely a stage between its infantile and adult forms. But this is where the problems started. In attempting to specify the significance of adolescence, psycho-analysis fell back on the recapitulation theory of Stanley Hall. Ernest Jones explicitly formulates a 'law' in which the adolescent replays in a heightened form, the early oedipal dramas of childhood. Against Freud's own model of sexuality this recap is invested with a predetermined developmental aim – to establish the primacy of genital hetero-sexuality over the earlier oral, anal and polymorphous phases. Anna Freud argued that this required that the truce between the ego and the id established during the latency period is upset to make room for the growing libido. Hence the emotional storms and stresses of adolescence came to be seen as a normative stage of development. Indeed, their *absence* is a sign of disturbance. The 'model' son or daughter is refusing to grow up, and is probably suffering from an overrepressive superego consequent on having a father whose word is law but whose presence continually incites its transgression.[28]

Psycho-analysis, or at least a certain version of it, has helped to popularise the notion of adolescent 'storm and stress', and in some cases (e.g. amongst the professional middle classes) to normalise it. There is, however, considerable evidence that 'pop-psy' has probably done more harm than good in the field of family relations. It has, for example, tended to strengthen certain forms of parent disavowal, viz. 'adolescent rebellion – it's just a phase you're going through' and much the same thing has been said about various kinds of youth movements. But even when such simple-minded applications are ruled out there is quite a lot wrong with the psycho-analytical theory of adolescence.

First, it assumes that adolescent conflict is necessarily focussed on family relations. But clearly there are many families in which, for various reasons, this is not the case. In working-class cultures, for example, oedipal patterns are displaced and organised through peer group forms to a large extent. Thus you can look at family interactions and find nothing remotely like the classical Freudian picture of adolescence. The Jewish middle-class family is another matter! And that's the point. Psycho-analytical accounts have largely ignored the importance of cultural and historical variations in family forms, and consequently tend to view its own construction of adolescence as a universal – or at least as universal as the patriarchal order.

Second, by setting up genital heterosexuality as the normative goal of all psycho-sexual development, not only are all other sexual practices treated as perverse and infantile, but the Whig interpretation of life history is, as it were, allowed in by the back door, and a door marked 'Men Only' at that.

To this scenario is added another equally dubious one – that of development as recapitulation. Undoubtedly this is a false extrapolation from the form which transference necessarily takes in the course of psycho-analytical treatment (including the phenomenon of repetition compulsion) to a general model of life history which reduces it to a simple reiteration of its repressed moments. How then to explain the fact that in certain forms of adolescence there is such a heightened sensitivity to time, to the discontinuities of past, present and future, that a special generational identity anchored to a particular historical conjuncture becomes possible? There is always *more* to adolescent identifications than the repeat of childhood infatuations, or the mourning for lost objects!

This diachronic weakness in psycho-analytical theory is, ironically enough, linked to its therapeutic method. Helping disturbed adolescents by freeing them from the compulsion to repeat neurotic patterns of the past, has largely been about uncovering childhood positions upon the assumption that once these are unfrozen, the process of 'growing up' will take care of itself. Thus the *shifters* between positions have remained largely unexplored, or else they are treated in a wholly uncritical and decontextualised way. Psycho-analysis's own markers of maturity in fact bear a strong resemblance to those of the inner-directed middle-class men who make up the bulk of the profession and its clientele. These developmental norms, drawn in varying combinations from the codes of vocation and career, are given a special ontological status, against which all other cultural formations are judged and found wanting. This is especially true of the (largely) American school of ego psychology, which has focussed on the treatment of disturbed adolescents. For ego psychologists the task of adolescence (and of adolescent counsellors) is to adapt instinctual drives through a process of cultural sublimation and social learning, to the roles and reality principles of the dominant society. The raw adolescent is thus cured (rather like ham) as the divided self is re-integrated into a unitary culture and society, belonging, in this case, to White Middle America.[29]

The most elaborate version of this model is to be found in the work of Erik Erikson.[30] Here the notion of development as recapitulation is carried to its logical – and some would say absurd – conclusion. Erikson is most famous for his emphasis on the adolescent identity crisis; but this is part of a larger, more ambitious theory which attempts to map out the epigenesis of the life cycle, and to locate it in terms of the culture and ideology which it reproduces. According to this model, each developmental stage is organised around a specific crisis, which can be resolved either positively or negatively. The subject position achieved at one stage lays the foundation for the way in which the next stage will be negotiated. Finally the polar outcomes that unfold through the life cycle (e.g. trust/mistrust, integrity/despair, etc.) represent a condensed statement of the cultural and ideological parameters within which the individual is formed.

For all its apparent sophistication this model pushes the theory of psychosexual development in the direction of a one dimensional teleology which Freud's own concept of over-determination precludes. Although Erikson shows a welcome sensitivity to cultural and historical mediations, the way he treats them effectively denies the relative autonomy of psychic reality itself. Instead, we are taken back to the view that each culture produces a 'basic personality structure' corresponding to it. Erikson has simply added a diachronic perspective and insisted more vigorously on the normative function of developmental crises, especially those of adolescence. But while there are definite historical and social patterns in the recognition and distribution of adolescent disorders (e.g. the narcissistic neuroses and schizophrenias have replaced the anxiety neuroses and hysteria of Freud's day) still there is no simple aetiology which rules that all Jewish boys suffer from Portnoy's complaint! What is decisive, and what Erikson leaves out of his account is the way the subject is positioned within a field of desire. This is not something that can be read off from cultural norms, but is, rather, a function of the way these norms are reworked within a particular family phantasy system. Yet how this grid of unconscious representations invests cultural markers of im/maturity remains quite unclear in Erikson's model.

In the USA psycho-analysis quickly became integrated into the self-improvement industry. Freud, it seems, had simply found a new way to turn the Jewish nightmare into an Interpretation of the American Dream! In Britain ego psychology, and its later variants such as 'transactional analysis', found a formidable adversary in the work of Melanie Klein and the 'object-relations school'.[31]

The early implantation of her ideas and techniques into educational and remedial settings (child guidance clinics, social casework, therapeutic communities for maladjusted children and young offenders) has ensured that Kleinian theories have developed within the straitjacket of an orthopaedic framework, and this has had certain effects. First, the focus of the theory on the earliest infantile subject positions (or object-relations) has resulted in little or no attention being paid to adolescence. Winnicott, for example, can analyse the 'transitional objects' of three-year-olds with great subtlety and clarity, but when it comes to fifteen-year-olds he can only see in youth culture a search for the lost teddy bear, or, in the peace movement, a desire to return to the breast! Finally, even if theoretically, the British psychoanalytical movement has stood against the 'social adjustment' bias of ego psychology, in practice, by virtue of its institutional setting, it has been forced to establish 'good' working relations with medical and judicial agencies whose primary function is repressive normalisation.[32]

As a result of these vagaries, many Marxists have been inclined to dismiss the whole psycho-analytic enterprise as either diversionary or reactionary nonsense. It seems the dreams and phantasies of the Young Proletarian have nothing to do with Narcissus or Oedipus; they are nothing but the mistranslation of class demands into the language of sexual desire – a special kind of false consciousness s/he will grow out of with a little help from dialectical materialism! Feminists have often been equally dismissive, in claiming that Freud failed to go beyond the patriarchal structures whose inner forms he excavated; psycho-analysis simply mistranslates women's desire into the language of male assumptions.[33]

A lot of these criticisms are not without foundation. Pyschoanalysis has often treated quite normative features of subordinate or minority cultures as pathogenic. Equally, any challenge to the 'law of the father' has been all too often dismissed as either an adolescent phase to be outgrown, or, if it persists, as a sign of neurotic fixation. Nevertheless I would argue that just as the classical sociologies of youth have bequeathed us a set of problems that will not go away by ignoring them, so psycho-analytical theories of adolescence show us the need to avoid certain traps rather than abandon the field to those who do not even see them. The trouble is that once you have decided to throw the baby out with the ideological bath water, it is not very easy to pay much attention to the adolescent with acne.

Someone who did, and who tried to bring Marxism and psychoanalysis closer together in the process, was Wilhelm Reich.

Freudo-Marxism, the family and the new frontiers

Wilhelm Reich was a hero of the 1960s counter-culture, hailed as a pioneer of body therapy, a guru of sexual liberation and intrepid explorer of the mysteries of the orgasm. Few people knew about his previous work in Germany and his attempt to introduce a new kind of sexual politics into the working-class movement there. Yet this was his real innovation. The 'Sex-Pol' movement as it was called, attempted to win working-class adolescents away from the Hitler Jugend, and towards involvement in the socialist youth movement, by running programmes of sex education, discussion groups, and other cultural activities in what today would be regarded as an exercise in mass conscious-ness raising. Reich was one of the few people on the Left to recognise that fascist ideology, especially its authoritarian and militaristic elements, had a deep-seated popular appeal, espe-cially to German youth from the lower middle and working class. He set out to both understand and combat the mass psychology of fascism. For his part he was expelled from the German Communist party, and ostracised from the psycho-analytic circle centred on Freud. What was so heretical about his project that it led to this double excommunication? His 'crime' was the very attempt to connect the fields of Marxism and psycho-analysis, and to apply their concepts in a practical form to the problem of working-class youth; for in doing so he exposed the failure of both theories to engage adequately with the cultural conditions and subjective factors behind the rise of fascism.[34]

Reich's thinking on the youth question was based on his analy-sis of the forms of sexual oppression in capitalist society. For him it was the structures of the bourgeois family, and the wider forms of patriarchal authority, which inculcated a guilt-ridden attitude to sex in the young. Alienated sexuality reinforced the exploita-tion of alienated labour, leading young workers to identify with the repressive authority of teachers, employers and political leaders, rather than to struggle for a freer sexual and political order. Reich was especially interested in the role of paramilitary and religious youth movements in perpetuating what he called the compulsive sex morality. He argued that their unconscious appeal to adolescents lay in the fact that they provided a set of defence mechanisms against the powerful sexual drives unleashed by puberty. The uniforms and drills clothed the adolescent body in a rigid 'character armour', while the ego was dissolved in an oceanic feeling of belonging to the mass, of being part of some-thing 'bigger' than the self, on condition of remaining in perma-nent subordination to 'elders and betters'. Rituals of initiation and other symbolisms of membership maintained this allegiance by fixing cultural sublimations to a collective ideal embodied in 'the leadership' and reinforced through various forms of peer group self-policing. Part of the appeal of the Hitler Youth, for example, was the promise of autonomy and even 'adventure' it offered to young people whose lives were otherwise heavily circumscribed. Yet this was a freedom which was encouraged only in so far as it supported the hierarchical structure which made it possible – the very formula of authoritarian populism.

To all this Reich sought to oppose an alternative body politics, based on the principles of what he called 'sex economy'. He argued that once libidinal energy was released from moral inhibitions or material constraints (e.g. poverty, overcrowding, ill-health), it would flow harmoniously into the struggle to build a new life-affirming culture and society. The task of psycho-analysis, transformed into a movement of mass therapy, was to loosen the moral blocks; that of Marxism and the workers movement to remove the economic privations. The more successful the sex-pols were at achieving the first aim, the more energy would be released for the second, and the more the living conditions of the working class improved, the better their love-making would become! Youth were potentially in the vanguard of struggle on both fronts: given the strength of the adolescent's sexual drive and the forces of bourgeois society pitted against its free expression, Reich saw German youth as the 'natural allies' of a libertarian socialism which recognised and responded to their needs.

Reich's optimism, and many of his preoccupations strike us as naive and old-fashioned today. Some at least of sex-pols demands, e.g. for free contraceptive advice and for abortion, have been realised; despite the efforts of Mary Whitehouse and her ilk, the kind of 'sex is a dirty secret' puritanism which pre-war adolescents were up against is a thing of the past. It has been replaced by positive celebration of 'proletarian sexuality' through the medium of Rock culture. Yet none of this has led to any growth of socialist consciousness. Quite the reverse. It has proved wholly consistent with the maintenance of both patriarchy and capitalism, giving the first a 'progressive gloss' and the second an added dimension to its forms of consumerism. Moreover, the emergence of the feminist and gay movements have given sexual politics a direction which Reich would almost certainly have opposed. If things did not turn out quite the way Reich expected, this tells us more than that he was just a man of his time'. For his conception of sexual politics was based on a reading of Marxism and psycho-analysis which was fundamentally flawed, and which was being actively opposed from a *progressive* standpoint within each school of thought even during the inter-war period.[35]

The method of Marx and Freud, Reich argued, had in common the fact that they were both 'materialists'. For him this meant in the first case that a society's superstructure (politics, ideology, culture) reflected its economic base (class relations) and in the second that personality structure reflected the infrastructure of instinctual drives (sex relations). In other words, an economistic model of class consciousness was added to an equally 'economistic' view of desire, reducing the former to a mere expression of relations of production and the latter to a bio-energetic system of sex drives. In the process Marx's theory of ideology and social reproduction was jettisoned, along with Freud's theory of phantasy and unconscious representation. For these possible but complex linkages Reich substituted his simple notion of 'character analysis' whose main object of study was to be the imprint of 'class conditioning' on the body. It was the positivistic model of causal determination which Reich applies to this 'bio-sociology' which led him to so disastrously overestimate the political effect of 'sexual liberation'.

There simply is no one-to-one correspondence between political and sexual practices. Some anarchists might have disturbed sex lives, some authoritarian personalities shed their 'character armour' in bed. Homosexuals and lesbians are to be found across the political spectrum. But it was not only his positivism which led Reich to make such facile connections. It was also due to the almost mystical role which he assigned to orgasm. The orgasm was as central to his orthopaedics of sexual technique as it was to his Utopia of 'wish fulfilment'. Here genital primacy ceases to be simply a tendency of sexual development, and becomes, in the form of 'orgastic potency', an index of both societal and individual health. The myth of the 'good' orgasm was born, and along with it the completely unwarranted assumption that good orgasms made good socialists! En passant (but it is far from an innocent move) an image of 'natural sexuality' is created, a sexuality which is not only free and uncorrupted by social inhibitions, but is not socially constructed at all. For the good orgasm only happens when character armour dissolves and 'culture surrenders to nature'. Counterposed to all this we have the 'bad orgasm' and 'unnatural sex', alias the mass neurosis and perversion of bourgeois society.

These kind of polarities are not only falsely premised, but lead
to quite reactionary conclusions vis-a-vis sexual politics. Certainly
Reich's vision of sexual liberation seems to leave existing gender
roles curiously undisturbed, and this is surely because he saw
repressed sexuality rather than gendered oppression as being the
primary motor of social change. Freud himself had no such illusions. He always maintained that the libido was highly conservative in its object choices; thus the satisfaction of sexual desire was
no more likely to make revolutionaries than its frustration. On
this reckoning, the power of adolescent sexuality might send
young people off in search of cultural sublimations, including
those offered by various political parties, but that in itself changed
nothing as far as the psychic structure was concerned. Indeed, it
ensured the maintenance of what Freud called the 'narcissism of
minor differences' on which so much displaced ideological
conflict is based.

Reich's theoretical apparatus was quite unable to deal with
questions of this complexity. But his was not the only kind of
'Freudo-Marxism'. Another, more sophisticated variant was simultaneously being developed in Germany by the Frankfurt School of
Social Research. They built on precisely the elements which Reich
jettisoned – Freud's metapsychology and cultural analysis; Marx's
sociology of knowledge and ideological critique. Less directly concerned with the youth question as such, their research has nevertheless proved far more fruitful for its investigation.[36]

The main focus of this research was on the new social and cultural forms thrown up in the transition from early to late capitalism and, in particular, the changing patterns of authority in the
family. It was clear even in the 1930s that the kind of patriarchal
structures on which Freud based his analysis of the oedipus
complex were already breaking down. When Father's word is no
longer Law he may cease to be a rival for sons, or an ideal for
daughters, and the peer group itself may increasingly fulfil this
function. At the same time, the consciousness industries (fashion,
music, etc.) exploit the blurring divisions of gender and generation by introducing their own brand of 'polymorphous perversity'
into popular culture. Advanced capitalism no longer wins consent
via the work ethic, but in terms of new pleasure principles which
ally self-gratification with particular commodity forms. While the
decline of the Father has made oedipal positions more difficult to

sustain, the rise of consumerism has elaborated a whole 'culture of narcissism' around pre-oedipal positions.[37]

There is broad agreement within the Frankfurt school on the general terms of this analysis; much less so on its political implications. Are these developments opening up a progressive life-style politics in which hitherto disenfranchised groups, such as young people, women and gays are playing a vanguard role? Or do they represent a retreat from the kinds of commitments and values on which the struggle for socialism depends? The pessimist tendency detects behind the genital facade of contemporary sexual practice a profound psychic regression, a flight from feeling in favour of an auto-erotic style of individualism, especially on the part of men. The counter-cultures of the 1960s exemplified this development, but subsequently it has increasingly penetrated into working-class cultures as well. The optimists, led by Thomas Ziehe, argue that much of this critique is sour grapes, a refusal to recognise that a new field of social contradiction and struggle has emerged outside the classic 'Marxist' sites of production and the state. The old politics dominated by authoritarian personalities and patriarchal forms is dying, along with the 'old' working class. But they point to the emergence of the peace movement and ecology parties (especially strong in Germany) to indicate that the new style libertarianism is capable of throwing up and sustaining its own organisational forms.

The ins and outs of this debate are perhaps best reflected in the work of Herbert Marcuse, the most famous 'export' of the Frankfurt School, another of the heroes of May '68 and all that. In *Eros and Civilisation* (1955) he is arguing for the abandonment of the reality principles of 'western civilisation' in favour of a new moral universe where work is transformed into play, where Narcissus and Orpheus are reinstated, and Oedipus and Prometheus dethroned – a culturalist version of Reich's erotic utopia. The Hippies, for a time, seemed to him to prefigure this, but by the end of the 1960s he was beginning to have second thoughts. Although he never embraced the pessimist analysis, he introduced the concept of 'repressive desublimation' to explain the peculiar ease with which the new pleasure principles and the old profit motives had been reconciled. And this notion was taken up and developed into a much more fully-fledged critique of certain kinds of cultural politics on the Left.

The main problem with the Frankfurt School is that most of their analyses, even the more substantive ones, ride at a very high level of generality. They often 'totalise' their critique of society on the basis of very selective evidence, and sometimes their results just do not add up. The youth question as such remains an epiphenomenon, albeit a highly symptomatic one. Yet they have succeeded in developing a critical approach to understanding the links between political socialisation, cultural change and structures of subjectivity which avoids the reductive materialism of Reich, in favour of a dialectics of history and the unconscious centred in the family.

In the last few years the articulation of Marxism and psychoanalysis has shifted into rather different ground – that of language, largely due to the influence of structuralism, and in particular the work of Althusser and Lacan.[38] According to this school of thought, ideology has no history, but is a compulsive repetition of certain structures of misrecognition embedded in discourse and ritual. Equally, the unconscious is no longer a repressed preverbal phantasy system, but a chain of signification structured like a language; it is the Discourse of the Other. Under the patriarchal order, Lacan argues, the place of the Other is occupied by the father as the bearer of a code which lays down the law of sexual difference.

Suprisingly, there is no discussion of the fact that the symbolic authority of the father is also founded on a system of generational relations. The phallocentric reading which Lacan gives to the construction of sexuality stems partly from his blindness to this other dimension of patriarchy. At the same time the family is reduced to a set of subject positions within a field of desire and its representations. Kinship structures, demographic regimes, strategies of social reproduction are deliberately ignored. Moreover, there is little room within this framework for the elaboration of a diachronic perspective, for a consideration of the *shifters* between positions and how they are encoded. Partly these blindnesses are the result of Lacan's determination to rescue the vision of psychoanalysis from its distortion as a therapeutic support for the 'American way of life'. And it is certainly the case that the subversive character of the Freudian theory of the subject is bound up with a topological model of the Unconscious which has invariably been sacrificed whenever attempts have been made to convert it into a psychology of human development.

Yet both the materialism and the dialectics of the analysis suffer when it is confined to a purely synchronic model of the psyche. This is a point made strongly in Timpanaro's critique of what he sees as the implicit idealism of the Lacanian approach.[39] Psychoanalysis, no less than a certain version of Marxism, is accused of having systematically ignored the primordial facts of birth, puberty, ageing and death. The basic co-ordinates of social existence change much more slowly than techniques of production or even state forms. They are not easily amenable to rapid social engineering such as five-year plans. They form the substrate of human experience in all societies, albeit one our own society thinks it has succeeded in controlling, only to forget all the more easily. Timpanaro's work emphasises precisely those dimensions of reproduction which Lacan ignores. Unfortunately in his anxiety to rescue Marxism from its structural marriage to psychoanalysis, he tends to fall back on a purely biological model of the life cycle, as a quasi-natural sequence of stages. The fact that different cultural paradigms of the life cycle fundamentally affect the way these stages are lived, is something with which a Marxist theory of reproduction and a Freudian theory of the subject must continue to grapple if they are to cohabit the same universe of discourse to productive effect.

The terms of that arrangement may indeed need renegotiating to emphasise the relative autonomy of the two partners, but there are some alternative approaches to looking at the family and the youth question which at least hold out this possibility. The first is centred on a macro-historical analysis of family relations in the transition to capitalism.[40] This body of research is beginning to show that the systems of apprenticeship and inheritance which regulated the position of youth in pre-industrial Europe did not simply dissolve into thin air with the supercession of artisan and peasant production. Rather they underwent a complex transformation in the context of transitional modes, linking forms of pre-capitalist industry to pre-industrial capitalism. One system of putting out (of surplus children as apprentices and servants to other households) was replaced by another (the capitalist putting out work to the family). This kind of cottage industry effectively transformed the whole family into wage labourers, who rented the means of production from the capitalist, and were paid for the finished product. Children could now earn their keep and more-

over no longer had to postpone marriage until they became entitled to their patrimony. Youth labour was now wage labour as
well as domestic labour, and yet this transformation took place
within the shell of a patriarchal order which continued to apprentice young people to an inheritance. This no longer consisted of
land, or tenures, or customary rights, but a 'patrimony of labour'.
This set of family/wage/labour relations was then transposed into
the early factory system, where it served to confirm the authority
of the father over both women and children in the workplace as
well as the home. The protective legislation which excluded children, officially, from the labour market and confined them to
wageless dependance in home and school, not only instituted a
new division between childhood and youth, but between youth
and adulthood as well. For the elimination of child labour from
the casual, unskilled and ancillary jobs, simply created a demand
for their replacement by older youth, who could still be paid a
'child wage'. In this way youth labour was forced into the category
of cheap 'fetch and carry' or proto-domestic labour, in opposition
to both adult labour and the family wage. This position was culturally reproduced through codes of apprenticeship and inheritance linking family, workplace and community, constituting the
basis on which much of what we now know as 'the youth question'
developed.

It is a complicated history, with a multiplicity of strands, discontinuities and anomalies, and it is one which is only now beginning
to be unearthed. It certainly presents a very different picture to
that of Talcott Parsons, yet it is one on which Marxists and feminists, demographers and social historians can usefully collabo-
rate, even if they do not always agree.

The second line of enquiry opening up new frontiers is that of
life-course analysis.[41] This arose out of a growing disatisfaction
amongst family historians and sociologists with functionalist
models of the life cycle. They wanted a more dynamic model
which would relate the transition strategies of individual members
of the household to the changing economic and social circumstances in which they found themselves in different historical
periods. This developed into a wider-ranged enquiry into the links
and disjunctures between 'macro-historical time' (e.g. changes in
labour processes, institutions of schooling, etc.) and the 'micro-
social time' of the family and domestic life. How, for instance, did

the Great Depression of the 1930s not only affect the transition strategies of that generation of school children, but the course of their later lives? How did the lived experience of childhood poverty affect subsequent adult experience of 'the affluent society' of the 1960s? How are biographic constructs modified by historical events, and how do they in turn modify the perception of the past and the present at different stages of the life cycle? In exploring these kinds of issues, life course analysts are concerned with the interaction of two diachronic chains of events, one belonging to the family and the other to the wider society, and with how they intersect to structure the life histories of individuals and groups. Here is perhaps a more sophisticated way of posing the question of generation which avoids the biologism/ historicism of the classical models. Certainly in sensitive hands it is capable of yielding rich insights. For example, it shows that the extent to which youth is perceived to be an especially formative stage of life varies according to a) whether it coincided with particularly significant national or world events, b) the type of transition strategy adopted in the family and c) subsequent life-historical events. An obvious enough point, but one which has never been systematically taken up, and which certainly gives the lie to those who argue that adolescence 'fixes' adult values in chronic moulds.

The third and final approach seeks, in a sense, to give an added dimension to the other two.[42] It stems from the work of oral historians who in the last decade have collected a wealth of autobiographical material, especially about childhood and youth, from groups who have hitherto been hidden from history. Until recently this material was simply regarded as providing documentary evidence about the lives, labours and loves of ordinary people ignored by the official archives. How things 'really were' amongst the working class. Yet this material raises issues which even life-course analysis has not begun to address. It is clear, for example, that these oral testimonies are constructed according to a very different narrative grammar from those deployed in the written autobiographies of the 'famous'. There is also a very complex and hidden relationship between the speaking subject (i.e. the old person who is telling their life story) and the spoken subject (e.g. the 16-year-old whose first romance is being recounted). In other words there is a set of unspoken subjects at work in generating these texts, organised into what we might call a hidden curriculum vitae; this hidden curriculum vitae weaves a web of associations between past, present and future, selecting and combining memories, phantasies and perceptions according to a set of underlying motifs. It is already clear that these motifs are normally drawn from certain strategic family representations which have the function of confirming a sense of positive identity, or life-historical continuity. But where do they come from? Freud is already waiting in the wings with a suggestion – the family romance.[43]

By the family romance Freud refers to those 'fairy stories' which children make up about parents or other members of their family, in which they play imaginary roles as heroes or villains in a larger-than-life drama. Later, in adolescence, film stars, rock idols, etc., will play a similar function in embodying, whether positively or negatively, the ego ideals of the culture. Yet the family romance is equally present in those other fairy stories spun by parents or grandparents about 'the uncle who made his fortune in America' or 'the sister-in-law who eloped with a rich businessman'. All these family narratives are the raw materials from which autobiographies are fashioned. Yet at the same time they have a peculiar ideological function in establishing relations of imaginary kinship with other classes. Thus it is possible to read a whole hidden history of class-cultural negotiation across these texts which speak in the language of the ideal self. Here, surely, is a rich field of study in which the methods of psycho-analysis and Marxist historiography can be most usefully combined to shed new light on the 'other scenes' of childhood and youth.[44]

Yet this is not exactly a new project. Already in the 1930s Walter Benjamin was applying the methods of cultural materialism and psycho-analysis to a reconsideration of the questions of generations.[45] In the Arcades Project, he approached the question from the standpoint of his theory of technology and the collective dream. He suggested that each generation, in its own childhood, seizes hold of the technology and material cultures produced by its predecessors, and reworks them in play and phantasy so that they conjure up imaginary visions of the future as well as of the past. It is on the basis of these childhood visions which are carried into adulthood that a new technology is born, and this in turn provides the raw materials with which a new generation can dream and eventually make the future out of its own past. This brief summary does scant justice to the subtlety of Benjamin's argument, still less to the poetry of his prose. But it may well be that it is Benjamin, rather than Mannheim, or Reich, or the other more orthodox Marxists of the Frankfurt school, who turns out to have most to say to a generation which has discovered the world of the micro-computer and the video arcade.

Rethinking the youth question

In taking a line of thought through this maze of theories, I have been less concerned to find 'Ariadne's thread' (i.e. the one and only correct line) than to illustrate through a number of examples some of the traps and deadends to which they sometimes lead. We started by looking at the classical models of unitary subjects in unified social systems (the biologistic/historicist reading) and went on to examine models of unitary subjects in divided societies (classical Marxist or feminist sociology) and of divided subjects in unitary societies (psycho-analysis). All these models were found to be inadequate for the purpose of rethinking the youth question, nor was some simple combination of them, a la social psychology, likely to deliver the goods. I suggested that the failure of Marxists and feminists to engage with the theoretical issues raised by Mannheim, Parsons and Stanley Hall had two consequences – it opened up a space for the new minotaurs of sociobiology and psycho-history to rephrase the classical reading of the youth question in even more reactionary terms – and strengthened the hand of 'ego-psychology' in the treatment of adolescence. Instead, we need to construct a model of multiply divided subjects in a multiply divided society; I tried to outline some of the terms in which a new collaboration between psychoanalysis and historical materialism might now be possible. I argued against the search for some 'Archimedean' point of reference beyond them, insofar as this led only to the idealist problematics of discourse analysis and semiology a la Foucault and Barthes. En route, as it were, I tried to show that the main intellectual premises on which current youth provision rests had little or no foundation. Young people did not constitute a unitary social category, even though 'youth' might be constructed as a singular site of state intervention or moral discourse. The notion of adolescence as ideologically formative and/or 'normally rebellious' had more to do with wishful thinking than concrete analysis. The idea that youth unemployment was of itself, causing an identity crisis amongst working-class youth, or that there was some simple correlation between the different forms of autonomy and dependance was criticised. The short case studies which I used in making this critique tried to exemplify a different approach – one based on a *differential* analysis of the youth question, and the *relative autonomy* of its instances.

This does *not* refer to some presumed ontological status of adolescence, as a half-way house between the absolute dependence of infancy and the absolute autonomy of adulthood. For a start, the notion of 'absolute autonomy', far from characterising adulthood, in fact belongs to those infantile phantasies of omnipotence which are first constructed as a defence against the recognition of helpless dependence on adults. The relativisation of these subject positions may be a worthy goal to aim at, it may even correspond to what Durkheim called 'organic solidarities' generated by an advanced division of labour. But it most surely is not the special prerogative of any developmental stage – certainly not of adolescence in the contemporary 'cultures of narcissism'. Rather, the relative autonomy of the youth question is founded on a *structural* principle – the relative autonomy of the political, economic and ideological structures of capitalist society. It is the discontinuity between these structures which poses the youth question as a specific instance of their articulation; this takes the paradoxical form of creating the conditions of an imaginary unity out of the real divisions which distribute young people to different social locations.

How do the discontinuities manifest themselves? First, in the different *places* to which 'youth' is assigned, for example as a category of labour, or popular discourse, or protective 'under-age' legislation; as a sexed child within the family romance, or a citizen pupil of the 'educational state', or a collective worker. There is no necessary or pre-given correspondence between these places – it has to be constructed through specialised practices.

Second, there are discontinuities in the structuring of *time*. For example, empty homogeneous clock time, the time of capitalist production, with its simple opposition between labour time and free time, may organise much of everyday experience, especially for those locked into the alienated routines of factory work or housework, but it is too impoverished to give meaning and direction to a life time. So also is its counterpart in bodily time, the chronic repetition of sexual tension and release, or the diurnal rhythms of waking and sleeping. Between these two tempi, and interrupting them, are other principles of duration: the cyclical time of generation and the seasons continue to rework the irreversible time of biological ageing to punctuate family time into phases. The reversible time of autobiography and popular memory ceaselessly plunders the conjunctural time of historical events to weave its own motifs of meaning. If youth has been constructed as such a dangerous time and place, it is because here so many conflicting principles of periodisation and predicament collide. Yet there is nothing random or arbitrary about this process; it is patterned in highly determinate ways.

The youth question is the site of a singular nexus of contradictions. Youth is simultaneously constituted as a place and time of marginality and powerlessness *and* as the bearer of a whole series of special symbolic powers. As a legal subject-form within a patriarchal order youth is a category of disqualification, a mere locus of lacks. But as a commodity form, manufactured by the consciousness industries, youth is a veritable cornucopia of desirable properties. The first position generates a discourse of proverbial wisdom – in which 'youth has its fling', 'old heads are placed on young shoulders'. The second places youth within a discourse of 'modernity' in which it is always and already 'the new', 'making history' only on condition that it transcends all historical determinations. The same pattern of contradiction embraces the youthful body, either strait-jacketing it within a rigid framework of 'proper dress, deportment or discipline' or alternatively, inciting or exciting the pleasures of adolescent sexuality.

In some social contexts, and some cultural forms, both modes of positioning are simultaneously present, trapping young people in a system of double binds. Equally the two modes may come into direct conflict, as for example in the struggle between 'improving' forms of rational recreation, and the 'devils music', rock'n'roll. Some times youth cultures mobilise the 'law of the father *against* the laws of capital and state, as in the case of practices of territoriality. Here the construction of imaginary kingdoms of youth (mis)rule feeds off and reinforces real positions of powerlessness. Certainly the marginality of youth within the official body politic tends to sponsor a rival 'body politics' centred on a culture of adolescent narcissism, which in turn even further alienates young people from organised politics.

Up until very recently this pattern of contradiction has been largely conjunctural for boys, part of a transition phase between childhood and adulthood. For girls, in contrast, it is structural; the patriarchal order traps them for life between a position as little wives and mothers, and as desirable objects who must remain eternally young if not eternally virgin. However, this may be changing. Girls are increasingly caught up in a conjunctural bind, between the discourses of adolescence and femininity. And boys may be facing a more structural crisis, as they are impelled ever younger into the arms of youth culture, while their entry into the adult labour market is more and more postponed. In the case of students and other sections of middle-class youth this may not represent much of a problem, since their culture allows for an extended adolescent moratorium. But the contradiction becomes all too acute for sections of black youth, at the other end of the social spectrum, who find themselves pushed permanently onto the economic scrapheap, while their cultures are praised, and ransacked, for their 'vitality'.

The singular contradiction thus takes a multiplicity of forms, and affects actual groups of young people in different ways. This fact is implicit in the notion of 'relative autonomy'. The youth question, I have insisted, is never not an issue of class, gender and ethnicity, but it poses these issues in a quite specific form. In my short case studies I suggested what this might consist of. In advanced capitalist societies, the distinctions between class cultures remain, and they remain based, in the last instance, on the fundamental division between mental and manual labour. But the forms in which that division is reproduced have changed, become more complex and fragmented, and they are no longer explainable solely in terms of the occupational structure or the educational system.

Class differences are now reproduced *indirectly* as different principles of articulation of gender, generational and race relations. In other words, class positions are rarely registered in a simple unmediated form (e.g. in the conflict between capital and labour) they are lived through a series of non-class positions which they invisibly connect and inflect *at the level of cultural reproduction.* Moreover, we have to deal not just with real relations of reproduction (e.g. demographic regimes or wage labour forms) but with the imaginary relations through which they are lived and symbolically represented. In other words – *reproduction codes.*[46] These codes constitute the subject positions through which contradictions, divisions, discontinuities, come to be experienced as their opposite – as the support of unitary categories and stable identities.

Each code weaves a web of imaginary correspondence between the disparate places and times occupied by the subject, throwing a distinctive grid of periodisation and predicament over the life cycle. In so far as this grid remains intact, a sense of life-historical continuity can be maintained in the face of even the most disjointed circumstances. For in constructing such an identity, each code fixes subject positions to certain paradigms of knowledge and power, as well as to retro-prospective markers of im/maturity. The code thus constitutes a synchronic grid of positions and a diachronic grid of 'shifters' between them.

The shifters constitute a chain of 'first times', or formative moments associated with specific objects or practices. For example, the first steps, the first cigarette, the first time you have sex, or leave home, the first wage packet and so on. These first times are formative but they are not necessarily traumative. In so far as they are embedded in normative sequencing rules, the markers become the focus of remarkable events, and as such constitute the building blocks of autobiography, and in particular of the family or peer group romance. Yet, however individually they are registered, there is nothing individual about their construction. They are culturally encoded, and vary according to gender, class and ethnicity. Unfortunately this micro level of life-course analysis has been singularly neglected. It is important here to stress that markers are reversible. What signifies being grown-up at one life-historical moment, becomes a sign of retardation at the next. (You're not *still* into dollies you're nearly five! Look at John, he doesn't even know how to ride his bike!) The markers become normative through a mixture of adult and peer-group pressures, and as such they index the ego or peer-group ideal to specific practices of mastery. Traditionally, these were focussed on techniques of the body, but increasingly they also involve a range of consumer technologies as in the series: tricycle, skateboard, BMX bike, motorbike, car. Such strings of markers not only engender the formation of specific peer-group generations, they can become landmarks for historical generations as well. For example, the division between the video game generation and 'Dungeons and Dragons' generation. At the same time the meaning of generational markers varies according to how they are encoded; for example, within the grid of working-class apprenticeships video games become the support of manual dexterities but under the middle-class code of career they are the source of mental fun and games. Here is a major focus of cultural innovation, as each generation recruits new objects and practices, fashions new markers to replace others which have become or been made redundant. In the age of hi-tech consumer capitalism, there is an increasing element of planned obsolescence built into the codes of cultural reproduction.

The study of reproduction codes is just beginning. At a macro-historical level, it involves mapping class-cultural struggles in terms of shifting lines of conflict and negotiation between different codes in specific sites of reproduction, e.g. family and educational regimes, ideological apparatuses, discourses, etc. This will be a history, and not an archaeology, because what is being unearthed are the deep structures of cultural hegemony, and the principles of resistance to them in specific conjunctures. While at a micro-social level, a theory of codes potentially enables us to delve beneath the conscious surface of life-plans or autobiographic narrative, to engage with a more hidden curriculum vitae, whose structures of recognition belong to Freud's 'other scenes'.

So far, four basic reproduction codes have been identified: inheritance, vocation, apprenticeship and career; their institutional configuration, and symbolic orders are currently being investigated from a number of angles.[47] The main principles of articulation are depicted in the schema shown in the figure on p. 229.

In this schema. the outer circle describes the class-cultural articulation of the codes as these have been historically sedimented in specific paradigms or referential models of socialisation. The inner grid maps the lines of tension or transformation between symbolic orders at a micro-social level. Thus each quadrant represents a matrix of subject positions and cultural forms within a particular

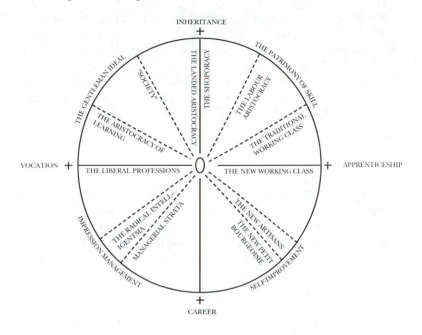

field of class reproduction. As positioning devices, codes may operate with varying degrees of normative strength, from strong (+) to weak (0). In the construction of referential models, one code usually furnishes the synchronic grid of positions (S), and another the diachronic shifters (D). Where there is a strong combination of codes, the same grid of representation governs all contexts of reproduction, and there is basic homology between family, sexual, educational, recreational, occupational and political forms. At the micro level strong codes provide stable identities (and differences) while strong combinations generate points of strong tension between the synchronic and diachronic orders *and* mechanisms for resolving them. Weak grids are another story. Here class cultural transmissions are fragmented, and social identities may be stabilised. A minimum condition for the existence of any class culture is a strong grid operating within its strategic site of reproduction (e.g. for the traditional petty bourgeoisie, within the family, and for the new middle class within the state education system) and it is here that the decisive struggle for the hegemony of its code over other configurations will take place.

The history of these articulations is clearly one of uneven and combined development; a given class culture will yield a different profile, a different pattern of code distributions, in different periods, and different places, reflecting both local relations of force and specific conjunctures (of historical compromise, accommodation, etc. with other codes). Perhaps the most interesting case is where a class culture weakens to the point where it splits up into its component codes; this may result in a new principle of internal differentiation, or its elementary structures may disintegrate as they are pulled along both the horizontal and vertical axis toward 'the zero point' where they may lose their independent existence, and be subsumed under rival codes. Yet this zero point is pregnant with other possibilities, for it is here that bricolage flourishes, and new cultural forms are thrown up, as symbolic elements from all four codes are selected and combined according to a pure semio-logic (of representation), unconstrained by socio-logistics (of reproduction). This needless to say is the space of youth cultures![48]

The symbolic orders of inheritance and career, or vocation and apprenticeship lie at opposite poles in terms of the subjectivities they construct. However, their incompatabilities have not precluded some 'marriages of convenience' as well as 'domestic conflict' ending in divorce. The history of popular education could, for example, largely be written in terms of the shifting pattern of conflict and alignment across both these axes. Initially, in the elementary school, relations between teacher and pupil continued to be modelled on those which have traditionally obtained between master and apprentice; it was only with the professionalisation of teaching and the introduction of new ways of measuring the pupil's performance against a developmental scale of age-graded competences, that the code of career could be said to have 'arrived'. Equally the liberal ideal that the school should enable the child to realise his or her inner potential for creative self-fulfilment, testifies to the independent strength of the vocation code within certain educational sub-regimes, its power to resist a popular fatalism concerning those who are 'born with brains' and those who 'congenitally' lack them. Nevertheless this code has only survived within the dominant ideology by becoming thoroughly instrumentalised, and in effect subsumed under the grid of career (i.e. vocationalism).

There are, inevitably, many situations in which young people find themselves caught between two contradictory structures of recognition belonging to rival codes. Most typically this occurs where the child or pupil is driven to climb the academic ladder because recognition is made dependent on the achievement of certain incremental norms of productivity (e.g. of speech, schoolwork, etc.), while at the same time his or her progress continues to be measured against certain fixed ascriptive categories of gender, race or class. The contradiction does not usually tear people apart because it is rationalised in terms of those who are 'born to succeed' and those who are 'bone idle'. In families it can be a different story. For example, where one parent points the child towards a social destination whose ambitions are quite different from the fixed 'destiny' recognised by the other parent, where consequently the hidden messages of career and inheritance codes are relayed through a system of conflicting parental injunctions (become what you strive to have *versus*. belong to what you always and already are) then a chronic double bind is inevitable. And there are certain moments in the social history of particular groups, for example, amongst socially mobile ethnic minorities, where this kind of thing frequently occurs; this is *not* because of any 'pathogenic' features of the culture, but because a conflict *within the host society* (i.e. between its code of possessive individualism, and its code of ascription) has penetrated certain family positions.

Although the study of reproductive codes is still in its infancy, it is also beginning to shed light on some of the ideological terms through which the 'discovery of adolescence' was made possible in the discourse of 19th-century psychology. Stanley Hall's theory contains the following elements: a) a model of history as the unfolding of an evolutionary process, moving step by step up a ladder of developmental stages, so that both individuals and societies can be ranked on a hierarchical scale of greater or lesser civilisation; b) a model of psychological growth in which the individual is 'congenitally destined' to repeat a fixed series of historical stages of social development in order to lay claim to its legacy of civilisation; c) a model of adolescence as a period of spiritual searching and emotional turmoil governed by a quest for both new experiences and lost certainties.

It is clear, then, that Hall's psychology of adolescence is constructed through a process of bricolage drawing on three codes.

His model of history is a transcription of the career code, but this in turn is transformed via a grid of inheritance to produce the notion of 'recapitulation'. Finally, the figure of the adolescent is fashioned in terms of the vocation code, with its paradigm of the life cycle unfolding at the imperious bidding of an ideal inner self, and its search for an authentic calling. In effect the grid of vocation mediates between the other two in combining an older sense of youth as a period of 'careering about' entertained by the aristocracy, with a newer sense of a 'moratorium' between child and adult phases of a bourgeois career. Paradoxically, an image of adolescent 'storm and stress' was produced out of this 'historical compromise' between the two leading cultural codes.

Yet there would always be points of tension between the vocation grid with its eternalisation of the adolescent quest, and the other codes which give youth a purely transitional status within a much more rigidly bounded framing of the life cycle. Today, for example, the career code and to a much lesser extent inheritance, continues to organise oedipal rivalries and give them an 'economic' function within the dominant culture; but at the level of the hidden curriculum vitae where the 'narcissism of minor differences' and pre-oedipal positions hold sway, the vocation code supports the growth of bohemian subcultures to be found in the elite art colleges and other finishing schools of the 'jeunesse dorée'. Meanwhile the psycho-drama of middle-class adolescence and its divided self, torn between the pursuit of an inner calling and the desire for public recognition, has become one of the staple ingredients of contemporary soap opera, most recently, and entertainingly, in the confessional diaries of one Adrian Mole!

So far we have considered only the left-hand side of the model, concerned with dominant ideologies of formation. But what of those who grow up on the other side of the tracks?

I suggested earlier that the 64,000-dollar question for anyone who wanted to get into the next round of the Generation Game was this: how has the decline in the political cultures of the manual working class, and the rise of structural youth unemployment affected the formation and outlook of non-student youth? Armed with this model of reproduction codes can we do any better than Tory futurologists, and Socialist impression managers? I have tried to show that until recently growing up working-class took the form of an apprenticeship to an inheritance; it involved a strong combination of these two codes, spanning familial, occupational, recreational, sexual and political practices and organising them into a single normative grid. This was, however, something of an ideal type, and was usually found only in occupational communities; elsewhere strong combinations were found in specific sites – for example, in family or recreational contexts rather than generalised through the class culture. The stronger and more extensive the grid, the more working-class boys experienced growing up as a process of progressive mastery over a fixed chain of quasi-congenital predicaments, and the more closely knit the successive positions of dependence and subordination occupied by girls. Thus one of the essential conditions for 'strong' class-cultural transmissions was the reproduction of a strong patriarchal order. As the latter has weakened so also has the former. Growing-up-working-class has become more a matter of growing up/working/class; the hyphenations on which a taken-for-granted sense of social identity depends are increasingly being broken, as the chain of associations between growing up and working and class are harder to sustain. But this is not just the material effect of youth unemployment on school transitions; it is about changes in the codes of cultural reproduction.

At one extreme the codes of apprenticeship and inheritance pull apart to constitute separate cultural forms. Where apprenticeship is to and for itself, youth ceases to be a transitional stage and is promoted to become a central reference point of the whole life cycle. In this case boys may be able to identify positively with certain aspects of their feminine positioning (instead of disavowing it) while girls may be freer to construct territories of desire quite independently of the peer group romance. But they can do so only in so far as they also dissociate themselves from fixed class positions synchronised through the code of inheritance. The resultant youth cultures offer new kinds of apprenticeship, especially in the sexual and recreational spheres, but they do *not* involve a search to retrieve some lost inheritance of struggle – that is a middle-class paradigm belonging to the vocation code, which is often projected on to them with disastrous effects.

There are, however, other possibilities. Youth cultures, for example, act selectively on codes to sometimes strengthen an otherwise weak combination. Most dangerously this can lead to the active racialisation of constructs of ethnicity associated with certain working-class codes. Especially where the transmission of cultural patrimonies is broken – whether through blocked transitions or family strife, racist discourses do provide a surrogate form of political apprenticeship into an imaginary 'lost' inheritance of kith and kin. The links between origins and destiny is thus restored via a sense of pride in belonging to a 'biological' community of labour whose territories are then staked out through a more or less violent body politics on the streets of the working-class city. This is a pattern largely confined to boys, because it depends precisely on mobilising structures of disavowal embedded within the 'strong' form of working-class masculinity.

For working-class girls, however, weak grids open up other more hopeful patterns of response. For example, elements of the family romance may be conserved but dependence on boys minimised. Mothers may still be strongly identified with, but their steps are not necessarily followed as far as the kitchen sink. In some cases, this may lead to a pattern of early pregnancy followed by setting up independent single-parent households. The pressure on unemployed girls to remain at home as unpaid skivvies is especially intense, so single parenthood offers one solution, offering both adult status, and some of the freedom traditionally associated with youth.

The third main pattern is where elements of working-class codes are incorporated within middle-class ones and vice versa. At the level of life-historical grammars this chiefly occurs through the medium of social mobility and the various kinds of individualism associated either with its achievement or with blocked aspirations. As increasing numbers of working-class children stay on into further education to avoid the dole, and as new regimes are introduced to skill them in various techniques of impression management, the pattern of code shifts is likely to become central to any understanding of ideological outcomes.

Already two tendencies can be detected. Where the incremental grid of career effectively subsumes that of apprenticeship, the transition from manual to mental cultures is likely to be relatively unproblematic. It is not likely to sensitise young people to class contradictions and their political attitudes are likely to remain individualistic and instrumental. In contrast, where the axis of code shift is from inheritance to vocation the relationship between social origins and destinies is likely to become a special

object of perception. The shift from a grammar in which the body
is constructed as the bearer of quasi-congenital messages to one
where the inner self functions as the voice of existential imperatives is likely to produce a highly charged expressive orientation
to a range of personal and political issues.

'Youth' unemployment

The case which finally has to be made for rethinking the youth
question is that it will help to clarify contemporary issues of youth
policy and provision. So let us return to the question of youth
unemployment.

It has often been argued that long term unemployment is constituting a new social stratum, an underclass, whose conditions of
existence prefigure a working class without work, and mark the
shape of things to come.[49] It is suggested that the long-term
unemployed are not only permanently marooned between school
and work, but that working-class apprenticeships and inheritances
have disintegrated to the point that they have been replaced by
purely statutory markers of im/maturity. In this context traditional labourist prescriptions – a return to full employment,
improved education and youth services, are not only unrealistic,
they are irrelvant. Instead the unemployed should be socially and
culturally waged, as well as politically enfranchised, through a new
apparatus of provision which is democratically controlled and
truly responsive to their needs. These suggestions must be taken
seriously, but we need also to think whether they do actually correspond to the way unemployment is actually experienced.

One of the implications of the kind of model I am arguing for,
is that unemployment will be experienced very differently according to whether it is lived through strong or weak grids of apprenticeship and inheritance, not to mention how its meaning will be
constructed through middle-class codes of vocation or career. To
take the working-class case first. It is clear that strong grids will be
found in certain types of community (e.g. occupational communities, single industry towns) and certain types of families (e.g. those
with a tradition of occupational succession). In these cases jobs
are still regarded as being held in trust by one generation for the
next; there will be fierce struggles to preserve trades and industries as a legacy to hand on to the children, and strong resistance

to selling jobs in return for productivity deals or redundancy payments. All sections of the community will, and have, been drawn into these struggles, including young people and the unemployed. Even though school leavers may never get apprenticeships or even jobs, they find themselves being politically apprenticed to the inheritance of struggle. At the same time strong grids make it possible to shift more easily from occupational to recreational modes, so that unemployed youth may be quite highly motivated to master a progression of new 'social and life skills' related to leisure pursuits, under the tutelage of 'old hands'.

New markers of maturity may be improvised, and new kinds of cultural apprenticeship carved out of older traditions. For example, the migration of many unemployed youth to seaside towns, where they lived in boarding houses and drew supplementary benefit, was an improvised, recreational variant of a traditional stage in a young persons working life, where the apprentice left home and lived in 'digs' preferably in another town. The young people who populated the 'costa del dole' had found a way of enjoying some kind of domestic autonomy which did not depend on the wage; but few of them had any illusions about its function. It was for them a transitional stage, a temporary stratagem, a means of growing up working-class without work, not a permanent way of life based on some Utopian pleasure principle.

This is only one side of the picture, the good news. The bad news is that strong communal grids generate a strong collective conscience centred on generational continuity; any break in this, especially in the transition to work, will be experienced as an exclusion from its 'body politic'. Young people in these areas are under much greater than normal pressure to find decent well paid work, and will feel more than usually depressed and worthless if they are unsuccessful. This tendency will be exacerbated if they have grown up in family cultures where life-historical messages are anyway transmitted in a confused or contradictory way. For then the ego ideal, which normally connects personal aspirations to those of class and community, will be correspondingly weak; at the slightest rebuff the adolescent beats a retreat into his or her ideal self, and/or a family or peer group romance which has become merely wishful thinking. Unfortunately this in turn leads to renewed feelings of guilt, as the dream world is shattered by a purely internal, but no less punitive voice of the 'collective conscience'. Young people in this position oscillate between magical private solutions, and self-blame.[50] They are very difficult to draw into involvement with other people around struggles to change or improve their lot. To be a member of a weak grid family in a strong grid community is to have the worst of all possible worlds.

Where the communal grid is weak, I suggested that the codes of inheritance and apprenticeship become highly polarised and produce insulated but experimental youth cultures, and insular/reactionary parent cultures. In so far as the youth cultures find a material base in the hidden economy they may offer one solution to blocked transitions. For in weak grids, unemployment is more easily associated with youth in a way that makes them both, if not equally desirable, then at least regarded as a permanent rather than temporary state: an apprenticeship to an apprenticeship. There is now no longer any need to grow up, working is for mugs, and class is pure style. However, even in its extreme form, the kind of mobile individualism which is now emerging amongst the most immobilised sections of unemployed youth is quite different from the response of the middle classes. For the graduate on the dole unemployment may be read as an extended adolescent moratorium, offering opportunities to set out in search of authentic selves, even to do a bit of 'careering about'. Some still expect to eventually get a professional job. But many are increasingly rejecting the career code, especially graduates from working-class backgrounds. They are combining elements of vocation and apprenticeship codes, alternative ideology and manual skills in a new, creative synthesis. These new artisans are as different from the hippies as they are from the old labour aristocracy. Yet from their ranks are to be found new sources of leadership, especially in inner-city areas where many of them are to be found in community organisations, co-ops and projects for unemployed youth. They offer strong 'global' grids in place of weak local ones. For this stratum, then, unemployment has been the stepping stone to alternative work. Ironically enough, this may give the ambitious few a leg up back onto the professional career ladder.

A final note on two key aspects of youth unemployment: gender and time. This analysis would suggest that the position of working-class girls is exactly the opposite of boys. They are 'better off' under weak grids as this gives them more cultural and existential room to improvise their own markers of maturity outside the domains where they are merely a prop to wounded male narcissism. For the problem of male youth unemployment within the culture of manual labour is that it hits below the belt in two places at once. Within these cultures unemployment is all too easily experienced as an emasculation – one of the more hidden injuries of class. And it forces the feminine positioning of boys vis-a-vis male elders all too abruptly to the surface of consciousness. Result: a defensive reassertion of existing macho practices. In strong-grid communities, with high levels of male youth unemployment, rules and rituals of territoriality tend to relay this reaction, and there may be an increasing level of street violence. Where territoriality comes home, the streets are quieter, but the level of male violence against women increases. In the case of weak-grid families in strong-grid communities, the result is an *implosion* of rage, leading to a range of self-destructive behaviours. Once again the pattern of youth provision must be geared up to respond more sensitively to the variety of experience to be found within working-class communities.

Time is a crucial dimension of unemployment, although one which is singularly neglected by social scientists. Is it the case that the unemployed measure out their lives, if not with coffee spoons, then with giro cheques? Do their dependent relations to the state lead them to set their clock by statutory definitions of time, as before workers were supposed to measure their lives by the rhythms of capitalist production? I think not. Amongst the young unemployed people I have interviewed it is however clear that there is a strong correlation between the meaning of 'the dole' and their sense of time. Where apprenticeship is enclosed in on itself, everything becomes very present tense, and people can live from day to day with some optimism and without feeling too overshadowed by a sense of permanent redundance. In contrast, where the code of inheritance becomes impacted on itself it throws a grid of chronic repetition over the whole life cycle and induces a profound sense of fatalism. The immediate present seems to stretch endlessly into the future, which is always and already the same as the past. It may, however, be possible to mobilise other kinds of time, the cyclical time of family life or sporting seasons and fixtures to impose other, more meaningful principles of periodisation on the predicament of unemployment – albeit ones which usually conserve existing gender divisions. It is clear then that what counts as short- or long-term unemployment varies considerably. What is long-term in one grid is short-term in another. One person's paradigm may be another person's poison.

The point of identifying the meaning of youth unemployment within a broader framework for understanding different life cycle paradigms is not simply a theoretical one. There can be no adequate youth policy which does not take into account other ages and stages of life and the ways they are changing. A failure to do so results in policies which reinforce the dominant ideology of ageism, and maroon young and old alike in ghettoised structures of provision. The current situation in which the state is institutionalising the youth question within a narrow framework of '16 to 19' training, whilst at the same time youth cultures are stretching at both ends to accelerate transitions from childhood and postpone entry into adulthood is one example of the kind of problem which can only be tackled practically from a standpoint of a life cycle politics informed by a theory of reproduction codes.

Perhaps the main reason for rethinking the youth question is to enable us to enable us to engage with these wider issues. But that in turn means abandoning the pervasive 'youthism' which continues to characterise most policy and practice, and whose intellectual and bio-political premises I have tried to trace in this chapter.

Notes and References

1. Paul Willis (1990) *Common Culture* (Milton Keynes: Open University).
2. Dick Hebdige (1988) *Hiding in the Light* (London: Comedia).
3. J. Bynner (1988) *Young People – Employment, Culture, Identity* (London: ESRC).
4. See Robin Cook, 'Why Labour needs kidology' in the *Guardian*, 9 December 1983, and the overview by David Smith, 'The Labour Party and youth policy' in *Youth and Policy*, 1, 2. For an historical analysis of the problem see Chapter 8 in this volume.
5. The debates on the political implications of structural and cultural change within the working class has, unfortunately, not begun to embrace the youth question. See, for example, M. Jacques and F. Hobsbawm (eds), *The Forward March of Labour Halted* (London, 1981), G. Stedman Jones, *Languages of Class* (Cambridge, 1983) and

Raymond Williams 'The end of an era' in *New Left Review*, 181. All of these contributions take the process of political socialisation for granted, as either a quasi-automatic process of cultural transmission or the inert effect of of political ideology. In this respect these studies have scarcely advanced beyond the crude readings of empiricist social science, which reduce political socialisation to the influence of political parties, the mass media or family traditions on voting behaviour. For a discussion of this field see T. Tapper and B. Salter, *Education and the Political Order* (London, 1978).

6. Much of what follows is based on material presented to my research seminar at the Institute of Education (1985–7). I am especially grateful to my students for their many helpful comments and criticisms.

7. One of the best critiques of Stanley Hall and Social Darwinism is to be found Carol Dyehouse, *Girls Growing Up in Late Victorian and Edwardian England* (London, 1981). See also the overview by John Springhall, 'The origins of adolescence' in *Youth and Policy*, 2, 3. Unfortunately the author of *Youth, Empire and Society* (London, 1977) does not here explore the connections between Woodcraft ideology and adolescence in the rational recreation movements or juvenile literature of the period. But as readers of *Wind in the Willows* can testify, the connections between taming the wildness within (Toad's adolescent passions) and civilising the wildness without (the proletarian 'jungle' inhabited by stoats and weasels) could be made most directly in the hunting and gathering of Good Deeds, preferably in the Great Outdoors. On this point see Norbert Elias, *The Civilising Process* (Oxford, 1994) (Vol. 1) and also E. Dudley and M. Novak (eds), *The Wild Man Within* (Pittsburgh, 1972).

8. Mannheim's classic text 'The problem of generations' appears in *Essays in the Sociology of Knowledge* (London, 1952). In Britain his influence on the sociology of knowledge has been far greater than on the sociology of youth. One notable exception is the work of the late Philip Abrahams. See 'Rites of passage – generational conflict in industrial society', reprinted in *Historical Sociology* (London, 1982). In Germany, Mannheim's influence was quickly eclipsed by that of the Frankfurt School (see note 32). For a good critique of Mannheim's historicism see J. Hood Williams, 'The problem with the problem of generations' (mimeo).

9. See Parsons, 'Age and sex in the social structure of the United States' (1942) and 'Youth in the context of American society' (1963), which, despite the 'particularism' of the titles, attempt to develop a general sociological model of youth. The most detailed application of Parsons' framework is to be found in S. N. Eisenstadt, *From Generation to Generation* (London, 1956). For an overview of this approach see D. M. Smith, 'Structural-functionalist accounts of youth' in *Youth and Policy*, 1, 3 (1983) and for an account of recent research within this problematic see L. Rosenmayr and R. Altenbeck, 'Youth and society' in *Current Sociology*, 27, 2–3 (1979).

10. The influence of sociobiology is paramount in the work of Peter Marsh on football ends, territoriality, and other aspects of male working-class youth culture. See *his Rules of Disorder* (London, 1976) and *Aggro* (London, 1979). For an alternative explanation of these phenomena see Chapter 3 in this volume. For a general critique of sociobiology see Lucy Bland 'It's only human nature', *Schooling and Culture*, 10 (1981).

11. Psycho-history draws its inspiration from the early work of Erik Erikson, and in the 1970s produced a spate of studies of childrearing practices in middle- and upper-class families in Europe since the 16th century. Perhaps the best of these is David Hunt's *Parents and Children in History* (New York, 1972). In cruder hands, e.g. Lloyd de Mause's *History of Childhood* (London, 1991), we get an obsessional detailing of early toilet training and anti-masturbation devices coupled with speculations about their effect on adult personality. Much psycho-history still depends on the old 'culture and personality' models of Mead and Kardiner in the 1940s. All this must be distinguished from the methodology of Aries and the French *Annales* school, where changing structures of feeling in parent/child relations are always analysed in terms of the social totality, political and economic realities, etc. For an overview of psycho-history see T. Rabb and R. Rotberg (eds), *The Family in History* (Cambridge, 1971), especially the essays by Kett, Kenniston, Hareven and Demos.

12. In addition to the work of Peter Marsh (see n. 10) perhaps the most florid example of 'back projectionism' is to be found in two early American anthologies edited by Louise Adelson: *The Universal Experience of Adolescence* (Chicago, 1964) and *Juvenile Delinquency for a 1,000 Years* (Chicago, 1966).

13. See George Duby, *Warriors and Peasants* (London, 1975). There *is* an interesting chain of association between the initiation practices described by Duby, the ritual enactment of 'Wild Man' cults, and the youth abbeys described by N. Z. Davis in *Society and Culture in Early Modern France* (London, 1975), but it will not be best traced by lumping these forms into a residual category as 'traditions of youth misrule'.

14. This is broadly the argument of Lewis Feuer in *The Conflict of Generations* (New York, 1978). The best account of German youth politics in the interwar period is still W. Laqueur, *Young Germany* (London, 1962). The most detailed account of the rise of *Hitler Youth* is given by H. J. Kock, in the book of that title (London, 1975). A good source book on the American student and hippy movements of the 1960s is C. Adelman, *Generations* (London, 1973); a critical reading of this material is to be found in C. Lasch, *The Culture Narcissism* (London, 1980).

15. Both the early attempt by F. Musgrove, *Youth and the Social Order*, (London, 1964) and the more sophisticated project of J. Gillis, *Youth and History* (New York, 1974) flounder on the unresolved relation between demographic regime and cultural practice in determining

changing forms of class reproduction. Sometimes demographic change becomes the sole motor of youth history; elsewhere it is linked to a principle of 'stratified diffusion of ideology' (or, what student youth get up to today working-class youth will do the day after tomorrow). Neither adequately locates youth history in a specific field of struggle, viz. between conflicting strategies of reproduction. For an alternative model see W. Secombe, 'Marxism and demography' in *New Left Review* 137 (1983). Also from a non-Marxist perspective see J. Kett, *Rites of Passage* (Chicago, 1977). The most sophisticated account is to be found in M. Mitterauer, *A History of Youth* (Oxford, 1992).

16. For example, the forms of truancy documented by Steven Humphries in *Hooligans or Rebels?* (Oxford, 1981) can all too easily be abstracted into a 'transgenerational' continuum of resistance to schooling. This is exactly what occurred in the TV programme by History Workshop with the same title. Local oral history projects rarely address the theoretical problems involved in constructing a valid inter-generational framework of comparison. For a critique of this see E. Hobsbawm and T. Ranger *The Invention of Tradition* (Cambridge, 1992).

17. It is the overwhelming virtue of Geoff Pearson's *Hooligans – A History of Respectable Fears* (London, 1983) that it unravels the various ideological threads in the civilising mission to youth as it crystallised in the 1880s, even though the attempt to explain their principles of articulation falls back on many of the arguments criticised here.

18. The most influential exponent of settlement sociology in the post-war period was J. B. Mays, author of *Growing Up in the City* (London, 1954), *Education and the Urban Child* (London, 1962), *The Young Pretenders* (London, 1968). The Institute of Community Studies took its distance from his attempt to combine urban sociology with moral reform. See P. Willmott, *Adolescent Boys in East London* (London, 1966). David Downes' *The Delinquent Solution* (London, 1966) was the first to explicitly break with this whole approach.

19. Longitudinal studies have now gone out of fashion, largely because they take so long and cost so much to carry out. Moreover, although studies like those of J. W. B. Douglas *Home and School* (St Albans, 1973), *All our Future* (London, 1971) did offer a statistical snapshot of the distributive effects of class inequality at different moments in the life cycle, they shed very little light on the actual mechanisms of their reproduction, let alone on the sexual and generational relations involved. The latter were bracketed off in a series of studies spawned by the mid-1960s moral panic about the permissive society and teenage promiscuity. See E. and E. M. Eppel, *Adolescents and Morality* (London, 1966). M. Schofield, *The Sexual Behaviour of Young Adults* (Harmondsworth, 1966), D. J. Stephenson, *The Development of Conscience* (New York, 1966).

20. The extent to which cultural relations between skilled workers and the labouring poor hardened into these moral categories in late

Victorian Britain, and the reasons for it have been much studied and debated by social historians. See, for example, H. MacLeod, *Religion and Class in a Victorian City* (London, 1978); P. Bailey, *Leisure and Class in Victorian England* (London, 1978); A. P. Donajgrodzki (ed.) *Social Control in Nineteenth-Century Britain* (London, 1977). But from our point of view what is important is the way these intra-class divisions were connected with sexual and generational ones. What role did different types of youth provision play in this? How come that artisans *and* costers sons had their own exclusive territorial codes, whereas their sisters remained confined within protocols of public propriety? Did this double standard in defining rough and respectable sexuality also powerfully disenfranchise 'youth' within the body politic of the labour movement? This is a largely unexplored area, but for some preliminary remarks see Chapter 8 in this volume, and also the contributions of M. Bommes and P. Wright to R. Johnson (ed.), *Making Histories* (London, 1983). There is much interesting contemporary data on the relations of moral economy and political geography in R. Jenkins, *Lads, Citizens and Ordinary Kids* (London, 1983).

21. Previous theories reduced all kinds of working-class culture to the status of sub-culture, and sub-cultures to juvenile delinquency and street crime. The attempt to problematise these connections came from two directions: radical criminology (c.f. S. Cohen, *Folk Devils and Moral Panics* (London, 1973) and radical community studies. This project demanded that the relation between class and culture be thought beyond the prevailing Marxist base/superstructure model. As discussed in the Introduction to Chapter 2, this was accomplished with the help of Gramsci's theory of hegemony, Althusser's theory of ideology, and Levi-Strauss's concept of bricolage – a synthesis most fully realised in the work of the Centre for Contemporary Cultural Studies, and more especially S. Hall and T. Jefferson (eds), *Resistance through Rituals* (London, 1975). For an overview of this whole development see M. Brake, *The Sociology of Youth Culture* (London, 1980) and J. Mungham and G. Pearson, *Working Class Youth Culture* (London, 1976).

22. The shift towards the work of Barthes, Foucault and the post-structuralists is most interestingly observed in the work of Dick Hebdige. See his *Sub-culture: The Meaning of Style* (London, 1979) and *Hiding in the Light* (London, 1979). The distance between the semiology of style and the sociology of subculture can be judged by reading D. O. Arnold, *The Sociology of Subculture* (1970) as a contrast to Hebdige. For a review of the wider intellectual debates in the field of cultural studies see the contributions to T. Bennett *et al.* (eds), *Culture, Ideology and Social Process* (London, 1981).

23. There are important differences in reproduction theory between the correspondence model of education/economy developed by S. Bowles and A. Gintis *Schooling in Capitalist America* (1976), the relative autonomy model of Althusser's 'Ideology and ideological state appara-

tus' in B. R. Cosin (ed.) *Education, Structure and Society* (London, 1971) and the multi-level model of Bourdieu, *Reproduction* (London, 1981). The transition studies influenced by these models tend to emphasise the common structural features of working-class resistance to schooling, though for P. Willis, *Learning to Labour* (London, 1978) these are to be found in cultural forms, while P. Corrigan *Schooling the Smash Street Kids* (London, 1980) locates them in the role of the state.

24. A vast literature of empiricist transition studies has accumulated over the past twenty years. Most of it deals with the job placement rates and patterns of school leavers, and provides a snapshot of the current state of local youth labour markets, and/or the effectiveness of careers guidance agencies. An interesting and more critical approach is to be found in J. Maizels, *Adolescent Needs and the Transition from School to Work* (London, 1978). The growth of youth unemployment through the 1980s has produced a new 'generation' of studies in much the same vein, but now of course focusing on 'transitions' to the dole queue, the hidden economy and the performance of youth training schemes. The most comprehensive of these is K. Roberts, *Transitions into Labour Markets* (Sheffield, 1991). A critical review of this literature, together with an alternative reading of the economic and institutional changes it documents is to be found in D. Finn, *Training without Jobs* (London, 1987) and R. Holland, *The Long Transition* (London, 1990).

25. The family is central to the account of school transitions given by R. W. Connell in *Making the Difference* (Brisbane, 1980) and also to my case study of a group of school leavers in South London in Chapter 10.

26. For a general feminist critique of youth culture research see A. McRobbie, *Feminism and Youth Culture* (London, 1991). See also the chapter by M. Nava on the impact of feminism on youth work in *Gender and Generation* (London, 1984). For a feminist reading of schooling and girls' transitions, see R. Deem (ed.), *Schooling for Women's Work* (London, 1980) and D. Spender and E. Sarah, *Learning to Lose* (London, 1980). Also M. Stanworth, *Gender and Schooling* (London, 1983) and A.-M. Wolpe, *Some Processes in Sexist Education* (London, 1978).

27. For the debate on the status of the concept of patriarchy see V. Beechey, 'On patriarchy' in *Feminist Review*, 3. For a feminist reading of generational relations see D. Leonard's study of working-class families, *Sex and Generation* (London, 1980). See also the contributions to A. McRobbie and M. Nava (eds), *Gender and Generation* (London, 1984), especially the chapter by Barbara Hudson on 'Adolescence and femininity'. The best account of sexual and generational divisions in the labour process is A. Pollert, *Girls, Wives, Factory Lives* (London, 1981).

28. Freud's own model of adolescence is sketched in *Three Essays on the Theory of Sexuality* (Harmondsworth, 1982). His later topographic

model of the psyche is applied in Anna Freud's classic statement on 'Adolescence' in *Psycho-analytical Study of the Child*, Vol. 13 (1960), and is further elaborated on the basis of clinical evidence in P. Blos, *On Adolescence* (London, 1962). Aichorn's *Wayward Youth* (London, 1928) was an early and influential attempt to apply psycho-analytical methods to the treatment of delinquents, and was taken up in Britain in the context of libertarian models of schooling (A. S. Neill) and rehabilitation of young offenders (David Wills). A good summary of current orthodox views is to be found in M. Laufer, *Adolescent Disturbance and Breakdown* (Harmondsworth, 1975) and L. Steinberg, *Adolescence*, 3rd edn (London, 1993). By far the best psycho-analytic account is L. Kaplan, *Adolescence – The Farewell to childhood* (London, 1986).

29. The American school of ego psychology was founded by Ernst Kris and Heinz Hartman, with their renewed emphasis on the adaptive and reality-testing functions of the ego. Ego strength, as a criterion of health, rather than normality, plays a key role in the 'radical school' represented by Karen Horney and Abraham Maslow, whilst many of the key concepts of ego psychology are to be found in the culturalist theory of personality developed by Kardiner. See J. Kruger (ed.), *Discussions in Ego Psychology* (New Jersey, 1994).

30. The major texts of Erikson in this context are *Childhood and Society* (London, 1951) and *Identity – Youth and Crisis* (London, 1978). See also his essay in 'psycho-history', *Young Man, Luther* (New York, 1995). A useful critique of Erikson is to be found in M. Poster, *Critical Theory of the Family* (London, 1978).

31. The 'object-relations' school is primarily associated with the work of Melanie Klein, who was herself influenced by Karl Abraham and Sandor Ferenczi. See her *Contributions to Psycho-analysis* (London, 1948). Her ideas were developed in the work of Balint (c.f. *Thrills and Regression,* (London, 1965), and, above all, D. W. Winnicott who is the only one to pay any attention to adolescence, c.f. *Playing and Reality* (London, 1991) *The Maturational Process and the Facilitating Environment* (London, 1990) and *Deprivation and Delinquency* (London, 1984).

32. It is a paradoxical fact that the most politically radical members of Freud's circle were often the most reactionary thinkers in terms of psycho-analytic theory. Alfred Adler is a classic case in point. Equally revolutionary ideas in psycho-analysis could often be accompanied by reactionary political attitudes, as in the case of George Groddeck, or of Freud himself. Sometimes, of course, cultural conservatism could be directly expressed in psycho-analytic terms (Jung's theory of racial archetypes). Only in the case of Otto Fenichel and his circle did a concern with changing political and psychic reality coincide. See Russell Jacobi, *The Repression of Psycho-analysis* (New York, 1984).

33. Not all critiques of psycho-analysis have been put in such crude terms of course. V. W. Volosinov in *Freudianism: A Marxist Critique* (New York and London, 1976) states the case for a materialist semiology

over and against Freud's theory of unconscious symbolism. Georges Politzer in *Foundations for a Materialist Psychology* (London, 1971) queries the epistemological status of infantile experience as providing the basis for explaining adult behaviour, whilst more recently, from the standpoint of a libertarian 'anti-psychiatry', G. Deleuze and F. Guettari in *Anti-Oedipus* (London, 1984) have attacked the 'familialism' of psycho-analysis and its refusal to engage with the wider social dynamics of the unconscious. Feminist responses have been equally diverse, from radical lesbian dismissal to socialist feminist approval. See J. Mitchell, *Feminism and Psycho-analysis* (Harmondsworth, 1986) for an overview, and the contributions to J. Smith and A. Mahfouz (eds), *Psychology, Feminism and the Future of Gender* (Baltimore, 1994).

34. The essential texts of Reich produced during this period are: *Dialectical Materialism and Psycho-analysis* (1929), *The Sexual Struggles of Youth* (1932), *What is Class Consciousness?* (1933), *Essays from Sex Pol* (1934–37) and *The Mass Psychology of Fascism* (London, 1991).

35. The best overview and critique of Reich is to be found in Mark Poster *A Critical Theory of the Family*. See also the comments by Michel Foucault in *History of Sexuality* (London, 1981).

36. A good collection of readings from the Frankfurt School is to be found in P. Connerton (ed.), *Critical Sociology* (Harmondsworth, 1976). The major studies in this tradition dealing with the youth question are A. and M. Mitscherlich, *Society Without the Father* (London, 1974), R. Reiche, *Sexuality and Class Struggle* (London, 1970) and Thomas Ziehe, *Pubertat and Narziss* (Frankfurt, 1984), a seminal text which has currently still not been translated.

37. Students of the debate on narcissism should start with Freud's original (1914) paper 'On narcissism', Vol. 14 of the *Collected Works*. Christopher Lasch is the main protagonist in the debate; see *Haven in a Heartless World* (London, 1974) and *Culture of Narcissism* (London, 1978). See also, in similar vein, R. Jaccobi, *Social Amnesia* (London, 1978). The feminist critique of Lasch's position is developed in M. McIntosh and M. Barrett, *The Anti-Social Family* (London, 1983).

38. In the Frankfurt perspective the 'language of the unconscious' tends to be treated as an example of 'distorted communication' (Habermas, Willener) rather than on its own terms. For the structuralist Marxist reappraisal the key text is L. Althusser, 'Freud with Lacan' in *New Left Review*, 190. Lacan's own work is difficult to the point of obscurantism, but there are some much more approachable studies by some of his colleagues. See in particular M. Mannoni, *The Child, His Illness and the Others* (London, 1970) and F. Dolto, *Dominique – Analysis of an Adolescent* (London, 1974).

39. Timpanaro's critique of psycho-analytic methods can be found in *The Freudian Slip* (London, 1976) and an article on Freud's Roman Phobia in *New Left Review*, 147. His own standpoint is developed in *On Materialism* (London, 1976).

40. There is now a vast literature on family history. For our purposes the best introduction to the whole field is to be found in M. Mitterauer and R. Sieder, *The European Family* (Oxford, 1982), and from a feminist standpoint L. Tilly and J. Scott, *Women, Work and Family* (New York 1978). More specialist works on the pre-capitalist period are P. Laslett, *Family Life and Illicit Love in Earlier Generations* (Cambridge, 1977) and J. L. Flandrin, *Families in Former Times* (Cambridge, Mass, 1979). On the crucial transition period see H. Medick, *Industrialisation before Industrialisation* (Cambridge, 1981), D. Levine, *Family Formation in Nascent Capitalism* (New York, 1977) and J. Rule *The Experience of Labour in 18th-Century Industry* (London, 1981). For the 19th century see M. Anderson, *Family Structure in 19th-Century Lancashire* (London 1971). A fruitful combination of Marxist and feminist methods is R. Hamilton, *The Liberation of Women* (London, 1978).

41. An early approach to life-course analysis can be found in J. Roth, *Timetables* (Chicago, 1966). The historical approach was developed by T. Hareven and colleagues in *Transitions* (New York, 1978) and *Family Time and Industrial Time* (Cambridge, 1982). A longer-range view is given by J. Modell in *Journal of Family History* (New Jersey, 1976) and by J. Kett, *Rites of Passage*. The difficulty with much of this work is that it takes for granted that the symbolic order of career provides the one and only paradigm of the life cycle. The research by Daniel Bertaux into French bakery apprentices gives the lie to this, even if he tends to fall back on a bio-energetic model of labour power in the process. See his contribution to *Life Sentences*, ed. R. Harre (London, 1976) and also *Biography and Society* (Chicago, 1981). The best application of this method is still the work of Glen Elder, see *Children of the Depression* (Chicago, 1981) and *Children in Time and Place* (Cambridge, 1993).

42. There are now a number of useful historical studies of autobiography, for example A. O. T. Cockshut, *The Art of Autobiography in 19th-20th Century England* (New York, 1984) and C. Steedman, *Past Tenses* (London, 1992). For a pathbreaking critique of naive realism in oral history see P. Thompson and R. Samuel, *Myths we Live by* (London, 1991). There is also some useful discussion in K. Plummer, *Documents of Life* (London, 1983). An attempt to theorise the deep structures of life stories, as well as to assess their ideological function can be found in a double issue of the *Revue des Sciences Humaines*, 191/2 (1984). A significant attempt to analyse the distinctive discursive features of life features and autobiography can be found in P. Lejeune, *La Pacte Autobiographique* (Paris, 1979).

43. For Freud's note on 'the family romance' see the *Collected Works*, Vol. 12. The concept is developed by V. Walkerdine in 'Some Day my Prince will Come' in A. McRobbie and M. Nava (eds), *Gender and Generation*.

44. See, for example, the approach to autobiography combining the methods of oral history and psycho-analysis in R. Fraser, *In Search of the Past* (London, 1984).

45. The two key texts of Walter Benjamin are *One Way Street* (London, 1979) and *Illuminations* (London, 1976). These give a good idea of his methodology as well as of his luminous prose style. Unfortunately they do no more than hint at his thesis on generation, technology and the collective dream contained in the *Passagen Werken* (Arcades Project) much of which remains unpublished, as well as untranslated. My comments here rely on the presentation of this work by Susan Buck-Morss in her *The Dialectics of Seeing – Walter Benjamin the Arcades Project* (London, 1989).

46. The notion of reproduction codes used here is close to Bourdieu's concept of Habitus in so far as it designates the symbolic devices through which specific forms of cultural power or powerlessness are internalised within the deep structures of subjectivity. However, rather than focusing on the formal features and functions of cultural reproduction from a sociological perspective, the main concern here is to identify the principles of variation which characterise rival codes, and to write the history of their articulation.

47. E. P. Thompson, in his seminal essay 'The grid of inheritance' in J. Goody *et al.* (ed), *Family and Inheritance* (London, 1976), was the first to focus on the 'rules and practices whereby particular social groups project forward provision for their future'; to insist that the grids of apprenticeship, vocation and career were worthy of study, and that there was more to inheritance than the transmission of material wealth. Noelle Bisseret in *Education, Class Language and Ideology* (London, 1976) examines the internal symbolic orders of inheritance, vocation and career in the context of the educational system.

48. Within this new theoretical framework several levels of youth culture can be isolated for investigation:
    1 at a macro level, what is selected and combined from which codes to furnish the stylistic identity of the youth culture;
    2 what rules of jurisdiction, social combination and discourse are mobilised in what specialised ritual practices to reproduce that identity;
    3 at a micro level, what subject positions are privileged and fixed within the peer group ideal.
       It is the third micro level which now needs to be looked at in more detail, especially from a psycho-analytic standpoint.

49. See the study by P. Willis and team, *The Social Conditions of Young People in Wolverhampton*, (Wolverhampton City Council, 1985). Despite my criticism of its line of argument, this is a pioneering study which deserves to be widely read and debated, not least because it is the first time a Labour council has taken youth policy seriously enough to commission a piece of research of this quality and scale.

50. Gregory Bateson's theory of the double bind (see *Steps to an Ecology of Mind* (London, 1987) suggests that in some families life historical messages are constructed in the form of paradoxical injunctions (of the type 'ignore this message'). But he never explains *why* this should

arise in some families and not others. It is clear, however, that life historical messages have both a spoken subject (i.e. attribution about
who or what the child is, or is expected to become) and an unspoken
subject, constituted by the adults' desire. Normally the two reinforce
each other, but where the grid of transmission is normatively weak,
what each parent unconsciously wishes the child to be for them, and
what they tell the child to become, can become the focus of intense,
if disowned, conflict.

Chapter 8

Losing the Generation Game

After the Labour Party's second election defeat by Mrs Thatcher, it decided to embark on a series of policy reviews. Under the slogan 'Labour Listens to Youth' front-bench politicians held meetings with carefully selected groups of young people up and down the country. At the same time, an agit prop outfit called Red Wedge was launched to spearhead a new cultural politics aimed at youth, and meetings were organised with 'youth experts' to advise the party on how to develop a range of new policies in this area. The initiative had a number of aims. It was designed to win back the youth vote which for the first time in half a century had gone more to the Tories than Labour, raising the spectre of a new 'yuppie generation' coming to power. And it was meant to reduce the influence of the Trotskyite-dominated Young Socialists who had been active around issues of youth training and unemployment and whose sectarian politics provided the Tory press with an ideal stick with which to beat Labour.

Eventually both these aims were achieved, but not, I am afraid, due to anything produced by the Youth Policy Review. As one of the people consulted, it quickly became apparent to me (and to others) that this was meant to be a purely cosmetic exercise, designed to produce the image of a

---

Chapter 8 originally appeared as two articles in the *New Socialist*, 3 (1982) and 14 (1983); this version of the text appeared in J. Curran (ed.), *The Future of the Left* (Cambridge: Polity Press, 1984).

rejuvenated Labour Party, without any substantive commitment to the kind of policies required to re-enfranchise the large numbers of young people who had been left stranded on the dole by Thatcherism.

Partly as a contribution to this debate, I wrote a series of articles for New Socialist and Marxism Today, which were then in the throes of rethinking the socialist project whilst still retaining some links, however tenuous, with the Western Marxist tradition. The articles were an attempt to locate the history of youth struggles in and against the patriarchal structures of Labourism and its political culture. I tried to show how these derived from sexual and generational divisions which had been set in place during the transition from artisanal to factory production, but which were now being rendered redundant by the advent of a post-Fordist economy. As a result, traditional forms of youth organisation, of whatever ideological tendency, were simply no longer appropriate vehicles of political education. The articles raised a howl of protest from readers who accused them of travestying the proud record of Labour fighting for youth. It seemed that there was a limit to what could be rethought in this particular political sphere. The subsequent collapse of both journals indicated not so much an exhaustion of their agendas – indeed the debate had just begun – but a failure to find a sufficiently supportive home within the shrinking environment of the Left to sustain them. It might be worth considering whether the current programme of 'New Labour' and its associated think tanks has picked up the threads of this earlier debate and given them a new twist, or merely given a communitarian gloss to the kind of divisive educational and youth policy pursued by the New Right.

Since Labour's 1983 election defeat there has been considerable discussion inside and outside the Labour Party on the question, Whatever happened to the youth vote? The evidence, on the face of it, seems pretty clear cut; the swing away from Labour was more marked amongst first-time voters than amongst other age-groups. Even more alarmingly, data from the school mock elections organized by the BBC showed a similar pattern of disaffection amongst those who will be first-time/voters at the next election. Concerned to demonstrate that a 'new generation' has come to power inside the Labour Party, the new leadership has since made strenuous efforts to appeal to young people, as part of a wider strategy to rejuvenate the movement (or at least its public image). And this seems to have paid off. Recent opinion polls show that the upward trend in Labour's electoral fortunes is much more marked amongst the 18- to 25-year-olds than any other group. But unfortunately for the optimists who have pinned their faith purely on electoral strategy, the apparent gains on these swings hide a continuing loss on the more roundabout movements of political ideology.

Only two things can be said with any degree of certainty about the contemporary youth vote. First, it is highly volatile; as an age group, first-voters' allegiances are less fixed than ever before within the ideological frameworks of customary political discourse. Second, it is not a bloc vote – and never has been. Class, gender and ethnicity all play a part in ensuring that there is no single experience of 'youth', no single social or cultural category. Though that is not to say 'youth' as a whole is not subject to common experiences or the target of common attacks.

It is becoming clear that the most volatile element in the first-time electorate is to be found amongst the new middle class. This group, largely comprising students in higher education, showed a large swing towards the Alliance in 1983, but an equally large swing back to Labour in 1984. The radicalism of this stratum has always had an instrumental, or frankly opportunist, aspect to it – in part bound up with the search for a political vehicle which would turn its cultural capital into more effective power. It is certainly important in electoral terms that the Labour Party recaptures this base of support, and there are already encouraging signs that it is capable of doing so. But there is also a great danger that success on this front may blind the party to disturbing evidence of a persistent trend in the opposite direction amongst young working-class voters.

A large and growing number of young workers, trainees, unemployed young people and early school leavers who will be voting for the first time in the next election, are consistently refusing even to consider voting Labour. Most of them say they will abstain altogether rather than support any kind of alternative politics, yet there is little comfort in that. This particular haemorrhage in the body politic of Labourism will not be healed by hiring a few media whizz-kids to liven up the party image, or by inviting Tony Blair on to a few teen-TV rock shows. The problem is structural. It concerns the disintegration of a whole political culture which once transmitted a version of socialism as a legacy of common sense and customary belief from one working-class generation to the next. And it concerns the failure of the Labour Party, or any other progressive movement, to construct a popular form of youth politics to fill the vacuum. The problem is either ignored in the hope that it will somehow go away, or rationalized in terms of a hedonistic 'apolitical phase' in the lifestyle of all working-class 'kids' – they'll rejoin the Labour fold once they settle down. But they don't and won't, largely because of the assumptions that lie behind this piece of wishful thinking.

Certainly, if their views are anything to go by (and I think they are) the young people I have interviewed give us few grounds for optimism, still less for complacency. I talked to a sample of early school leavers, who were either unemployed or on youth training schemes in London. One group came from Labour-voting families, the others did not. Yet despite the differences in emphasis in what they had to say, both groups were united in their hostility to Thatcherism *and* in their belief that the Labour Party had little or nothing to offer their generation. I was left with an overwhelming impression of cynicism about politicians of every kind and a general disbelief in the solutions to the crisis put forward by socialists.

These young people, did, however, have some specific demands. They wanted decent, preferably skilled, jobs with proper trade training and a living wage. They wanted cheap public housing for single young people so that they could afford some privacy and independence. They wanted better cultural and educational facilities for the unemployed. And they wanted democratically run organizations which would represent their views and give them some real bargaining power. These are modest enough aspirations which ought to be supported by all sections of the Labour movement – and are indeed written into the party's manifesto for youth. Yet they were voiced hesitantly, almost apologetically, as if I would think them unrealistic, asking for the moon. Above all, they were not connected to any existing form of youth politics.

There are always people calling for a new socialist youth movement. But a look at the history of such movements shows that initiatives in that direction are unlikely to regenerate socialism. The story of the various youth wings sprouted by the Labour party, the ILP, the Communist Party and organizations of the far left, makes fascinating, if depressing, reading. It is a tale of chronic feuds, sectarian rivalries and battles with the parent bodies. The details are not important here. What matters is why it happened like this, and how it militated against any of these groups breaking through to achieve solid, popular support.

Until recently, growing up working-class has meant being apprenticed to a special kind of 'inheritance'. In this, destinies were fixed to origins through an *active* mastery of shared techniques and conditions of labour. As a child you were both 'set on' to tasks related to a future function on the shop or kitchen floor, and thereby aquired a sense of being 'born and bred' into your class place.

This code operated through, and linked, the cultures of family, work-place and community. Within it, boys were placed in a subordinate position *vis*-a-vis male elders; while girls were trained in passive support for the lads' counter-assertion of manhood and maturity. These same forms governed customary practices of initiation into working-class politics. The young novitiate was first taken on as a fetcher and carrier of the political message, a skivvy-cum-errand boy, then graduated to the position of 'time server' and finally 'improver' when the craft of running the party or trade union machine had been mastered. Political apprenticeships into the Labour movement thus mirrored the occupational form, but often took considerably longer. 'Young' socialists were expected to reach political maturity only in early middle age. Through this system socialist ideas were entailed in a legacy of struggle. Political knowledge, like trade skills and even jobs, was to be held in trust by one generation for the next. But it was only by accepting the tutelage of elders who 'knew better' that youth could legitimately come into possession of this patrimony.

In my shop, the older men were always talking politics and arguing with each other. Half the time I didn't understand a word they were on about, but gradually bits and pieces I heard began to fit together. Of course I didn't dare interrupt them, or ask questions – I'd only get shown up as an ignorant kid. But I think that just eavesdropping, as it were, was what first awakened my interest in socialism. (Engineering apprentice, 1920s)

Socialism could be transmitted as an oral tradition within entire communities as well. In some working-class districts, 9 and 10-year-olds might get a political education from one of the 'speakers' corners'. One East Ender had this memory of the 1930s:

Becton Road corner used to be called the East End's university. The Labour League of Youth, the ILP, the Communist Party, they all used to put up speakers regular, Wednesdays of an evening and Sunday afternoon. I used to go up there with my mates to bunk off Sunday School. We used to go to hear Will Thorne; he was an old man then, but still a fine speaker. These places, stumping grounds we called them, they were traditional, passed on from generation to generation and the law knew well enough not to interfere.

The transmission did not then depend on family influences, as this Jewish girl, also from the East End, made clear:

My father regarded himself as working-class and a socialist even though he never took an active part in politics. But I didn't get my ideas from him. The ideas were there, all around us, as we were growing up. It was simply regarded as the correct thing for Jewish immigrants, as well as Irish dockers, to vote Labour.

If socialism was constructed as a patrimony, then it might also be appropriated as a birthright, something you felt you had 'in your bones'. It was then no longer a legacy dependent on the power of elders. This could lead to some remarkable examples of what we would now regard as political precocity, as in this story from Liverpool:

I came rather late to politics – when I was 13. I knew kids of 11 who were more politically advanced than me. We used to organize public meetings in the streets, by ourselves, without any adults at all. We would get up and talk about unemployment and injustice and the threat of fascism. We used to get quite a crowd around us. There were lots of arguments and hecklers.

Some grown-ups would come to take the piss, but sometimes they stayed to listen. I think they were impressed that we knew what we were talking about, even if we didn't win them over. Yes, we were only 12 or 13 then, still at school. It seems ever so young by today's standards, but in those days it wasn't.

This kind of political culture only ever socialized small numbers of young people for socialism. They were drawn overwhelmingly from the ranks of the Labour aristocracy, or from the Jewish and Irish communities. In both cases, though for different reasons, the codes of apprenticeship and inheritance were strong, locking into a mesh of political loyalties rooted in everyday life. The youth wings of the Labour and Communist parties were largely recruited from these social bases, and in their official policies and practices did little to challenge the patriarchal assumptions of such codes. The notion of politics as patrimony corresponded to the idea that youth organizations should be handmaidens to their parent bodies. They were granted autonomy partly to *minimize* their bargaining power. Young socialists were excluded effectively from adult policy-making and often found themselves confined to purely social and recreational activities, or routine tasks of propaganda.

There is a pattern common to the history of Labour and Communist youth movements, despite (or rather because of) their intense rivalry. Whenever trusteeship of the party's ideological inheritance is under threat, its elder statesmen move to tighten up the system of political apprenticeship to ensure that youth toes the correct line. In the case of the CP this has been bound up with a particular view of the working class as almost congenitally destined to overthrow capitalism – a destiny inscribed in a historical master plan unfolding in stages according to iron laws of development. Consequently any practice which does not conform to these laws becomes defined as adventurist. Adventurism is then identified as the besetting sin of youth. Underlying this view is a curious kind of political Darwinism. Different class fractions or social groups are ranked on an evolutionary scale of 'consciousness'. Adherence to party discipline or programme is seen as a sign of advanced development equated with maturity; resistance to the dictates of party elders thus becomes a sign of chronic backwardness. Ironically the most politically precocious young people, those who claimed socialism as a birthright rather than a legacy, and who therefore refused to take the handmaiden role lying down, found themselves diagnosed as suffering from Lenin's famous infantile disorder, and were often booted out.

The Labour Party's policy towards its youth wing has been no less oppressive in periods when it has been dominated by the great fear of being infiltrated from the left. Yet the problem has been managed in such a way as virtually to guarantee that this would happen. Far left groups have operated with a very different model of youth organization in class politics. What were youthful vices for the other parties became political virtues for groups with a more voluntarist reading of history, where spontaneous forms of direct action or rank-and-file struggle are seen as the key to proletarian advance. The so-called adventurism of youth is here hailed as a sign that young people are ready to be promoted into the front line, a strategy which often has disastrous results. Yet at least it puts these youth vanguards in a strong position to exploit the discontent generated by the handmaiden models of the other parties. Thereupon the party hierarchy moves to impose even tighter controls over its 'handmaidens', which in turn drives the youth wing yet further into the arms of the 'opposition'.

Labour's youth and the YCL have frequently sprouted Trotskyist or libertarian wings which have flapped about and made a good deal of noise, but never got off the ground in terms of popular membership or influence. The immediate reason is that they have remained locked in chronic conflict with each other and their parent bodies in a way which has alienated large numbers of potential working-class recruits. The real victims in all this have been young socialists themselves, beleaguered by entryists, belaboured by party elders, bewildered by factional in-fights. The very stuff of politics for some, who graduate to positions of adult responsibility having mastered the required techniques of impression management. But the drop-out rate has always been high. For all too many, what began as a political birthright ends in a legacy of disillusionment and personal defeat.

The Labour movement has, however, developed some defence mechanisms to deal with the problem. Youthful militancy, including militancy of the far left, can be treated as a kind of rite of passage – a way of sowing political wild oats before settling down into an adult career as a party or trade union official. The biographies of Labour leaders provide countless examples of this. Usually the cycle is rationalized in terms of the idealism of youth 'naturally' giving way to the wisdom (or realpolitik) of maturity. In fact it has more to do with the way generations replace themselves inside relatively inert political organizations. New issues, social forces and tactics are continually being thrown up from the grass roots of the movement, but these are only belatedly given official status and representation within the Labour Party apparatus, usually after a long struggle. Thus each generation tends to see the policies and practices it pioneered fall back to the point where they come into conflict with the priorities and persuasions of the next wave of new socialists. A recent example of this was the way some Labour leaders tried to apply strategies for campaigning against unemployment and fascism in the 1930s to the very different conditions of racism and recession today.

Of course, the current state of the Labour Party and the disenchantment of young people cannot be put down to these institutional factors or to some simple generation gap. They are bound up with profound changes in working-class culture, politics, and the position of youth. If I have talked about socialist youth movements in the past tense it is because they have proved incapable of adapting to these changes, despite the often heroic attempts of their members to do so. Instead they have preyed upon new forms of youth politics which have developed outside the old class-and-party lines. What has been gained, and what lost, in the process?

The clash with Keir Hardie

Since the Second World War the culture of work-place and community, which relayed the socialist message most effectively from one generation to another, has had its back broken. The restructuring of labour in the interests of capital, policies of urban renewal and industrial relocation, deskilling and new technologies all had their cumulative effect. At the same time the spectacular gearing of the 'consciousness industries' such as television or the music and fashion businesses around the manufacture of whole new ranges of consumer demand, served to privatize or make redundant many of the practices hitherto organized through a distinctively proletarian public realm. The stumping ground and the workshop stove gave way to the TV panel and studio audience as centres of political debate. A political culture which had rested on oral tradition began to wither. The chains of association between family, work place and community weakened too. Here is an experience of growing up in the East End in the late 1950s:

> It was just everybody working at the Penal Colony down the road, coming home, up the pub for a quick pint, and then home to watch the telly. Trade unionism and politics were never talked about. It was the 60-year-olds, the grandparents, who used to try and talk socialism to us. So I grew up with the idea that socialism was just a lot of old people going on about the past. It had nothing to do with us youngsters.

Where socialist ideas were still bequeathed in the old way, their transmission tended to be confined to individual families. The political patrimony thus became more easily embroiled in emotional conflicts between parents and adolescent children. Even if the legacy of elders was not rejected outright, its reception tended to be complicated, often in mutually unproductive ways.

In the early 1960s, Ray Gosling was one of the first socialists to sound the alarm bells about what was happening. In an early issue of *New Left Review* he wrote: 'In general, the youth clubs, the Church of England, the Labour Party, the trade unions, are talking a language that doesn't make contact with the new world that has arisen, the new conditions, the new codes of behaviour and living which have grown up amongst this younger generation of workers.' The new codes belonged to the mods and rockers, teds, skinheads and the rest. Each in their own way explored lines of continuity and rupture between the old and new working class. But on the terrain mapped out by these youth cultures, ways of 'showing class' were dramatically dislocated from real divisions of labour.

The youth service tried to learn the new language and modernize its image. Not so the labour movement. Here it seemed that all the youth demands that had been fought for and enshrined in the welfare state – comprehensive schooling, raising the school-leaving age (ROSLA), further education – were being rejected by this new generation in favour of rock'n'roll. One Clydesdale shop steward, in his forties, echoed the complaints of many socialists during the so-called youth revolution of the 1960s:

> Most of the lads in the yard have grown their hair long; they are more interested in drugs and discos than going to college. They've lost interest in any ideas of self improvement that even some of their parents had. The labour movement fought for 50 years to ensure lads like these got a decent education. Now it looks as if they'll be fighting for another 50 to get out of it.

State schooling had never been popular. But the tradition of self-improvement and rational recreation could simply not compete against the glittering array of youth cultures. The painful fact was that they attracted not only the unskilled, the unorganized, and the unemployed, but young people who would previously have grown up socialists. With the arrival of hard times the appeal has persisted. Today youth cultures offer an even more dazzling mirror image of the fragmentation of class identities.

There have been two main responses to these developments on the left. On one side are the Jeremiahs who wring their hands over what went wrong, and conclude that Labour has sold its socialist soul for a mess of capitalist potage – higher wages, home ownership, holidays in the Costa Brava and ever higher fi. Seen in this light youth cultures are Machiavellian devices designed to seduce the working class away from its historic mission to build the New Jerusalem. The appeal to the Labour movement is to return to its authentic roots, located in some golden age of uncorrupted consciousness before the consumerist Fall. This myth addresses itself to an imaginary subject, an idealized vision of the 'old' working class. The truth is that the mutual aid of the labouring poor was always tempered by large doses of penny capitalism; the militancy of the skilled worker shot through with petty bourgeois aspirations of 'being your own boss'. Working-class youth cultures have resisted these 'seductions' neither more nor less than the old forms.

There are, however, strategic objections to be raised against the attempt to outdo Thatcherism: a return to our own version of Victorian values is neither possible nor desirable. In my *New Socialist* articles, I tried to show how the inheritance of socialist ideology was realized through certain patriarchal forms of 'apprenticeship', but that whole system of political patrimony is in irreversible decline: it is not a question of keeping the good bits, and getting rid of the bad. Those who wish to restore this old political culture end up by tacitly endorsing all those practices which confined women and young people to subordinate positions within it. As for those who wax lyrical about growing up with socialism in their bones, perhaps we should remind them that this sense of political ancestry not only included the image of the free-born English*man* but all too often that of an inherently superior Anglo-Saxon race.

The weakening of traditional allegiances has helped open the field to hitherto disenfranchised groups. They are not, by definition, based on class or party ideology; indeed they may explicitly reject the old codes in favour of personal politics which give priority to issues of gender, age and race. The response from some sections of the left has been to endorse these new developments uncritically and then, in some cases, to try and co-opt them. Will these new movements succeed in mobilizing mass resistance to Thatcherism where Labour has so obviously failed?

The most successful attempt so far to politicize youth culture was organized by the Anti-Nazi League. The ANL tried to bring white and black youth together around two-tone music, to build a progressive anti-racist movement with its roots on the streets of the working-class city. But the ANL failed to hold together the volatile constituencies it had mobilized so brilliantly, not just because it lacked the organizational structure but because to have succeeded would have deprived youth culture of its *raison d'etre.*

Youth cultures work by scrambling fixed signs of identity into more fluid and imaginary configurations of differences based on style. They thrive on what Freud called the narcissism of minor differences, already powerfully installed in adolescence and now vastly amplified by the fashion and music industries. But if they can only operate in an arena of stylistic oppositions and rival codes, they cannot be unified under any single political banner. They remain inherently unstable forms, resisting anchorage to any political ideology or movement.

It is doubtful, too, whether rock groups, however committed their lyrics, can ever be effective political educators while for the majority of their followers the medium is the only message that counts. Moreover the ambiguity of the populist message which most rock ideologues purvey can all too easily allow the music to dissociate itself from the politics. Perhaps it is no coincidence that The Clash's 'White Riot' was a hit with both the racist and anti-racist youth movements. Certainly the skinheads I worked with saw no contradiction between going along to ANL rallies because they liked the music, and continuing to attack black people on the street. If numbers of potential recruits were persuaded that the NF was No Fun it was not, in my experience, because they had rocked against racism. Rather they had learnt that involvement in racialist politics might mean being subjected to counter-attack by the black community, or even, occasionally, getting into trouble with the police. Only the hard core fanatics felt it was worth getting your head kicked in for your beliefs. Not that the majority were converted to an anti-racist position; they simply became rather more circumspect about how they expressed their preju-dice. Finally, if the National Front were No Fun it was for much the same reason as any other political party. Active membership involved more than going on marches and hurling abuse or broken bottles at the enemy; it meant attending meetings, addressing envelopes, delivering leaflets and all the other humdrum tasks attractive only to the committed few.

None of these points should be taken to imply that the ANL or Rock Against Racism was a waste of time. They succeeded in dra-matizing the issue of racism in a way that the labour movement never even tried to do. And they opened opportunities for a whole new generation of middle-class youth, who then went on to become active in the peace movement and feminist or left-wing politics. Unfortunately the impact on white working-class youth was far more problematic.

The history of the schools movement during the 1970s confirms this picture. The shift from a politics of class to one of subjectivity is encapsulated in the movement's two key moments. The strike of 1971 was led by the Schools Action Union armed with a 'Marxist-Leninist' analysis and the slogan 'smash the dictatorship of the Head'. Its paper *Vanguard* was filled with dense Maoist rhetoric about the need for revolutionary discipline and the correct proletarian line. In contrast, the National Union of School Students went through a reformist phase and then discov-ered sexual politics. Its magazine *Blot* carried articles cham-pioning the cause of masturbation, feminism, gay rights,

paedophilia, not to mention drugs and rock'n'roll. This version of
the cultural revolution could not have been further from the
clenched-fist puritanism of the SAU, and would have had the
poor Chairman turning in his grave. But through all these ideological swings and roundabouts the movement remained the preserve of a small rebel sixth-form elite who had a material stake in
the education system as well as a privileged awareness of its contradictions. Working-class pupils had neither, and their cultures
of resistance to schooling obstinately refused to be connected to
either kind of ideology. Plagued by sectarian rivalries and lacking
organized support from teachers, the schools movement
eventually collapsed.

To understand why neither the old political culture, nor the new
cultural politics cuts much ice with a generation of school leavers
headed for youth training schemes or the dole, it is necessary to
look both at how the links between growing up, working and class
have changed, and at how these hubs of identity have become disconnected from each other, and from the transmission belts of
organized ideology. Quite simply, as the codes of inheritance and
apprenticeship have weakened, they have increasingly pulled apart
into separate, cultural forms. When inheritance is only to and for
itself, its frame of reference contracts to the immediate confines of
kith and kin. Family relations become the epicentre of a war of
fixed position waged between genders and generations, stalemated
in the old patriarchal binds. Growing up no longer means striving
to take control of one's own destiny, but simply going through the
motions of a more or less preordained fate.

Amongst the unemployed young people I interviewed this was
certainly one clear pattern. Colin, for example, came from a
strong socialist and trade union background. His father, once a
YCL militant, had had an accident at work which had left him dis-
abled; he was now a somewhat embittered armchair critic of politics. Colin said of him:

My dad's a Communist. It's all he ever talks about. He makes
me sick. He sits in front of the telly all day and argues with
them. But he never does anything about it. He just sits there.
Everyone I know, it's just as if they've been sitting all their lives.
Then I realized why. There was no reason to try and stand.
There was no point. Life makes you like that, my mate says.

Instead of the father's injury evoking a sense of anger and injustice in the son, his physical immobility becomes a metaphor for Colin's own passivity – which is then justified in terms of a more general sense of class defeat. Instead of renewing a family tradition of militancy, Colin has inherited a fatalism which makes the struggle to grow up or stand up seem simply irrelevant.

In contrast, where apprenticeships turn in on themselves, youth is promoted to the centre stage where it busily constructs a world in its own image, proclaiming its freedom from the legacies of class. The political connections are often hard to make. Consider this encounter from a TV debate between Joan Lestor, representing the old code, and The Clash, thoughtful and committed exponents of the new:

> *The Clash*: Politics is just so remote from young people. You don't feel part of it, that you can change it or affect it in any way. You learnt in school how it's supposed to work. It was just boring. The problem is politics works in terms of what's going to happen in ten years, amounts of time like that. You say ten years to a young person and you might as well say eternity. You're thinking about what you're going to do tonight, what you're going to wear tomorrow. You're thinking in terms of half an hour, not ten years. Politics is just a big mess and you just feel like 'well, I don't want to have anything to do with it, I'll go and hear a good record instead'.

> *Joan Lestor*: But it's not only young people who want to see things happen quickly. Most people do. People who have been waiting years to get rehoused. People a lot older than you probably share your disillusionment. We have certainly got problems in this country, with the recession, which are not of our own making – and certain things have to take priority and certain things have to wait. What would you put forward in place of the system we've got at the present time?

A lot of people would like the answer to be socialism! Clearly we are going to have to wait some time for that. Meanwhile we have not even begun to articulate the terms in which a real dialogue between these two attitudes could take place. Joan Lestor's views are widespread in all sections and tendencies within the Labour

Party. The essential message is 'young people must learn to wait' – until, presumably, they are old enough to join the silent majority who vote against Labour!

Enfranchising young people

From this perspective, the fact that young working-class people are already at the back of the queue for housing and jobs is either ignored, taken for granted or even held to be a good thing. Yet their consequent dependence on continued family support pushes these school leavers to seek autonomy in a 'body politic' whose pleasure principles, as indicated by The Clash quote, distance them even further from organized struggles. The whole process is a self-fulfilling prophecy, and one for which the labour movement bears considerable responsibility, not least for the way in which it has disenfranchised youth within its own ranks.

None of this will be changed by writing a new Youth Charter, with yet another shopping list of reforms. The first-time electorate may not have much of a memory for broken promises, but it does not go by party manifestos or policy statements. The Labour Party will be judged by its performance in practice. And here it is all too clear that for the majority of Labour administrations, both locally and nationally, the youth question has a very low priority. Where it is tackled, the approach has been either unpopular (ROSLA) or cosmetic (youth service provision), or both (youth opportunity schemes).

There are, of course, notable exceptions to this rule. The Greater London Council consistently supported progressive youth movements, campaigns and projects. Wolverhampton Council appointed a senior youth policy advisor to cut through the red tape and produce a comprehensive programme aimed at the basic material and social needs of school leavers, young workers and unemployed young people. At present such initiatives are few and far between. The success of Youth Aid as a campaigning agency in the field of provision for 16–19 year-olds, and the growth of a national network of radical professionals around the magazine *Youth and Policy* are encouraging signs of a more co-ordinated response.

The problem with all these developments is that by definition they are not originated by young people themselves; they are designed to implement changes in state policy and provision which may hopefully benefit specific categories of youth, but in which youth itself has little or no say or stake. The real test of a youth policy, especially one that claims to be socialist, must be the extent to which it creates the conditions for the emergence of genuinely popular and democratic forms of progressive youth politics. Such politics could only be based on places where young people are already concentrated in large numbers – schools, training schemes, work-places and housing estates – and whatever forms of self-organization and collective representation were constructed would also have to break down existing patterns of exclusion and discrimination based on gender or race. Are there any new developments in political education and youth work which point in this direction?

Bernard Crick, in association with the Hansard Society, recently launched a programme to radicalize the teaching of 'civics' in schools. This started from the correct view that re-enfranchising the young involves more than lowering the voting age or the age of consent. In Crick's view, it is conditional on young people acquiring 'political literacy'. Essentially, this involves mastering the skills and protocol of democratic procedure and public debate as established within the framework of the parliamentary tradition. Crick's approach has been rather more successful in the context of youth and community work than in schools themselves; it is particularly geared to raising issues of civil liberties affecting groups of young people who are more than usually deprived of them. Some very interesting work has been done with young people in care on this basis; the move to establish youth councils as politically representative bodies for local youth organizations is inspired by similar principles. But the problem with this approach is that in challenging existing monopolies over due political process, it also rules out of order as politically illiterate, undemocratic or immature many of the key practices of popular struggle within the working-class community. In particular it reinforces the 'great moral divide' between respectable sheep, who join youth clubs, sit on committees and so on and the rough goats, whose main idea of collective bargaining is to riot. This in turn echoes a fatal split in socialist conceptions of youth politics – between the Labourists who recognize only bureaucratically organized youth activities, and libertarians who romanticize youth's more spectacular subcultural manifestations. Needless to say, the majority of working-class boys and girls, black and white, do not fall into either of these camps!

A rather more promising approach to political education – one, I believe, that at least tries to avoid these crude prescriptive classifications – derives from the Marxist tradition of cultural studies. Originally inspired by the work of Raymond Williams, and increasingly influenced by the feminist and oral history movements, this approach sets out to enable school students to locate their own contemporary practices within some sense of a wider history and geography. The aim is both to challenge dominant constructs of class, gender and ethnicity, and to equip young people with the skills they need to gain more effective control over the production of their own cultures. At its best, this approach makes continual cross-reference between the personal and the political, between what is historical and what is unconscious, between the constraining realities of schooling and unemployment and the pleasures which can still be set against them. This strategy is a long way from the techniques of inculcation advocated by the traditional left. Its success is not to be measured in terms of propaganda/recruitment but by the extent to which it shifts the ground of common sense towards a more open discourse, where socialist or feminist ideas can be tried and tested for their realism and their relevance to a new generation.

However, it has to be admitted that no programme of political education will make a decisive impact if it is confined to institutional sites and captive audiences. Indeed if the socialist, feminist, or anti-racist message is only relayed through the medium of teachers, youth workers and other professionals, the majority of working-class girls and boys will continue to turn a deaf ear. For example, despite the important gains being made by feminists at the level of youth policy and provision, and the growth and popularity of girls' projects, working-class girls remain a tiny minority within the women's liberation movement and continue to leave the initiative to their middle-class sisters when it comes to fighting sexism in schools. This is primarily a result of the deep subordination of girls within working-class culture, and the intensity of their sexual harassment by boys. Far from moving them towards active political engagement, such pressures force them back into the arms of the women's magazines and their own versions of the peer-group romance. With obstacles like these to overcome, feminism would undoubtedly have to take a militantly separatist line if it were eventually to capture the hearts and minds of working-class girls – a line hostile to any attempt to connect it with socialism.

This is already the pattern amongst the new wave of youth organizations emerging from sexual and ethnic minorities. Gay teenagers' groups, The Black Sisters, The Southall Youth Movement – there are many encouraging signs that in dealing with specific sites of oppression new kinds of political apprenticeship are being constructed. Yet by the same token a cultural politics of separatism makes alliances harder, not easier, to sustain and alienates these groups even further from the Labour Party and its traditional working-class base.

The difficulties of mobilizing a sizeable youth vote thus mirror the wider problems facing the Labour Party. But there is also a special problem of credibility on this front, concerning the issue of youth unemployment. All sections of young people agree in identifying this as the number one political issue. Yet it is also the issue about which they are the most fatalistic, believing that no political party or policy can make much difference. And it is an issue on which the labour movement and the left are deeply divided.

The optimists believe that a reflationary economic policy will do the trick and restore something like full employment for all 16- to 19-year-olds who want to work rather than continue in some form of education or training. The alternative optimists take the completely opposite view and argue that new technology is ushering us towards the New Jerusalem of the leisure society, and that young people will not miss full-time paid employment, since they have never known it and so are in the best position to experiment with new lifestyles and alternative kinds of work. The pessimist tendency, of which I confess to being a fully unpaid-up member, believes that both kinds of dream ticket offer a one-way ride to cloud-cuckoo-land. If a British economic miracle were to happen tomorrow, the displacement of youth labour as a result of the automation of its servicing functions or the elimination of its more unproductive forms, would more than counterbalance the rate of absorption from the growth. Moreover, to train the reserve army of youth for employment as low-grade people-minders within an expanded welfare state is no more a socialist solution than to encourage them to find 'alternative work' in the hidden economy, or in do-it-yourself forms of small business enterprise – which is what the other optimists seem to have in mind.

It is also becoming clear that structural unemployment is having an increasingly regressive effect on both girls' and boys' cultures of transition from school. Working-class girls have customarily been trapped in a position of chronic maturity – as little wives and mothers apprenticed to housework, child care and other 'labours of love' while still at school. Waged work may have echoed many of the features of their domestic servitude, but it also offered them a brief interlude of economic independence before marriage and this is now being drastically threatened. Unemployed daughters are under enormous pressure to go on 'making themselves useful about the house' in return for their continued upkeep. For many girls, the only way out of this impasse lies in early motherhood – though not necessarily marriage. Getting pregnant and becoming a single parent may not be a calculated choice, but it's a way of qualifying for council housing. As one girl put it to me, it may be out of the frying pan into the fire – but at least it's your own hearth! Such a course of action tends not to predispose these girls towards challenging central aspects of their subordination.

Unemployed boys are subjected to the opposite pressure – of feeling that unless they earn money to pay their way at home they are not entitled to be there, or be accorded adult status. They may even begin to feel guilty about treating their mums and sisters like skivvies! Some respond by acting the hard man, others by taking to their beds; but either way the increased sense of powerlessness tends to addict them to cultural activities which support the more infantile modes of male omnipotence. Walk round almost any inner-city housing estate and you will see how easily patterns of boredom and drug use interact to turn these lads into imaginary kings of castles in the air, while locking them into the most vicious kinds of territorial rivalry.

If structural youth unemployment is here to stay, and if it is armouring working-class girls and boys against feminist or socialist politics, it seems that all we are left with is a counsel of despair – concentrate on student, ethnic and sexual minority youth and ignore the rest. Certainly, given the Labour Party's scarce resources it might seem sensible to concentrate them where they are likely to reap the most immediate electoral benefit. In my view this would be a short-sighted policy; and it would mean a massive abstention amongst potential first-time Labour voters at the next election – something that need not happen. For there *is* an alternative.

It is necessary to conceive of a long-term strategy for building the material and ideological conditions of a new kind of autonomy for working-class youth – one that is no longer conditional on being paid a wage or on continued parental support, still less on regressive cultural practices or the kind of 'mobile privatization' sponsored by consumer capitalism. The central *material* condition for this is the provision of cheap public housing available to all 16- to 19 year-olds not in full-time education, as part of a massive programme of rehousing in the inner cities. To recognize this group as a priority for housing may seem unrealistic, but in terms of the likely saving on health and on social services it certainly makes welfare sense. It would also, of course, ease transitions for young working-class people. Boys would be more strongly motivated to 'grow up', learn how to look after themselves and do the housework; girls would be able to set up their own independent households without having to have a baby to 'legitimate' the move. The combination of sexual privacy with forms of collective self-management and sharing would provide at least a framework within which a more desirable form of autonomy could be developed than that offered either by the marketplace or the work-place. Finally, a youth housing programme would not only attract widespread support from existing youth organizations, it would give feminists and socialists who are working with ordinary 'apolitical' young people in working-class areas a chance to introduce a material stake around which ideological issues could be anchored.

I have few illusions that this suggestion will be discussed seriously within the Labour movement, let alone acted upon. Yet if we look at the solutions which school leavers and unemployed young people are themselves improvising to weather the crisis, we can see the starkly opposed directions in which the search for a sense of their own place leads. One way points towards a restless individualism anchored by various kinds of territorial chauvinism and petty delinquency; the other towards a more open and equal relationship between the domestic and the communal, and between the masculine and feminine spheres. Out of this a popular and democratic youth politics might just emerge. Labour may have more to lose than the youth vote if it fails to respond positively to *this* youth question.

Part III

Unsentimental Education

Chapter 9

Teaching Enterprise Culture: Individualism, Vocationalism and the New Right

Perhaps the most enduring legacy of the Thatcher years is the reshaping of the educational system. This is not just a matter of the great structural reforms – the introduction of the National Curriculum, the local management of schools, the creation of a new system of post-school vocational training; it concerns the way in which the New Right vision of Enterprise Culture has come to be widely accepted as defining the skills and values to which all children and young people should aspire. Few educationalists and politicians now question this 'commonsense' philosophy even if they may disagree about how its goals can best be achieved.

Working at the Institute of Education's Post 16 Centre at this time was a strange and not always pleasant experience. As we prepared to meet the industrialists and state bureaucrats who were beginning their long slow march through the committees and quangos which came to preside over this bold new experiment, I remember the enthusiasm with which

Originally Chapter 3 in I. Taylor (ed.), *The Social Effect of Market Policies* (Brighton: Harvester/Wheatsheet, 1990).

*some colleagues embraced the 'new realism' and buried the Utopian edu-
cational sentiments of their youth. Of course we had all of us failed,
failed to engage the hearts, minds, and above all the material self-interest
of the vast majority of parents and children in any feasible vision of education as a democratic enterprise. And that was why the Thatcherite
agenda was so patently popular. But it seemed to me that what was called
for was a double critique – a critique both of radical education and of the
new vocationalism, as a precursor to moving on from both. This chapter
is a stab at the first part of that project. It focuses on what Foucault calls
the microphysics of knowledge and power as these are articulated in the
hidden curriculum of vocational education and training. Through a
detailed reading of the teaching materials which were produced for use in
social and life skills and youth training schemes I try to unpack the elementary structures of the new individualism and its relation to the post-
Fordist economy. It was written in 1985. Since then how much has
changed?*

Thatcherism as a fairy story

Fairy stories, unlike myths, are woven out of the materials of everyday life, and, unlike daydreams or fantasies, show us how we can
symbolically overcome the frustrations engendered by our
encounters with the social structures we inhabit, in order to 'live
happily ever after'. Adults tell them to children in order that they
may learn to grow up without illusions as to the difficulties in
store for them, but with some sense of hope that they may win
out in the end.[1] Political ideologies, if they are to work, in the
sense of carrying the persuasive force of common sense, must also
construct narratives which convince us that the promises they
make not only articulate our real wishes, but also possess the
means to ensure that they will come true, so that we too will live
happily ever after – at least until the next election. According to
this view the success of Thatcherism does not lie in the coherence
of its policies or even in its strategies of 'impression management'
centred on the public persona of the Iron Lady herself, but in the
way a certain kind of fairy story has been told to convince us that
we can indeed overcome our problems and reach a happy ending,
provided we realize that there is no alternative to the plot which is
being unfolded before us.

The central theme in the Thatcherite fairy story is that of a nation enslaved by the illusions of socialism being set free and converted into an enterprise culture, thus regaining the greatness which belongs to it by tradition and historical destiny. It is a story made to be told to children because they have a special role to play within it, and it goes something like this:

Once upon a time, Britain was a nation of shopkeepers which became the workshop of the world. Industry and trade prospered, while from an early age fair Albion's sons and daughters prepared themselves diligently for a life of service and toil. But then along came some nasty people with a lot of foreign ideas about poetry and politics, none of which was any good for helping them earn a living or learning the skills which Britain needed to compete in the market-place and stay Great. And so industry declined and trade ceased to prosper, and even some of the shopkeepers went bankrupt. Things got so bad it was decided to have a Great Debate, so that everybody could blame somebody else for the state of affairs. Trade unionists blamed the employers, industrialists blamed the teachers, teachers blamed the government, politicians blamed the world economy, moralists pointed the finger at the permissive society, while ecologists put it down to the impact of new technologies and almost everyone blamed young people and the working class for failing to adapt to the new realities. But help was at hand. In England's darkest hour a second Britannia appeared to lead the nation's children into a new and promised land – a land where sunrise industries flourished, trade unions were kept in check, everyone knew their place and lived within their means, and young people priced themselves back into jobs, or set up new businesses. The messiah had a simple message: 'God helps those who train themselves – and God help those who don't.' Many were converted to the new vocationalist faith, and those who continued to voice doubts were told to keep quiet and make way for those made of sterner stuff. Schools were rapidly converted into training centres, youth unemployment was declared illegal and the British economy was once more set on the road to recovery. For like all fairy stories there is only one possible happy ending.

There are a number of reasons why education should have provided the privileged terrain for this exercise in wish fulfilment. It
was here that the State of the Nation Debate with its historical
links to 'Victorian' values was most easily and directly connected
to strategies for 'modernizing' British capitalism. The so-called
Black Papers produced by a group of New Right educationalists in
the 1970s succeeded in yoking an archaic vision of the body
politic to a futuristic image of a 'post-industrial' society.[2]
Secondly, educational issues in Britain have always tended to condense and displace other, wider, relations of conflict in society,
and given them a particular inflection. Mrs Thatcher grasped the
fact that the 'battle for hearts and minds' could be more easily
won over in education than in other areas of social policy. It was
relatively easy to caricature the policies of left-wing Labour administrations – or the practices of anti-racist teachers – as vicious
forms of political indoctrination aiming to 'brainwash' innocent
children, to the detriment of 'standards' and 'discipline'. By
appearing to side with parents against both teachers and educational experts she was able to exploit a deep vein of popular
resentment against state schools.[3] The spectacle of Mrs T teaching
the teachers a lesson and giving them a good ticking off must
have struck a responsive chord in the hearts and minds of many
working-class parents who had been made to suffer in the classrooms of the 1950s and 1960s; the rhetoric of parental choice was
even sweeter music to the ears of their classmates who had been
the official success stories and who now wanted to ensure that
their own children followed in their footsteps into the new middle
class. Not for nothing has the Great Educational Reform Bill
(GERBIL) been called a 'Yuppies' Charter'.

However, it is only the most sentimental fairy story which relies
on an actual fairy to wave her wand and make everything come
true. Whatever her personal delusions of grandeur Mrs Thatcher
had no special magical powers to turn her policies into practice.
The Thatcherite project would not have got off the ground if
certain elements in its programme had not won the active support
of mainstream educationalists. In fact there has been a conver-
gence of opinion over the last decade on what constitutes 'good
education' and 'effective schooling'. And central to this new settlement is the idea that school should equip children from all
social backgrounds with a greater understanding and experience

of the world of work, and in the process equip them with social and technical skills required by employers. The test of the relevance of any subject, its place in the hierarchy of classroom knowledge, depends not on the insight it gives into the fundamental workings of nature or culture, nor the extent to which it develops particular creative or critical sensibilities, but how far it contributes to the formation of general dispositions for manual or mental labour in capitalist or bureaucratic organizations.[4]

The ideology of the new vocationalism is appropriately summed up in an advertisement for a 'progressive' system of vocational qualifications. The poster shows a young woman 'flying high' against the background of a modernist office (or polytechnic) block, over a caption which reads 'If you want more than a job, get more than an education'. This poster juxtaposes the meritocratic vision of technical training with the elitism of liberal education, and privileges the former over the latter. The implicit message is that if you want to fly high, to have a career, rather than just a job, then it's no good burying your head in a lot of useless academic books. Mental labour must become thoroughly rationalized and trained up for its occupational functions in much the same way as manual labour has been. The poster cleverly plays upon popular prejudices against 'academics' and 'intellectuals', whilst at the same time appealing to working-class aspirations to join the ranks of the new petty bourgeoisie. And there is a set of apparently progressive arguments to back it all up. For example it is often claimed that to vocationalize all levels of education thoroughly in this way is to remove the privileges of the traditional aristocracy of learning, as well as to sweep away the last bastions of the apprenticeship system associated with the old aristocracy of labour.

Vocationalism is a modernizing strategy which finally removes the structures of inheritance from the transmission of cultural capital. Of course it does nothing of the kind, given the way mechanisms of parental choice will harden the tripartite structure of public education – to say nothing of the growth of private, fee-paying schools, and the persistence of patriarchal structures in the skilled manual trades. A liberal education is indeed still the preferred formation of the professional and managerial élite, and a skilled trade is still the preferred route for boys from the manual working class. If the Thatcherite project was to carry through a bourgeois revolution in education it has won something of a pyrrhic victory. For the more these 'aristocratic' codes have been marginalized within the educational apparatus, the greater their pulling power as referential models seems to have become.

It is, however, amongst people of working-class origins, who have been denied access to the traditional kinds of intellectual or technical apprenticeship, that the anti-elitist rhetoric of the new vocationalism has gained hold, articulating their aspirations for betterment in a way that the language of 'equal opportunities' and 'comprehensivization' no longer does. This bit of the fairy story works partly because so many people, for different reasons, want it to come true. The education of popular desires by the mass media of the enterprise culture has, at least for the time being, taken the place of the desire for popular education as a means of social emancipation. Really useful knowledge has come to mean skills which help you get on and make it, not insights that help you combine with others to build a better world. But it also convinces because it corresponds to real changes in labour processes, both mental and manual, which have been brought about by the introduction of new information technologies within a 'post-Fordist' framework for acquiring and transmitting knowledge.[5]

The essential shift is from a long apprenticeship an inherited body of general or fundamental knowledge (whether belonging to a manual trade or profession) towards the learning of functional skills and specialized routines related to the manipulation of operationally defined 'information environments'. A modular curriculum which allows maximum scope for selecting and combining given 'bits' of knowledge in an opportunistic way, plus an active pedagogy based on hands-on experience is the essential format for this vocational model and it is one which is increasingly institutionalized within Higher and Further Education. Applied to the professional training of various kinds of public servants and industrial managers it produces skilled mental technicians who can be flexibly deployed to supervise various systems of work but who are unable to innovate at a deeper level or respond imaginatively to emergent change outside their own immediate field. In other words their dynamism is superficial and this can sometimes cause more problems than it solves, as witness the disarray which is currently being produced in many corporate man-power planning strategies by the advent of the integrated European Community (EC) market in 1992.

Ironically it is the more elitist and conservative forms of intel-lectual apprenticeship which retain the ability to generate really new knowledge (i.e. thought which anticipates and creates, rather than passively adapts to, change), by equipping people with the means firstly to grasp and then to question inherited structures of understanding in their totality. This is why many large corpora-tions still prefer to recruit graduates with firsts in such 'useless' and 'unvocational' subjects as classics and philosophy; but by the same token the use value of this knowledge to society is often rad-ically curtailed, or else is forced into the mould of a new ortho-doxy. This outcome might seem to be the worst of all possible worlds; nevertheless a techno-meritocracy for the masses super-vised by a new modernizing elite, whose dynamism is still con-tained within essentially conservative structures of thought and action, would seem to be a winning formula for Thatcherism. In fact the prolonged series of cuts in university funding, the aboli-tion of academic tenure, and populist onslaughts on 'experts' have ensured that Mrs Thatcher has effectively united and mobi-lized most of the intelligentsia against the effects of her policies, if not always against the vision of education and society they represent.

Further down the line, in secondary schools and youth training schemes, government policies designed to promote the new voca-tionalism have met with much greater success.[6] Here the idioms and practices of liberal education, with its emphasis on child-centredness and individual self-enhancement, have been sub-sumed and re-articulated within a more competitive and utilitarian framework to produce a whole series of new pedagogic and disciplinary regimes. In the process, radical critiques of working-class schooling, made by parents and children as well as by educationalists, have often been appropriated and turned against the teaching profession itself. Two discourses have been critical in negotiating this shift.

The first belongs to what Foucault has called bio-politics – the science of surveillance and control over subject populations.[7] One branch of this has been particularly focused on policing the youthful body, whether by subordinating adolescent desires to the disciplines of work, protecting juveniles from undesirable forms of popular pleasure, promoting 'improving' or 'rational' forms of recreation amongst the poor, or rescuing delinquents from their deprived environments. These concerns helped to organize the moral panic over youth unemployment which rose to a peak in the wake of the 1981 riots in many inner city areas. The spectacle of black and white youths confronting police on the street, creating no-go areas, burning and looting shops, played on all the traditional fears of the hooligan mob, and invoked the usual authoritarian response, a call for a tightening of discipline in the family and school, more effective policing, a closing of ranks against 'these barbarians encamped in our midst'.[8]

Racism undoubtedly fanned the flames not only in enumerating the grievances of the 'silent' white majority, but by defining the whole problem of youth unemployment in terms of the numbers game. Blacks, like youth, are always and only seen as a problem when there are too many of them, never when there are too few. The problem then was to find new ways of warehousing this surplus population, of disciplining the reserve army of youth labour, perhaps by bringing in some form of conscription and/or removing them from the labour market altogether. This was the solution favoured by the neo-conservative wing of the New Right. They succeeded in getting unemployment benefit withdrawn from 16- and 17-year-olds, and prevented young people from moving to seaside towns in search of casual work while continuing to claim the dole; school-leavers were thus both immobilized in areas of high unemployment, made absolutely dependent on family support and forced to sign on to Youth Training Schemes (hereafter YTS) – which many of them regarded, rightly or wrongly, as slave labour.[9] The neo-conservative rationale for all this was simply that the intervention of a strong state was needed to hold the line against these new 'dangerous classes', until, with a declining birth-rate, and possibly a little assisted emigration, their numbers dropped. These are the people who now proclaim that the youth question is officially solved, because the demographic 'bulge' of the 1960s cohort is past.

In contrast, neo-liberal tendencies on the New Right saw the problem of balancing the supply and demand for youth labour in terms of quality, not quantity. The problem was that schools were not equipping young people with the right skills and personal dispositions to make themselves sufficiently attractive to employers. Here was a chance to reform secondary schooling, and restructure the transition to work in a way which conformed to the requirements of the 'post-Fordist' economy. At the same time, the fact that the traditional system of apprenticeship had become obsolescent, creating unnecessary bottlenecks in the production process, also provided an opportunity to dismantle the cultural forms which supported working-class solidarities and powers of resistance. For the neo-liberals, it was not a question of holding the mob at bay until their numbers fell by natural attrition, but of developing a positive strategy for remaking the working class in its own image, by endowing a new generation of young workers with the individualistic values and practices associated with enterprise culture.

This is where the second major discourse comes into play, aiming not to confine or repress youthful energies but to empower them as agents of capital rather than labour. We might call this an orthopaedic strategy in that it aims at the correct formation of children's attitudes by controlling the conditions under which they acquire basic skills. Given that this strategy is so important to the hidden curriculum of the new vocationalism it is perhaps worth looking at it in more detail.

A short history of skill

One of the constant refrains of employers since the 1970s has been the chronic shortage of properly skilled workers. The poor performance of the British economy compared with West Germany or Japan has frequently been attributed to this factor, which in turn is put down to poor quality of training. In all these debates the issue of what constitutes a skill is rarely discussed. The skilled worker is trained and the unskilled worker is not. It's as simple as that! The notion that skill might itself be an ideological construct, rather than a simple material factor in the labour process, that the same practice might be regarded as skilled, semi-skilled or unskilled according to the particular occupational culture within which it was transmitted, or the gender of the worker performing it, such ideas have been discussed only on the academic fringes of public debate. Nevertheless it is not possible to understand the true import of recent innovations in vocational training without looking at the historical discourses of skill in and against which they are located.

The dominant construct of skill is the outcome of a historical compromise between two leading reproduction codes – the code of the aristocracy, with its paradigm of the amateur and the gentleman, and the code of the bourgeoisie predicated on the position of the professional and the self-made man.[10] Under the former, skill is constructed as a natural aptitude, an *inheritance* of cultural capital, a birthright and a legacy of effortless mastery. The latter code, in contrast, defines skill in terms of personal initiative and drive, measured through an incremental grid of status or *career*. The rise of the 'career code' can be traced in the history of its meaning. From its eighteenth-century usage as a largely derogatory term applied to the rake's progress of younger sons of the aristocracy ('careering about'), the word gradually took on the sense of orderly progress up an occupational ladder associated with competitive success in examinations. By the end of the nineteenth century careerists have made their appearance, and by the 1960s we not only have a careers service for young people whose school 'careers' have disqualified them from pursuing one, but even criminals and delinquents are said to have 'careers', albeit ones closer to the original meaning of the word! The extent to which it is a male construct can be judged from the derogatory connotations of 'career woman'.

However, the code of inheritance is far from having been eclipsed. It continues to dominate common-sense constructs of skill, such as the 'natural athlete', the 'born teacher', etc. In combination, the two codes thus relay a contradictory message: skill is both an inherent property and a socially achieved practice, both the cause and the effect of mastery.

There is, though, another major construct of skill, which increasingly mediates between the terms of this contradiction. It has its own distinctive history, and moreover has come to lend its name, if not its substance, to the preparation of young people for work.

From the time of the seventeenth-century Puritan revolution, the code of vocation has offered an image of skill as a special gift or calling, acquired through a purely interior process, governed by the voice of conscience or the presence of an 'inner light'. Skill here becomes a sign of grace, which may be spiritual, aesthetic or purely physical in mode. In any case it remains the prerogative of the self-elected few.

This code was open to multiple articulations. In one such, the notion of natural aptitude is reworked; it is divorced from its rendering as a congenital mark of birth or breeding, and constructed instead as an 'inner bent', a decidedly more mystical reading of 'innate dispositions'! A quite different set of relays enabled careerists to claim that personal drive had nothing to do with a material quest for fame and fortune, but was simply the realization of a 'God-given' gift. But in its most powerful and popular articulation the code invested the 'congenital destiny' to labour for capital, with a special sense of inner-directed purpose or mission. For according to the protestant work ethic, skill, like virtue, was to be its own reward, measured as an index of an inner, moral worth, rather than in terms of wage differentials.

Yet the vocation code also retained an independent existence albeit one confined to feminine, or Bohemian, pursuits, both, of course, being regarded as equally 'unproductive'. If these activities continued to be valued as skills, it was precisely in so far as they remained economically marginal or unpaid – as generations of housewives, artists, nurses and others have found to their cost! The code thus instructed middle- and upper-class girls that their true calling was caring for men, rather than the 'selfish' pursuit of career. Motherhood was constructed as an exercise in creative self-fulfilment, on the same plane as the male pursuit of the Muse. Whereas the code of inheritance reproduced the patriarchal order as a quasi-biological grid of origins and destinies, under the vocation code this was inscribed in the subject as a project of desire – a far more insidious mechanism.

Working-class ideologies of skill, though no less patriarchal, operate according to quite different principles. Here skill is constructed under the sign of an *apprenticeship*, as the progressive mastery of techniques of dexterity associated with the performance of manual labour, both in the home and for wages. However, these skills could only be legitimately mastered from a position of subordination *vis-a-vis* elders – who always 'know better'. Apprenticeship, in other words, has customarily been to an inheritance of sorts, a patrimony of concrete skills, transmitted through the family, the shop-floor or the wider institutions of the class-culture and community. This entailed a whole process of socialization into the customary practices of the work-place, including special rituals of initiation and the mastery of skills associated with practices of informal bargaining and a resistance to line management. Learning a trade under the tutelage of 'old hands' meant informally absorbing the folklore of the trade, and often an oral history of shop-floor struggle. This was not something confined to the indentured few; it characterized the 'on-the-job training' of young people in a whole range of officially unskilled occupations, from textile factories to street markets, and involved girls as well as boys. Moreover, similar modes of learning informed practices of popular pleasure, for example in the structures of sexual apprenticeship to be found in many working-class communities. Political apprenticeships were often modelled on the occupational form, and in the autobiographies of many working-class leaders we can read just how closely technical training and political education went hand in glove.[11]

There are several consequences of this kind of code. It is strongly patriarchal, the power of male elders, as guardians of both the class patrimony and the family wage, over both women and children being almost absolute. Secondly, resistance to technical innovation and social change is intense. Where jobs are regarded as being held in trust by one generation for the next, they will not so easily be sold for productivity deals or redundancy payments. The code has thus been a major stumbling block to attempts to impose a properly capitalist rationality on both the immediate labour process and the labour market.

However, in the post-war period there has occurred a pervasive weakening and fragmentation of these grids. Cultural apprenticeships are no longer so easily or frequently connected to occupational inheritances. The practice of dexterity is no longer anchored to the sign of manual labour; it takes place increasingly in leisure contexts, in the mastery of popular dance forms or video games, for example. As a result positions of 'skill' and 'unskill' are no longer tied so rigidly to divisions of labour or their relations of generational transmission, but are negotiated primarily through the peer group. The body is no longer engendered solely as a bearer of labour power, specialized according to productive (male) or reproductive (female) functions. One effect of this is to make the forms of adolescent sexuality more dependent on what Freud called 'the narcissism' of minor differences, i.e.

differences of taste, clothes and personal life-style. Whether the escape routes this opens up are more imaginary than real, and just how far they undermine working-class sexism, may be open to debate. But the desire to escape a universe of fixed reference, whether of gender or class, could potentially be connected to the kind of mobile individualism currently being promoted through the new regimes of skilling.

The systematic preparation of school-leavers for their future occupational roles, by state agencies, is a relatively recent development. It is designed to gear the transition from school to the requirements of the economy in a way which, it is argued, neither individual employers, nor market forces, alone can do. It is no coincidence that these initiatives came to be defined as *vocational* guidance and preparation, or that a *careers* service should initially have been put in charge of implementing them – since the aim is precisely to establish the hegemony of these codes over working-class constructs of skill.

It is in this context that attempts to introduce new regimes and strategies of vocational training must be understood. Their hidden agenda is to complete the disintegration of the apprenticeship–inheritance model and to strengthen all those forms of working-class individualism which can be articulated within the enterprise culture. This manoeuvre pivots on a redefinition of the functions and meaning of skill. First, skills are dissociated from specific practices of manual labour, or from general forms of mental coordination exercised by workers over the immediate labour process. Secondly, skills are divorced from their historical association within particular trades or occupational cultures, and their acquisition is no longer entailed in a power of social combination tied to a process of cultural apprenticeship. Instead work practices are reclassified into 'occupational training families' defined according to a set of purely functional properties of coordination between atomized operations of mind–body–machine interfacing within the same 'information environment'. In this discourse skills have become abstract universal properties of the labour process. This indeed is what is supposed to make them transferable between one industry and another. In fact training in transferable skills is essentially training for what Marx called abstract labour – that is labour considered in its generic commodity form as an interchangeable unit/factor of production. What transferable skilling corresponds to in reality is the process of deskilling set in motion by information technologies – a process which is here represented as its opposite: an occasion for perpetual reskilling. The main function of this redescription is in fact to undermine the residual forms of control exercised by conventionally skilled workers by increasing elasticities of substitution between different occupational categories. This ploy is usually code-named 'flexibility'.

One of the most notable features of the obsessive inventories and check-lists which are generated by this discourse is the way in which a language of abstraction is deployed to describe labour processes as if they were models of impersonal or bureaucratic rationality. This produces a managerialist perspective which bears little or no real relation to actual working conditions. In so far as this model is applied to concrete forms of manual labour, the resulting descriptions can be positively surreal – as for example in Table 9.1, from a document prepared by the Scottish Education

Table 9.1 *New voxspeak*

Learning outcomes	The student should: 1. communicate effectively with the client to determine requirements; 2. analyse the hair, devise a cutting strategy, and select appropriate tools and equipment; 3. perform the cut safely and effectively.
Content/context	*Corresponding to learning outcomes 1–3:* 1. Good questioning technique; interpretation of client's wishes; communication of possible difficulties with tact and reaching of agreement over any necessary compromise. 2. Consideration of client's personal characteristics and beard/moustache idiosyncracies; selection of method taking account of possible hair growth limitations. 3. Methodical pattern of work; avoidance or correction of scissor marks; check cutting; the achievement of a balanced result to the client's satisfaction.

Department, which modestly describes itself as a 'Specialist Module to enable the student to enhance his/her haircutting skills in the specialist area of beards and moustaches'.

However, when it comes down to 'suggested learning and teaching approaches' it becomes quite clear that these involve quite traditional forms of apprenticeship: the technique is demonstrated, the apprentice watches; the apprentice then copies, while being watched and given advice on how to improve. Moreover since the module is 'salon-based' we might well suspect that other traditional aspects of hairdressing apprenticeship are also likely to be reproduced. Having learnt how to 'put together two metal blades unpowered' (use a pair of scissors) students may find themselves 'operating an unpowered cleaning device suitable for removing superfluous material' (sweeping up) and 'operating electrical equipment to produce steam pressure' (boiling a kettle to make the staff tea).

These elements of 'proto-domestic' labour have been an integral part of the cultural apprenticeships of most young workers; being made to fetch and carry, run errands, sweep up, etc., is something which marks their subordinate quasi-feminine status *vis*-a-vis others, i.e. male/elders, and constitutes the first stage of their initiation into adult shop-floor culture. Yet there is a more positive side to this process. As well as being treated as a dogsbody, the hairdressing apprentice may pick up lots of 'really useful knowledge' about how to deal with awkward customers, or salon managers, how to maximize earnings from tips, even how (or not) to run your own business. But because the vocationalist approach is committed to an ideal hyper-rationalized model of the labour process, it cannot admit many of these real techniques which young workers actually need to learn if they are both to humanize their work and combine effectively – and hence productively – with others. It could be argued that it is these skills of resistance and accommodation to work discipline which are the truly transferable ones.

Along with the abstraction of the labour form goes an individualization of the pedagogic regimes through which labour is skilled and disciplined. The trainee is inducted into methods of learning which focus not on the social relations of production, but on the formation of 'correct' personal attitudes and interpersonal competences. Here also the new vocationalism has introduced a decisive innovation. For the aim is to teach youth trainees how to sell themselves to customers, clients or employers, by learning specific techniques of self-presentation. These techniques are designed to enable the individual to manipulate or project a 'positive image', or at least to conform with occupational norms whilst successfully controlling any anger or resentment this may produce. Training in these so-called social and life skills is essentially training in behavioural etiquettes which concretize in a subject form the general commodity form of abstract labour. What is in reality a position of class subjection (the selling of labour power) is thus represented as its opposite – a position of individual mastery (the marketing of a self-image).

There is also a gendered dimension to this inversion. The aim here is to replace the old masculinist disciplines of apprenticeship, including the arcane rituals of humiliation designed to 'toughen' the young worker, with a code based on the positive acquisition of 'feminine' techniques of tension and impression management. Not that this change necessarily undermines the sexual division of labour. Indeed, given that these skills are so clearly tailored to work in personal service industries, their impact is likely to confine girls even more tightly to occupational roles in this sector. As for boys, learning these skills may help to shift them into non-traditional gender roles, whilst also serving to wean them away from their more 'boisterous' forms of resistance to the exploitative 'protodomestic' features of youth labour. In either case what is often represented as a progressive move to liberate young people from repressive patriarchal structures, turns out on closer inspection to be a device for subjecting them secretly and individually, and hence all the more effectively, to the 'discipline' of market forces.

This shift in methods of work discipline, from a system of external controls and negative sanctions tightly policed by line management, to a more invisible process of self-regulation on the part of individual employees is an essential part of the strategy for remaking the working class for its functions in a post-Fordist economy. But the ideology of the enterprise culture has a much wider remit than that. Its hegemonic project is to reshape the aspirations of all social classes according to a new model of individualism, and it is to this we must now turn.

The enterprise culture as a morality tale: from Samuel Smiles to Richard Branson

When I was growing up in the early 1950s it was still possible to get given 'improving books' for one's birthday, consisting of biographies of self-made men, engineers, inventors, industrialists, entrepreneurs, philanthropists and the like. These men, and they were all men, had usually lived in the 'heroic' age of nineteenth-century capitalism and the books themselves were clearly prepared for the edification of the young. I soon learnt to ignore these 'worthy lives' along with the earnest enjoinders written on the flyleaf to 'go forth and do likewise'; instead like many of my friends I turned to more modern and exciting figures; Dan Dare followed by Dick Barton, Special Agent, and then, in turn, Elvis, Camus, Dylan, Sartre and the Rolling Stones.

Whereas the old heroes triumphed over adversity through hard work and persistent effort, our new role models celebrated their transcendence of all the more mundane concerns of life and labour in favour of Bohemian adventures, philosophizing about the absurdity of human existence or playing in a rock'n'roll band, preferably all three at once!

It is tempting, then, to characterize the cultural politics of Thatcherism as a kind of counter-revolution – the reinstatement of Victorian values swept aside by the 'swinging sixties'; what sweeter revenge for all those lower-middle-class youths at grammar school and university who stayed in to study while everyone else was out having a good time? That subtext seems to be the one which Mrs Thatcher prefers, which is as good a reason as any for questioning its salience. Perhaps, after all, Thatcherism is more complicated than she herself supposes?[12]

For example, one of the move genuinely remarkable figures thrown up by Thatcherism is Richard Branson. A 'hippy entrepreneur' made even better than good, who turned Virgin Records from a small 'alternative' label into a multinational company with interests in every section of the leisure industry, including tourism and airlines, Branson cultivates a careful public image which combines swashbuckling adventures out of the pages of *Boy's Own Paper* with all the classical capitalist virtues and just a touch of bohemianism thrown in for good measure. Here is a romantic individualism in which the protestant work ethic and a libertarian life-style have been effortlessly reconciled. Branson may indeed be the Yuppies' great folk hero; there is certainly no parallel to be found amongst the eminent Victorians, or even the more eccentric Edwardian entrepreneurs. The contemporary forms of self-improvement have a quite different *raison d'être* from the original Victorian version. The figure of Richard Branson has a complex and contradictory provenance which takes some unravelling. In tracing a line of descent from Samuel Smiles, through the Dale Carnegie era between the two World Wars, personal growth movements of the 1960s up to the social and life skill pedagogies of today, the tensions and breaks between those successive forms are as significant as their continuities.[13]

For example, the nineteenth-century version did not always relay an individualistic message about 'pulling oneself up by one's own bootstraps'. It did not necessarily involve the deferential imitation of the manners and morals of 'elders and betters'. It also informed the movement for independent working-class education, supported popular demands for better cultural amenities and living conditions and it has been an element in both the religious and secular visions of socialism. In other words it can take on cooperative forms which stand against the ethic of possessive individualism. In sharp contrast the dominant model gave an aggressive competitive edge to the notion of betterment. Here self-improvement is an exercise in contest mobility, not forelock-touching. The typical mortality tale which features in this literature concerns the hero (almost always male and usually the author) setting out on life's journey, beset by the temptations of pleasure and 'vice' at every turn. The road to fame and fortune follows a very straight and narrow path dictated by conscience and ambition marching hand in hand. Along the way tempters and failures would be met, individuals whose early promise had been confounded by the evils of drink or sex, their role as much to introduce an element of suspense – would the hero fall, be led astray? – as to underline the terrible consequences of ignoring the prescriptive code laid down as the key to success. A very ancient theme, but what is original about this code is the way it legitimizes competition, makes rivalry respectable; the message often seems to be 'stand on your own feet, even if it means treading on other people's toes'.

In the last thirty years, the cooperative vision of self-improvement has virtually disintegrated, while the competitive model has undergone a series of rapid transformations. Many of the old links between material and moral betterment have snapped, but new ones have taken their place. State education promised to provide an institutionalized route to social mobility, in a way that made the lonely struggles of the autodidact or the self-made man stand out as 'heroic' exceptions to the rule. Consumer life-styles emerged in which new and improved self-images could be bought, fully-fashioned, and changed as easily as clothes. These developments are exemplified in post-Second World War forms of rational recreation, always the mainstay of self-improvers. These forms have either become privatized and embedded in costly technologies of leisure consumption; or taken in under state provision. In the first case they constitute symbols of success, rather than a means of achieving it; in the second, they have become a means of providing 'safe activities' for 'dangerous' groups (such as the young, black, unemployed, etc.) rather than a leg up the social ladder. But perhaps the most significant shift has been the way a whole range of bodily pleasures and expressive forms which had hitherto been ruled out of bounds have been legitimized as 'rational recreation' and incorporated within strategies of self-improvement adapted to the codes of the new middle class. At last the old moral economy of fixed and sublimated drives gave way to a liberal therapeutics of 'personal growth' whose slogan might be 'incremental insight equals interpersonal effectiveness equals success in work and play!' Creative individualism has here become a recipe for social success, rather than a symbol of Bohemian excess. In contrast to Smiles, the subject to be improved is a private or inner self rather than a public one, yet the object is still 'promotion'. In effect, the inner-directed features of the vocation code, and the other-directed features of the career code have become inextricably fused, or rather confused!

In the diverse elements which compose social and life-skill (SLS) training, both the Smiles and the liberal therapeutic models have their place. The former has been operationalized in so-called 'assertion training' and given a radical, though no less individualistic, edge; the latter can be found in various kinds of counselling for adolescents in schools and youth projects. Yet at present both approaches remain marginal to the core curriculum of SLS. The reason is not hard to find. The translation of a self-improvement programme into the formal pedagogic context of the state school or training scheme imposes its own selective constraints. What had essentially been a method of self-help, learned through the personal example of mentors who had themselves successfully mastered it, hardly provided a model for institutional provision on a large scale, nor did it fit in with the prevailing relations of educational transmission. It is nevertheless highly significant that it was at the point where the notion of *skill* was made central to self-improvement that the apprenticeship model was dropped in favour of the behaviouristic model of learning applied to the whole field of vocational preparation.[14]

Initially SLS emerged out of an apparently radical critique of state schooling, designed to expose the irrelevance of academic curricula to working-class pupils, and concerned to develop an alternative approach to learning related to their real lives outside the school gates. How did it come to be, so quickly and easily, incorporated within youth training schemes?

Of course the notion that schools or training schemes should be preparing young people for 'life' as well as labour does help give a nice liberal gloss to an otherwise all too crude utilitarian philosophy, and it also provides a convenient safety clause when trainees reach the end of the job-training programmes and find there are still no jobs for them. But the promotion of SLS is not the story of the corruption of an ideal. From the beginning it was conceived as a form of compensatory education suitable for 'non-academic' children; and what had to be compensated for was not only the inadequacy of existing forms of classroom knowledge, but the deficiencies of the pupils' cultures as well. It was a *double* deficit model in which the school's failure to connect with the 'real world of work' was mirrored in a failure of the working-class family to transmit the kinds of communication skills and interpersonal competencies which employers were now demanding for white collar jobs. But, never mind, those skills and competencies could be taught in the *same way* as woodwork or metalwork.

From the outset, then, a new micro-technology of self-improvement is proposed; the social is dissolved into the interpersonal as a condition of the expressive becoming fully instrumentalized. Behaviourist theories of learning were thus the most appropriate pedagogic model for social- and life-skilling. Amongst the pioneers in the field was the Industrial Training Research Unit with its programme entitled CRAMP (Comprehension, Reflex learning, Attitude development, Memorization, Procedural learning).

Even more significant was the work carried out by a group of social psychologists under the direction of Michael Argyle at Oxford. Inspired by ethological studies of animal and human communication, this team set out to devise a rehabilitation programme for long-term inmates of prisons and mental hospitals. This started from the somewhat circular proposition that 'social deviants' had failed to learn 'normal' techniques of social interaction. In the case of mental patients and prisoners we might suspect that their long periods of incarceration might have had something to do with it but, never mind, they could at least now be taught how to behave themselves in public once they were released! The programme consisted of a crash course in verbal and non-verbal communication techniques (rules for eye contact and body posture in various social settings, how to pick up and respond to social cues, how and when to smile appropriately, conversational rituals, etc.). It was assumed that once the subject had learnt to release these signals 'correctly', social relations would become unproblematic.

In many ways Michael Argyle is the Frederick Winslow Taylor of the human relations industry. Just as Taylor attempted to establish a science of production-line management based on time and motion studies, so Argyle is aiming at a science of impression management also based on breaking down social practices into standardized, quantified and controllable units of 'interaction'. But where Taylorism was concerned to maximize the physical efficiency and output of the factory worker, Argyle's programme is somewhat more ambitious. For the norms of interpersonal efficiency he uses make the notion of 'social skill' highly transferable between a whole range of contexts. They are not only designed to increase the productivity of the white-collar worker, but also that of the housewife (tension management!). These are techniques for selling yourself to a prospective lover as well as to a personnel manager. The very transferability of these 'skills' is an index of their real disciplinary function and scope. For their effect is to anatomize the speaking body into a set of 'proper' features silently regulated by law – the law of 'free and equal exchange' (Argyle's 'interaction') – which systematically conceals the structural inequalities in power governing the production of the discourse. Despite the claims that this legal body has an 'instinctual foundation', it turns out to be the bearer of a behavioural ideology combining the calculating rationality of the boardroom with the social niceties of the bourgeois drawing-room. As for the reality principles behind this project, it is perhaps worth noting that the result of the proposed 'reskilling' of the mental patient or prisoner seems a lot closer to the fragmented routines of the deskilled labourer than to the 'whole personality of the informed citizen' that is claimed.

Given this, it might seem at first sight rather odd that social and life skills should have been taken up so enthusiastically by educationalists; but the paradigm was all too easily recast in terms of demands for a 'relevant' curriculum for early leavers. For here was a method which would teach them 'how to communicate effectively, how to make, keep and end relationships, how to make effective transitions, how to be positive about oneself, how to manage negative emotions, how to cope with unemployment, how to cope with stress, and how to be an effective member of a group' and much else besides.[15] A veritable panacea for those concerned to free working-class pupils from the 'double tyranny' of mechanical solidarity and abstract thought.

Yet the essential appeal, to teachers as well as pupils, was the promise to forge new and more substantive links between self-improvement and self-employment. To be your own boss was still supposed to mean not simply being in control of your own self-image, but to own and control a small business. In many ways the career of Richard Branson dramatizes that articulation between new and old versions of petty bourgeois individualism. But this merger of enterprise culture with youth culture, like Branson's own preferred strategy for success, is in reality a take-over bid. And as Thatcherism strengthened its hold, it was private philanthropy rather than public education which took the initiative in promoting the view that the answer to youth unemployment was to 'create yourself a job'. From 1982 onwards the argument was increasingly heard that self-employment, whether in the hidden economy or in small enterprises based on the new cultural industries, was the most fruitful way in which young people could turn skills and interests generated by their life-styles into a means of livelihood. Dance, music and other elements of do-it-yourself culture could all be turned to good account. What is practised for pleasure can be practised with profit!

In this way the initial threat posed by the emergence of (especially black) counter-cultures was significantly neutralized. The Prince Charles Trust, for example, sponsored training schemes which aimed to turn unemployed youth into cultural capitalists of one sort or another. One of its advertising posters shows a scowling skinhead with the caption 'Help him to create wealth, not aggro'; another shows a black youth and reads 'Help him keep the right company – his own'. These are rhetorical images designed to construct a certain kind of Thatcherite common sense to the effect that anyone (even blacks!) can make it if they try, provided they have a little help from their elders and betters (like Prince Charles). A poster advertising 'Youth Action 89' – a display of youthful endeavour promoted by the Government's enterprise allowance scheme – is even more explicit in its message; a picture of Norman Tebbit (then Mrs Thatcher's right-hand man – Chairman of the Conservative Party) dressed in a preparatory school uniform with the caption 'if he hadn't realized his potential he might have ended up on a park bench, not the Front Bench'. The rags-to-riches story is here given a subtle twist to convey a hidden threat to all those who do not subscribe to dreams of ambition and career success.

Many of the small self-help enterprises set up and run by young people with starter finance from public funds were initially inspired by an alternative and altogether more cooperative vision. However, they often involve the kind of work already performed by young people in domestic or leisure contexts – so many variations on the 'odd job' collective, doing window cleaning, babysitting, gardening, decorating, household and bike repairs. Traditionally this kind of work was included in the category of blind alley occupations, but now it is redescribed as a stepping-stone to a better future. Often these set-ups only survive by drastically undercutting rates for the job charged by unionized firms or qualified workers. So although they may start with good intentions about creating socially useful jobs and organizing themselves according to principles of democratic self-management, all too many of them are forced by the economic logic of their situation to subscribe tacitly or openly to the values of the enterprise

culture. The names they choose for themselves – Bootstraps',
'Ladders', etc. – give the game away.

The combination of romantic individualism and penny capitalism exemplified in many of these schemes has a potentially wide
appeal to young people whose traditional routes into wage labour
have been blocked. The 'greening' of Mrs Thatcher in the late
1980s – however superficial – may give added impetus to this kind
of solution. The slogan 'small is beautiful' thus reaches its final
apotheosis in giving a slightly more hedonistic or human face to
popular capitalism. But once again this is a morality tale with a
complex genealogy. It originated in a historical compromise
between the bourgeois work ethic and aristocratic pleasure principles in mid-Victorian Britian, a compromise cemented in the rational recreation movement and the civilizing mission to the
working classes. Mr Gradgrind was forced to admit that 'all work
and no play made Jack a dull boy' (though it made Jill a good
wife!), while the Marquess of Queensbery wrote 'Leisure Earned is
the Devil Spurned' into his rule book. The construction of the
Great Outdoors as a playground for the urban masses was designed
both to spur them on to greater industry and channel their interests away from politics and crime. But, more than that, it symbol-
ized a peculiar alliance between different sections of the governing
class, which in turn made it easier to neutralize popular anti-industrial sentiment and even convert it to a programme for modernizing both capital and state. In this unique coalition of forces, the
dissenting voice of English socialism, as represented by Morris and
Ruskin, was squeezed to the margins of public debate, where it was
tolerated as an eccentric or merely Utopian presence.

Today socialists who wish to reclaim self-improvement or other
elements of petty bourgeois radicalism have to start from this
weak point. They also have to compete with the New Right's own
vision of a return to England's 'green and pleasant land' based on
'organic', family-centred and home-owning communities, small-
scale hi-tech production units, and freedom from state control.
The training of young people in practices which militate against
their identification with organized labour, the displacement of
job creation to the un- or deregulated margins of the economy,
the construction of 'leisure' as a cottage industry for the unemployed, all help to ensure that the vision of the 'New Jerusalem'
remains captive to the enterprise culture.

However, it is also important to realize some of the limitations of this strategy as a means of incorporating the underclass as a whole. Historically, self-improvement, of whatever kind, has appealed only to those sections of the lower middle and upper working classes whose social aspirations have, for one reason or another, been structurally blocked. It has never caught on amongst the poor, the unskilled and the unemployed. But is this changing? Will the present generation of school-leavers, living, as they say, 'on the rock and roll', find more survival value in techniques of self-improvement than their predecessors did? Certainly the handbooks, teaching kits, visual aids and other SLS materials that were introduced at this time took great pains to dress up their improving message in fashionable clothes. A closer look at some of this literature may therefore be useful, both to give us a clearer idea of the kind of discursive strategies being employed by these latter-day Samuel Smileses, and to help us assess what is likely to be their impact on their young readerships.

Janet and John in Thatcherland

All the texts I looked at[16] were designed to appeal to young people whom the publicity handouts variously described as 'non-academic', 'under-achievers' or 'poor readers with short attention spans' – in other words, the 'residuum'. It was clear from the handouts (and the materials themselves) that a common set of assumptions was being made about 'the kids': they are ignorant of their rights and weakly motivated to defend them. They lack any kind of work experience. They have no access to useful information and advice other than that provided by official agencies and professional experts. They have difficulty in organizing their lives in a rational or satisfactory way.

Now this does not remotely add up to an accurate account of the way school-leavers deal with their real situation. It is simply a deficit model of working-class culture used to provide a rationale for SLS as a form of compensatory education. As to their actual content, all the texts offered very similar information and advice about looking for a job, going for an interview, fitting in at work, claiming state benefits and getting on training or further education courses. A section on safe sex was usually included in the package, along with advice on 'personal relations'. Youth politics, whether to do with unemployment, housing or cultural questions, is conspicuous by its absence. What were, in effect, pills of information and advice were offered in an easily digestible form; the objective seemed to be to give the reader quick-acting, if not permanent, relief from a range of social ills (poverty, boredom, discrimination, etc.). 'If you take this advice regularly (before and after interviews?), you'll be OK' was the basic comforting message.

But perhaps the messages are not quite so straightforwardly reassuring as the authors intended. The explicit prescriptions – the texts are full of check-lists of do's and don'ts – also have to stake their claim to credibility or 'realism' by acknowledging unpleasant facts, such as unemployment, homelessness or racism. Yet the anxieties these situations may arouse in young people are in no way assuaged by the way the issues are actually dealt with. For instead of explaining the origins and causes of these phenomena, or documenting the struggles which are being waged against them, they are presented as social calamities which can neither be understood nor prevented, but whose effects may be avoided by purely individual measures of precaution. Yet the guarantees of 'personal safety' which this offers are not likely to stand up against the lived experience of school-leavers, especially in areas of high unemployment. Nor is the attempt to sugar the pill by wrapping the exhortatory messages in photo-stories or cartoons likely to take away the bitter taste which is left.

It is in their claim to be purely factual or practical that these materials reveal themselves as ideological through and through. School-leavers are indeed being invited to enter into an imaginary relation to their predicaments; not because the ways suggested for dealing with them are in themselves impracticable, or inexact, but because they are premised on a *subject position* which turns real relations to capital or the state upside down and inside out. For the reader who is addressed, whether directly, or indirectly, is always a *legal* subject, i.e. an individual centre of contractual rights and obligations, free and equal before the law. It is from this position that we are urged to join a trade union, resist racism and sexism, start our own business, be polite to policemen and dress sensibly for interviews. It is also, as a legal subject, that the reader is supposed to recognize the situations shown, identify with the 'exemplary' figures of youth portrayed in them, and clutching a check-list of prescriptions in hand, go and do likewise.

But this is not just an exercise in conforming to external rules and regulations. These texts counsel young people to police their own behaviour, not by appealing to the wisdom or authority of 'elders and betters', but by referencing the experience of peers. The testimonies of young people who have apparently followed the advice and succeeded is a recurring device used to lend credibility, or realism, to the text. In the process, the legal subject is subtly converted into a *judicious self*, a super-ego, based not on the father (whose word is no longer law) but on an imaginary peer, a double representing the reader's 'better self'.

Through this beguiling figure, the voice of self-improvement speaks, and constructs its special effects of meaning. But of course everything now depends on whether readers do indeed recognize themselves in the mirror images projected by these 'judicious selves'. I showed a sample of this literature to a group of twenty unemployed school-leavers in north London; I asked them whether they thought the situations that were portrayed in the photo-stories or cartoons were realistic, and whether the information and advice amounted to really useful knowledge. The response was almost entirely negative. They found the story-lines artificial, the language used patronizing, and the information and advice completely abstracted from the real social context of their lives.

To illustrate this, let us look in more detail at one fairly typical example of the genre. *The School Leaver's Guide* (Symonds, 1981) sticks very closely to the core curriculum of SLS. A separate topic is dealt with on each double-page spread, and the format consists of a photo or cartoon story accompanied by a checklist of do's and don'ts. In the stories, all the young people are shown dressed sensibly, as if for interviews. They spend most of their time posed in empty space, occasionally framed by the odd corner of a table, or brick wall, saying things like 'Hi Sheila, I've been told to leave my job because I'm pregnant' or 'Magic, it's my cheque from the *DSS* [Department of Social Security]. I'll cash it and have some money to spend at last.'[16] The characters are continually hailing each other, and the reader, with lines like 'Hi. Last week I went for my seventh interview and I think I've finally got it right. I thought I'd pass on a few ideas to you.' Sometimes we get what passes for a dialogue:

Girl A   Hi! I haven't seen you for a few months, did you get a
          job after all?
Girl B   No, but I took your advice and applied for a place at
          college.
Girl C   Colleges have typing, nursing, mechanics, electrical
          work, dressmaking, engineering, photography, art,
          catering, maths, hairdressing and loads of other
          courses and you don't always need exams to get in.
Girl A   I started last week. It's OK.

As you can see, these youngsters are not arresting conversational-
ists despite all the hailing that goes on. They would, however,
provide great material for a Monty Python sketch! Even when
relaxing at the youth club, they are likely to have earnest discussions about the role of industrial tribunals, or social security
appeal procedures. They are surrounded by kindly officials,
including the police who are presented as a more or less benevo-
lent agency of the welfare state. The section entitled 'Arrest'
begins:

> Most people only contact the police when they have some sort
> of a problem. They go to the police station voluntarily to regis-
> ter a complaint or seek information. However there are occa-
> sions when the police may seek your help. You may wish to help
> them, but you should also know your rights.

An even more strenuous exercise in wish fulfilment is to be
found in the section dealing with trade unions. A West Indian boy
and girl are shown having an argument about the pros and cons
of joining one. The girl is initially hostile, but is finally won over
by the lad's assertion that unions are in the vanguard of the fight
against sex and race discrimination!
    The script throughout is written in a bizarre mixture of child-
ish language and 'bureaucratese'. There is no real dialogue or
debate between the characters because whatever their role,
everyone speaks either in the name of the law or in the language
of the judicious self. The Everyboys and Girls who people the
stories are persons without personalities, ventriloquists'
dummies manipulated by the hidden hand of an ideology not
their own. The device of putting official information and advice

into the mouths of a multi-ethnic cast of working-class teenagers may strike you as a rather pathetic piece of sleight-of-hand, one which says a lot about the authors' patronizing attitudes. But the point is, it is *structurally* necessary to maintain the coherence of this particular universe of discourse. The problem the authors had to solve, whether they recognized it or not, was this: if the text is to work, in the sense of getting the message across, then readers have to identify with its 'senders' (the characters) as speaking on their behalf, or in some way representing the real world. But if the text is to work as an enunciation of official codes of practice, then everything which would enable working-class school-leavers to identify with the characters in terms of language, culture or ideology has to be cut out. In trying to get round this problem – which the use of familiar graphic forms highlights, but does not solve – the authors are impelled to construct a story-line which is both mystifying and obtuse. Let us look at a typical case in point.

Really cool knowledge?

Two pages of the book deal with applying for a job by phone (see figure on p. 306). A white boy and black girl are shown ringing up a garage in reply to an advertisement for a salesperson. The boy does it all wrong, while the girl follows all the correct procedures as laid down in the accompanying check-list. However *both* applicants are turned down. The manager thanks them for ringing but says 'there are a lot of people we have to interview'. No other explanation is given. On the face of it, then, the implication seems to be that there is no pay-off for learning 'good' interview techniques, since they make absolutely no difference to the outcome. That, indeed, is the conclusion which the young people reading this sequence reached. Why should a book which is devoted to life and social skills put across such a self-defeating message? Why was not the black girl, shown as such an adept at 'impression management', rewarded by being offered an interview, while the lad who is made to break all the rules, has to suffer the consequences?

One reason is that if the book is to maintain any credibility with the reader, it has to maintain a semblance of economic realism. It has to take into account the fact that in a situation of structural unemployment *and* credential inflation, the links between educability and employability on which so much of the teachers' authority rests, can no longer be made with any degree of conviction. School-leavers are coming to realize that no matter how impressive their interview manners, how good their personal or academic credentials, irrespective of how many dozens of immaculately written letters they send out or how diligently they follow the instructions in their job-hunter kits, the cards have already been dealt and theirs read 'sorry, no vacancies'.

How then to motivate them, to cool out their immediate demands for real work at a living wage, and persuade them to go on a training scheme instead, without simultaneously practising a cruel deception? This is the problem which teachers face, and which this sequence (and the whole book) tries to solve. It does so not by suppressing the contradiction, but by displacing its terms into a magical resolution: the salvage of individual victories out of collective defeats.

How is this effect achieved here? Consider for a moment the position of the garage manager. Despite the marked differences between the two applicants, in terms of race, gender and class 'attributes', he is shown addressing them identically throughout. Obviously an equal opportunities employer, he rejects them both!

In other words the manager is constructed as an exemplary legal subject. He conforms to employment legislation (the Race Relations and Sex Discrimination Acts) and this in turn legitimates his freedom to hire and fire according to the laws of the market (lots of others to interview, sorry). What in fact is being guaranteed is his freedom *not* to hire and *not* to give any substantive reason why. The applicants are left with their 'freedom' to remain unemployed. The interview is presented as an equal exchange between free subjects, rather than what it is, an unequal power relation between capital and labour mediated by patterns of social discrimination institutionalized by the state. The symmetry of the manager's responses is necessary to maintain the legal fiction and suppress the social facts.

If he had been shown differentiating between the boy and girl, following a policy of either negative or positive discrimination, then the real relations in play would have had to be depicted simply to maintain the congruity of the story-line. His silences are equally functional. Because this is an exercise in public propriety we are not told what he might be thinking or feeling in contradistinction to what he says. No advantage can thus be taken, here or elsewhere, of the cartoon's capacity to demystify, e.g. by using 'think-bubbles' to articulate a sub-text of what is truly going on but is censored, distorted or covered over in official discourse. In the process, the power of the interviewer to remain silent, to withhold information or to lie, and the interviewee's powerlessness to challenge these prerogatives without offending against the code, all this is massively endorsed – and this in a book which ostensibly upholds young people's rights!

There is, however, a further twist to the tale, which concerns the type of qualities associated with the occupation chosen for the exercise. 'Salesperson in a garage' can refer equally to men's work (car salesman) or women's work (behind the counter) *without* putting in question the fundamental rule governing the sexual division of labour (the closer the job is to operating the machine, the more likely it is to be a masculine preserve).

Moreover no school-leaver would be taken on as a car salesman – it is indeed regarded as a 'man's' job, not a boy's. Salesperson therefore in this context has the connotation of shop girl. The qualities which are normally demanded for shop work – selling one's self to sell the product, looking good to make the customer feel good – are of course constructed as 'essentially feminine'. Now none of this is problematized in the text. Instead the girl is shown as having effortlessly mastered the art of selling herself whereas the boy apparently sees no reason even to try. Her 'success', his 'failure', does not therefore represent some role reversal. It reinforces gender stereotypes in the crudest possible way.

At the same time a far more subtle and insidious displacement is effected in the story-line. As I have said, the even-handedness of the garage manager is mystifying, in that it works to conceal the real asymmetry between his class position and that of the young people, but the asymmetry that *is* shown operating between the two job applicants is no less mystifying. For the distinction between right and wrong interview manners not only cancels the real differences between them but also conceals the fact that they are being positioned *symmetrically* within *the same system of double binds*. How does this occur?

The lad is allowed to drop his aitches, confess he doesn't really want the job, run out of money for the telephone and forget the

name of the 'bloke in charge'. The nearest anyone in this book is ever permitted to come to a position with which the reader could identify! This character can be a 'speaking subject' within a certain code of working-class masculinity, affirm something like a cultural identity, but only as an index of *social disqualification*, a transgressor of 'the law'.

The black girl, in contrast, is made to give a flawless perform- ance of deference to white middle-class etiquette. Even when she gets the brush-off, she politely thanks the manager for his help! But she is allowed to exist only as a subject spoken for by the dom- inant culture, one who suppresses anything that would affirm her real identity. The line that is drawn between the two characters is not one of gender, ethnicity or class; that would destroy the whole fragile grid of legal subjectivity on which the story rests. In con- trast, the distinction that *is* made reinforces the grid, for it rests on the opposition between judicious and injudicious selves.

Injudicious selves 'show themselves up', 'give themselves away', 'lose control'. Judicious selves remain *self-possessed*, on condition that they first *disown* everything that would invest them with the properties of speaking subjects. Which is better? To remain calm, cool and collected by taking the role of 'The Other' or show your- self up as being incompetent or worse, 'uncool', by 'being your- self'. That is the double bind into which *both* these characters are implicitly locked.

Self-possession has been turned into a highly convertible cur- rency – both a selling-point for prospective employers and an insurance policy against feelings of indignation or disappoint- ment triggered by rejection; a 'therapeutic' for dealing with anxi- eties of the first interview or the traumas of a first date. It is by these means that young people are supposed to conjure individ- ual victories out of collective defeats, or, as here, black girls do better than white boys. Instead of being helped to confront their shared predicaments within a wider framework of knowledge and action, they are offered a purely personal tactic of disavowal.

What this means in classroom practice, as I found, is that even when a political issue, such as job discrimination, is implicitly posed, it cannot be clarified or made explicit within the terms of reference set out. I asked my group why they thought the garage manager had turned the applicants down. Was it because the girl was black and he was a racist? 'Well, no, because he couldn't see

her, and she talked posh, so he couldn't tell by what she said.' Was
it because she was a girl? 'No, because it wasn't a particularly male
job anyway.' Why did the boy get rejected? 'He messed up the interview ... no it couldn't be that 'cos the girl did everything right and
she got the brush off too.' Did the manager then turn them down
on different grounds? 'No.' Why? 'Because he said the same to
both, treated them the same way.' But he might have been thinking
different things about them? 'Well, you couldn't know, could you?'
So what was the point of the story? 'We don't know. It's pointless,
stupid. The people who wrote it must be mad!'

They are not mad, but they are certainly unconscious of the way
their ideological grammar serves to close off any space for critical
engagement by the reader, subverting their own undoubtedly progressive intentions.

I have tried to show how here the ideal of 'self-possession' plays a
key role in shifting the ideology of self-improvement onto a new
terrain. In the classic Samuel Smiles version, it was at least recognized that legal subjects were free to negotiate or bargain with real
competitors in the market-place, to find the highest price for their
labour and so on. I think it is very significant that no one in this
book is shown doing so. The competition between the boy and girl
is not set up in these terms at all. Rather it is invisibly structured by
a purely symbolic exchange, a system of trade-offs between a public
and a private self. The public self is made to adjust to undesirable
realities (viz., the Youth Training Scheme or unemployment) by
suppressing its real features (as in the case of the black girl). By the
same token, the private self is made the focus of unrealizable
desires (the dream job, or the job you really want, as with the boy).
Subtly, the right of collective bargaining is transmuted into the
obligation to conduct a purely interior negotiation between two
halves of a divided self. Impression management makes its cultural
capital out of just that split, even as it promises to resolve it. The full
formula for its 'therapeutic' double bind should be written: 'privatize what you publicly are – publicize what you privately
are not', and *enjoy* the duplicity for the sense of power it gives you
over the means of self-representation.

Clearly we have come a long way from old-style bourgeois individualism. There is no place for the strong inner-directed ego,
voice of conscience and morality in this scenario. Nor are young
people being trained to measure themselves competitively against

their peers, to run and win in the rat race. Yet elements of both the vocation and career codes are still in play; they have been transposed into the figures of a new individualism, more flexible and 'desirable' than the old, capable of adapting itself continually to the changing demands of market forces, while sustaining the illusion of its autonomy from them. It all adds up to a subject form ideally suited to a 'Hi-tech' version of consumer capitalism and one that is increasingly being mobilized against the residual forms of resistance which this is throwing up.[17]

The 'cooling out' of school-leavers' aspirations is no longer being left to the cumulative effect of educational failure, or the sudden pressures of the labour market. A new set of pedagogic and counselling devices is being developed, of which existing forms of careers guidance and SLS are but the crude prototypes. So let us take a brief look at some possible trends for the future.

I think it is possible to envisage a scenario in which the whole process of disqualification was turned to rather different account; instead of being coerced into conformity or bribed into better ways, classroom resisters would be encouraged to follow the example of those of their peers who have learned to win against the system by pretending to play its game. In other words they could be officially counselled how to 'play it cool'.

There are probably as many styles of playing it cool as there are terms to describe the practice. It is part of the survival tactics of every subordinate group, a way of neutralizing the consequences of powerlessness without challenging the prerogatives of power. Playing it cool avoids the risks of open defiance and the humiliation of abject surrender to the dominant norm. Indeed the very success of this game depends on how skilfully the ambiguous status of the practice is played upon. Its basic elements involve the following:

1. The construction of a position of inner detachment or mental reserve which enables people to dissociate themselves from acts of compliance imposed upon them by a superior authority.
2. The systematic inhibition of spontaneous feelings, whether positive or negative, in contexts where this would be interpreted as a sign of weakness.[18]

The central paradox of this whole manoeuvre is that it preserves the integrity of an oppositional identity only by practising a calculated duplicity: you pretend to be playing according to the official rules, whilst secretly bending them to the advantage of your own, rather different, game – that of 'loser wins'. Thus, for example, a 'cool' way for young soldiers to get a free discharge from the army may be to pretend that they are gay. But if you are really gay, and happen to like army life, then the 'cool' thing to do is to pretend that you are as heterosexual as the other lads, while in secret, in the company of your gay friends, continuing to 'be yourself'.

As this example shows, 'playing it cool' is a very double-edged weapon. In some contexts it may be a rational survival tactic; in others it may be profoundly self-destructive, and it is often very difficult to tell which is which – who is playing whose power game, who is losing and who winning – first because the game involves the suppression of true feelings (which is why it is a predominantly masculine technique) and second because this form of one-upmanship is simply a mirror image of real power relations, a way, precisely, of conjuring imaginary victories out of positions of real defeat.

'Playing it cool' is thus a rather more 'hip' version of the techniques of impression management already being taught to school-leavers in SLS. The cultural contexts may be different but the mechanisms (of splitting, etc.) are essentially the same, and this is what some of the new vocationalists are beginning to realize.

In our telephone interview story, if the black girl is represented as someone whose conformity to the dominant code involves the abject surrender of her identity, few readers will support her position – especially not black girls. The boy, in contrast, becomes a popular hero. But what if the story-line is contextualized in a slightly different way? What if the black girl is represented as *pretending* to play 'whitey's' game, while secretly laughing up her sleeve at him? Why, then she is 'playing it cool' and it is the boy who is being stupidly 'uncool'. I offered just such a reading to a control group of school-leavers and that indeed was their response.

The question this leaves us with is a disturbing one. For we seem to be looking at a mode of resistance which systematically fractures and undermines the inner strengths required to sustain a collective sense of predicament and struggle. But is this the only possible outcome? Or is the enterprise culture truly digging its

own grave by releasing ambitions which cannot possibly be realized within the political and economic frameworks at its disposal?
Is there a new and specifically post-modernist form of individualism which subverts the kinds of identifications which Thatcherism
seeks to promote? Meanwhile, on the other side of the equation,
are there alternative forms of vocational education or youth
training which can promote a more cooperative vision of self-
improvement and really useful knowledge?

Negative capabilities: taking after Thatcherism?

The creation of an enterprise culture is central to the Thatcher
'revolution'; it is here that the political, economic and ideological
dimensions of the programme are most clearly and decisively integrated. The privatization of the public realm, the permeation of
market values into the most intimate reaches of social life, the
modernization of traditional forms of individualism, these aims
required the creation of an institutional framework, cutting across
and linking industry and education, civil society and the state in a
radically new way. Other elements of the New Right philosophy,
for example, its espousal of monetarism and 'Little Englander'
nationalism, are important, but they remained essentially tactical
interventions, to be jettisoned as soon as they had outlived their
usefulness. The question still to be decided is whether the construction of an enterprise culture does indeed represent a
genuine process of socio-economic transformation or whether it
too is yet another heraldic device, lacking real substance. Will it
survive as a permanent monument to Thatcherism, or is its fate
too intimately bound up with that of the Iron Lady herself? Will
the spell of the fairy story be finally broken now that the economic miracle it forecast has so evidently failed to come to pass?[19]

   When Harold Macmillan was asked this question he answered
by quoting the Victorian adage 'children often run to Nurse, for
fear of finding something worse'. The image of Mrs Thatcher as a
nanny figure, a stern governess who keeps our noses to the grind-
stone while holding socialism and the permissive society at bay,
may indeed speak to infantile fears and fantasies, especially on the
part of men who had an upbringing in which such authoritarian
figures played a central role. But by the same token it can hardly
have the same appeal to all those who have lost out under her

regime – and that includes large sections of the professional middle class, women, organized labour and the black underclass.

It could be argued that the enterprise culture never depended solely on material indicators of prosperity. It was much more a moral crusade, whose fervour was not dented by the high failure rate of small businesses. After all, even the appeal to monetarism turned out to have more to do with the moral economy of family budgeting and the iconography of 'sound money' than with actual fiscal policy.

A slightly more realistic argument is that the spell worked only as long as there were just enough people visibly better-off to make even those who were not think that it might one day happen to them. In other words as long as the economy (and especially the housing market) was sufficiently buoyant to transform the neurotic envies of relative deprivation into a soothing daydream of affluence just around the corner. But the impact of the Poll Tax, coupled with high interest rates and the return of 'stagflation', was enough to dispel this hope. For an increasing number the Thatcherite dream has begun to turn into a waking nightmare.

However useful such an argument is against the tendency to over-estimate the 'special effects' of Thatcherism, it still cannot explain the fact that however socially polarized Britain has become, however manifestly unjust or inequitable some of the policies, there has been no corresponding movement to the Left; indeed the political opposition is now largely fighting on the ground staked out by the New Right. For example, the strategic importance of consumer choice, the new stress on individual as opposed to collective solutions, the development of more flexible work practices, the property- and share-owning democracy, all these themes pioneered by the New Right have been taken up in the New Labour Party's recent policy reviews. This exercise has clearly succeeded in convincing many floating voters that Labour would continue to support the central values and structures of the enterprise culture, merely ensuring that hitherto disadvantaged groups would have greater opportunity to participate in them. *En route* any alternative or more generous vision of social justice (let alone socialist policies) has been made unthinkable as well as unworkable.[20]

The continual reiteration of 'There is no alternative' seems to have worked as a self-fulfilling prophecy! But if so much of the

New Right's thinking has come to be accepted as common sense, then this is only because it articulates basic changes in the structure of economy and society which in turn have created the ideological conditions for its hegemony. This is not just a passive process, or a matter of 'values'. Everyone who sets up their own business as a result of the Enterprise Allowance Scheme, or who buys their own council house, has a material stake in a particular kind of vision of society. Of course Mrs Thatcher is famous for her belief that 'society' is an abstraction dreamed up by Marxist sociologists, to make life awkward. But perhaps, after all, a little sociology might help us to understand the changing terrain on which the battle for hearts and minds has now to be fought?

Clearly we are living through a period in which the mechanical solidarities of kith and kin, neighbourhood and community, workplace and trade union are fast disintegrating; where they remain they take on increasingly overt – and violent – racist and sexist overtones. At the same time the political ideologies and institutions predicated on this type of solidarity have undergone a similar decay. Both state socialism and the collectivist ethic associated with classical parties of the Left are withering away.

Marx and Durkheim in their different ways foresaw this process, if not always the consequences, as the division of labour became increasingly specialized, and as new technologies replaced 'living labour' in the production process.[21] Durkheim thought it would usher in a new era of pluralistic socialism, based upon 'organic' solidarities, i.e. loose-knit associations between functionally differentiated but interdependent groups of producers and citizens. Marx argued that in principle the increased productivity of labour could liberate workers from the tyranny of the immediate labour process and help create the conditions for an eventual erosion of the basic divisions between manual and mental work. Obviously we are a long way from this state of affairs, though the emergence of a new kind of cultural worker, and new forms of organization in the 'alternative' movements (black, gay and feminist) based on networking and affinity groups seems to point, partially, in this direction.

The actual situation is most hopefully characterized as a long-drawn-out and painful process of transition between Durkheim's two types of solidarity. There are no grounds for thinking that we have reached the end of history, let alone ideology, as the philosophers of the New Right have claimed. In any case, I have argued that it is more useful to consider the present conjuncture as the advent of a new technology of individualism which is better adapted to the formation of the 'collective worker' in a Hi-tech system of production as well as to the organization of popular consumption. I have tried to show how this has occurred within the shell of 'old' occupational and pedagogic forms and how, in the process, the desire to be different is both fuelled by a sense of powerlessness and social atomization, but also works to invest positions of subjection with an aura of false mastery. The 'modern religion' of individualism is so powerful precisely because it offers a source of integration which can never be attained under the existing divisions of labour, and which for that very reason stimulates an insatiable quest for its possession.

Here I believe lies the key to understanding why the fairy story of self-improvement continues to be believed even and especially when the economic indicators of success are so evidently absent. For if others fail then that is all the more reason to redouble one's own efforts, pushing oneself to the limits of self-exploitation and beyond, in order to grasp the holy grail of 'being your own boss', or 'being your own person'. In this context the actual splitting of social identity does not so much liberate people from 'totalizing' ideologies and 'fixed positions' as the post-modernists claim, as furnish them with strategies of dissociation, based on magical positions of omnipotence, reinforcing their real conditions of oppression.[22]

Yet to stop the analysis at this point is to ignore the energies which the enterprise culture has so clearly released. We have to recognize that the majority of people do feel empowered by owning their own home or small business in a way they do not by participating in more collective forms of undertaking. It is useless to argue that they are simply suffering from 'false consciousness'; equally the desire to be recognized in the first person singular is an existential imperative, not just the product of the machinations of 'Thatcherism'. For example, children in school do not want to be recognized as 'Green Class' or 'working-class under-achievers' or 'ethnic minority pupils' or even as 'black' if it means that they stop being treated as human subjects with unique personal histories. Teachers are valued pre-

cisely in so far as they are able to relate in a distinctively appropriate way to particular children, rather than simply pigeon-
holing them. Moreover the way in which children negotiate and
make sense of the social structures they inhabit does indeed vary
dramatically from one to another, even where common patterns
can be discerned. The kind of sociology which recognizes
people as only the bearers of structures or functions has proved
conspicuously unable to grasp these more intimate and subtle
dialectics.

One attempt to do just that is to be found in the work of
Roberto Unger.[23] For Unger, the motor for social change lies in
what he calls (after Keats rather than Hermann Khan) negative
capability – the permanent ability of human beings to transcend
the given conditions of their social existence either through elementary acts of refusal, or through the active imagination of alter-
natives. In the absence of institutional structures which allow this
sociological imagination to flourish at the level of policy making
as well as everyday life, negative capabilities will necessarily take
on individualistic, nihilistic or regressive forms, and this is precisely what the enterprise culture has so successfully engineered.
There are many signs of this: the rampant careerism which has
penetrated into large sections of the oppositional intelligentsia;
the business ethics practised by many organizations supposedly
committed to alternative codes of conduct; the cultural politics of
narcissism based on making capital out of one's own specific
oppression rather than making links with other, different, struggles. The rhetorics of hate and envy turn the demand for social
justice into a drive for revenge.

But Unger argues that this is not the end of the story. He
appeals to the tradition of artisan and petty bourgeois radicalism
as an indication of the small-scale, decentralized and cooperative forms which negative capabilities might yet take, within the
framework of a pluralistic socialism; it is not always clear from
his account how these forms might be renewed under late capitalism or how they might overcome the sectarianism and fragmentation of current opposition, but perhaps this is less
important than the purchase his model gives us on the contradictory tendencies of the present. A lot of contemporary cultural
practice begins to make sense as the site of a continuing struggle
between these two, reactionary and progressive, versions of neg-

ative capability, or rather as forms of compromise solution between them.

For example, to be 'young, gifted and black' is to experience the tensions between the drive to individual success and the adherence to a communal sense of roots. Recently those tensions have been explored in the humour of Lenny Henry, which pokes fun at black Yuppies and white racists with equal glee. Sharp dressing, cynical, street-wise, above all self-possessed, Henry's humour comes precisely from situations in which he 'blows his cool' *and* succeeds in disarming his adversaries, with a wisecrack or a bit of fancy footwork. He has the best of both worlds: this is the key to his success.

The Lenny Henry persona may be used to advertise the virtues of health foods to the new black middle class, but his style is still recognizably part of the experience of the black underclass. His symbolic importance lies in the way he straddles these two worlds, worlds which increasingly exist side by side in inner city neigh-bourhoods which have been gentrified. The relations of mutual exploitation which obtain between these two groups indeed provide the source of much of his best jokes. But if the tensions are resolved through his humour, the Lenny Henry laugh remains just nervous enough to signal that the contradictions remain and it might just be 'the fire next time'.

Perhaps the best case study in the contradictory articulation of enterprise culture and youth culture, showing how the two sides of negative capability are actually being lived out, is to be found in Manfred Karge's play *The Conquest of the South Pole*. The play tells the story of four unemployed young men who make a last-ditch attempt to stave off total depression by beginning to act out the story of Amundsen's successful expedition to the Antarctic. The fantasy takes over their lives to varying degrees. For one of them it comes to represent an absolute, self-enclosed universe of meaning in which everything which is no longer available to him in the real world (a heroic sense of masculinity, comradeship, a purpose and direction to life, the triumph over adverse conditions) is magically retrieved and celebrated. For one of his friends, with a wife and child to support, the game is merely an interesting interlude, a brief moment of escape before returning to the painful realities of the dole queue and the search for work. The other two members of the game use the situation in yet another way, to work out their attitudes to life and death. At one point, one of them proposes changing the script, to base it on Shackleton's expedition, because, as he says:

> It's not triumph we need to act out. We do failures better. They're our staple diet. Every trip to the Job Centre, every phone call about a job is a failure. Even work is a failure, a paid failure, a badly paid failure. And so the failure must go on until we're all sick to death. It's only when you're up to your eyes in shit, desperately gasping for air, when you're really on your last legs, that the vomit might rise so high in your throat that you lash out in all directions … We are Shackleton and his crew, poor buggers who can see their goal ahead of them however hazily, somewhere there in the distance. (Karge, 1988)

This is an extreme version of the power of negative capability to conjure victories out of defeats. The question posed by the play is what is lost and gained in these 'victories'. The family man eventually settles down and is able to afford a package holiday in which he actually gets to visit the South Pole, though only as a tourist in the comfort of a Boeing 707! Meanwhile his friend remains at home, unemployed and immobilized by his imaginary conquests. The play seems to be saying that neither the actual fruits of consumerism nor the fairy tale successes of the enterprise culture offer sustainable identities to these youths; nevertheless, these young men continue to struggle towards an alternative sense of their lives, even if this is only immediately representable through the medium of fantasy or myth.

But do more material and overt practices of resistance offer a more hopeful resolution? Certainly a good deal of Unger's analysis is borne out by recent responses to the Government's education policies. There has been no shortage of 'negative capability' on the part of both teachers and pupils! Both have developed quite sophisticated strategies for reworking what is imposed upon them in the name of education or training, subverting or neutralizing the more extreme effects, while adapting other elements to their own, often conflicting purposes. For example, personal and social education (PSE), which was officially supposed to instil social and life skills, has in many cases provided a haven for critical pedagogies ousted from the core curriculum. The Tories' call for schools to educate 'active citizens' has similarly given a boost to forms of political literacy which put in question the processes which disenfranchise particular social groups. Within pre-vocational education, media studies work has been extended from teaching 'communication skills' to undertaking various kinds of cultural studies, in which that kind of instrumental attitude towards language is 'deconstructed' by the students themselves. Young people on YTS have not been cowed or dragooned into becoming model workers, but have sometimes used the opportunity, with or without official encouragement, to exercise their own kind of sociological imagination via '*samizdat* publications' and graffiti art attacking the more repressive aspects of the regime.

Meanwhile, further up the line, public and private service workers who have undergone assertiveness training may find that it helps them stand up to their bosses as well as their customers. Finally, recent research has shown that a significant number of working-class girls are putting their own personal ambitions first, and boyfriends and marriage later or last. This not only brings them up against the entrenched sexisms of male working-class culture, but may also push them towards non-traditional occupations. This may not turn them into ideological feminists, but it is likely to orient them towards forms of collective action which undermine the competitive logic of market relations.[24]

In many cases, these are *ad hoc* initiatives, improvised and unco-ordinated responses. There are at present no structures which could transform negative capabilities into positive ones, acts of refusal into the envisaging of a different kind of education and society. Nevertheless the range and diversity of these examples may give us some realistic grounds for hope. It is to these practices that we should be looking for the elements of a new kind of really useful knowledge, one which may resist incorporation into particular curricula or pedagogic forms, but which nevertheless does point us beyond the narrow pragmatics of vocationalism and towards a different sense of enterprise.[25]

Notes

1. For an analysis of fairy tales see Bettelheim (1978). A classic psycho-analytic view of political ideology as wish fulfilment is to be found in the work of Lasswell (1948). However the position taken here is that

political ideologies are necessarily programmatic, and propose strategies premised on a rational framework of implementation. However the relationship which is asserted between means and ends may be purely magical, and involve various kinds of primary process thinking. This follows the line of thinking developed by Murray Edelman (1977 and 1988), who argues that both the realism and the rationality of political ideologies is constructed through particular kinds of narrative devices, employed as part of their persuasive rhetoric.

2. The first Black Paper appeared in 1969, as a set of dissenting right-wing essays. By 1975 the fourth such paper laid out the terms of what subsequently became known as the Great Debate inaugurated by the then Labour Prime Minister James Callaghan. In her first government Mrs Thatcher appointed one of the Black Paper editors as Minister for Higher Education and subsequently many of the ideas first put forward by this group have been taken up and elaborated by right-wing think-tanks and influential journals such as the *Salisbury Review*. The original 'state of the nation' debate took place in the 1890s and centred on the lack of mental and physical fitness of working-class youth to meet the demands of a modern industrial economy. On this first 'Great Debate' see M. Weiner (1982) and the rather different interpretation of J. Ahier (1989).

3. For a good account of the way Thatcherism exploited the weakness of Labour's education policy see CCCS (1981). For an analysis of the different tendencies within New Right Educationalism see Johnson (1989). For a more general discussion of New Right ideology see the contributions to Levitas (1986).

4. It has been the major argument of sociologists of education that schools reproduce the division between manual and mental labour precisely through the forms of knowledge and subjectivity to which they give priority. In this perspective, the new vocationalism simply makes explicit the principles of power and division hitherto 'buried' in the hidden curriculum. See the contributions to Dale (ed.) (1985).

5. For a discussion of this complex of changes see Hall and Jacques (1983) and Hall (1988); also Lash and Urry (1987). An analytic framework which makes these changes central to the problematics of education can be found in Apple (1982). The concept of 'post-Fordism' has been used to describe a structural shift away from the material culture of mass production associated with an industrial working class, as originally described by Gramsci (1971), towards a service economy segmented into particular consumer markets and powered by capital intensive information technologies. This thesis is developed in Murray (1989).

6. The basic programme of the new vocationalism was first spelt out in a series of policy documents produced by the Manpower Services Commission (MSC) concerning the introduction of youth training schemes to deal with the high levels of youth unemployment experienced in the 1970s and early '80s. See Rees and Atkinson (1982).

The role of the MSC was then extended backwards into secondary education with the creation of the Technical and Vocational Education Initiative (TVEI) and the Certificate in Pre-Vocational Education (CPVE). This latter was designed to provide otherwise unqualified school-leavers with sufficient training in work discipline to make them attractive to employers. For the development of the MSC see Finn (1987) and also the contributions to Benn and Fairley (1986). More recently an attempt has been made to rationalize the whole structure by abolishing the MSC and putting in its place a network of Training and Enterprise Councils. These are supposed to provide local bases of cooperation between employers, education authorities and training agencies. This is not however a partnership between equals, but rather a framework within which the hegemony of the enterprise culture can be established over education as well as training.

7. Foucault (1977) has argued that discipline is not a purely repressive force but actively empowers the subject through its regulation of bodies. Conversely it could be argued that skill regulates the subject through the mastery of techniques. Both these aspects of socialization are present in the 'bio-political' strategies discussed below. Foucault's concept of a 'technology of the self' is also useful in pin-pointing some of the discursive strategies which are deployed in and through youth training regimes.

8. The phrase is that of John Biggs-Davidson, a member of the extreme 'Old Right' within the Tory Party. For a history of the moral panics focused on youth see Pearson (1983).

9. The best studies of YTS, combining ethnography with structural analysis, are Cockburn (1988) and Hollands (1990).

10. For an account of how this historical compromise functioned to con-struct an 'anti-industrial spirit' at the time when Britain was suppos-edly the 'workshop of the world' see Weiner (1982). For an account of the role which codes of inheritance, vocation and career have played in the formation of educational and class ideologies see the work of Bisseret (1978). For their role in constructing notions of skill see More (1980).

11. For a historical analysis of changing forms of political socialization within working-class culture see Chapter 8.

12. See the contributions to Hall and Jacques (1983), and the critique of this position in Jessop *et al.* (1987).

13. Historical accounts of youth policy and provision have tended to over-emphasize these continuities. See, for example, the otherwise interesting study by Horne (1984). Historical studies of rational recreation and self-improvement movements such as Bailey (1978) and Morris (1970) are useful but do not focus on the kinds of dis-course which were mobilized by them. In contrast, the work of Ahier (1989) provides a much more sophisticated reading of these kinds of ideological text. Samuel Smiles's works (1859, 1894) would repay similar close analysis. Lasch (1980) puts forward a trenchant critique

of the post-war personal growth movement and this is developed further in Richards (1989). Both studies, however, remain at the level of 'histories of ideas'; a discourse analysis of popular ideologies of self-help in contemporary psychology is to be found in Treacher (1989).

14. In tracing the provenance of the disparate elements which make up SLS ideology I have followed Griffith (1983) in concentrating on its core elements and forms of implantation. For this reason I have taken the work of Argyle (1978, 1980) as paradigmatic because it maps out the main framework within which this set of practices has developed. This is not to deny the specificity of purely educational variants such as Priestley and Maguire (1978) or Hopson and Scally (1981a, 1981b) and the extent to which these adaptations may modify some aspects of Argyle's own behaviourism.

15. Quotation from Hopson and Scally (1981a).

16. The materials reviewed here were all published between 1979 and 1984. Many of them were produced in association with the National Extension College and linked to a 'new wave' of Teen TV programmes which combined pop music, 'life-style' issues and practical advice on training and work. They include 'Roadshow', 'JobMate', '16 Up', 'Help', 'Just the Job' and 'The Job Hunter Kit'. *The School Leaver's Guide*, which is quoted in this and the following section, was published by Longman's as part of a pre-vocational educational package. More recently Life Skills Associates have produced some rather more sophisticated and interactive texts for use in personal and social education (PSE). See also the materials published by the Careers Research Advisory Centre (CRAC), which belong to the more traditional genre of careers guide.

17. The classic study of individualism by Macpherson (1962) deals only with its *strong* bourgeois form and its conditions of reproduction as a *political* ideology. The approach which has been adopted here draws largely on the pioneering work of Bernard Edelman (1979). Edelman outlines the constitution of legal subjectivity in civil society and then looks at how this is transformed by the advent of new consciousness industries. Unlike the theories of 'post-modernism', developed by Jameson (1984), Lyotard (1984) or Baudrillard (1988), Edelman does not relate changing modes of individualism to some generalized 'cultural logic' or 'structural tendency' of advanced capitalism, but to specific transformations of property relations and to the way these relations are represented, articulated or lived in particular contexts. See Abercrombie *et al.* (1986) for an attempt to develop an equally grounded and differential model of individualism. Williams (1983) also makes some characteristically insightful comments on what he calls 'mobile privatization' as a point of transmutation between competitive and self-possessive modes of individualism. The weakness in all these accounts lies in the failure to grasp the power of individualism as an *existential* ideology; this is being remedied in recent studies

influenced by the psycho-analytic theories; see for example the contributions to Henriques *et al.* (1984) and Rustin (1989).

18. Winnicott (1965), from a Kleinian perspective, argues that the splitting mechanisms described here are attributable to specific developmental difficulties which prevent a normal process of integration
taking place. Post-modernists, influenced by Lacan, tend to celebrate
this fragmentation and argue that integration is an illusory quest on
the part of a decentred or split subject. The view taken here is that if,
indeed, splitting is a necessary defence mechanism, it appears to be
one which is especially characteristic of the subcultures produced by
oppressed groups. However, most strategies of consciousness-raising
involving such groups attempt to challenge splitting at the level of
individual consciousness by setting in motion a process of collective
self-affirmation. Nevertheless this often involves conserving splitting
at a higher level of abstraction, i.e. by dividing the world into good
and bad reference groups. On this point see the contributions by
Hoggett and Richards in Richards (1989).

19. A good summary of debates on the enterprise culture is to be found
in the journal *Theory, Culture and Society* (1985).

20. The Labour Party's Policy Review (1987–9) was an attempt to
outflank the fundamentalist Left and to distance the party apparatus from its trade union base. To defeat both labourism and ultra-
leftism it was necessary to mobilize some of the more libertarian
elements of New Left thinking against the central tenets of
'command socialism', whilst at the same time moving the party to
the right to capture the political centre ground from the then
emergent Alliance parties. This in turn meant abandoning unpopular aspects of Labour party policy, most notably its commitment to
unilateralism. The policy review was thus essentially a strategic
device for strengthening Kinnock's base of support inside the party
and signalling to the mass media the rout of its favourite 'loony
lefties', such as Tony Benn and 'Red Ken' Livingstone. Not surprisingly it did not produce any substantively new policies in the field
of education and youth training, but it has proved an exceptionally
effective electoral device.

21. For a discussion of some points of correspondence between Marx
and Durkheim see Schnorrer (1984). For the political implications of
these changes for the labour movement see Gorz (1982).

22. The play by Catherine Johnson (shown at the 1989 Edinburgh
Festival), 'Boys Mean Business', provided a brilliant exploration of
forms of self-exploitation current within youth-enterprise culture.
See also the discussion in Hebdige (1987).

23. The concept of negative capability as outlined in Unger (1983 and
1987) is very close to Sartre's theory of *depassment* and Sartre's work is
indeed a central influence on his thought. A useful overview of
Unger's work is given by Anderson (1989).

24. For strategies of resistance to YTS, see Hollands (1990) and, with particular reference to girls' transitions, Cockburn (1988). For a general

discussion of girls' cultures see the contributions to McRobbie and Nava (1984).

25. The 'No Kidding' project, directed by the author of this chapter, 1984–7, set out to develop such an alternative approach to pre-vocational education based on the critical pedagogy of cultural studies. For a detailed account see Chapter 10.

Bibliography and References

Abercrombie, N., S. Hill and B. Turner (1986) *The Sovereign Individuals of Capitalism* (London: Allen & Unwin).

Ahier, J. (1989) *Industry, Children and the Nation* (London: Falmer).

Anderson, P. (1989) 'Politics, passion, plasticity', *New Left Review* 173.

Apple, M. (1982) *Education and Power* (London: Routledge & Kegan Paul).

Argyle, M. (1978) *Social Skills and Mental Health* (London: Methuen).

Argyle, M. (1980) *Social Skills and Work* (London: Methuen).

Bailey, P. (1978) *Leisure and Class in Victorian Britain* (London: Routledge & Kegan Paul).

Bates, I. *et al.* (1984) *Schooling for the Dole* (London: Macmillan).

Baudrillard, J. (1988) *Selected Writings* (Cambridge: Polity Press).

Benn, C. and J. Fairley (eds) (1986) *Challenging the MSC* (London: Pluto).

Bettelheim, B. (1978) *The Uses of Enchantment* (Harmondsworth: Penguin).

Bisseret, N. (1978) *Education, Class Language and Ideology* (London: Routledge & Kegan Paul).

CCCS (1981) *Unpopular Education* (London: Hutchinson).

Cockburn, C. (1988) *Two Track Training* (London: Macmillan).

Curran, J. (ed.) (1984) *The Future of the Left* (Cambridge: Polity Press).

Dale, R. (ed.) (1985) *Education, Training and Employment* (Oxford: Pergamon).

Edelman, B. (1979) *Ownership of the Image* (London: Routledge & Kegan Paul).

Edelman, M. (1977) *Political Language* (London: Academic Press).

Edelman, M. (1988) *Constructing the Political Spectacle* (Chicago: University of Chicago Press).

Finn, D. (1987) *Training without Jobs* (London: Macmillan).

Foucault, M. (1977) *Discipline and Punish* (London: Allen Lane).

Gleeson, D. (1984) *Youth Training and the Search for Work* (London: Routledge & Kegan Paul).

Gorz, A. (1982) *Farewell to the Working Class* (London: Pluto).

Gramsci, C. (1971) *Prison Notebooks* (London: Lawrence & Wishart).

Griffith, T. (1983) *Skilling for Life* (Toronto: OISE).

Grossberg, C. and Grossberg, L. (eds) (1988) *Marxism and the Interpretation of Culture* (London: Macmillan).

Hall, S. (1988) 'The Toad in the Garden: Thatcherism among the theorists', in C. and L. Grossberg (eds) (1988).

Hall, S. and M. Jacques (eds) (1983) *The Politics of Thatcherism* (London: Lawrence & Wishart).

Hebdige, D. (1987) *Hiding in the Light* (London: Comedia).

Henriques, J. *et al.* (1984) *Changing the Subject* (London: Methuen).

Hoggett, P. (1989) 'The culture of uncertainty', in B. Richards (1989).

Hollands, R. (1990) *The Long Transition* (London: Macmillan).

Hopson, B. and M. Scally (1981a) *Life Skills Training* (London: Tavistock).

Hopson, B. and M. Scally (1981b) 'Life skills teaching in schools and colleges', *Liberal Education*, 44.

Horne, J. (1984) 'Youth unemployment programmes – A historical perspective', in D. Gleeson, *Youth Training and the Search for Work* (London: Routledge & Kegan Paul).

Jameson, F. (1984) 'Postmodernism or the cultural logic of capital', *New Left Review*, 146.

Jessop, R. *et al.* (1987) 'Thatcher and the Left', *New Left Review*, 165.

Johnson, R. (1989) 'Thatcherism and English education', *History of Education* **18**, 2.

Karge, M. (1988) *The Conquest of the South Pole* (Edinburgh: Traverse).

Lasch, C. (1980) *The Culture of Narcissism*, London: Abacus.

Lash, S. and J. Urry (1987) *The End of Organised Capitalism*, Cambridge: Polity Press.

Lasswell, H. (1948) *Power and Personality*, (New York: Norton).

Levitas, R. (ed.) (1986) *The Ideology of the New Right* (Cambridge: Polity Press).

Lyotard, J. -F. (1984) *The Post Modern Condition* (Manchester: Manchester University Press).

Macpherson, P. (1962) *The Political Theory of Possessive Individualism* (Oxford: Oxford University Press).

McRobbie, A. and M. Nava (eds) (1984) *Gender and Generation* (London: Macmillan).

More, C. (1980) *Skill and the Working Class* (London: Croom Helm).

Morris, R. J. (1970) 'The history of self help', *New Society*, 167.

Murray, R. (1989) *Life After Ford* (Cambridge: Polity Press).

Nelson, C. and L. Grossberg (eds) (1988) *Marxism and the Interpretation of Culture* (London: Macmillan).

Pearson, G. (1983) *Hooligans – A History of Respectable Fears* (London: Macmillan).

Priestley, J. and H. Maguire (1978) *Social Skills and Personal Problem Solving* (London: Tavistock).

Rees, T. and P. Atkinson (1982) *Youth Unemployment and State Intervention* (London: Routledge & Kegan Paul).

Richards, B. (ed.) (1989) *Crises of the Self* (London: FAB).

Rustin, M. (1989) 'Post Kleinian psychoanalysis and the post-modern', *New Left Review* **173**.

Schnorrer, P. (1984) *Marx, Durkheim and the Post Modern World* (Calcutta: New Perspective Books).

Smiles, S. (1859) *Self Help* (London: Murray).

Smiles, S. (1894) *Character* (London: Murray).
Symonds, G. D. R. (1981) *The School Leaver's Guide* (Harlow: Longman).
Theory, Culture and Society (1985) *The Fate of Modernity* 2, 3, special issue.
Treacher, A. (1989) 'Be your own person', in B. Richards (ed.), *Crises of the Self* (London: FAB).
Unger, R. (1983) *Passion – An Essay on Personality* (New York: New York Free Press).
Unger, R. (1987) *Plasticity into Power* (Cambridge: Cambridge University Press).
Weiner, M. (1982) *English Culture and the Decline of the Industrial Spirit* (Cambridge: Cambridge University Press).
Williams, R. (1983) 'The end of an era', *New Left Review*, 181.
Winnicott, D. W. (1965) *The Maturational Process and the Facilitating Environment* (London: Tavistock).
Young, M. F. D. (ed.) (1971) *Knowledge and Control* (London: Macmillan).

Chapter 10

Cultural Studies in School Transitions

This chapter describes the No Kidding Project which set out to develop an alternative approach to vocational education with school leavers. The project sought *to examine the transition from school from the point of view of young people themselves and to understand the languages of gender and class which they used to give it meaning. Photography was the main medium of self-representation and working with different groups we produced a series of exhibitions, photo-texts and other curriculum materials, with funds from the Greater London Council. It was an essay in applied cultural studies in which we tried to integrate critical pedagogy, ethnographic research and curriculum development within a single reflexive arc based upon the theoretical model outlined in 'Rethinking'.*

The project collaborated closely with the Cockpit Cultural Studies Department which had pioneered the use of photography as a critical pedagogy in schools, and whose magazine, Schooling and Culture, *was for many years the major conduit through which the work of the Birmingham School percolated through to the staffroom. Nevertheless, No Kidding took its distance from the celebratory populism/culturalism which characterised much of the Cockpit's work with young people (and my own earlier work), and also introduced a psycho-analytic dimension which was foreign to their approach.*

The chapter is a shortened version of *Really Useful Knowledge: Photography and Cultural Studies in the Transition from School* (Trentham Books, 1990).

No Kidding was not popular with the gurus of the new vocationalism, but at least it succeeded in demonstrating that, given adequate time and resources, ordinary teachers and students could work together to produce sophisticated statements about the complexities and contradictions of the educational process. How far it actually shifted commonsense assumptions about the worlds of school and work, and underlying notions of class and and gender, is more problematic.

Today, at any rate, it would be much less possible to create a space within which this kind of work might be undertaken, and valued, although similar methods have been employed more recently in the field of multicultural education. This is a slightly abridged version of the original report, but still, I hope conveys enough of substance to let the reader judge the potential and the limitations of the approach.

Towards a cultural studies model of pre-vocational education

In September 1983 a group of us, cultural studies teachers and social researchers, came together around a common set of inter-ests and concerns in the field of pre-vocational education. We were looking for a new way of reading school transitions, one which was sensitive both to the first person singular ways these are negotiated and lived, and to the impact of structural changes (viz. in state provisions, labour market and working-class culture) on patterns of political socialisation. Secondly, we were searching for ways in which the kinds of really useful knowledge which had been marginalised by the new vocationalism, could be recentred with a pedagogy and curriculum informed by this reading of the youth question. Thirdly, we wanted to explore the limits and con-ditions of collaboration between researchers, teachers, and working-class students in contexts which challenged the 'normal' (i.e. hierarchical) power structures and instead tried to move towards a more open division of mental labour.

In setting ourselves these aims, we deliberately rejected any 'going back', whether to the original models of independent working-class education, child-centred progressivism, or 'insur-gent sociology'. Instead we tried to explore some of the *educa-tional* connections between recent theoretical advances in the human sciences, and certain political developments, at the level, of both consciousness and organisation, amongst young people. These connections were above all to be found in the field of cultural studies, where many of the debates (viz. on ideology and modernity) despite their obtuseness, prefigured real movements in identity politics in which young women, ethnic and sexual minority youth have played a leading role.[1]

At a theoretical level this pointed our research in the direction of a cultural history of the codes through which identities of gender, class and ethnicity are articulated, complemented by a reading of the autobiographical constructs or subject positions which these codes made possible.[2] At a more practical level, cultural studies provided a link between technical and political education, and here our chosen medium was photography.[3] At once a technical skill and a popular cultural practice, a means of social investigation, and device for exploring self images, photography was an essential element in the short courses and project work which we undertook with various groups of school leavers and unemployed youth. The material which they produced in turn provided the basis for a series of photo-text exhibitions, classroom readers, and other teaching materials, designed to help develop an alternative cultural studies model of pre-vocational education, focusing on major aspects of the youth question.[4]

Through this four-year programme, we therefore struggled to achieve as close an interaction possible between theoretical research, empirical investigation, educational work with young people, and curriculum development. It proved far from easy to integrate these various levels. The story was one of uneven, rather than combined development. But the attempt was worthwhile, if only because it enabled us to discover some new possibilities, as well as old problems.

The substantive focus of our work was on the varieties of working class experience of family, school and community transition, as this was constructed through the interplay of gender, generation and race. We were dissatisfied with the pigeon holes into which school leavers were put both by teachers and sociologists. We found ourselves working with young people who could not be classified as 'resisters' or 'conformists', 'lads' or 'earoles', 'underachievers' or 'academic', 'punks' or 'skinheads', and yet who were far from being loners or eccentrics. Indeed, they were part of a 'silent majority' of working-class pupils whose perspectives and pre-occupations had been singularly ignored. We tried to develop a more sensitive reading of transitions which would pick up some of these 'subliminal' positions, a project which took us in a number of different directions at once. For example, we began to explore the ways in which working-class boys are placed in a quasi-feminine position *vis-a-vis* male elders through various cultural practices in the family, workplace and community; we looked at how this position is underwritten by traditional youth labour and wage forms, and at how it is denied or displaced in traditional codes of masculinity as these become active in peer group practices, especially in the process of sexual apprenticeship. Of course this system is breaking down fast, although not necessarily in ways which propel working-class boys into an 'adolescent identity crisis'. These dynamics proved crucial to understanding some of the new ways boys are reconstructing working-class identities in the context of extended schooling, training or unemployment.[5]

However, all this was not just a 'research project'. The ideas as well as the data were originally generated through a series of short pre-vocational courses which we ran for early leavers. The words and images which they produced provided the basis for a photographic exhibition exploring the tensions between official and unofficial transitions, as well as giving us food for further thought in developing a cultural analysis of the material.[6] This in turn led into a second phase of work in which we concentrated on the autobiographical grammars through which these positions are lived and given meaning. A context was provided by the Hackney Unemployed School Leavers project, and resulted in an extended project with one particular boy who, in his own words, was a semi-professional truant.[7] This focused on his memories and phantasies about primary and secondary school, particularly as these were triggered off by revisiting and photographing the sites of key childhood experiences associated with family and friends. Gradually what began to emerge from these representations, was a *hidden* curriculum vitae, one which had been censored in response to family or peer group pressures, and which had equally gone unrecognised by the school. In making some of these 'other scenes' of childhood and adolescence more accessible, an often painful process, the boy's own sense of where he had come from and where he wanted to go, came into sharper focus, as well as delineating for us some of the more hidden injuries inflicted on those who have to grow up working-class. Bringing *these* structures of feeling to the surface was one way of beginning to peel away the 'hard'-edged image of male school counter-culture which continues to dominate most sociological accounts, as well as opening up some suggestive approaches to an alternative practice of vocational guidance and counselling.

A second strand of our work, carried on at the same time, concerned the position of girls. A community care course for a group of (mostly black) girls staying on into the new one-year sixth form provided the starting point.[8] Our project explored the conjuncture of pressures from family, school and work which were forcing these girls into a traditional servicing role. We looked at the ways their domestic apprenticeships at home were being 'naturalised' in their schooling, routing them into jobs (e.g. as nursery nurses) which reinforced the multiple oppressions of gender, race and class.[9] Much of the work focused on the double standards of parental (and still, teacher) expectation; home work for these girls meant washing, cleaning, cooking, while for boys it meant studying for exams undisturbed by domestic demands; relations with boys as brothers and boyfriends highlighted this process. The girls' own positive responses in challenging aspects of their subordination, sometimes aided by their mums, emerged with growing strength as the course progressed. Even though the extent of the pressures on them told against any radical revision of occupational choices at this late stage in their school careers, our intervention did serve to problematise aspects of their vocational preparation in a way which proved less than comfortable for the teaching staff concerned.

The theme of gendered transitions was then developed in a further project looking at the position of women in popular music.[10] We worked with a girls band, who were in the process of making the difficult transition from amateur to semi-professional status. The practical difficulties of combining their musical interests with having to earn a living by other means, the desire to 'make it' on the music scene without exploiting their femininity either ideologically or commercially, the excitements and anxieties of 'doing a gig', the construction of a group image, the pain and sweat of getting it all together, these were some of the themes which the girls addressed in their collective self-portrait. The purpose of the exercise, from our point of view, was to encourage more girls to form their own bands, and to put into question some of the assumptions behind music teaching in schools. The model of political socialisation which began to emerge from this work, was markedly different from the sociological accounts which have so far influenced programmes of political literacy in schools.[11] Instead of measuring the impact, or lack of it, of macro-political ideologies and apparatuses on young people's overt attitudes and behaviour – an approach which inevitably shows working-class youths up as 'don't knows and don't cares' – we concentrated on bringing to light the cultural practices which positioned boys and girls subliminally (and asymetrically) within various fields of 'personal' discourse centred on the youth question. The problem we encountered here was not one of apathy, but rather of getting young people to *stop* talking before we ran out of tape, and the time to transcribe it!

Our final initiative was in the field of anti-racist teaching. We worked with a group of unemployed boys who were active supporters of the National Front and responsible for a number of vicious attacks on black families in their neighbourhood. Clearly neither 'multiculturalism' nor 'moralism', neither appeals to 'reason' nor 'facts' were likely to prove effective with such a group. Instead through weekly discussion we encouraged them to talk their racism out to the point where it began to exhaust its limited repertoire of meanings, and alternative ways of making sense of their personal and collective histories became possible. Although we never succeeded in shifting the hard core, we did manage to get some of the group to begin to review and revise their beliefs. Through these means we came to understand much more about the ways in which the racist imagination works through popular cultural forms to establish itself as common sense, and this in turn led us to develop an alternative 'cultural studies' approach to anti-racist work with white working class youth.[12]

Differences and difficulties

It may be useful to spell out some of the differences between the No Kidding project and more conventional approaches, not least because it was from these differences that many of our difficulties arose.

Firstly, as against the social studies model, we did not set out to examine social issues from an objectifying standpoint, nor, like civics, did we equate Civil Society and the State with an 'adult world' of which young people were supposedly ignorant Unlike Social and Life Skills we did not operate with a deficit model of working-class cultures and competencies. Instead we tried to connect social issues in and through their relation to youth policies, while at the same time questioning the construction of youth as a special problem category; we tried to build on and make explicit the really useful knowledge which our students already possessed – especially relating to work and community life; yet we also tried to critically explore those defensive aspects of youth culture which constructed imaginary positions of omnipotence, largely through racist and sexist practices, while simultaneously leaving real subordinations, of generation and class, intact.

We did not however adopt a prescriptive or normative approach, as is frequently done in anti-sexist or anti-racist work; nor did we address students as citizen/consumers defined by legal rights or moral responsibilities based on individual choices – as occurs in many 'value-free' models of political or religious education. Instead we focused on the shared predicaments which arose in concrete contexts of everyday life and the ways in which particular power structures co-opted or invalidated grassroots forms of decision-making; here we laid special emphasis on giving historical and contemporary examples of the way specific groups of young people had organised themselves, to define their own needs and exert greater control over their own lives.

Thirdly, we set out to overcome the divisions of form and content, process and product, which bedevil most strategies of curriculum development in the field of pre-vocational education; we sought to do this by involving both teachers and students in the development of educational materials in which a critical/reflexive reading of texts was an integral part of the process of their production. In that sense we tried to give some real substance to the rhetorics of active learning and negotiated curriculum. All this, as we soon discovered, was a lot easier said than done! It was, however, in struggling to get to grips with the problems we encountered, that the limits and conditions of our cultural studies model became clarified.

The first and most obvious problem we had to overcome was that of misunderstanding. Although the project initially generated considerable enthusiasm amongst academics, classroom teachers and students, this was largely based on the assumption that its aims coincided with their own. But No Kidding was not just another piece of action/research, nor was it simply a rather more radical version of lifeskills; nor was it all fun and games out of school, to take the three most frequently expressed hopes. And, of course, when initial expectations are not fulfilled, sour grapes are high on the menu of response. Academic colleagues could not see what producing comics[13] or organising youth conferences[14] had to do with 'serious' educational research; the enthusiasm of some classroom teachers tended to wane when we started publishing students' material which implied criticism of their own approach; many people were suspicious of the projects' theoretical/research dimension, especially in so far as this was informed by the intellectual traditions of Marxist historiography, critical theory, and psychoanalysis. The very attempt to combine theory and practice thus led to attacks from both sides. The young people with whom we worked presented a rather different problem. In some cases the extent of their commitment intensified their resistance to other kinds of schooling, and in others the material they produced brought up painful personal memories, with which they (and we) found it hard to deal.

Now many, if not all of these problems could perhaps be overcome with persistence over time. But they also bear on certain *structural* tensions within the project, which are not so easily argued away. Inevitably these tensions centre on the different positions which researchers, teachers and students occupy in the division of mental labour. There is no way these positions can simply be 'equalised' – any collaboration has to be based on a mutual recognition of what each contributes to the overall process, and product. But at every stage there are likely to be conflicting priorities. Consequently we found ourselves operating what amounted to a split-level operation. At the first level (and stage) researcher and teacher worked together and alongside the students in 'reading' the written and visual material which the latter produced as a result of site visits or autobiographical exercises; from these feedback and debriefing sessions we all gained insights, albeit of a different order, from and into what was going on, whether in the group, in individual lives, or in wider social and cultural contexts. However, there was a further process involved in which these materials had to be shaped into a coherent form for publication and re-use in the classroom. It was at this point that the conflicting priorities, attenuated during the earlier phase, came to a head. In so far as the students exerted control over the final text, they often tended to include material which we regarded as unsuitable on educational grounds (ie the references were sexist, racist, etc); alternatively they censored out anything which they thought would show them up in a less than favourable light, and in consequence produced dull sanitised images which were little improvement, from our point of view, on the model young citizens/pupils/workers who fill the pages of lifeskill workbooks. In so far as the teachers had a say in matters, they tended to edit the texts so that they conformed to existing vocationalist ideology, and in the process removed everything (and that meant most of the students' own cultural material) which contradicted these views. The combination of these constraints meant that the final form and content of the curriculum materials was in danger of being much less interesting and useful than the actual educational work which had generated them.

In the event, a number of compromises and trade-offs proved necessary to ensure that particular projects were completed. In some cases we devised 'split texts' – i.e. texts in which the different points of view of teacher, researcher and students could be explicitly articulated. In *Now and Then* for example, an introduction sets out some of the theoretical and pedagogic problems involved in doing intensive autobiographical work, and this is followed up by the 'Truant's Tale' and then the 'Teacher's Tale' so we get quite contrasting perspectives on the same piece of work. The book can thus be used by quite different readerships; 15-and 16-year-olds will read the Truant's Tale and ignore the rest, whereas students on PGCE courses may be expected to get more out of the Teacher's Tale, and cultural studies buffs might want to use the text to reflect further on class and autobiography. Similarly, the girls in *Dolls House* were quite adamant that they did not want to be represented as part of any feminist project, and this wish was respected in the classroom reader. However, a second text, written for teachers and designed to accompany the exhibition, was produced to supply the missing feminist links.[15]

Now clearly neither of these are ideal solutions. They indicate the gulf that continued to exist between the perspectives of middle-class teachers and working-class students, despite the intense collaboration which had taken place between them.

Readers and texts

A rather different set of problems centred on the issue of reading practices and textual forms; here the tension was between the idioms of popular pleasure and those of academic instruction. In a number of SLS readers we looked at a rather pathetic attempt had been made to reconcile the two by borrowing photo-story formats and other graphic devices from commercial teenage magazines, to try and 'pep up' the educational message – a device which in my experience fools no one. Even those school leavers' guides which were not patronising, or an insult to the reader's intelligence, tended to confine themselves to highly prescriptive types of information, geared to the official transition routes of the model young citizen, in a way which ignored many of the reality principles transmitted by working-class cultures. Youth politics was also conspicuous by its absence, presumably on the grounds that the issues it raises are too controversial to be acceptable to teachers or YTS managers. Yet to include these missing elements created its own difficulties Firstly, because there is little point in producing a text which simply reflects back to readers what they already know, or can get from other sources. Secondly, because the youth scene changes so fast that the more 'with it' the approach the quicker it is likely to go out of date. Not only is the whole system of youth provision in a state of flux, but youth styles are being recycled at an ever increasing rate. Today's news is tomorrow's 'history'. Finally, youth is not a unitary category, and any general text which attempts to connect the various aspects of the youth question has to be capable of addressing a readership differentiated not only in terms of gender and race but also by the more subtle inflections of these positions in young people's lives.

In preparing our own school leavers' guide to Youth Training Schemes we were therefore all too aware of the potential pitfalls. Moreover, there is at present a pervasive flight from the text in the field of pre-vocational education. The evangelists of 'experiential learning' tend to regard written texts as purely academic instruments, quite unsuitable for their severely 'practical purposes'. Why not make a video instead? This view is not without justification, given the form and content of most school textbooks and the resistance of many students to them. However, our project was founded on the belief that the practice of reading, whether of visual or written texts, was essential to the development of critical attitudes amongst students and should remain central to popular education. At the same time, it was important to produce a text with which readers could *interact* rather than being set up as purely passive recipients of 'knowledge'.

We decided to approach the problem by looking at how the young people we worked with actually read teenage magazines and similar youth culture material for pleasure. Clearly they did not start at the beginning and work their way through until they came to the end; they flipped through pages, moving back and forth scanning the captions and pictures, until something caught their attention for a while, before once again moving on. Their choice of next item was significantly influenced, we might say overdetermined, by the item they had just read, and certainly the way they contextualised each item was affected in this way. They were constructing an individual reading route through the text, but one which did not go in a straight line, corresponding to the step by step development of analytical reasoning; rather they operated according to a more subliminal logic of 'free' association. Yet there was nothing random about the way they jumped about, nor was it a matter of calculated preferences or 'consumer choice'. It was governed by a set of relations to the text in and through which readers were being inscribed in its particular discourse in front of their own eyes, yet in ways they could not see, precisely because they were just 'doing their own thing'. Was it possible to construct another kind of text in which the same model of reading would serve a rather different purpose, actively interrupting the conventions of realism and the 'natural attitude' by tracing connections between items which are normally radically dissociated from each other in 'common sense' views of the world?

We were especially fortunate then, in having the involvement of the 'Soul Searchers' a group of unemployed young people from Telford, who had made a number of video programmes for

Channel Four. The photo-text which they finally produced for us provides an open and imaginative reading of the issues surrounding youth training at the present time.[16] In its verbal and visual wit, it is as far away from the stodgy, sanitised world of the 'pre-voc' manual, as it is from the political rhetoric of the Militant Tendency. Here, at last, we felt, with some relief, was a text which young people might actually want to read, and argue with!

Working on the School Leaver's Guide had led us in a new and completely unexpected direction – we found ourselves in the world of role playing games. In the 1980s, this had become a major growth industry at the present time largely thanks to the impetus of computer and video games. At this period a whole youth culture had elaborated itself around 'Dungeons and Dragons' and similar fantasy games, based on the action maze principle. Here players take on a larger than life characters drawn from mediaeval legends or science fiction, before embarking on a series of 'adventures', in which magic and violence usually 'rule OK'. These games are explicitly designed as an escape from the reality principles modelled in educational simulations and are no doubt all the more popular and pleasurable for that. Yet the opposition between the two kinds of role playing is not always as clear cut as it might seem. To encourage a 16-year-old boy who finds difficulty in reading and writing, to play at being his own boss is nothing if not to entertain his phantasies. But equally if the same lad plays a 'thief' in a D and D scenario he may be closer to the practices of his everyday life, than his teachers would like to suppose!

Clearly from our point of view the main drawback with pure simulation is that it models social reality as it is, usually in its dominant forms, and only 'problematises' it at the level of *individual* options.[17] This is hardly a way to encourage the development of a properly sociological imagination amongst students whose own cultural practices either predispose them to individualistic solutions or to forms of collective resistance which leave existing power structures intact. In contrast we wanted to devise a system in which the rules and roles of the school leaving 'game' were open to both individual variation and collective challenge.

The other problem is that the surface realism of 'simulations' is quickly exhausted and there is not enough cognitive depth to these games to make them worth playing twice. In so far as this 'ludic' dimension is addressed, we tend to be offered disguised versions of snakes and ladders, or Monopoly. Young people would rather play the 'real thing'. So we needed to find a set of strategic devices which made the game interesting to play, without making it either too difficult, or too easy, or so exciting that players got totally absorbed in its internal mechanisms, at the expense of what they represented.

The game we eventually produced involves a range of cognitive skills related to problem solving and decision making, related to differential payoffs for official and unofficial transition routes from school.[18] But 'Livelihoods' is not just an exercise in 'pre voc'; it also includes an important element of political literacy work in presenting players, as a group, with constantly changing circumstances – a strike, a riot, a new government policy – which they have to negotiate round by round; at the same time it is possible to challenge and change some of the rules of the game, especially those relating to sex and race discrimination, provided that players can reach agreement. The game can be played co-operatively or competitively, and at different levels of skill and complexity. Players with moderate learning difficulties might concentrate on mastering the travel economy and the mechanisms of choice built into the game. With an A level group, it is possible to use the game as an extended exercise in sociological imagination either to produce a historical version set in the world of Mayhew and Booth, or to engage in a form of futurology.

The strength of cultural studies in schools has been the way it has engaged with the lived experience of young people outside the classroom – in their families, peer groups, and part time work places; if these sites of common sense understanding are to be transformed into sources of really useful knowledge, then they have to be recognised for what they are – the product of a complex negotiation between official ideologies and popular cultures, between dominant discourse and subordinate codes. To vocationalise cultural studies is not to eliminate that tension, but to use it as a primary educational resource, a means of equipping young people with the confidence and competence to negotiate it on their own terms, and in the light of their own preferred readings.

A case in point was a course for school leavers which we organised in a South London School. Because it illustrates so concretely the problems and possibilities of this approach. I have analysed the processes involved in some depth.

Rethinking really useful knowledge

When we first began to think about putting together a course for school leavers, we asked some fifth-year pupils what kind of preparation they had already received. First there was 'careers'. 'A lady came down and asked us what we wanted to do, and told us about these schemes.' Then there was social studies: 'We went to a hospital, and they showed us a film about unemployment and that'. They seemed thoroughly bored with the whole idea. More alarming was their total lack of interest or knowledge about the local training schemes they might be forced to enter within months. None of this was exactly the teaching staff's fault. They had had a social education programme for 4th and 5th years imposed on them, following an inspectorate report, and had neither the time nor resources to plan or implement it fully. The result was a mishmash of health and sex education, careers and life skills taught by resentful staff to bored pupils.

Yet the problem of devising a more appropriate curriculum was never going to be an easy one to solve. For example to offer our students a 'beginners guide' to the local economy and state provision might be to insult their own local intelligence of these matters (an instant recipe for disaster); it would also beg a series of tricky but important questions we wanted to explore with them.

These questions had to do with the way learning, labour and leisure are currently being redefined, not only by the discourses of the powerful, but within working-class cultures as well. Just how much of a minefield we were walking into, quickly became apparent, when the first draft of the course came out with all emphasis placed on learning and leisure, on the assumption that none of our school leavers would find jobs, and therefore would not be interested in workplace issues. The first premise might turn out to be true, but the second one did not follow on from it. The fact is that unconsciously we had been drawn into constructing a course on the very grounds we wanted to question – the idea that the transition from school to work has now, inevitably, to pass through YTS, for the majority of 'non-academic' pupils.'

This idea was common sense to most of the local teachers, youth workers, careers officers and training managers we talked to. Although many of them were strongly opposed to the effect of Tory policies on their own particular sector of provision, their overall view had much in common with Thatcherite perspectives: 1) there is a need for a new kind of worker, no longer tied to specific trade practices or occupational loyalties, but highly mobile and possessing 'transferable skills'; 2) self-employment in the hidden economy or small enterprises will be the only source of job creation for young people in the foreseeable future. Structural youth unemployment is here to stay. There is no alternative economic strategy, 3) as a result of new technologies we are moving from a society based on a work ethic to one based on a leisure ethic. This means developing new forms of rational recreation and expanding their provision especially to youth; 4) the education and training of young people should reflect these trends. That is what the new vocationalism is all about.

Over and against this we set out to develop an alternative version of really useful knowledge, in which the dichotomies between general education and technical training, 'the academic' and the vocational would be superceded. There was of course no going back to the old 19th-century formulas of independent working-class education; it is no longer possible to directly link technical and political apprenticeships in the old way, given the organisation of the labour process under advanced capitalism; moreover the patriarchal order of shop floor culture is nowhere more oppressive than in its practices of youth initiation. To attempt to restore either the traditional corpus of 'work-related knowledge' or the social relations in which it is embedded is a retrograde step. That does not mean however that we have no alternative but to embrace the 'Thatcherite revolution' in education and training. We too may deplore the elitism of the 'old' aristocracies of labour and learning if for rather different reasons, but we have learnt, and from Gramsci above all, that neither the skills which co-ordinate production, nor the governing forms of knowledge in society should be despised just because they are the preserve of a privileged minority of workers or intellectuals. It is, however, not just a question of widening access to them via 'quality training' or further education as some of the more reformist 'Gramscians' suppose. The issue is how to develop a curriculum and pedagogy which actually transforms the relations between 'theory' and 'practice' within the new cultural forms and social sites which post fordism has created.

The popular cultures which have formed around computers, video, photography, and HIFI, are one obvious site where technologies are being to some extent transformed by the social relations of their use; here the privatisation of experience through the medium of home consumption, comes up against new forms of public communication which are simultaneously released; the enlarged reproduction of dominant imagery is potentially interrupted by new facilities for do-it-yourself culture. Moreover the concept of political literacy has increasingly come to include the ability to decode ideological messages relayed through cultural industries, industries which are major potential sites of employment of the 'new' working class.

Technical and political education could therefore find a new point of engagement around a critical theory and practice of cultural production. But that possibility is expressly ruled out within the new vocational curriculum with its technicist concept of communication skills, and its phobia about anything 'political'. In contrast we wanted to demonstrate that on these *educational* grounds a new version of really useful knowledge might yet be constructed.

We decided to base our course around photography, for a number of reasons; it was an accessible low cost technology whose basics are easily learnt; it was a popular cultural practice – in the form of holiday snapshots and family albums – with which our students might be already conversant; finally it was a medium of social documentation and self-portraiture which might also be used to 'deconstruct' some of the more hidden ideological messages which shape images of self and other. In the event we found ourselves exploiting all these potentialities of the medium to the full.

Some starting points

The course began by teaching basic photographic skills; the use of cameras, developing, processing, and general darkroom procedures. We took some trouble to avoid teaching these skills in a technicist manner; practical demonstrations of working methods were always accompanied as far as possible with anecdotal illustrations drawing on the folklore of the trade. Initiating young people into such 'trade secrets' involves them in a process of *cultural* apprenticeship, giving them a sense of access to body of knowledge produced by workers themselves. This means that even greater care has to be taken to ensure that boys do not monopolise either equipment or cultural capital. In the event it was the girls who proved quicker on the uptake, as evidenced by the quality of their early prints.

At the same time we began to explore with them some of the hidden messages contained in images of work. For this purpose we worked from various examples of careers literature, examining stereotypes of gender, race and class to be found therein. In particular we looked at the whole ideology of vocation and career, and contrasted it with the very different kinds of cultural associations produced around working-class and women's jobs. As part of this we got the group to devise their own definitions and profiles of skill, across a range of social contexts. It was the boys who showed greatest awareness of the class dimensions of these constructs; some of the girls had the greatest difficulty in recognising in housework, or leisure activities, or indeed in anything they did, the practice of worthwhile skills, reflecting the general devaluation of women's roles in society.

We finished these sessions by getting the students to compose an 'alternative' careers pamphlet, writing a new text and/or finding new images to illustrate the worker's view of the job. Again the girls tended to be more conservative in their approach, whilst the boys had a field day with alternative versions of life in the army and police force, or a 'career' as a postman!

After the preparatory exercises, the main part of the course consisted in group visits to a number of work and training sites. These were chosen because they illustrated specific issues viz sexual divisions of labour, managerial structures, attitudes and aspirations of workers/trainers, state strategies towards youth unemployment etc. Each visit was documented, the students interviewing both managers, and the 'rank and file', and taking photographs. These experiences were then explored thematically via group discussions and photo-story work, enabling students to interpret the emerging issues in the light of their own concerns.

Finally the material was worked up to produce a statement in words and images on a series of presentation boards.

The other major component was the homework exercise. This ran in tandem with the day time visits. Students were lent cameras and tape recorders to take home, to build up a personal portrait of the people, places, and practices which were significant for them. The aim here was to help students contextualise the issues arising from the visits, in terms of a sharpened sense of their own social and cultural priorities.

There were four main variables which shaped the course and its outcomes – our institutional negotiations, the composition of the student group, the working conditions and facilities, and, not least, our own capacities and limitations as tutors. We will deal with each briefly in turn.

Getting past the gatekeepers

We were very fortunate in our choice of school. The course was discussed in outline with the head of Social Studies, who was very enthusiastic, and went out of his way to meet our requirements. Our problems only started when we began to make arrangements for visiting local work and training sites. We assumed that these would have to be negotiated officially, and that meant going through the local MSC clearing house. This agency proved to be a masterpiece of bureaucratic gatekeeping. Our proposals were subjected to endless vetting, and referral, the effect being to gradually whittle down our options till they fitted in with the agencies own model of what our course should be. In other words we were experiencing the very procedures of assessment that school leavers have to endure! And like many of them, we eventually decided to strike out on our own, and negotiate directly with employers. Here the similarity ended, for we found much to our surprise that we were welcomed with open arms. From their point of view, the course may have looked like a good exercise in public relations. We did not disillusion them!

Finding the group

Initially we had asked the school for a group of a dozen early leavers, half girls, half boys. We ended up with ten – seven boys, three girls. We were unahppy about the imbalance; given that the tutors were both male, it would be difficult to avoid a male emphasis in looking at the sexual politics of the transition, even though we were determined to maintain an anti-sexist teaching style. But we were presented with a fait accompli, two days before the course was due to start. We had anticipated that we would get the resisters, those the school would be only too pleased to get rid of for a while. In this we were proved wrong. The group we got, formed part of that middle stratum whose school lives had neither been academically rewarding, nor spectacularly troubled. Being neither 'bright' nor 'bother' from the teachers point of view, they had tended to be neglected. Sending them on this course was one way the school could make it up to them, for at least we could give them the personal attention they had not received before.

Three things united them as a group, even though they had been drawn from different classes in school. The first was their low regard for exams as a credential for finding work. Second, their desire to leave school at the earliest possible opportunity. And third, their determination to 'make it' by any other means. These are all interrelated, of course, but it was interesting that their personal aspirations had in no way been dented by their experience of failure at school, nor were they deterred, *at this stage*, by the recognition that real job prospects were bleak.

Space (and Time)

Our teaching premises were in a large, rambling community settlement, full of narrow staircases, winding passageways, and all sorts of mysterious nooks and crannies. An ideal place for games of hide and seek. The building housed a wide assortment of projects from an old people's luncheon club to a nursery, and included a rather dilapidated youth club in the basement. Our teaching space was concentrated around a large urban studies room, and included the use of reprographic facilities, and a small teaching dark room next door.

Every room in the building was brightly labelled with the occupant's name and function; because of the many break-ins, there was much locking and unlocking of doors to be done to get from one part of the settlement to the other. We spent a lot of our time doing that! Some attempt then had been made to impose order on this otherwise chaotic space.

It quite suited us. It meant we could split the students up into small groups easily, and they could move from one site of activity to another (e.g. from the darkroom to drying room) without us having to act as traffic cops. The students too made themselves at home. They liked the higgledy-piggledy layout, so different from the tight institutional grid of school, closer to their own preferred reading of social space. This could create some problems though. During the first week, at lunch breaks the main classroom was instantly converted into a kind of 'den'. We would return to find a mountain of half-eaten packed lunches, coke cans, etc. strewn amidst their project work, while the students lounged about, feet on tables, listening to records. A picture of the kind of mess they would have liked to make at home, but weren't allowed to, perhaps? Stronger 'boundary maintenance' was called for, we felt, as we grimly stood over them while they cleared up! In the event the youth club was pressed into service as a lunchtime canteen, while the word went out, especially to the lads 'making yourself at home means you also have to do the housework'.

The organisation of time followed a similar pattern. Some activities, like the visits, were more strongly framed, others like the photo-story exercises, much less so. A variety in educational tempo suited them, as it does most adolescents, providing the principle of variation is made explicit and is held to. Thus, if the pace got too hot, or too tightly regulated, there were also cooler, less structured times. We had decided from the outset to set the students a target – the presentation of their work in an exhibitable form. This was not without its risks, but it gave the course a dramatic structure, which drew all the students into involvement. The last few days became a race against time, to finish all the work, but one we managed to construct so that the group as a whole could win.

All this was only possible, because the school had allowed us a block release period for the course. We had the students every day for a fortnight. This enabled us to work with them in a concentrated and continuous way, yet retain an element of flexibility. It was the fact that the course was both off site, and offered them an extended period away from school, which made it such an attractive proposition to our group. Working on a sessional basis, say one day a week, through a term (our original plan) would have made it much more difficult to hold their interest. As it was, their attention spans stretched to more than match ours, as the course progressed.

A more pressing problem was the way students might perceive the course. Whatever we said about its aims, they might still see it as a means of railroading them through from school to YTS. Most of the professionals we talked to certainly took it for granted that this was our 'real' function. One reason perhaps we got the level of cooperation we did.

There was a wider issue at stake in this. Normally school leavers are made to start off from an assumed position of ignorance, incompetence, unskill. They are then supposed to shift to a position of knowledge, social maturity, and expertise through various kinds of training. It all seems very reasonable, until you realise, as many working-class pupils do, that there is never not a time *throughout* their school lives, when someone is not defining them in some way as inadequate or lacking in essential qualities. So what appears to be a conjunctural issue around training and transition, turns out to concern a wider pattern – the distribution of knowledge and power in society, and the way a certain process of disqualification repeats itself over time.

Our aim was to interrupt that pattern, to build on the resources students already valued and possessed, while extending them into new areas of experience. The shift we sought, was from a position of individual fatalism or dog eat dog, to one of greater confidence in their ability to not just read but question the official signposts. That meant we somehow had to interrupt the 'normative' sequencing rules for 'successful' transitions in planning our timetable. In fact we decided to reverse them. We would *start* the course by looking at work regimes and local labour markets, move back to inspect government training schemes, and only towards the end of the fortnight deal with the mechanics of leaving school, signing on, and job search.

What might at first sight seem a back-to-front approach was designed to underwrite young people's own priorities. We had to resist some gentle pressure from the local Unemployed Centre which had just opened its doors, and was understandably keen to use the course to promote its facilities and focus on its concerns.

But we were determined after our false start, that the course would not be another kind of schooling for the dole.

In the event our strategy paid off. Reversing the normal order of progression seemed to give the students space to explore some of the key disjunctions between the official rules, and their own, a space which both released their sense of imagination (and humour) and opened up issues around the three 'L's in a way that made sense to them.

From social studies to cultural practice

When we came to consider our general approach to teaching the course we decided to opt initially for a version of the 'social studies' model. This consists in turning students into 'social investigators' in the belief, or hope, that this generates a more critical perspective on society. We had some reservations about this model. It was already known to our students from school, and familiarity seemed to have bred contempt, if our pre-course discussion with them was anything to go by. But it had the big advantage that it seemed well suited to the documentation of our day-time visits. We remained, in any case, agnostic. We would see how our group took to this way of working. How far could they push it in the direction of their own interests and concerns?

Partly to test this, we chose strongly contrasting types of workplace or training regime for our 'investigations'. For example, a workers' co-op, a small non-unionised family firm, a large public corporation. However this was not simply to be an exercise in the appreciation of diversity, or even to examine, critically, different forms of ownership and control; we rejected these more orthodox versions of the social studies approach as being too objectivist for our purposes. Instead we sought to construct an experiential framework of comparison, which corresponded to the actual range of conditions likely to be met by young workers or trainees, in the hope that out of this a number of key political issues might emerge for further discussion and project work. How similar or different were the attitudes of small co-ops to those of small businesses? What difference did the presence or absence of trade unions make to the position of women workers? etc. Now clearly, as tutors, we could have taken the lead in formulating these and similar questions. Yet even within the confines of the social studies

model, we felt it might be counterproductive to artificially prioritise issues on behalf of the group. For the danger was that the students' own concerns might then become marginalised, at best
developed 'off script'.

What we could, and did, do, was help the group script, the
issues as they imagined they would find them, and that meant
things they wanted to find out about, however instrumentally. Alas
for non- directiveness, the interview scripting that emerged from
the early briefing sessions was often wooden and inflexible when
put into practice.

A case in point occurred on the second day, when as a limber-
ing up exercise, the group went on a local walkabout, interviewing
people they saw at work. They met some Telecom engineers
repairing a cable in the street. The scripted questions about
skilling and training opportunities failed to yield much response.
In the embarrassed silence that followed, one of the girls asked
diffidently enough whether the job had any special perks.
"Talking to young girls in the street", replied one jack the lad.
But our boys didn't find the ritual sexist quip at all funny for
once. *This* was something they wanted to hear about. In fact Sue's
question released a flow of stories from the men about moonlight-
ing and other fiddles, the skyves they used to get up to when they
were apprentices, and the importance of not having the gaffer on
your back. Despite the initial hiccup, a real rapport was established around the commonalities of an experience which
embraced both school and work. In the process, important, but
hitherto unscripted issues, concerning discipline and resistance,
control over labour processes, the hidden economy, and not least,
the routine sexism of working life, emerged in a way which
allowed the students to give them proper weight; these were to be
the major themes in the material they subsequently produced. It
seemed at this stage of the course that being thrown in the deep
end was less of a problem for them, than it was for us!

By the third day, something like a group practice had crystallised, with the students beginning to work well together, taking
turns to do interviews, operating the darkroom on a rota, tran-
scribing tapes. The inevitable beginners' mistakes (underexposed
film, tapes erased, etc) did nothing to dampen the general enthusiasm. Their ability to master the technical rudiments, to work
quickly and accurately, and increasingly under their own steam,

was truly impressive. The classroom began to take on the frenzied appearance of the editorial offices of some latter day *Picture Post*, with prints spreading round the walls, tapes and transcripts accumulating in an ordered clutter on the desks.

Undoubtedly much of this initial energy must be credited to the new experience of compiling evidence through the production of photo-texts. This was not quite like the social studies they had done at school. But underlying this was a more significant response. The group were beginning to take collective responsibility for generating material which reflected their, not our, concerns.

A small breakthrough occurred on Day 5, when for the first time, on a visit (to some co-ops) they told us to stop chaperoning them about, and leave them alone to get on with the job. They had discovered something in *this* labour process which, like the Telecom workers, they could control and turn to their advantage. They didn't need us, as gaffers, on their back!

Group work seemed to exemplify the best aspects of this media version of social studies. But in other respects we were becoming aware of some of its limitations. It seemed that holding our group within this investigative frame could serve them as a strategy of *dissociation* when it came to looking at some of the more painful realities of working-class life and labour. Actually social scientists do not have this problem, because normally the conditions they investigate don't directly touch the world. But our students were not in this privileged position. What happened when they were confronted with such realities is well illustrated by their visit to a local pickle factory. This was housed in a squalid Dickensian building, with plant to match; the relaxed and informal atmosphere on the shop floor belied its rigid division of labour – women worked the lines, bottling, labelling, and packing, the men did all the heavy, skilled, and supervisory jobs. The management policies of this small family firm can be judged from the fact that they refused to employ any relatives of women workers, on the grounds that family rows would disrupt production, and they had promptly sacked the only woman who had tried to join a union. The declared loyalty of the women to the firm (many had been there more than twenty years, the manager told us with pride) was in fact built on a profound fatalism. Conditions weren't good, the wages low, but that's the way life is, isn't it?

We had chosen this site because we thought it would force the group to address all those issues about women's work, which a screening of *Rosie the Riveter* had earlier failed to spark off. We were wrong.

As they chatted informally to the women, they made their own assessment of the place. "It's a dump. I wouldn't work here if they paid me!"

Sharon thought that even marriage might be better than this kind of 'slave labour'. The married women who were paid to do just that agreed with her! They wouldn't want their teenage daughters to end up in the same boat. But this consensus expressed no closure of a generation gap, no solidarity of sisterhood in class. Quite the opposite. The investigative frame had simply enabled our group to protect themselves from having to take in the whole painful experience; they distanced it in terms of age and gender ("it was OK for these od bags") in much the same way as, in reverse, the women insulated themselves from the situation by projecting their hopes for a better life onto a future generation (at least the youngsters might find something better to do than this). Neither view sought to challenge the appalling conditions in the factory.

When we got back to base we asked the group to identify which aspects of the visit had affected them most. As they sifted through the source materials, it soon became clear that the only images they felt confident in shaping up were neutral descriptions of technical processes (the plant, the production stages). There was enormous resistance to representing the social relations of the workplace. This can be seen in the panels about the visit that were eventually produced – a literal reading of the labour process, followed by excerpts from the firm's publicity handout and some uncontexted quotes from manager and employees.

We began to see a pattern to the successes and failures of the social studies model. In situations where students felt at home, where they could empathise to some extent with the people they were interviewing, then they felt able to shape the experience within the documentary form, even treat it 'objectively'. But where they felt they were entering a hostile evironment, or when they could not identify in some way with the subjects 'under investigation' then they could not objectify the experience, or shape it into a coherent representation. The visits to the youth training centres confirmed this 'law'.

We had chosen them because of the strong contrast between the form and content of the two regimes. At the Kilburn scheme a wide range of trade skills was offered, the atmosphere was informal but purposeful and the relations between trainers and trainees good-

Source: Trentham Books, *Really Useful Knowledge*, p. 27.

humoured and based on mutual respect (See p. 000). Significantly this was no ordinary MSC scheme but one which had been set up by local community activists, with a very different philosophy in mind. Our group thoroughly enjoyed their stay; they were shown round by some of the trainees, encouraged to ask awkward questions, and generally made to feel welcome. In fact it turned into something of a love affair, with students vowing that this was definitely the scheme for them, it was better even than a job! In the afternoon, we visited another training scheme in Southwark (See p. 000). The contrast could not have been more complete.

An showpiece, costing all of £1½ million, it had been opened by Mr Callaghan, and looked like an open borstal. On this occasion our group were not even accorded the status of would-be recruits, let alone thinking school leavers. Instead they were subjected to a monologue about the requirements of work and family discipline by the training manager, before being given a short guided tour. This kind of verbal assault, not to say its theme, was nothing new to most of them – they had met with both often enough during their school lives, and their way of dealing with it was familiar too. A kind of sullen dumbness overcame the group. Undoubtedly this only served to reinforce the manager's view that working-class 'kids' were insolent, lazy and disinterested. Not surprisingly, our group's comments on leaving the site were equally dismissive – 'He's not interested in talking to us, only at us; he didn't listen to anything we said.'

The anger and resentment they felt towards the manager, but were prevented from openly showing, was quickly turned on us. When we got back to the settlement, we split the group into two, each dealing with material from one of the visits. The contrast between the two training regimes was now instantly reproduced in the classroom. In one room, an enthusiastic and attentive group discussed the Kilburn visit, and engaged with some of the wider issues around the role of trade unions and Britain's economic prospects. Our most successful example of the social studies model to date. But in the other room, the 'Southwark' group presented a very different picture. Bored and resentful, they sat about making a few desultory attempts to muck about, steadfastly refusing to discuss the issues at all. They were not interested in trying to explain their reactions to the scheme, in terms of cause and effect!

Source: Trentham Books, *Really Useful Knowledge*, p. 27.

And why should they be? The fact is that to construct these pupils as 'social scientists' is to put them into an imaginary position to which nothing corresponds in their own social location or discursive practice. The hope is that somehow the imaginary will become real, and some of the critical insights that can be generated within this privileged educational frame, will somehow rub off on the rest of their lives. The secret to the model's success lies in finding situations where its illusions can be sustained. But what happens when students find themselves subjected to real relations of knowledge and power, for example, by that authoritarian training manager at Southwark? Then the whole fragile construction collapses, or rather is revealed for what it is. At this point the position of 'critical detachment' capsizes into one far more organic to working-class experience, that of a passive observer, someone to whom 'things simply happen', because the real processes which determine them are seen to be beyond understanding or control. A pedagogic approach which sets out to give students the confidence to question social norms, thus paradoxically can end by inducing a fatalistic acceptance of them. In the case of the Southwark episode, our students found themselves trapped between two equally untenable positions. They could not ask the scripted questions, the manager had seen to that. But nor could they simply become 'flies on the wall'; they were all too easily swatted down from there. Neither finally could they effectively become flies in the MSC ointment by 'answering back'. That position had been foreclosed by the nature of the whole exercise. They were there to document the place, not tear it apart. The group was locked into the worst of all possible worlds. No wonder they were struck dumb, or later took their anger out on us.

Meanwhile back in the classroom, it was obviously too late to reprogramme the students as 'social scientists'! One of the group had met a friend of his who was on the scheme, during the Southwark visit (much to their mutual embarrassment). So we suggested they explore what it might feel like to be a trainee on such a scheme. Initially that idea too got a hostile reception. The last thing they wanted to envisage was the possibility of ending up in a place like that. But then someone mentioned how trainees in another scheme had sabotaged an 'open day'. The possibility of resistance instantly galvanised the group into imaginative life. They had noticed some graffiti on one of the workshop walls. They now set to, to produce sheets of work in similar vein. Some of it more or less inspired by the visit itself (and addressed to the manager!), but also drawing on popular political slogans and a rich repertoire of what is politely called scatological humour. But the lesson was clear enough. It was only through these resources of meaning, these discourses and cultural forms, that the students were prepared to confront the more painful possibilities of what might lie in store for them. *They* had pushed us beyond the social studies model, in the direction of their own cultural practices, and the forms of popular resistance they connected with.

Materials and media/tions

More generally, and importantly, it signified their desire to shift from a position as observers of 'society' (whether critical or passive) to one of active participation in a process of cultural production.

Now we had already, with the introduction of homework exercises, deliberately built that possibility into the course from Day One. These exercises were closer to a cultural studies model. They were designed to foreground resources of meaning which are normally treated as background information by teachers, careers officers and employers. It was these references, belonging to a more hidden curriculum vitae, which we felt it was important to take up in providing a space where they could be represented *in their own terms*.

The advantage of this method had already been shown in our preparatory work with students on personal inventories and constructs of skill. Although this was focussed on specifying unofficial routes into wage labour, the commentaries that were generated had much wider terms of reference. These were autobiographical, and centred on family and peer group experiences not necessarily confined to particular problems of transition. It was this wider-angled view that the students began to explore, through their homework activity and the personal panels they produced from this.

Photography was again a central practice here, but it differed in some important respects from the way it was being used in the day-time visits. In the first place the homework photography was not intended to function as social documentation – information captured by an 'objective eye'. Taking pictures around the house, of friends, or cars, or playing pool, was centred on a more subjective position, of an 'I related to an 'us' – personal worlds, yet also, of course, socially constructed ones. This work was therefore closer to the conventions of the family album, highlighted by an emphasis on 'being in the picture' surrounded by references that confirmed their present positions as well as future aspirations. The photographs asserted a positive self-image, whose terms are constructed through a particular use of photography, a use that already had currency as a popular cultural practice through the 'snapshot'. Although the technology they were using was more sophisticated (35mm rather than instamatics for instance) it was nevertheless handled in the family or peer group context, in a way that typified instamatic photography.

By the beginning of the second week, the material from the homework was beginning to cohere into a series of personal statements-in-images on our presentation boards. Sometimes the key references were imaginary – wish fulfillments revolving around high life and fast cars. Significantly it was the boys who were more likely to indulge in fantasies of spectacular consumption. More usually the portraits represented everyday experiences – interests, places to go, commitments at home. The girls' statements tended to emphasise these grounded references more than the boys. This is not to say that elements of romance did not enter in, but it took a significantly different form from that of the boys. We were beginning to see a 'double standard' or representation emerging.

It is interesting, in this respect to compare the panels produced by Mark and Lynne.

Mark's panel is a lyrical celebration of working-class masculinity, in what feminists would see as its most sexist form. The panel is centred on the family, and the family romance. Mark sits in the father's place, at the top of the montage, all too comfortably embracing the images of family and friends below. Signifiers of inheritance (the males grouped in a line) and the apprenticeships to it ('the mastery of 'manual' techniques) are represented side by side. It is a strong grid, which no female presence is allowed to enter or disturb.

MARK

I live on East Lane, on top of shops and I might get a job underneath. If I can't get that I'll go across the road to Marks and Spencer working on the tills in there. Underneath is a butcher's, my dad knows the bloke who runs it. I'd like it working as a butcher.

I'm a fairly optimistic person really. I've felt that all through school. My mum wants me to stay on in the 6th form because there's no jobs — and she thinks I need to get a qualification. But I've had enough of school. I've seen the careers lady. She goes "er . . . you look like you're a bit handy with your hands. You can be a postman or work on building sites". Well that's alright really 'cos most of my options I picked I have to use my hands. She sent me a letter 2 days later saying when you leave school come down and see me and I'll help you try to get a job.

I like going to youth clubs. I go down to Ammersham and Northchurch: we go on trips sometimes, it's good ice-skating. Sometimes they take you to schemes like weight training, or courses like the fire brigade or police. But we organise things for ourselves — we have quite a lot to say in running the club — it's different from school. There's a committee — 5 girls and 5 boys and youth workers — they take it seriously.

Source: Trentham Books, *Really Useful Knowledge*, p. 29.

A portrait of patriarchal closure then, and yet... And yet if you thought Mark was quite like this you would be wrong. This is how Mark imagined himself to be, even wanted to be seen, a little hard man. Yet he did not come across to us in this way at all. He was not 'one of the lads' on the course. He was very keen on the girls (especially Lynne) but he did not behave towards them in a 'brutally sexist' manner. His main aim was to get the girls to show him how to dance. He was receptive to them, and their skills, in a way most of the other boys were not. If you like, he was able to show a softer, more 'feminine' side in relation to them. And perhaps this was a relief. Being the youngest and smallest in his family, he must have found it difficult to live up to the hard man image all the time. So in his social relations (with girls) he was actually trying to break out of the patriarchal closure represented in his personal portrait of a family romance.

In contrast to Mark, Lynne's panel more accurately mirrors her real position in the group (see p. 359). It is much more decentred than his. The world does not revolve around her, but around others – her boyfriend, sister, and her home life. Images of romance run like a thread through the panel, connecting the images, smoothing out the contradictions they contain, without ever privileging her own desires. A portrait of a closure around the domestic world (she says she rarely goes out) which shows everything that Mark's panel leaves out. In the context of the course, Lynne was the only girl who fell into a traditional woman's role. Or was she pushed? She was the only member of the group who possessed any typing skills, and continually 'volunteered' to type up transcripts, saying she preferred this to other work. As tutors we tried to continualy interrupt the prevailing sexual division of labour in the way tasks were assigned. But as the pressure of our deadline increased, so did the demands on Lynne to fulfill the role of office secretary. We were all too aware, that neither in this panel, nor in the course as a whole, were we adequately able to prioritise this issue.

More positively, what these two panels show is the importance of reading these kinds of cultural texts, in the light of the social context of which they are produced. For instance, unless you knew something about the social relations in the group, you would be seriously in danger of misreading some of the portraits, of missing the tensions, and contradictions, between these imaginary positions and real practices, between these forms of representation, and the experience they depict. The way these contradictions are handled also leaves its traces 'between the lines', of these texts.

Source: Trentham Books, *Really Useful Knowledge*, p. 30.

This became apparent when the students came to prepare the final edition of their portraits for public exhibition. They now became aware that they would be addressing these statements to a wider audience than the group itself. This created some anxiety. What would parents, friends, the school, let alone 'members of the general public' think about it? Would they be able to live up to the image of themselves they had so carefully constructed. Or in some cases, be ever able to live them down?

Terry, for example, didn't want to be 'shown up' by the picture of him posed against a luridly exotic poster outside a sexshop in Soho. Martin wasn't keen to include a reference to his dad, as a ted, which cut across his own enthusiasm for punk. In both cases it was seen as a case of 'washing dirty linen' in public. They wanted these images cut out.

Should we endorse this self-censorship? Would that place us on the side of a sanitised image of sexuality and harmonious family life? Or would it signify a stance against pornography and for the rebellious voice of punk? As we talked the issue through with them it became clear that simply excising these images would do nothing to tackle the underlying conflicts they represented. It would simply be a case of out of sight, out of mind. Better then, perhaps, to argue for their inclusion and signal the issues which they raise, in a way that could taken up in discussion around the exhibition itself.

Evidently though, the course had privileged a space of representation which temporarily suspended some of the protocols of public propriety which normally apply. But as soon as it was a question of going public, then these protocols, and the censor's code came straight back into force. In other words, as the social relations between author and audience changed so too did the texts themselves, often in subtle ways. This is something we ourselves have had to guard against in preparing the exhibition. It is a constant temptation to edit out weaknesses in the students' work, and our own, which of course must be resisted. We have tried!

A second set of issues revolved around the relationship between the two kinds of media the students were using, the strategies for putting images and words together, and more generally, the balance between the photographic and literacy work.

Initially we were concerned that if the tape recorder was privileged as a means of asking questions, on the site visits, then the camera might be relegated to a purely naturalising role – collecting snapshot souvenirs for the 'group album'. In practice this did not happen at all. Students weighted both media equally as different but complementary recording devices. Back in the classroom, we had the opposite worry – that the popularity of photography as a technical process might only heighten the students' already developed resistance to producing written texts. But this fear too proved exaggerated. For as students began to assemble their prints onto presentation boards, there was a gradual recognition of the power of written texts to 'load' the reading of images. 'Reading' and 'writing' became important acts of self-definition. This did not however happen all at once or overnight!

The students' first attempts at captioning their photographs was purely literal. The words neither added nor subtracted meaning but reiterated the information carried by the image. To try and overcome this redundancy effect, we did some simple caption/picture exercises with them to illustrate the special effects of meaning that came into play. We started with discrete word/image units and once they'd got the hang of it moved on to series, looking at sequencing rules and how changing them altered the narrative meaning too. All this is, of course, standard practice in media studies work on 'deconstructing' texts. But our approach had a different emphasis. We were not just interested in skilling the students in 'decoding images' (an interesting game for the armchair critic of ideology, but hardly much use to anybody else), but in devising a strategy which would help them transpose their own cultural practices into a textual form which did justices to the richness and complexity of their lived meanings.

We approached this problem in two ways. First by introducing the group to elementary techniques of photomontage, and secondly by working with them on constructing a series of photo-stories related to themes in both the workplace and home material. Through both these methods we tried to loosen up the fixed (reified) relation between form and content in their work, by encouraging them to *play* with the signifiers which represented them as subjects in the text. We met with varying degrees of success. The photo-stories provide the best illustration of how far we got.

One group decided to construct a photo narrative based on a visit they had made to a London Transport garage. The central theme – the stresses of the driver's job, ways of resisting it, the possible disciplinary consequence – suggested itself from interviews with bus crews and their earlier encounter with the British Telecom lads. But this theme was now *anchored* more firmly in their own experience by its re-organisation around a fragment of peer group narrative, one centred on a subject they all knew – Martin. Martin had a reputation as a daydreamer in school. Stories were told of his prodigious feats in this department. So his way of resisting the boredom and confinement of the classroom was now transposed to the busdriver in his lonely cabin – daydreaming of the 'good life'.

The narrative theme cross references the discipline of school and work in terms of a common desire to escape both. But where? In the denouement of this story there is clearly no elsewhere than the dole queue. The driver does not get away with it (as Martin might have done in the classroom); he is sacked. A morality tale then whose implicit message seems to be: it's OK to daydream when you are a kid but any worker who mistakes dreams for reality will come to a bad end. Interestingly enough, this group complained that school was not strict enough. The fact that teachers let them get away with things, and didn't push them to work for exams, they read as a sign of indifference and neglect. A recognition then that discipline empowers its subjects in a way that resistance, for them, did not. The realism of the content of this message is mirrored in the realism of its photo-form.

Further work would have needed to be done with the group to draw out these issues, but as in so much else in their project work, we did not have the time. In Martin's own photo-story, though, we were able to take things a stage further and emerge with a slightly more hopeful message. He went off one day with Terry to document his dad at work. Dad was a stonemason and Martin often went along to help him, fetching and carrying the paving slabs, as any apprentice would. But he had no intention of following in his father's footsteps, and not just in terms of work. Dad, as we said, had been a ted. Still was, by his son's account, frequenting rocker pubs and occasionally playing in a band. Now of all the post-war youth cultures, the teds are the only ones to largely run in families. Father and son combinations are a marked feature of teddy boy reunions. But in Martin's case this cultural inheritance was explicitly rejected. His dad was a source of embarrassment; he never asked about the early days of rock'n roll. Ironical this, since punk was supposed to be about getting back to roots, and Martin was an apprentice punk. But there has been no

Source: Trentham Books, *Really Useful Knowledge*, p. 33.

love lost between teds and punks. How then was love to be won between father and son? That is the underlying issue on which his photo-story turns. But to understand this you also have to know something about the history of its production.

On the day in question Martin and Terry turned up with cameras to 'snap' the old man at work. But they quickly got tired of this, and started mucking about. This too they recorded. At this stage it was a purely documentary exercise. The notion of making it into a photo-story had not been raised. But when we subsequently started to work on the materials, it soon became clear that they did not fit. There was a 'pickle factory' type sequence depict-

Source: Trentham Books, *Really Useful Knowledge*, pp. 35–6.

ing the stone-mason's labour process and some odd shots of the two of them larking about 'off script'. Then they hit upon a solution. They would turn the whole thing into a story about two 'riotous' apprentices versus the authority of the craftsman. An ancient theme, but one which Martin now proceeded to give a

more contemporary and personal twist. We were having a brain-
storming session trying to think up a title. How about 'Stiff Little
Fingers', Martin suggested. It was the name of a new wave band
he was quite keen on. But what else did the words signify?
Martin's associations were both to his father and himself.

'Stiff Little Fingers' was an occupational hazard for the stone
mason ('all those heavy slabs') *and* for his sexually frustrated son
('too much wanking!'). The double entendre of the title worked
both as a metaphor of their relationship, signifying both their
similarities and differences. But there was more where this came
from. The captions he produced continued the punning,
weaving an intricate chain of associations around the photo text.
He was learning how to *play* with signifiers, but also how to put
them to work in representing some of his more complicated and
contradictory feelings. For example the caption which turns the
stone mason into a sculptor, is at once ironic and affectionate. 'A
real work of Art' may be read as a sarcasm directed against a
workmate who is getting 'above himself', *and* the expression of
shared pride in skill. Martin's ambivalence towards his father
here rejoins a wider tension within working class culture –
between art and craft, work and pleasure. Yet the caption also
points towards a possible resolution; it reconciles the son's creative ambitions, as a Punk, with the father's manual skills, and
this identification is made possible by mobilising a certain kind
of deprecatory humour, in which some of the more hidden
wounds of class are for once, revealed. This is a humour which
softens the impacts of the blows which life deals out, but does
not, in itself, heal. This is made clear in another frame showing
Martin's father at work and en.titiled 'Beckenham Beach'. The
sand 'discovered' under the paving stone only serves to emphasise how far away the reality principles of life and labour in this
working-class community are from the pleasures of the beach.
Martin's caption is a long way in context and consciousness from
the Utopian sentimentality of the famous May '68 slogan 'Sous
Les Paves, la Plage'. For Martin, paving stones are still the materials of a labour process rather than for building barricades, let
alone a new society. Yet his materialism does not stifle his imagination; on the contrary it furnishes and landscapes its particular
spaces of representation. For what the whole photo-story points
towards is the whole laborious – and playful – process of

unearthing a world of meaning which is submerged under the official discourses of learning and labour.

Portraits in transition

We have suggested some of the ways in which cultural texts can be read, to put author and audience (and their *social*/relations) back in the picture. But the people, places and practices which figured in the students' own panels also belonged to a deeper set of references. For through the homework exercises elements of a more hidden curriculum vitae began to emerge. How are we to read *these* subtexts, these 'other scenes' of growing up working class, and the predicaments they engender?

Not according to those primers of 'adolescent psychology' which are inflicted on teachers at training college. Not, therefore, in terms of those 'stages' of mental or psycho-social development we learn to recite like the three times table – and which add up to a normative grid where anyone who is not male, white and middle-class shows up as hopelessly precocious or retarded. The dangers of psychologising the crisis (e.g. youth unemployment viewed as a crisis in adolescent identity, rather than in the political and economic structure) are all too evident. Nevertheless, to ignore the subjective aspects of transition, or to reduce them to the simple social effect of class, gender or ethnic position, is *really* to throw the baby out with the ideological bathwater. For there are dramatic variations in the way these positions are individually assumed and lived, as we discovered with our group. These 'little differences' can make a big difference to outcomes within limits and conditions fixed by social formation. But they are not random, or unique to particular lives, they are not reducible to 'personality types' or 'the vicissitudes of the instincts'. How then, as teachers, should we recognise them? Let's take a closer look at two members of our student group.

Jane was going to be a hairdresser. She was the most definite and confident member of the group when it came to discussing plans for leaving school. Indeed her disinterest in school (she rarely went) stemmed from the strength of her commitment to what she saw as her 'career'. But then she had already made the transition to work, at home. She had, as she put it, grown up with hairdressing. It was in her family; her mother, aunt, elder brother, cousins too, were all in the business. As a little girl she had watched her mum doing friends' hair at home. Quite early on she had been taught how to shampoo and set; later she had worked as a helper in the family salon. And from these sources she had picked up a wealth of knowledge, about styles and techniques, how to deal with customers – cultural capital she fully intended to cash in. It was through the family network too that she was now hoping to find a job.

The fact that she constructed hairdressing as a career had less to do with the industry's attempt to professionalise its training structures (which in any case she had sidestepped) than the way the appalling conditions in the industry (low pay for long hours) are justified as leading step by step to the promised land of self-employment (running your own salon). Few ever make it of course, but the ambition runs deep. Jane's 'family salon' turned out to mean merely the salon where members of her family worked – part of a chain owned by a leisure combine!

Jane may have been in love with hairdressing, but she had few illusions about the actual job, especially the apprentices' lot. The photo-story she put together on this theme shows her getting the rough end of the deal from both manager and client. Equally, her description of her own, domestic, apprenticeship, may have been tinged with elements of a 'family romance', but if she was dreaming of becoming a princess of the salons, she was most certainly not waiting around for some Prince Charming to make it all come true. This comes out strongly in her comments about her boyfriend, which she included in her personal statement. It is clear from these that she was far from charmed by his attempts to lord it over her!

At the same time, Jane said, in a significant phrase, that she had grown up with hairdressing *in her fingers*. Skill for her was a natural aptitude, a cultural legacy literally emboided in her, providing a quasi-congenital link between her origins and her destiny. In fact, in this family, occupational succession was both a female and male tradition stretching back to the grandparents' generation. Thus for Jane, growing-up was most definitely an apprenticeship to an inheritance. But if she was positioned within a *strong* grid, that also meant that she experienced the tension between the two codes, between the positions of active appropriation made possible by the former and the positions of passive reproduction

Source: Trentham Books, *Really Useful Knowledge*, p. 37.

imposed by the latter, in a particularly acute way. This emerged clearly when she came to montage her personal portrait. She had plenty of images of herself as an active subject – 'an active person who likes playing snooker and pool' as she put it. But she also had photographs of herself passively playing out the 'little woman' role. In the first version of her panel, she positioned a large picture of herself holding a kettle in the left foreground, dominating the other, more active images. But in the final version the emphasis is reversed. The domestic image is reduced in size, and 'bleached' so that it fades into the background against the dynamic image of her at the pool-table. Wish fulfilment or an actual process of negotiation? Jane may have wanted to follow in

I handle the cue pretty well.
I'm not very photogenic.
I always used to go in the Cafe — talk to my mates, play on the machines. The photograph of me holding the kettle . . . whenever I go to someone's house it's always me that ends up making the tea. They're always saying "Jane put the kettle on". I'm just a dogsbody.
But I'm a very active person. Donna, Nicola and me we're the only ones who play pool at Nick's Cafe across the road from where Donna lives. Well I used to go in there all the time but now I've stopped; that's because of my boyfriend. He doesn't like me going in there. He's too possessive. If I go to the Cafe to get some fags he goes "who was there, who'd you talk to?" Well when I'm at home I get up and go out on purpose sometimes. He likes to stay in now — since he's been going out with me he doesn't want to go out. He likes to stay in with me but I don't. I like pool, darts and discos.

Source: Trentham Books, *Really Useful Knowledge*, p. 38.

her mother's footsteps, but this was into hairdressing, not the kitchen sink. The purely domestic register of both codes *was* being rejected. She was struggling to challenge male preserves (as pool-player and breadwinner) while still maintaining a style of

femininity (in her clothes, make-up, etc.) Which was conventionally glamorous. This was possible for two reasons in her case – first
because strong grids provide adolescents with a sense of continuity between where they are 'coming from' as children and where
they are 'going to' as adults in terms of a class place. But this itinerary did not have to follow every signpost of the family romance,
despite her boyfriend's attempt to trap her in the 'Great indoors'.
Jane's position was sufficiently decentred within a wider network
of affiliation, to enable her struggle for autonomy to be endorsed
as expressing kinship with other members of the family, who also
had resisted the closures of 'the couple'. Her father was as proud
of his daugther's skill at pool, as her mother was of the fact that
Jane stood up to her boyfriend so well. She was 'taking after' her
mother's brother and father's sister in these respects! A similar
set of relays came into play in supporting Jane through the immediate transition from school. At first the promised job failed to
materialise. It looked as if, at this critical moment, all her family
connections in the business would fail to deliver the goods. Yet
there were also plenty of family precedents for both this situation
and for her decision to stick it out; she refused to go on a YTS
scheme; she would wait until what she wanted turned up as
indeed it eventually did – a position as a junior in a flourishing
high-street salon.

Most working-class girls do not have so much room for manoeuvre of course. The grid of inheritance locks them into a
chronic position of maturity from an early age, whence they are
simultaneously exploited and idealised as 'little wives and
mothers' (i.e. domestic apprentices) both at home and in the
labour market. Moreover, once they take a step outside the protective frame of their own peer-group romance, girls find themselves trapped back in the double-bind positions always and
already assigned to them by the system of male sexual apprenticeship: baby-faced virgins or old whores.

The difference between girls' and boys' transitions is the difference between the rephrasing of a structural subordination and
the resolution of a conjunctural contradiction. For girls the wage
form offers a brief encounter with an autonomy which bears all
the traces of 'domestication'; but for boys it signifies a licence to
deny the fact of continued dependence on the family, in assum-
ing masculine rights without adult responsibilities. This stems

from the split positioning of boys within working-class culture.
The rites of passage into shopfloor cultures customarily place the
lad in a quasi-feminine position *vis-a-vis* male elders; he is subjected to sexual teasing, treated as a skivvy, sent on errands for
'left-handed spanners' and generally 'shown up' as soft or incompetent by the older men. At the same time, in the family culture,
the boy is held in a quasi-infantile position *vis-a-vis* female elders;
he is fed, cleaned up, has his clothes washed for him, and is generally babied. His assumption of masculinity and maturity involves
the unconscious conservation of this infantile position in and
through the disavowal of all the despised 'feminine' features associated with his 'other place'. The sexual and economic power of
male elders is thus not confronted directly; rather their role at
work and in the family is assumed by the boy through a series of
inversions and transpositions of its symbolic terms played out in
relation to mothers, sisters, girlfriends and other boys. These patterns of transference are encoded in both the family romance and
in youth-cultural forms, especially in the structures of sexual
apprenticeship which link both to a line of male inheritances. For
example shopfloor custom has traditionally 'apprenticed' the
'virgin worker' to the 'woman who is old enough to be his
mother' who sexually initiates him only to be confirmed a 'slag'.
This is followed by a phase in which the young 'improver' per-
fects his mastery of sexual technique by seducing younger, preferably virgin girls. Out on the street meanwhile, groups of 'hard
men' play at king-of-the-castle by elaborating a whole series of territorial devices to feminise and belittle other boys from the neighbourhood. Once indoors, however, the hard nut metamorphoses
into the 'family man' as soon as he pays over a proportion of his
wage packet to his mum for board and lodging – the payment
making him feel grown up about continuing to be babied.

Unemployment, and the weakening of cultural supports, has
simply had the effect of privatising these structures, restricting
them to the level of phantasy, rather than elaborating them in
peer-group ritual or myth. Jamie's story and personal portrait
illustrate this all too clearly.

Jamie, like Jane, presented a picture of self-confidence. It was
not that he had no plans for leaving school, he had too many.
He could work with his stepfather on the lorries, or with
his brother in catering, or get a job as a despatch rider with his

Source: Trentham Books, *Really Useful Knowledge*, p. 40.

new motor bike, or even become a photographer (after our course!). His only problem, it seemed, was an embarrassment of riches.

It was hard to tell fact from phantasy. By his account his family connections included a famous uncle who played in a rock band

and 'knew Bert Weedon', and an Aunt who had a villa in the South of France. All that we could discover about his real family was that his stepfather was an unemployed bricklayer and did not get on with Jamie at all.

Throughout the course Jamie plied us with questions. Questions like 'Please, Sir, can I borrow the camera tonight?' 'Please, Sir, what kind of bike did you have?' 'Please, Sir, do you like Black Sabbath?' all asked in the tones of a little boy asking for sweets. Was he really thirsting for knowledge, or was it all an elaborate wind-up? The answer is 'both, and neither'. At one level he was drawing a caricature of the model son or pupil, which he might once have tried and failed to become. But as soon as we responded to his questions we found ourselves led by the nose for a bit and then slapped down by a sudden sarcasm or withdrawal, put back in our place (as teachers and male elders) *and in his.* For what Jamie was doing was leading us into a trap which had been sprung on him at school and in his family.

What is the primary experience of schooling for most working-class children? It is the experience of being constantly encouraged to answer teachers' questions and then as soon as they rise to the bait (and fail to get it right) being slapped down. And what do most working-class children start out wanting to do at school? Go into any infants' class and you'll see. They want to 'please sir or miss' because that is the only way their desire to be recognised in the first person singular gets recognised by that strange anonymous figure the state has substituted for their mum or dad. But if Jamie's name is called by the teacher it is normally only to summon him back to a legal place of attendance as a 'pupil', in which nothing that makes him Jamie counts for much. At which point his desire for recognition flies out the window to the playground, or familiar streets, or imaginary landscapes peopled with real incidents, and above all friends. But of course if Jamie wants school friends then one way he does *not* want his difference recognised is as teacher's pet! One way out of that bind is to get a name for yourself as a classroom saboteur, winning recognition from both sides. But Jamie was not a troublemaker. He had evolved a more subtle line of attack. He exploited our desire as teachers to impart knowledge, while satisfying his own for personal attention, and at the same time sent the whole process up so that he could shine as a piss artist in the eyes of his peers. He won either way, or so he thought, while trapping us in his own cleft stick. That was the perverse pleasure he got from his game of "please sir".

Undoubtedly his strategy was overdetermined by a family history. We could only guess at that. But it seems likely that he had been subjected to a system of perversely conflicting signals, which he read as a sequence of seduction and rejection. He was treating us to the way he had been treated as a child. Yet this was also part of a wider pattern – built into the way working-class masculinity is constructed. I have argued earlier that boy labour is essentially proto-domestic labour. The lad starting on the shop floor is made to serve as skivvy to the older men, as well as a general fetcher and carrier about the place. This feminine positioning is reproduced within the family too, in so far as the son is his dad's best mate. But this is normally only part of a toughening up process of 'growingup', whereby the boy has to prove that he is not soft like a girl, but a little hard man, or jack the lad, by disavowing all the despised feminine features associated with his place. But for one reason or another that route had been blocked off for Jamie. He chose another route to the same goal. He borrowed 'feminine' techniques of seductiveness and transformed them into props of his male self-esteem. He began by flattering us, feeding us questions, apparently hangling on our every word, the way girls have been traditionally taught to 'hook their man'. But as soon as we picked up his words, they began to function in quite a different discourse. They strung us along, they took us for a ride, until he got tired of it, and told us where to get off. A very masculine technique!

Yet behind all this there was still a little boy lost struggling to grow up. If Jamie was such a willing apprentice, it was not primarily to acquire our actual skills, but to find a framework within which whatever was transmitted by elders came as a *birthright*, not a legacy corrupted by a seductive power game called education or love. Behind all the questions he asked, was one he could not put into words, about his origins and his destiny, and what means he had to master to connect the two. For where grids of apprenticeship and inheritance are weak or confused, neither the question nor the answers are easy to articulate.

This is not to say they were not to be found elsewhere, outside the family/school couple. For example, in his personal panel a

quite different face of Jamie emerges. The little boy lost is suddenly transfigured into the sauve young man about town. This
represented another mode of seduction he deployed, not towards
us, but towards his peers. Jamie fancied himself as a ladies' man,
something of a Don Juan, attractive to older women, irresistable
to younger girls. He was already looking forward to going steady
and getting married though. An unproblematic inheritance of
good looks supported *this* structure of apprenticeship. This all
tied into the peer group romance for the point about all the real
or imaginary sexual conquests of course is to shine in front of
your other 'mates'. This was where Jamie's skills at impression
management came into their own. If school in his account was so
brilliant (though he couldn't wait to leave) it was maybe because
it at least provided a stage where he could show them off. Perhaps
this was as well, because from our observations he was very shy
with girls.

Jamie's main concern then was to maintain a one-up position
centred on an ideal self. This comes through strongly in his self-
portrait, a mirror image in which signs of past, present and future
are montaged together in a seamless trajectory. In this representation his world still looks like an oyster full of hidden pearls. But it
actually signifies a closure, not a way of keeping real options
open. It is one way of dealing with the symbolic wounds of
growing up working-class, but not unfortunately of healing them.
That requires a process of social engagement which relativises the
self. But that is also what is beginning to happen in the accompanying text, though it is Andy who initially brings Jamie back down
to earth in the exchange about work. It is a small shift, but an
important one.

All very interesting, you may be thinking by now, but what possible practical use is all this to the teacher? The short answer is that
any analysis which gives us a sharper, more sensitive reading of
these little differences in positioning, can also help us pinpoint
more accurately the small differences that our own practice can
legitimately make to them. In Jane and Jamie's case our achievements were slight enough; a confirmation of Jane's positive stance
towards her predicament as a working-class girl, a partial opening
beyond Jamie's fixed universe of self-reference. Neither's basic
strategies of transition would change, but maybe one or two of their
tactics might. That at least gave us as teachers some cause for hope.

This brings us back to a central issue raised by our two portraits of transition. How are we as teachers to draw the thin line between those of our practices which support real moves, however small, towards greater political awareness and social autonomy, and those which collusively support forms of self-regard which leave existing patterns of subordination intact?

Is the escape into fantasy always a regressive one? Are some defences against the harshening reality principles of youth unemployment necessary, even a sign of health? If so, which?

To be a 16-year-old school leaver, living on the Aylesbury estate in south London is to have experienced more than your fair share of blows to self-esteem, from teachers, policemen, parents, and, not least, peers. Yet all the members of our group had managed, with varying degrees of success, to carve a sense of pride out of the oppressive circumstances of their young lives. Pride in appearance, clothes, looks, sexuality, style. Pride in skills, as a disco dancer, pool player, handyman, or wit. Pride even in their area, bound up with an assertive sense of territory. These prides are easily injured, *but they are also capable of injuring others.* For they also realy a range of racist and sexist practices which take on a brutal enough form, even when they do not lead to actual violence. The problem is, that as the links between growing up (apprenticeship) and working-class (inheritance) weaken or break, the narcissism of minor differences, already installed in adolescence, emerges along a negative path to charge all the real divsions which exist within the culture and community.

We had a small example of how this can happen in our course. For as soon as students began to take pride in their work (for the first time, in a long time, in some cases, we guessed) other purely destructive feelings were mobilised – envy, petty jealousy, greed – these triggered off all the divisions implanted, socially, within the group.

The fact that these feelings came to the surface at all is some indication of the depth of involvement the students came to have in their work. But this was also a source of strength. For it was the sense of collective investment, a common enterprise in which each member had an equal but specific stake and share, which eventually prevailed over individual attempts to make capital out of it. The damage was made good, and the group managed to complete all their projects much to their own satisfaction and ours. A happy ending then. But one which raised for us as many questions as it answered, both about our personal practice as teachers and the wider, political context of the course.

Post script: questioning cultural studies?

How has cultural studies developed in schools and what role has photography played?

One of the central weaknesses of Cultural Studies is that in order to stake its claim to a legitimate place in higher education it has had to sacrifice its more generous sense of applicability to a much narrower and more academic definition of scope.

At the same time, outside the university there has developed a cultural politics dominated by populist ideologies in which the methods of critical pedagogy have been sacrificed to rhetorics of 'positive images' and self-affirmation. In my view neither theoreticist or populist positions offers a way forward for teachers in schools.

Cultural Studies in schools has in any case taken a different direction. In part its intellectual and political agendas have been subsumed by Media and Social Studies; it has never been accepted as a subject discipline in its own right, and this has been a source of both strength and weakness. It has meant that the original cross-curricular and interdisciplinary character of CS has been maintained but of course it has also led to marginalisation. The one area where it has bee maintained a distinctive presence, is via Photography in Education. There is no doubt that the interplay between Cultural Studies and Photography has been mutually productive. It has helped develop a pedagogy which works well with both 'academic' and 'non-academic' children.

The role which photography actually plays may however vary considerably. It may be absolutely central, as with the Cockpit's work; it may be used in conjunction with other media, as in the No Kidding work; or it may be used as a means of doing something else—like language development or political literacy work; finally it may simply be used instrumentally to open up various kinds of conventional, media studies work. Getting children to take photographs is after all a relatively cheap and easy way of ensuring that you have lots of material to put up around the classroom walls to impress parents and school inspectors! As schools polish up their techniques of impression management to project a 'positive image' and meet the criteria of the National Curriculum I am very much afraid that photography will be relegated to this purely decorative function.

In what ways can Cultural Studies contribute to a redefinition in the form and content of 'really useful knowledge'?

The first thing we have to recognise is that for the vast majority of pupils and their parents, the only knowledge that counts is knowledge you can cash in, whether to get a job, or to deal practically with immediate problems of living. This instrumental view of learning is neither peculiar to the working class, nor originated there; it is to be found in every social stratum, and has intensified as a result of credential inflation, a process which has developed alongside the educational system itself. The higher up the educational ladder you go, the more commodified – and reified – knowledge becomes. Now it is possible to bemoan the fact that the ideals of liberal education have been sacrificed on the altar of market values, but it is not a very useful stance to take. The disinterested pursuit of learning has only every been the prerogative of relatively small and privileged groups – the gentleman scholar, the lady of leisure, the working-class autodidact, the 'pure' scientist.

For the rest, education has never not been 'vocational' in the narrow utilitarian sense of the word. Classics, for example, was studied at public and grammar schools primarily because it was required for entry to university, and certain of the professions, not because reading Plato or Cicero was going to equip you with a cultivated sensibility!

What is new about the new vocationalism is not its utilitarian or instrumental vision of learning, but the technocratic ideology and methods through which that vision is being realised. This is indeed a bureaucratic revolution, submitting every aspect of the educational process, including the most intimate, and subjective aspects to the rule of an impersonal and calculating rationality. The chief beneficiaries of this revolution, if indeed it is successfully carried through, will appropriately enough, be a new kind of middle class, one whose cultural capital is embodied in technical skills related to the management, control, ownership, and distribution of specialised forms of knowledge. But as Marx was the first to remind us, you cannot produce a bourgeoisie without also at the same time, producing a proletariat. This is the other half of the vocationalist programme – to train up a new service class in the 'transferable skills' or 'techniques of impression management' which are the condition of its deployment into expanding sectors of the service economy. In the process, we are seeing class divisions, not so much redrawn, as being given a new educational form.

What has Cultural Studies got to do with all this? Well, one thing it is not about is making a rearguard stand for old-style liberal education. CS has long since outgrown its origins in 'Eng Lit'. Its critique of techno-bureaucratic forms no longer proceeds from the kind of anti-industrial spirit which informed the Leavisite tradition. Instead what CS has to offer is a detailed case study of the growth of cultural industries in post-war society, and the role which various technologies of power play in everyday life and labour. Where its critical dimension becomes apparent, is in its rejection of any naive equation between technological and social progress, its exploration of social contradictions, cultural variables, patterns of discontinuity in historical change. Understanding of these issues seems to me to be a vital component of any prevocational curriculum, since it provides students with the widest possible basis on which to make informed occupational choices. But this refers us at once, not just to the dimensions of class, but to those of gender and race. Here too, I believe Cultural Studies is beginning to make a special contribution.

Today the old brand of 'really useful knowledge' is being powerfully renewed by the black supplementary school movement. Basic numeracy and literacy skills are taught in a context which also encourages the students to see themselves as a force capable of transforming society. The teaching methods involved tend to be authoritarian, even patriarchal in form, as indeed they were in the days of the 19th-century movement for independent working-class education. For this reason, I do not think we can look to this initiative, important though it is, for a general model. Instead we need to develop a pedagogy which is properly anti-racist – that is which opens up a space of cultural affirmation for ethnic minorities, and at the same time engages with the roots of common-sense racism in white cultures. Because of the kinds of media it uses, and its 'reading between the lines', Cultural Studies is well placed to advance this pedagogy beyond the naive prescriptive stance on 'positive images' which currently dominates so much anti-racist work.

Equally anti-sexist initiatives have tended to concentrate on changing the content or context of girls' education, but have been remarkably unadventurous in pedagogy, tending to simply adapt existing models of experimential learning, to their purposes. This is all the more ironic, in so far as it is feminists who, in the last few years, have pioneered so many of the formal innovations in cultural media such as video, photography, and the other visual arts, which have put into question the status of both experience and reason. It is once again, at this level of teaching method, that I think Cultural Studies has such a decisive contribution to make to a reappraisal of what is to count as 'really useful knowledge'. For above all this is a method which does not divorce the personal from the political, and which is centred on a practice of literacy in which the technical and aesthetic, cognitive skills and imaginative resources are closely integrated.

In what way is the Cultural Studies approach different from 'experimential learning'?

Certainly the documentation of lived experience forms a central part of many Social Studies courses. This is already to place the student at a critical remove from immediate impressions, since it involves a conscious reflection on the content and context of experience, rather than the naive assumption that experience as such automatically leads to 'learning'. But in moving from social to cultural studies a further dimension is added, namely, that related to the practice of representation itself. At this level the hidden agendas of 'common sense' and their social construction can become an explicit focus of educational attentional as students learn how they have unconsciously 'learnt' certain ideas. What so-called 'experiential learning' does is to *abstract* the student from the real determinants of experience, whereas Cultural Studies moves in the opposite direction – to ground the student within concrete contexts of meaning. Cultural Studies deals in images which are all too immediate in the emotional power they exercise, but instead of making them the object of a purely intellectual critique we use them as the basis for practical project work in a variety of expressive media. Above all our pedagogy does not operate in terms of the traditional opposition between abstract thought and immediate feelings; our raw materials are precisely those popular cultural forms in which structures of phantasy and belief are inextricably entwined.

How do you think the National Curriculum will affect the development of Cultural Studies and photography in education?

One things is for sure. Whatever the circumstances this kind of work always has to push against the professional ideologies and educational discourses in which both the singularities and shared experiences of gender, race and class are ignored, travestied, or conscripted into quite alien categories of representation. For although we work in and through the medium of everyday cultural practices, it is always against the grain of dominant commonsense construction that our essential engagement proceeds.

Notes

1. For a discussion of 1980s cultural politics related to the youth question, see 'Beyond Youthopia' *Marxism Today* (Autumn 1985).
2. See Chapter 7 in this volume.
3. See, for example, *Cultural Studies in Schools* (Cockpit, 1986); also A. Dewdney and M. Lister, *Youth Culture and Photography* (Macmillan, 1988).
4. Many of these materials are now out of print, but some are available from the New Ethnicities Unit at the University of East London.
5. See Chapter 8 in this volume.
6. Material from this 'Leavers Believers' exhibition is discussed later in this chapter.
7. See the introduction to *Now and Then* (No Kidding Publications, London, 1985).
8. See *Staying On* (No Kidding Publications, London, 1986).
9. See C. Cockburn, *Two Track Training* (Macmillan, London, 1987).
10. See *Dolls House* (No Kidding Publications, London, 1985).
11. See, for example, R. Stradling, *Political Literacy and the School Leaver* (London, 1978).
12. See Chapter 6 for an account of this project. Also P. Cohen, *Racism and Popular Culture* (Institute of Education, 1987).

13. See *Whatever Happened to Janet and John?* (No Kidding Publications, London, 1986).
14. See *Livelihoods – the video* (No Kidding Publications, London, 1987).
15. See *Listen to All They Say* (No Kidding Publications, London, 1987).
16. See *Schools Out* (No Kidding Publications, London 1987).
17. See M. Alverado: 'Simulation as method', *Science Education*, 14 (1975).
18. See *Livelihoods* published by New Ethnicities Unit.

Select bibliography

Berger, John and Mohr, Jean (1988) *Another Way of Telling* (London: Verso).
Dewdney, Andrew and Lister, Martin (1987) *Using Photography in Schools* (London: *Cockpit)*
————(1987) *Youth, Culture and Photography* (London, Macmillan).
Hollands, Robert (1990) *The Long Transition* (London: Macmillan).
Johnson, Richard (1988) 'Really Useful Knowledge – memories for education in the '80s', in T. Lovett (ed.), *Radical Arguments for Adult Education* (London, Routledge & Kegan Paul).
Reynolds, J. (1976) *Camera in the Classroom* (London Longman Paul).
Spence, Jo. (1986) *Putting Myself in the Picture* (London: Camden Press).
Wagner, J. (ed.) (1979) *Images of Information* (London, Sage).

Chapter 11

Negative Capabilities: On Pedagogy and Post-Modernity

Shortly before I left the Institute of Education, after a ten-year stint, I was invited by Bob Ferguson, head of the Media Studies Department to give a valedictory lecture.

The occasion gave me a chance to reflect on the politics of knowledge as it was played out within the field of educational policy and research, and also allowed me to take a line of thought for a walk in search of an alternative paradigm.

Although the text is critical of the post-modern framing of the knowledge/power issue in education, it does at least indicate an area in which the grand narratives of enlightenment can be held up to quizzical inspection. But it is also suggested that techniques of 'deconstruction', however useful in literary criticism or media studies, do not offer an epistemology which could inform everyday classroom practice, let alone curriculum development. The real quest is for a versatile and accessible model or method of critical investigation which is as good for pedagogic as for research purposes.

In this text I argue the case for introducing a hermeneutics based upon psycho-analytic notions of the 'unknown' and 'potential space'. Although this might seem like a frivolously impracticable suggestion for a profession that spends most of its time trying to keep order in the classroom while managing diminishing resources, it does speak to what inspired so many people to become teachers in the first place – the desire to create a symbolic framework which enables children to explore and make their own discoveries about the world, rather that merely train up their minds or discipline their bodies. One of the more hopeful signs of the times is perhaps the growing awareness at every level that without a structure which encourages this room for manoeuvre, the very kinds of initiative and self-confidence which are extolled as being so essential to national as well as individual well-being are unlikely to flourish.

Overviews

The grand narratives in which education played a central role as an agency of human emancipation and social justice, as a means of transforming wider structures of state and civil society, are today in disarray. Whether or not they were fairy stories, the happy endings which they promised have failed to materialise; the larger hopes they nourished have been crushed, not just by the political forces ranged against them, but because the whole historical project of the Enlightenment, of which they are a central part, turned out to be more fatally compromised in the knowledge/power game than we ever realised in the heady days of 1960s and '70s radicalism.

If it is more difficult today to believe in this version of reason or progress, if, to take a specific case, we can no longer take for granted the civilising mission of English in popular education, it is not primarily because the meaning of these terms have been twisted and debased, but because the discourses themselves were always on the side of the big battalions (either those of the 'bourgeoisie' or 'the masses', the public man or the traditional intelligentsia). They served to marginalise all those 'others' who lacked an organised political voice (women, children, the petit bourgeoisie, ethnic minorities, the artist and bohemian, the 'underclass'). These groups were regarded as so many backward, irrational and deviant elements, who were to be seen for the purposes of intellectual scrutiny, but certainly not heard in their own write.

Now if the onward march of those big battalions who were supposed to be on the side of freedom, justice and the New

Jerusalem has been halted far short of these goals, it is perhaps
worth remembering that history tends to proceed by its bad side
and the angels never had a monopoly of these rhetorics. Reason
and Progress proved just as able mercenaries on the other side,
on the side of those whose project was to conform education to
the rationality of the market place or the industrial enterprise,
and who today measure the pupils' and the teachers' progress in
terms of norms of profitability or productivity derived from business management.

One of the crueller ironies of recent intellectual history has
been the way a certain version of Marxism claiming to possess a
higher rationality successfully undermined the humanist positions
associated with the Young Marx, which had supported so many
emancipatory educational projects (Freire, Illich, *et al.*) In their
place was put a functionalist account of schooling as a mode of
reproduction of (according to choice) the dominant ideology,
cultural capital or the social divisions of labour, a model where
the mechanisms of structural inequality were oiled by resistance
and opposition and no one was in a position to throw a spanner
in the works. So, instead of the idealisation of the teacher as a
visionary setting out to change the world both inside and outside
the classroom (the story I grew up with), we were given an image
of the state functionary whose room for manoeuvre was virtually
nil.

It did not take the educationalists of the New Right long to see
that this was less an account of how schools or teachers actually
worked, than of how they ought to be. And, indeed, how they
could be if only their local autonomies could be sufficiently
shaped. If the curriculum was thoroughly vocationalised, and
nationalised, if methods of teaching and evaluation could be fully
subordinated as a means to that end, then a New Right Jerusalem
could be attained. Schooling would at last be fully rational and
progressive, enabling anyone (but especially blacks, women and
the working class) to make it into the new middle class if they
really tried. Although there was some dispute over whether these
people should pull themselves up by their own bootstraps
(contest mobility) or be given a helping hand (sponsored mobility) the important thing was that the elements of a success story
had been found and articulated. Teachers had a key role to play
in its telling; those who clung to the old emancipatory narratives

were the new folk devils in moral panics about falling standards and economic decline. Those who embraced the Cause were cast in the role of evangelical bureaucrats, in the front line of the crusade to make Britain great again.

In the 1980s educational initiatives were thus no longer insured against failure by appealing to historical laws or tendencies, or long-distance principles of hope; instead, under the watchwords of Back to Basics, or Victorian Values, or Parental Choice, or (more recently) Active Citizenship, a new educational managerialism was installed, guaranteed by more immediate and tractable models of means and ends, the ubiquitous checklists of aims and objectives, the prescriptive, quasi-performative statements of intent, which disguise the dictation of political goals in the language of bureaucratic imperatives. And lo and behold, rationalist pedagogies and child-centred methods of learning now appear as the new way to manage learning processes and promote the skills and values associated with the enterprise culture. Reason, turned into a character in a Thatcherite Pilgrims Progress, was told to stop daydreaming about dialectics and contradiction and get on with the job of promoting the New Realism.

As a result it has become less easy to appeal to some grand narrative of reason and progress which somehow transcends these instances as the basis from which to conduct a critical overview of educational policies and practices. Those who have still tried to do so have been sidelined, turned into armchair critics, excluded from the corridors of power even within the educational system itself. In so far as we are forced to write from the confinement of the library or the word processor, we may console ourselves with the thought that all the world's a text, and that all we need to do to keep up with the knowledge/power game is give the latest policy statement from the DES the once over with a little help from discourse analysis; but that does not hide from us or anyone else the fact that the more ambitious our critique of current initiatives the less credence and effective purchase it is likely to have on actual decision-making.

Placing ourselves on some imaginary summit of understanding, on the assumption that this affords critical distance and lends a necessary disenchantment to the view, has been a fatally seductive option for radical intellectuals who neither wish to nor have the chance to be actively implicated in social changes to which they remain fundamentally opposed. They become omniscient talking heads as a cover story to gloss over actual powerlessness within the body politic of education. The problem is that when this form of dissociation no longer works, it lends itself to a slow capitulation to the very reality principles which had been hitherto been disavowed. The intransigent radical becomes a New Realist, an often fervent convert to the pragmatics of the knowledge/power game, caught up opportunistically in the slipstream of events that s/he still does not control and realising the worst fears of what would happen once there is a letting go of Olympian world views.

Still, with or without the help of the gods, there are different ways of doing overviews, and I want for the moment to look at some of the options.

The first type of overview tries to cut the present down to size, by setting it in some wider, even global, historical perspective, to restore a sense of contingency to what otherwise seems immutable (and it seems not even Thatcherism goes on for ever). But such historical overviews are not always as liberatory in their effect as they are intended to be. Sometimes this is because in making the present seem to be the culmination of past struggles, they fall back on Whig interpretations of history – the onward march of the big battalions of educational enlightenment and progress: the labour movement in one version, the liberal intelligentsia in another, and industrial reformers in yet a third.

There is another version of this which sets out to rescue educational experiments and struggles that failed to change the course of history from E. P. Thompson's 'enormous condescension of posterity', but only by locating them in a kind of alternative teleology of the oppressed. We tunnel back into the past stopping wherever we can document a school strike, a womens caucus, a black presence, and then retrospectively link together all these instances as part of a continuous tradition of underground resistance. This is history as genealogy; it seeks to empower the struggles of the present generation, to give them a sense of legitimacy and even direction by referring them to a chain of precedents set by those who came before. Obviously it is important to retrieve these histories in their own right, if only to grasp the discontinuities involved and avoid projecting the present onto the past. The work of Richard Johnson is exemplary in this respect. But the issue is the uses to which this work is put. Roots radicalism may be an effective form of therapy, it may be a useful exercise in faith healing, but does it actually help to devise strategies which will lead us from the present to a better future? And is this not a crucial question for education which is nothing if not a struggle to shape a better future for our children?

That issue arises with special force in the second kind of overview which take the narrative form of a soap opera. Here the basic plot never changes. Capitalism, racism, patriarchy is always and essentially the same old story of exploitation and oppression. The surface details may vary, dramatis personae come and go, but the drama revolves endlessly around the same depressing or reassuringly familiar conflicts. The basic rule is that each episode must culminate in a crisis, but the resolution is permanently postponed. The struggle is always to be continued because it is always the fire next time. This is the preferred model of conspiracy theories – the workers are always on the point of finally winning but are then betrayed at the last minute by their leaders. This may get some people hooked on the edge of their seat waiting for the next instalment, but for those of us not so addicted, the element of chronic repetition is all very demoralising. If the present is merely a replay of the past, if it is always a case of *déja vu* and *plus ça change*, then why bother to struggle on? It is a recipe for cynicism not commitment. Or perhaps for the kind of grim satisfaction which comes from experiencing events in everyday life as a kind of objective correlative of some earlier historical injustice done to one's community. It is in this context that the construction of a collective memory through the invention of tradition can become a block on understanding what is specifically different or new about the present.

That, however, is the special province of the third type of overview: the conjunctural analysis which surveys current developments and aims to set an agenda for debate. This usually takes the form of a state of the art or state of the nation address (or, more modestly, a literature review). At its best it may be a ground-clearing exercise, a necessary precursor to rethinking an issue which helps people get their bearings and see the wood from the trees. At its worst and least generous, it becomes an exercise in summary justice and settling old scores, measuring everything against a preferred paradigm and finding it inevitably wanting: A hatchet job with a hint of self-congratulation. Or a sermon on the mount preaching to the converted. These days, when triumphalism is out of fashion, this kind of overview is often delivered in the magisterial tone of a public school headmaster/mistress presenting an end of term report. Achievements are enumerated, prizes handed out. Bad marks and worse examples are cited to exhort us to redouble our efforts in dealing with problems to come. Under cover of these *excathedra* pronouncements personal hobby horses can be ridden for all their worth. It is a useful device for building one's own empire and knocking down others', extending or defending the boundaries of an existing discipline, establishing orthodoxies, or staking a claim to a new field. For all these reasons this kind of overview in both its good and bad aspects has become a professorial prerogative, and appropriately so since the inaugural lecture is a rite of passage to a chair, which is supposed to mark a new move in a particular knowledge/power game. For similar reasons it is the conventional genre of the swan song, a pretext for a few parting shots.

The final type of overview professes to subvert the knowledge power game but in fact extends it in a new direction. It operates according to the principle of bricolage, drawing bits and pieces of evidence and argument from here, there and everywhere, and threading them together around a common, discursive theme. The game is either to make as many unusual connections between disparate phenomena (free associations) or establish as many different articulations of a single instance as the chosen theme permits (intertextuality). We have arrived at the post-modernist overview, one which does not privilege any of the elements in play, or inscribe its own juxtapositions within any fixed or closed hierarchy of meaning, but juggles around trying to keep as many ideas in the air at once as it can. This approach specialises in transgressing established academic boundaries, hyphenating disciplines, and wrenching texts out of their historical context and making them play intellectual games with each other. Wittgenstein meets Vico under the banner of gay science; Nietzsche is dressed in drag and goes to the ball with Foucault. Rousseau shares a wet dream with Derrida or an argument about social order with Lenin. Now this can make for exciting reading; it can work like Eisenstein's theory of montage – juxtaposing different elements to generate a new, and more dialectical concept. But in the wrong hands it can quickly degenerate into collage and pastiche in which everything is rendered equivalent in the cultural supermarket of ideas; for example, the meaning or value of a text is not considered in its own terms for what strategic insights or oversights it might contain about its subject-matter; it is judged solely or primarily in relation to another text of which it is only regarded as a supplementary reading, i.e. what does it add or subtract to what has already been said before? Criticism becomes the art of usually invidious comparison carried out solely for the benefit of a select professional audience who play this *particular* language game. We are in the world of radical intellectual chic and BIFF cartoons, and not one confined to cultural or media studies unfortunately. We can see the same principles at work in the construction of modular curricula in which students acquire bits and pieces of highly mediated information generated from different and often incompatible perspectives which are then stitched together into an apparently seamless thematic web, without for all that giving any real purchase on the subject.

It is like living in the House that Jack or Jill built, an architecture with an infinite number of stories but no solid foundations. There is a principle of planned obsolescence built into the supermarket of ideas. And the result is that some of the most difficult and therefore interesting ideas are simply shelved rather than being worked through in any depth or detail simply because people are already rushing onto the next bright idea in the hope that this will provide the missing key. In fact, behind much of the post-modernist frenzy lies the pressure of a very old, and certainly pre-modern quest which is disavowed – for the book of books. The overview to end all overviews, will discover the key, but hitherto missing text, which lies forgotten and buried in obscurity but will finally somehow sum it all up. The momentum this generates is all rather good for business. Post-modernism appears to dismantle the hierarchy of knowledge but in fact represents its final fetishism as a commodity form. In this I am with Jameson and against Baudrillard.

One thing that all these kinds of overview have in common is that they tend to reach foregone conclusions and beg a lot of questions en route. In particular they tend to select only that evidence which confirms their particular line of thought. Here is one statement of the method involved, from the authors of an

influential book about the dominant ideology thesis, which presented a historical overview of the development of western societies from feudalism to late capitalism and set out to prove that
ideology played only a secondary role in the maintenance of the
class structure and popular consent:

> What we propose to do is to follow the current practice of
> mixing second order and occasionally impressionistic evidence
> with a priori reasoning so as to arrive at a construct which
> appears plausible.

This rather dis/ingenuously gives the whole game away. The OED
gives the definition of 'Plausible' as: 'deserving of applause,
acceptable, ingratiating, having a show of truth, specious.'

Not so much a search for understanding but an exercise in
impression management, designed to win over the audience at
all costs. Primary sources are not consulted or used as a control
or check on theorisation; instead, secondary studies are
ransacked for any quotes which may lend an appearance of credibility to the argument or give a sense of realism to the story
line.

If most of us resort to this method at some time or another
(and some people do it most of the time) it is partly because of
the current difficulties in carrying out the kind of empirical
research which could meaningfully address the kind of larger
questions addressed in the overview. It is to the politics of
research that I now want to turn.

Heuristics

In the last decade there has been a growing rift between the
highflown theoretical debates between the big ideas of Marxism,
structuralism, feminism, post-structuralism and all the other
isms, which do not depend on generating new evidence, and
the development of educational research which has been forced
into an ever more narrow, empiricist and technically specialised framework which inhibits engagement with these wider
issues.

In a recent lecture by the chairman of the British Educational
Research Foundation, research was defined as including 'any dis-

ciplined enquiry which serves educational judgement, or decisions, or which is conducted in an educational setting'.

In his view the role of the research community was to 'render
the process of educational policy-making and implementation
more rational and more efficient'.

Undoubtedly this was intended as a broad definition and to
include a multiplicity of approaches. But what he did not seem to
realise was that he was describing the final incorporation of educational research into the governmental structure; the researcher
becomes a mental technician who services the Department of
Education and Science or the National Curriculum Council, or
their successors, with information they can refer to (and even
occasionally defer to) if they need to legitimate the decisions they
take, as realistic, rational or responsible (the new 3 Rs) within the
parameters established by central government. Those parameters,
which make up the more or less hidden premises of 'policy oriented' research, are not themselves supposed to be open to question, still less investigation. They are simply bracketed out of the
research design – best left to academics who engage in overviews
to worry about.

Of course there are many researchers who write these issues back
in, suitably disguised and embedded within the cover story of the
research proposal. The general move, however, is to integrate
research within the new managerialism. The model is that of an R
& D Department of a large industrial enterprise. The task is to
design, test and evaluate the likely impact of a new product (in this
case a particular policy or curriculum) on the educational market
place. How cost-effective is it? What are the likely forms of consumer (i.e. teacher or pupil) resistance and how can they be overcome? How should the product be packaged and sold to maintain
brand loyalty? The researcher is a kind of backroom girl or boy,
who finds solutions to the problems of management, which the
workers – in this case the rank-and-file teachers – are supposed to
implement. This model not only downgrades research, it deskills
the teacher. It is not that some kind of educational market research
may not be necessary, but whether there should be rather more to
curriculum development and evaluation than this. And again there
are cover stories which enable the wider agenda to be retained.

However, no such cover is needed for the kind of large-scale
number-crunching research which is still the most successful in

terms of its measurable impact on official thinking. Of course it is expensive and can only be undertaken with adequate public funding and institutional support. It is successful partly because these agencies have such a large investment in disseminating the findings, and have the power and resources to do so effectively. It is also successfull because of the form it takes – surveying large populations, using sophisticated methods of statistical analysis to establish cause or correlation, all this impresses politicians and policy-makers as being properly scientific; putting numbers to instances somehow magically turns conjectures about them into hard facts.

Unfortunately the conceptual basis of this type of research is often very weak, and the constructions which are placed upon the data correspondingly flimsy. In many cases this does not matter, since the success of the story does not depend on concepts, but on the way findings can be used to confirm, in an apparently objective way, central tenets of common sense.

The final paradigm of educational research makes no such large claims on resources, although in its own more modest way it is often used to underwrite common sense. Action research and the ethnographic case study became popular with funding bodies as a low-cost alternative to number crunching at the point where their apparent radicalism of purpose – to enable teachers to investigate for themselves what happened when they introduced small-scale changes in professional practice, or to provide a 'view from below' of educational processes – could be safely reconciled with a conservative philosophy of managerialism which bracketed out larger structural questions, questions of power etc., or simply took them as given.

Once again, many of us promptly tried to write these issues back into the script, but even when done successfully the qualitative methodologies to which we were committed were not always well suited to the purpose. Detailed ethnographic studies of teacher – pupil interaction, classroom process or school counter-cultures are often entertainingly written, and strong on local colour; sometimes done in the form of a living novel, with the researcher as narrator/hero-ine, the genre effectively exploited the socially committed voyeurism of its readers – the desire to know what life is life on the other side of the tracks. More positively, these accounts could also furnish useful icono-

graphies for the budding teacher or youth worker who had yet
to encounter the real thing, and wanted to get a feel for it.

But even, and especially, when these accounts were interleaved
with heavy dollops of theory, as a means of making generalised
interpretations of the material, they were never taken seriously by
politicians or policy-makers. It was just too easy for them to
dismiss *Learning to Labour* as being about ten working-class lads in
Wolverhampton or, more recently, *Murder in the Playground* as
being about what went wrong in one school with a bad head in
Manchester, in order to deny any wider significance to their
uncomfortable conclusions about class, gender or race.

The political and moral economy of educational research, as
I've described it, has worked to eliminate various kinds of theoretical research which seeks to produce new concepts, and/or
develop new methodologies in order to open up a new field of
investigation.

Imagine you are the director of a well-known foundation which
commits substantial funds to social research. One morning a
letter arrives on your desk which goes something like this:

> The applicant wishes to conduct a study of the role of dreams
> in mental life. The study will undertake a critical review of
> existing theories of dreams, both popular and scientific. It will
> draw on both clinical and autobiographical material to
> develop an alternative model of interpretation. A typology of
> dream processes will be constructed and their characteristic
> mechanisms of representation described. From this model a
> general theory of memory, desire and the unconscious will be
> derived and its implications for understanding both normal
> functioning and forms of mental illness will be drawn out. It is
> hoped that this research will be disseminated widely amongst
> the caring professions and lead to changes in many areas of
> their activity.

Our grants director has got out of bed the wrong side this
morning, after a disturbed night in which he had yet another
dream in which he was trapped in a derelict building being
besieged by angry researchers who all look like his mother. He is
not in the best of moods. Reaching for a copy of the foundation's
Guidelines to Applicants, he writes back:

Dear Dr Freud, Thank you very much for your interesting proposal. Unfortunately, I have to tell you that it does not fall within our present terms of reference. The proposal, although academically competent, fails to meet the overwhelmingly important criterion of policy relevance. Nor is it at all clear in what way your proposed research would change the practice of educationalists or the medical profession, or indeed be of direct benefit to their clients. You do not include any suggestion as to how the effectiveness of treatment based on your method of dream interpretation could be evaluated compared with other approaches. Your sampling procedure, based as it is on a small, and dare I say it, unrepresentative sample of the population, does not inspire confidence in the sweeping claims which you make for your discovery. I am sorry not to be more encouraging. It is a great pity that your promising early work on hypnosis, and the uses of novacaine in dental treatment, did not lead you to pursue your enquiries in these fields.

The second area of exclusion is longitudinal research. Following a cohort over a long duration, making periodic surveys, produces a kind of speeded-up version of how the social structure changes or reproduces itself in and through life histories. The problem with the studies undertaken when it was still possible to fund them was that they used rather crude questionnaires and only succeeded in producing blurred snapshots of the processes involved. But if we want to understand how different experiences of schooling not only determine but are subsequently reconstructed in autobiographies, as these are in turn shaped by changing circumstances and conjunctures, then clearly we need more sensitive qualitative methods which allow people to tell the stories which have invested their inner lives with social meaning.

I think that the absence of these two kinds of enquiry crucially inhibits the contribution which research could make to widening and deepening the terms of public debate over educational futures. But there are other factors, too, which militate against this.

Although the pressures of the academic rat race (publish or perish) ensure that the quantity of literature continues to increase at a rate which would make it more than a full-time job for anyone just to read what was relevant to their own area of interest, never mind do any of their own research, its range of reference continues to narrow down to the point where most of it is, perhaps fortunately, of little importance to anything except the author's own CV.

Example: Volume 1 of *Das Kapital* is 800 pages long, and has only 200 bibliographic references, over half of which are to works outside the area of political economy. Freud's *Interpretation of Dreams* is 671 pages long and contains 310 references, of which over two-thirds are to works of art, literature or philosophy. In contrast, a 30-page article published in the journal *History Workshop* on 'Plebeian spiritualism, 1853–1913' contained 214 footnotes and even more references, none of which were drawn from outside its immediate research area. The fact that writers of case studies or monographs feel they have to authorise almost every sentence in this way is not I think just about a ritual display of scholarship; it speaks volumes about the kind of panic which can set in once the safety nets and guarantees hitherto furnished by grand narratives are taken away.

The proliferation of competing paradigms, the multiplication of foci, the shift from the initial emphasis on class to include gender and race, the increasing specialisation of fields of enquiry, not to mention the growing complexity of change in education and society – all this, coupled with the increased competition for research funds, means a continuing fragmentation of knowledge and an intensification of the power games which are played around its production and dissemination. At the same time there is an increasing demand for overviews, maps to help students or teachers find a path through the ideological minefields and intellectual mazes, at a time when, for the reasons I discussed, they yield diminishing returns. No amount of neat pigeon-holing of ideas will recover the middle ground which has been lost between atomised forms of 'general knowledge' and the necessarily specialised forms of academic discourse.

Publishers' policies also ensure that the texts which are written are less likely to rebuild these bridges. They want books which are neither too rooted in concrete analyses to confine their sales to the UK market, nor too intellectually demanding to prevent them being put on the reading lists of undergraduate courses, nor too like a work of art or literature to disqualify them from serious academic consideration and review. These constraints operating at the end of the research process have much the same debilitating effect as funding policies do at the beginning in limiting the kinds of stories that educational research can tell and the kinds of issues and audiences it can address.

As a result of these foreclosures, the kind of debate which has developed in the last few years, as educational issues have been pushed ever higher up the political agenda, has tended to oscillate between phases of intense in-fighting within and between different academic specialisms, and rhetorics which have faint echoes of the grand narrative, but are now reduced to a language of dumb generalities.

As an example of the latter, consider the following contribution to a recent Labour party policy review on education:

> The task of a publicly funded system of education is to bring all our children to the point of being intellectually, socially and emotionally able to take their place as caring, critical and intelligent citizens of our community.

Now who could possibly disagree with that? The only problem is that it is just another end-of-term speech. It can mean all things to all people and as soon as you try and translate it into concrete terms it disintegrates into a multiplicity of different prescriptions, priorities and practices, all of which would claim, with about equal plausability, to do the business. Finally, of course, it begs the central question of *whose* community. Who is 'us'? It simply assumes some kind of unitary and egalitarian form of civil society, which is to be inhabited by these model citizen pupils, a utopia which, for better or worse, is as distant from the pragmatics of educational reform as it is from the differences which dominate the real everyday lives of parents, teachers and children in today's state schools.

So the task we face, is to find another way of getting our bearings, of reconstructing a middle ground of discourse which hopefully is neither political platitude or academic pontification, to build some real bridges between theory and practice, the high ground and the profane realpolitiks of staffroom and classroom. So let us look at the kind of resources that could be committed to such an enterprise, and at some of the problems and possibilities which arise.

Conjectures

In *The Book of Laughter and Forgetting,* Milan Kundera writes about his hero's mother in the following terms:

> She has an unfortunate tendency to see things in a different perspective from everyone else. What was large for them was small for her, and what were stones for them were houses for her. One night the tanks of a foreign country invaded and the shock was so great and so terrible that no one could think or talk of anything else. Mother, however, only worried about the fact that a neighbour is so preoccupied with these events that he forgets to come and collect some pears from her garden. Her son is infuriated by her pettiness. 'Everyone is thinking about tanks and all you can think about is pears' he yells at her. But then he began to think. Are tanks really more important than pears? As time passed he began to realise that the answer was not so obvious as it seemed at first. And he began to sympathise secretly with his mother's perspective: a big pear in the foreground and somewhere, off in the distance, a tank, tiny as a ladybird, ready at any moment to take wing and disappear from sight. So mother was right after all, tanks are mortal and pears immortal.

Now it seems to me that you do not have to agree with the conclusion, which may be a recipe for quietism, to see something fruitful in this change of standpoint. At a time when we are witnessing the horrific results of a so-called new world order, lead by the biggest of big battalions, it may seem as if Kundera is asking us to simply cultivate our own gardens, to hang out a sign saying small is beautiful and let everything else go hang. But that is not the case. He is simply inviting us not to let these large-scale events so overpower our imaginations that we are incapable of envisaging another kind of world, in which they would not be possible, and indeed of actually constructing this world as a basis of everyday resistance to the big batallions. It might be a world in which the small cruelties and injustices of the classroom and playground loomed very large, as they do indeed for the children who have to suffer them, a perspective in which, instead of sorting pupils into broad social categories, of gender, race or class, we paid more attention to the different ways individual children negotiated these positions, and made sense or nonsense of them in their daily lives.

The problem with Kundera's image is that it proposes a rather too simple and mechanical reversal – looking at the world through the 'wrong end of the telescope' may not in fact bring the possibility of getting our bearings any nearer. To enlarge the view from below may cut the discourse of the big battalions down to size, but it may also, I suggest, create its own overblown rhetorics, its own delusions of grandeur. However, let us stay with the pear and the tank a little longer and see what else they have to tell us. Let us think of it as a photo-construction.

Roland Barthes makes a useful distinction between two kinds of photographs; there are those pictures which speak in generalities, in which the subject matter is unitary and dominates our reading of it, and which, as he says, 'constructs reality without doubling it or making it vacillate'. And there are photographs in which there is an element of discontinuity, or shock, which disturbs our common sense understanding of the subject matter. This element, which Barthes calls a punctum, consists of an often untoward detail – a particular texture, the fold of a dress, a sticking plaster on a finger clenched into a fist – a detail which functions as a memory trace, evoking a chain of images belonging to a particular lived history, a singular narrative. The first kind of photograph may instruct, inform and even interest us, but it does not draw anything out from us, it does not engage our imaginations, elicit stories; it cannot educate in the proper sense. Only the second kind of picture, which Kundera is offering us here, can do that. And paradoxically it does so by virtue of something which neither its composition nor its rhetoric can control – a potential space of meaning between what is depicted and what it can be made to represent. It is that potential space which allows Kundera to take a line of thought for a walk, and it leads him in a direction which overturns the ideological power of the big battalions, and their narratives of laughter and forgetting.

This idea is far from new. Paul Klee starts his *Pedagogical Sketchbook* by recommending just such an itinerary for the art student:

An active line, moving freely, without goal. A walk for a walk's sake. The mobility agent is a point shifting its position forward, accompanied by complimentary forms, circumscribing itself, undergoing many transformations.

We are very close to Walter Benjamin's 'art of wandering': 'to lose oneself in a city, as one loses oneself in a forest, calls for quite a different schooling'. This certainly seems to take us a long way from the current aims and objectives of teacher training! But Klee was a great teacher as well as a great artist, and he is very far from recommending a romantic retreat into the world of the 19th-century dilettante or flaneur.

What he was getting at was a method of investigation which is both ancient and modern, popular and scientific, and in fact takes many different forms. Carlo Ginzberg was the first to describe the history and principles of this conjectural method, which he argues provides us with an alternative way of explaining the world to that offered by the rationalist pedagogies and hermaneutics of the Enlightenment. In his essay 'Morelli, Freud and Sherlock Holmes' he draws our attention to the similarities between a method for establishing the provenance of paintings, the procedures of psychoanalytic interpretation, and the narrative devices of the detective story. These consist in the following operations: 1) focussing on small, apparently insignificant details, the way a hand or a nose is painted, a slip of the tongue, or a throwaway remark made in association to a dream, a broken twig or cigarette ash at the scene of the crime; 2) treating these elements as clues or material signs of a history which has to be reconstructed by means of an imaginative interplay of inductive and deductive reasoning – taking a line of thought for a walk to the point where 'the penny drops' – the famous 'aha erlebnis' praised by the phenomenologists; 3) En route, judgement is suspended about discourses which focus exclusively on the dominant features of the phenomena: thematic studies of painting, the patient's secondary elaborations, circumstantial evidence.

This seems to me to describe quite a lot of activities. It has often been a preferred method of a poetics of the material imagination, for example in the work of William Carlos Williams or Mroslav Holub, who, perhaps by no coincidence both apply the diagnostic skills of the doctor and research scientist to tracing the weight of particular histories on the communities in which they live. It also happens to describe rather well how research in the human sciences actually proceeds, even if it is not so often reported like this. You spend a lot of time ferreting about amongst primary sources, looking for things which other people may have overlooked, but which might give you a clue to unravelling the particular problem you are addressing. You suspend judgement on the secondary literature. A lot of the time you get lost, you go up blind alleys and reach dead ends, and then, hopefully just before the grant runs out, the penny drops and the picture falls into place. If you're lucky it has a large blue pear of a type no one has noted before in the foreground, and a large and nasty 'ism', which was getting in your way has turned into a pink elephant and is about to take flight.

As for the conjectural method of teaching, it involves constructing a framework which enables children to take ideas for a walk to see where they will lead, rather than merely reaching foregone conclusions. Is that not a rather good definition of what education is all about? And if we are to get back to basics, to the root of things, perhaps it is worth noting the local homegrown etymology of 'teaching' – from the Old English *taecan*, Gothic *taekjan*, the word can ultimately be traced back to the Greek *deiknunai* – which means to show, or make manifest the meaning of something. Interestingly enough *taekjan* is also the root of token, which in its transitive sense means to signify, or symbolise. Teaching, like research, is above all a semiotic activity, a practice of signification, a negotiation of meaning. It is this excess of meaning which differentiates teaching and learning, from schooling and training.

The detective story seems a useful analogy for what is involved in both research and education, and above all in educational research. We can, of course, cheat, and turn to the end of the story to find out who or what dunnit, or introduce a *deus ex machina* to make it all come out as 'the right answer' – the redemptive happy ending promised us if we adopt the correct ideological position. But that way nothing is learnt about learning, or about much else. It is much more useful to allow the story to unfold at its own pace, to play the detective and try to unravel the mystery, even if it means running the risk of getting it wrong.

Potential spaces

Marion Milner, in a commentary on the implications for teachers of Blake's portrayal of Job's torment, suggested that it could be read as a parable about the sin of pride, which is a permanent danger for those of us who think we have a recipe for making the world a better place to live in. It is a sin which she associates with overdependence on conscious rational thought processes, and their ability to control things, and also the desire to at all costs present a positive image of reality. Teachers, especially under the impact of the new managerialism, are under enormous pressure to do both. But the result is that the unconscious processes which dominate the 'other scenes' of school life, for children as well as staff, are split off or denied, or otherwise held at bay, but in any event are not tackled properly so that they when they surface, as they inevitably do, especially in the playground, they come to seem even more threatening and overpowering than they actually are or need be.

A proper strategy of management must therefore involve devising ways of bringing these structures of feeling more out into the open, of working through, as well as against them, especially in order to disconnect them from the racist and sexist practices in which they are so often enmeshed. Only in that way can these practices, which recruit for the big battalions, be robbed of the pleasure principles which give them their power over young people, a power which stems from the imaginary positions of omnipotence which they promise those who are in so many other areas of their lives all too powerless.

When Marion Milner argues that teachers need to take responsibility for dis-illusioning children, she does not mean that we should join forces with an educational system which all too surely shatters the hopes and limits the aspirations of so many; she is not advocating a new realism. Nor is she arguing that we should use the power of some superior reasoning to demystify their false consciousness as the classical Marxists would have us do. She is arguing, instead, for the creation of a potential space in which these knowledge/power games are temporarily put in abeyance, and where consequently it is possible to conduct the kind of negotiations in which children can actually learn to find their own voice, not by shouting loudest, but by listening and putting into words what has been silenced by what they have been made to echo. One of the conditions of that possibility is that teachers and pupils learn to practise what Keats calls 'negative capability' – the ability to entertain uncertainties, mysteries, doubts, without any irritable reaching after reason or fact.

As an example of what may then occur I would like to end by quoting from a discussion amongst a group of four 10-year-old girls: Chinese, Irish, Afro-Caribbean and white English. I simply drew an outline figure and invited them to fill it in. What they then created within this potential space was a character they came to call the Indian Cowgirl Warrior. And this is what they said about her:

> She's called Sandy ... No Jo ... Sandy Jo ... she fights and bangs people's heads together but only the baddies ... she's a warrior ... she's a bad warrior ... no a good warrior ... cos if people beat up their best friends she helps them out ... sometimes she's mad ... she's mad about the baddies shooting people dead ... she chases after them and bangs their heads together, saying 'pack it in'...

In the next sequence, the *mise-en-scene* shifts and the 'Warrior' finds herself suddenly transported to the Wild West. But this re-location in turn sparks off a debate about her ontological status – is she real or imaginary?

> She's a cowgirl ... a cowgirl warrior ... I saw one in a film, she had boots on and these prickly things on behind [spurs] ... I like Supergirls ... so do I ... the cowgirl lives in heaven ... No Way ... No Way ... she lives in a desert. Every morning she gets up, she cleans everything up, and she goes to work ... she does something very important ... she's not real, is she? 'cos she's just in a film ... she cleans everything up then she goes to the man making the film and says 'can I have a cup of tea first' cos I've come a long way to get here...

The class and gender status of the figure having been resolved the debate now moves onto another terrain of confusion: her 'race' of ethnic origins. Rachel is doing her face and announces ~'I'm going to do the colour of the skin'. Thereupon Amanda speaks for the first time: 'Do it yellow.' But Rachel refuses. 'No, I'm going to do it brown ... I know let's make her an Indian ... an Indian cowgirl.' And this suggestion is greeted with a chorus of Yeses from Yolande and Sharon, but not from Amanda, who looks hurt. Yolande then turns to Amanda and says in a comforting

tone of voice, 'You're an Indian.' But this is immediately contradicted by Sharon, 'No, she's not,' at which Rachel and Sharon
break out into giggles.

This is partly because there is an ambiguity about the term
'Indian' in this context. Are they referring to American Indians,
or the inhabitants of India? At this point I intervened for the first
time to ask them what they knew about 'Indians'. Where did they
come from? Rachel suggested Africa; Yolande, loyal to Amanda,
suggested Hong Kong, while Rachel said simply 'the desert'.
Their answers thus revealed a personal geography of
identification with the figure which had little or nothing to do
with the real world. Yet this also made their own creation wholly
'other'. How then, could they then reclaim it as the product of a
shared multi-ethnic enterprise?

For this purpose it was necessary to construct a new myth of
origins. And now it became clear to which *mise-en-scène* this
Indian belonged:

> First there were cowboys ... no, the Indians ... then the cowboys
> came along ... they were looking for treasure ... a great big
> block of gold ... they fight a lot ... they fight about money ...
> and princesses ... the Indians come along ... they're warriors ...
> they bang the baddies' heads together and tell them to stop.

In this dialogue Amanda for the first time fully joined in. She
could bring her gift for story telling to bear in reclaiming the
figure for everyone. Sharon starts by stating the traditional colonial mythology of the American frontier. But this is quickly contradicted by Rachel, who knows better – the Indians were there
first. Amanda now suggests one of the real motives behind the
settlement of the American West – they were looking for gold.
This appeals to Sharon's material imagination-there were a lot
of fights about money. But for Amanda gold and buried treasure
clearly have a more mythological significance and she persists in
adding a fairy tale theme about princesses to the scenario. When
the Indians make their entry it is, implicitly, to avenge this
pillage and rape. Naturally they are warriors, and in a reprise of
the opening motif, they are invested with a legislative and peace-
keeping role. They bang the cowboys heads together and tell
them to stop.

The cowboys in question do not however belong only to a distant and imaginary 'wild west', but to the all too real and immediate frontiers of racial prejudice which some of these girls encounter every day in the playground and streets. The concluding sentence is a form of wishfullment. If only teachers would come to their rescue and bang the baddies heads together and make them stop their racist taunts. And if the teachers cannot be relied upon then maybe it really is up to 'the Indians' and other ethnic minority communities to exert their power and put an end to harrassment.

In working through these themes, in taking these lines of thought for a walk, through the stories which the figure draws out of them, crystallising in a demand for social justice, it seems to me that these girls are demonstrating in practice that excess of reach for meaning which education should exert over schooling and training. The proper job of curriculum planning and classroom management in a 'post modern frame' is not to substitute itself for this kind of semiotic activity or supress it in the name of 'academic standards', but to create the conditions for its widest possible dissemination. Only in so far as that occurs as a matter of whole school policy can children be properly equipped for active citizenship in a multinational state and a multicultural society.

References

Abercrombie, N. *et al* (1980) *The Dominant Ideology Thesis* (London: Allen & Unwin).
Barthes, R. (1988) *Camera Lucida* (London: Flamingo).
Baudrillard, J. (1988) *Selected Writings* (Cambridge: Polity).
Benjamin, W. (1986) *Reflections* (New York: Schocken).
Carlos Williams, W. (1976) *Selected Poems* (Harmondsworth: Penguin).
Freire, P. (1982) *A Pedagogy for Liberation* (London: Macmillan).
Ginzberg, C. (1990) *Myths, Emblems, Clues* (London, Hutchinson).
Holub, M. (1990) *The Present Moment* (London: Faber).
Illich, I. (1991) *In the Mirror of the Past* (London: Boyars).
Jameson, F. (1991) *Post-Modernism or the Cultural Logic of Late Capitalism* (London: Verso).
Johnson, R. W. (1990) *Heroes and Villains* (Harvester/ Wheatsheaf).
Klee, P. (1989) *Pedagogical Sketchbook* (London: Faber).
Kundera, M. *The Book of Laughter and Forgetting* (London: Faber)
Lyotard, J.-E. (ed.) (1995) *Education and the Post Modern Condition* (London: Croom Helm).

Macdonald, I. (1989) *Murder in the Playground* (London: Longsight).
Milner, M. (1987) *Eternity's Sunrise* (London: Virago).
Thompson, E. P. ((1980) *Writing by Candlelight* (London: Merlin).
Willis, P. (1993) *Learning to Labour* (Ashgate: Aldershot).

Index

409